D0116616

# The Lion
## in the North

# The Lion in the North

*One thousand years of Scotland's history*

## John Prebble

**DORSET PRESS**
**NEW YORK**

*This book was designed and produced by*
*George Rainbird Ltd.*
*27 Wrights Lane, Kensington*
*London W8 5TZ*

*House editor: Yorke Crompton*
*Picture research and indexing: Ellen Crampton*
*Design: Pauline Harrison*

*First published in the United States of America 1971*
*Reprinted 1983*
*This edition published in 1986 by Dorset Press,*
*a division of Marboro Books Corporation,*
*by arrangement with George Rainbird Ltd.*

*Printed in Singapore*

*Library of Congress Cataloging in Publication*

*Prebble, John, 1915 –*
*The Lion in the North*

*Originally published: London: Secker & Warburg 1971*
*Bibliography: p.*
*Includes index*
*I. Scotland – History. I. Title*
*[DA760. P73 1983] 941.1 83–7814*

*ISBN 0-88029-090-0*

*For James Robertson-Justice*

# Contents

# Colour Plates

# PART I

# The Union of Peoples

'...dreadful clashings of wars'

Eleven centuries ago Kenneth the Hardy, son of Alpin and the descendant of forty tribal kings, became the first King of Alba, of *Albainn* the land of the Scots. The small mountain kingdom of these eponymous people would in time extend to the Caithness coast and the Northumbrian hills, and they would be a minority in a national fusion of Pict and Scot, Briton and Norseman, Norman and Angle.

They were all incomers, and there had been earlier ethnic tides. Three thousand years before the birth of Christ simple flint-users had come from Ireland to Kintyre, from England and from Norway. Neolithic men from the Mediterranean crucible of man-kind, makers of fire and polished axes, herders of sheep and sowers of grain, passing into oblivion through their great chambered cairns. Beaker People from the estuaries of northern Europe, merging with the cairn-builders in one of the first of the racial unions that have made the people of Scotland. A thousand years of Bronze Age men, lost dust in cremation urns. Three hundred years before Christ, iron-users came in from the North Sea, builders of stone and timber forts that were vitrified in the fires of unending wars. In the west other immigrants, perhaps from Ireland again, built hill-top defences known as duns. In the far north and on the isles, mysterious and unidentifiable men raised tall, circular towers of dry-stone slabs. These brochs stood in groups, by harvest fields at the sea's edge, and though they were plainly shelters from sudden attack, the enemy their builders feared is still conjectural – hostile men from the mountains, or slave-galleys from Rome. Their usefulness is believed to have been brief, and before they were abandoned there was another great ethnic flood, a Celtic population moving northward as the Belgic tribes invaded England, the outer ripple from some Central European spring. In the Lowlands of Scotland they overran and enslaved the earlier inhabitants, or drove them into the mountains. They built forts on floating islands, earth-houses, hill-towns of round huts. They used horses for war and for the field. They wore tunics of bright colours, created kings and aristocracies from the valorous, and left wistful echoes of their civilization, glazed pottery brought from Gaul, bronze swords and the simple beauty of their ornaments.

The Romans came to Scotland, but never subdued it or made a peaceful colonial people of its inhabitants. Toward the end of the first century A.D. they fought a great battle, called Mons Graupius by the historian Tacitus. There, on an unknown hill-slope in the north-east,[1] his father-in-law Julius Agricola vanquished an army of tall, red-haired men who fought bravely with long swords and round shields. Their slaughtered leader was Calgacus, the Swordsman, and if name and man were not invented by Tacitus he is the first inhabitant of Scotland to have a recorded identity. Prehistory ends with his appearance, and what has been called the long brawl of Scottish history begins with his fierce defiance of the Romans: 'They make a desert, and they call it peace!'

Agricola was recalled to Rome before he could prove his claim that this mountain land might be subdued. Thereafter the legions held its foothills under arms, and there is no record and no relic of their occupation north of Loch Earn and the Tay. To contain the northern people they called Caledonians, they established a slender line of forts from Callander to Perth. At Inchtuthil on the Tay, where Agricola had based his Ninth

---

[1] The sixteenth-century historian Hector Boece misspelt the name of the battle as Mons Grampius, and from this literary oversight the mountain mass of the Grampians acquired its name.

*Skara Brae, Orkney, the site of a prehistoric village, c. 1500 B.C. Right Hadrian's Wall at Housesteads (called Vercovicium in Roman times), in Northumberland.*

Legion, was built the great fortified camp of Pinnata Castra. North of the seven ditches that surrounded its fifty acres was a roadless wilderness of mountains, marsh and forest, wildcat and wolf, and the hidden hostility of relentless enemies. Within thirty years, as the garrisons of Britain were reduced to reinforce the German wars of Rome, the Caledonians had isolated or destroyed these Tayside forts, and the Ninth Legion, marching north to their relief, was silently lost in an unrecorded massacre.

The Romans fell back to the Tyne and the Solway. There the Emperor Hadrian, deciding that Caledonia was not worth the loss of another legion, built his great wall, seventy miles from sea to sea, a wide ditch, a causeway of stone, forts, castles, camps and signal-towers, a formidable tribute to the strength of the enemy it was meant to contain. So constant were the attacks upon the wall, and so great the risk of a sympathetic rebellion behind it, that the Romans were forced to advance their frontier again, to the

*The broch at Dornadilla, Sutherland, has a wall that in places is 20 feet high. Right These remarkable Standing Stones at Callernish, Lewis, Outer Hebrides, were connected with sun worship.*

narrow neck of Scotland between the Forth and Clyde. There was built another wall, a rampart of earth ten feet high, thirty-nine miles long and studded with twenty forts. This Antonine Wall, named for the Emperor Antoninus Pius, was also furiously attacked, its forts lost, retaken, and lost again by the Second, Sixth and Twentieth Legions who held it during the forty years of its existence. Toward the end of the second century it was finally abandoned, and the exhausted legionaries retired from a northern sky black with the smoke of their burning barracks. In 208 the valiant old Emperor Severus took a fleet into the Firth of Forth, landed a punitive army on its north shore, and fought a bloody, burning campaign across Fife and the valley of the Tay. The old man took the surrender or the heads of the chieftains he defeated, but the land itself was unconquerable, and he too was soon dead. But the lesson taught by his spearmen was dutifully learnt, and for almost a century there was an uneasy peace. The Romans held their wall and the protectorate beyond it, the Caledonian tribes stayed in their brooding hills.

With the beginning of the fourth century the lava of a dreadful turbulence poured forth again from those volcanic mountains. As Scot, Frank and Saxon raided the southern coasts of Britain, the mountain tribes of the north, now called Picts by their enemies, terrorized the North Britons of the protectorate and hammered at the wall. Decade by decade until, in 367, they broke through to the soft provinces of northern England. They were repulsed, but when they came again in 383 most of the garrison troops had been withdrawn from the wall, and this time the damage done to causeway and forts was never repaired. The dying empire of Rome was contracting, its colonial governors and generals taking their legions home to fight for the possession of its body. In 409 the Britons of the protectorate were told to defend themselves, no legion would help them. This they did well, and out of need created a powerful kingdom, a stubborn and independent spirit that would endure, in one political and religious form or another, until the end of the seventeenth century.

There is a darkness now over much of the knowledge we would have, ill-lit by legend and myth, a black mantle upon which shine the jewelled names of seventy Pictish kings and the red-gold of their battles. These kings, doubtfully recorded in the annals of their conquerors, are names without substance. The Picts are a lost race, and were remembered without charity. Apostates, said the Columban monks, unworthy and most evil. Even the name is not their own, its meaning still indeterminable. The Irish called them Cruithni, the equivalent of Pritani or Britons, more poetically the people of the designs. To the Romans they were *picti*, the painted ones, a foot-soldier's affectionate distortion perhaps. There is not, and probably may never be, agreement on their origin. Tacitus decided from their yellow-red hair and great limbs that they came from Germany, later classical writers speak of Gaul, and of hair not so red, limbs not so great. That they were alien, incomers, is open to dispute, that they were the aboriginal broch-builders is unproven. No body of evidence survives about their laws, their legends, or their religion, no consecutive words, no enlightening sentence written in their language. This tongue, which philologists aridly call P-Celtic, to distinguish its non-existence from the Q-Celtic of the Gaels, thinly survives in place-names and the Gaelic that replaced it.

They were never a united people until the last few years of their independence. From the warring groups of earlier centuries there did emerge two dominant tribes whom the Romans called the 'greatest peoples', the Caledonii of the north and the Maeatae of the south. Separated by the natural barrier of the Mounth, between Strathspey and the Dee,

*Relics of Roman glass: a jug found in Aberdeenshire, a bowl, the fragment of a bottle.*
*Overleaf David I and his grandson Malcolm IV, from the Charter of Kelso Abbey.*

uco
faun
quar
pro
S; 1
uene
locus

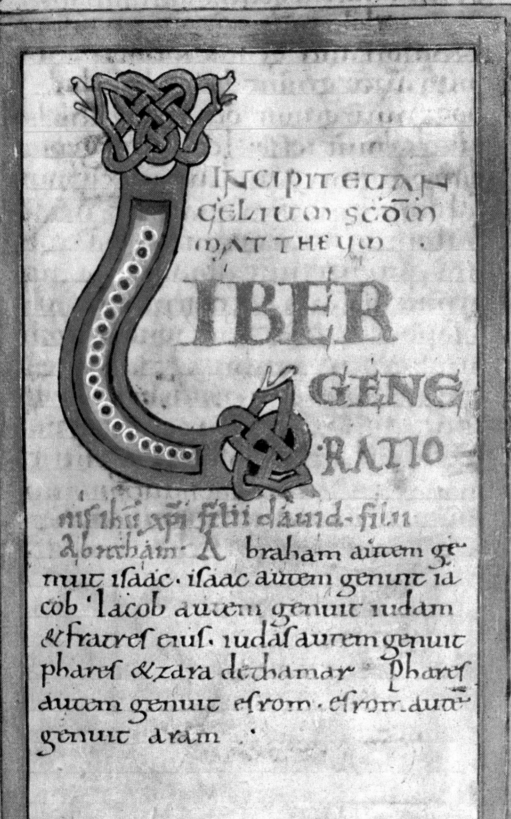

INCIPIT EUAN
GELIUM SCDM
MATTHEUM

LIBER

GENE
RATIO

nis ihu xpi filii dauid · filii
Abraham · Abraham autem ge
nuit isaac · isaac autem genuit ia
cob · Iacob autem genuit iudam
& fratres eius · iudas autem genuit
phares & zara dethamar · Phares
autem genuit esrom · esrom autem
genuit aram ·

their wasting conflicts lasted until the savage struggle with Scot and Norseman brought a brief union. They left little that a man may touch with his hand and wonder, but the tangible relics that do exist are strangely moving. Five score standing-stones and symbol-stones of evocative alliteration, on hill-slope and seaward cliff, a carving on a cave-wall, a wooden box that may have held a leather-worker's tools. The silver relics found in the ruins of their late Christianity, a hoard buried in haste, brooches, pins, a bowl. The symbol-stones mark the extent of Pictland, from Shetland and Orkney, by the Dornoch and Moray firths, across the shires of Nairn, Banff and Aberdeen, down the land of Fife. On the early stones the incised carvings are clean, pure and lovely. A goose with backward-turning neck, a bull with lowered head and splendid loins, a curling serpent, an antlered deer, a stallion with hoof raised, about to walk from the rock face. And there are beasts unrecognizable, slack-jawed and narrow-flanked, grotesquely entwined, crescents, broken arrows, and bars of lightning. A wolf, a falcon, a boar, simply cut, and then again reversed, forming a ritualistic pattern of lost meaning. A moving frieze of huntsmen, of grazing cattle, tall soldiers in long tunics, carrying longer spears and square shields, a drawn bow, a suckling faun, the soundless beat of hooves and a running hound. The strangeness is that these carvings show no spectacular slaughter of man by man.

Although the Antonine Wall had long been deserted by the legions, its crumbling rampart and burnt forts still formed the loose, southern frontier of Pictland. By the sixth century the abandoned North Britons of the Roman protectorate had become a unifying kingdom of Strathclyde, stretching from that river's northern bank to the fringe of Wales, with whom its people had common tongue and kinship. It was an aristocratic, organized and disciplined society, hill-towns, farms, and palisaded manors, cavalry that rode to war in powerful divisions, resolute chieftains and kings, of whom one may have been Arthur. Its heroics and cradle songs were immortalized in the elegiac body of poems known as the *Gododdin* which, although Welsh, is sometimes boldly called the oldest Scottish poem. The hold which these Strathclyde men had on the eastern Lowlands was already loosening before the upward thrust of the Angles from Northumbria, two contentious kingdoms dividing the land between York and the Forth. Neither Briton nor Angle was yet a serious menace to the Picts. When that came it was from Ireland, from a Gaelic-speaking people who were burning the western coasts of Britain before the last legion went home. By the end of the fifth century the Hebrides were theirs to dispute with the Vikings, and their ships were beached in the western sea-lochs of Pictland.

Scot, it is said, is a corruption of an Irish word for raider, and if so it was apt.[1] They were Goidelic Celts, they were Gaels, and that is an anglicized form of the Gaelic derivation of *Gwyddel*, the name given to the Irish by the Welsh. In their own land they were the Féni, but it is as Scots that history remembers them, and for whom the land is named. They came from Northern Ireland to the south-western corner of Pictland, to the green finger of Kintyre, the mountains of Knapdale and Lorn. At the beginning of the sixth century they came as settlers, not raiders. One hundred and fifty men, according to the legends, grounded their ships on the coast of Argyll, the land of the Gael. They were led by three sons of Erc, King of Dalriada in Ireland, and they divided their little conquest between them, creating rival dynasties. That which Gabhran established

---

[1] The Gaelic for a raider, a pillager, is *creachadair*, and one may make what one wishes of that. The earliest form is the Latin *Scottus*, about A.D. 400.

*Detail from the* Gospels of St Margaret, *wife of Malcolm III, who used*
'*the Word of God against the defenders of perverted customs*'.

17

in Knapdale, building his fortress on the rock of Dunadd, gave Scotland its crooked line of kings.

What resistance, if any, there was to this enclave is unknown. Bede said that it was created by friendship or the sword, and it may be that long before the coming of the sons of Erc the Scots were allies of the Picts against the Romans, and later took or were given the land in payment. Within half a century, however, they were in conflict, and in the energy of battle the province of Dalriada in Pictland expanded and contracted like a breathing lung. The Picts were now on the defensive, aggressively attacked by the Scots in the west, and menaced in the south by Briton and Angle. The kings of Strathclyde built their capital fortress on the basalt rock of Dumbarton, challenging both Pict and Scot. In the east their kinsmen of Manaw Gododdin held the southern shore of the Forth and the Stirling plain, until they were driven into Strathclyde by the Northumbrian English. Between all four peoples there were uneasy frontiers and ceaseless battles, murder, marriage, truce and treachery. They can be seen as a turning wheel, the movement of Scot against Pict, and Angle against Briton. The main sources of the fragmentary and frequently suppositional story are the Irish *Annals of Tigernach* and Adamnan's *Life of Columba*. Few men can be seen clearly in the mist of blood, and scarcely heard in Adamnan's 'dreadful clashings of wars'. There are the dates of kings and the deaths of kings, clouds of horsemen and red-sailed fleets. Here and there a name holds the

*The Glamis Stone in Angus is one of the earliest Christian monuments in Scotland and a fine example of Pictish skill. On one side is carved a cross in high relief, on the other appear a serpent, fish, and mirror.*

*This Pictish incised stonework is both simple and evocative. The goose and bull were found in Moray at Burghead and the deer inland at Grantown. The relief work showing mounted warriors is from a cross slab in Aberlemno churchyard, Angus.*

imagination. Aidan of the house of Gabhran, leading an allied army of Scots and Britons against the Angles in Liddesdale, dedicating a humble tenth of his booty to Christ, and filling the church of Iona with the banners of his enemies. Bridei, son of Maelcon, King of the Picts and a descendant of Welsh princes. A most powerful king, said Bede, who ruled all Pictland during a brief period of union. A Christian convert who carried a charmed pebble sent to him by Columba, though it helped him little when the southern Picts rose and killed him in battle.

In the seventh century the Scots pushed their frontier far up the Great Glen, and an exultant army, led by Aidan's grandson, came within a morning's march of Inverness before it was defeated. In the south the Angles crossed both Forth and Tay with horse, foot, and godly standards, and held the Mounth for thirty years, until another Bridei drove them from it, slaughtering their leader and all his shield-wall on the edge of an Angus bog. Like his namesake before, this Bridei united Pictland, but upon his surprisingly peaceful death it was splintered again, and the last two centuries of Pictish independence were drained of blood by wars of succession and the carrion hunger of Scot and Angle. From the welter of the last fratricidal battle, in 729, Oengus became King of all Picts. A man of desperate ambition and pride, of military skill and political craft, he made peace with the Angles and fell upon the Scots. He captured the citadels of Dunadd and Dunolly, drowned one Dalriadic king in triumphant execution, and forced others to the seaboard and their ships. After ten years of war, culminating in two battles that may have been fought in Ireland, he broke the power of Dalriada and made it subject. Foolishly then, he turned against Strathclyde, marching upon Dumbarton Rock with Northumbrian allies. His army was annihilated, and by treachery it seems, for the Britons had surrendered ten days before the battle. And then there is silence in

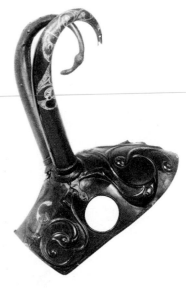

*A gravestone showing 'Tall soldiers in long tunics, carrying longer spears and square shields'. Right A Celtic horse-mask in bronze, 200 B.C., similar to the chamfrein of medieval horse-armour.*

the annals. He died in 761, five years after this disaster, and the monks who continued Bede's work gave him no happy valediction. He was, they said, a 'tyrannical murderer who from the beginning to the end of his reign persisted in the performance of bloody crime'. The same might have been said of his opponents, but the Picts did not write the annals.

And in these years, too, men broke the meagre soil, planted grain, hunted on their beloved horses, herded cattle, bred falcons, carved their stones with loving care, built Christian churches and pagan fires, feasted, gave birth, and grieved.

There was a new enemy, and the enemy of all. The slender longships of Norse raiders, resolute and hardy men with horned heads, monk-killers, the terrible 'gentiles' of the chronicles. By the ninth century their piratical onslaughts upon Britain, France and Ireland had become invading armies, singing men in shirts of mail, leaving their ships and taking to horse, settling where they conquered. In 839, when the Picts were fighting rebellious Scots under Alpin of Gabhran's house, a great army of Norsemen came upon their rear. Though Alpin was killed, and his head impaled, the Pictish army which then turned to meet the Norsemen was destroyed by them, dying 'almost without number'. Eoghann, last King of the Picts, may have died with them, for there was now no leader to oppose the Scots. In the simple words of a later chronicler, 'Kenneth passed into the remaining territories of the Picts.' Kenneth the Hardy, avenging son of Alpin, occupied their stronghold of Fortriu, of Forteviot in Perthshire, and at a banquet in Scone, it is said, murdered seven earls of Dalriada, kinsmen who might have disputed his claim to be King of Scots and Picts, *Ard-righ Albainn*.

Dramatically, the end of the long struggle should have been some climactic battle between Scot and Pict, and annalists of the next century said there was one at Fortriu, but the union was also a more gradual process. Locked in conflict for so long, subject and subjecting, like metals under a great heat the two peoples became fused, then annealed by a cooling Christianity. Since the triumph of Oengus, Pictish kings had occupied the

Dalriadic throne as well, and the Scots pretenders, like Kenneth, sometimes had Pictish names. There was a mingling of blood in marriage, and since the Pictish law of inheritance was through the female line, it has been said that Kenneth MacAlpin's mother gave him a right to the Pictland throne. Contemporary chronicles are dark and unhelpful, and one gives Providence credit for the end of Pictish independence. 'For God deigned to make them alien from and void of their heritage, by reason of their wickedness; because they not only spurned the Lord's mass and precept, but also refused to be held

*Centuries of migration, war and intermarriage created a fiercely independent race from Pict and Scot, Briton, Angle and Viking, which even the addition of Norman blood could not quell.*

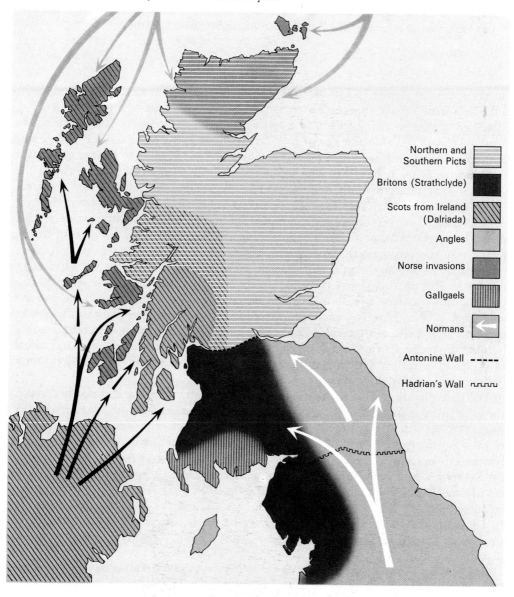

equal to others in the law of justice.' It is a churlish dismissal of those distant horsemen, the carvers of symbol-stones, the painted ones, makers of designs.

The Irish *Annals* refer to Kenneth as 'King of the Picts', and the same title is given to the brother and son who succeeded him, but his descendants were soon buried on Iona as *Ard-righ Albainn*. The Picts pass from history, and with them the kingdom of Dalriada, though the evocative memory of that would last for a thousand years among the western clans. The Scots spread northward and eastward, absorbing or suffocating the culture and the customs and the language of the Picts. The seat of kings was moved to Scone, sacred centre of Pictland, and the royal sons of Alpin accepted their inheritance upon a stone slab which tradition believes was taken from Tara in Ireland, built into the wall of Dunstaffnage Castle, and then brought reverently to Scone.

Geologists say it is Lower Old Red Sandstone, and quarried nearby.

2

Southern Britain already had its saints and martyrs before the foundation of the Celtic Church, before Patrick, himself a Strathclyde Briton, converted the north of Ireland. Whether the British or the Irish may take the credit for bringing the faith of Christ to Scotland was always a dispute out of harmony with the spirit of its subject, and is now of no great consequence. In his *Historica Ecclesiastica*, Bede briefly recorded the tradition of Nynia the Briton, a holy man who studied under St Martin at Tours, who taught the southern Picts to accept the Cross long before the coming of Columba and the great Age of Saints of the sixth century. A Celtic life of St Ninian is lost, and there are legends only. Not the least beguiling of these is that he built a house of white stone (a most unusual thing for a Briton to do, thought Bede), and from thence set out on his perilous journeys to the pagan north. Until the Reformation, grieving kings made a footsore pilgrimage to a Ninian shrine at Whithorn in Galloway, the centre of a Christian community in Roman times, and there archaeologists have since found the remains of a building that may have been Ninian's *Candida Casa*. The evidence of his mission to the wild Picts is thin, however, and has more substance in Victorian paintings where he appears as the well-born incumbent of a Church of England parish, reminding sturdy bucolics dressed as warriors of the tithes due from them. Yet he and his monastic school in Galloway were lovingly remembered, and later priests and kings would long for a return to his simple goodness.

The strong figure of Columcille, Colmkil, Columba the elder,[1] strides clearly through the mist that surrounds Ninian, and our picture of him owes much to his hagiographer Adamnan. Born in Donegal of the O'Neill clan, a descendant of kings and a presbyter of the Church, he came to Dalriada in Scotland in 563, when he was forty-two, and laboured there for the next thirty-six years. Though his Gaelic name was reformed into the Latin for a dove, he seems to have been more of a hawk in his youth, and for much of his life was loud-voiced, aggressive and authoritarian, characteristics more useful to an organizer, perhaps, than saintly reserve. Adamnan said that he left Ireland, 'wishing to be a pilgrim', two years after the battle of Cuil-dremne, where the O'Neills and their Connaught allies fought against the High King of Ireland. According to one tradition,

---

[1] His contemporary, Columba the younger, St Columbanus, was also Irish. He became Abbot of Luxeuil in Burgundy, and upheld the spirited independence of his native church with vigour and courage.

Columba's hot blood was responsible for the savage slaughter. Ordered by the King to return a psalter he had borrowed without permission, he appealed to his clan instead, and three thousand men died to prove he was no thief. Adamnan wrote nothing of this, but he did say that when Columba was called before a synod to face excommunication for 'certain venial and excusable causes', he was preceded by a wondrous column of light. At least, St Brendan of Birr claimed it was there, and he persuaded the rest of the synod that a man so miraculously attended was surely ordained by God and should not be cast out. To escape the King's anger, to further the work of the Church, or both, Columba then left Ireland with twelve apostles. They landed on a small, wild island off the Ross of Mull, given to them by Bridei of the Picts or by the Dalriadic king to whom Columba was related. A scrap of earth, of grass, hill and heather, it became known as I-Colmkil, from the Gaelic Hy or I, an isle, and later by the adjectival form Iona.

In its lack of central organization, in the power of its independent monastic communities and the abbots who led them, the Irish Church was markedly different from the Roman. Its great strength lay in its many 'saints' who left one community to set up their own among the unconverted, usually on small islands, held by sea and sky as if in the palm of God. Iona was in this tradition, and eventually pre-eminent. About a green rise, and upon the site of a heathen altar, were built an abbot's house and a refectory, hospice, barns, a mill and byre, and an oratory so small that its congregation sat outside, singing psalms above the waves and the wind. Columba, abbot father of the monastic family, set the pattern for those who followed him in office. Angelic in appearance, said one of those successors Adamnan, graceful in speech and holy in work, he could not let an hour pass without prayer, or a day without fast or vigil, living 'as a soldier of Christ upon an island'. An evangelizing mission took him up the Great Glen to Bridei's fortress. The open-jawed monster of Loch Ness submerged at his command, pagan priests were confounded by his stentorian version of the Forty-fifth Psalm, and the gates of the stronghold were miraculously opened by his touch. If Bridei son of Maelcon was not immediately converted by all this, he was impressed enough to give Columba his protection among the Picts, receiving that curative pebble in return.

As the Ionan community grew, with Britons and Saxons among its novitiates, it became a sacred centre, the heart of an ecclesiastical dominion from which kings would draw their spiritual power, and lesser men find compensation for their suffering. The interdependence of Crown and Church was established in 574, when Columba chose Aidan of Gabhran's house to be King of Dalriada, laying hands upon him and saying, 'Believe firmly, O Aidan, that none of your enemies will be able to resist you unless you first deal falsely against me and my successors.' To this he added 'or my relatives in Ireland', and if he meant the O'Neills, and not his family in Christ, he gave the politician priests of Scotland their first example of spiritual blackmail.

Columba died prophesying that his island would in time be honoured by all men, not only kings of the Scots but 'rulers of barbarous and foreign nations'. Over the next two centuries Christianity played its part – with conquest, marriage and murder – in unifying the peoples of Scotland, and the graveyard of Iona was floored with the funeral slabs of Scottish, Pictish and Viking kings. Remote from Rome, sturdy in independence, the Columban Church had taken its separate path before its founder died, and before Augustine had begun his southern evangelizing with the conversion of the King of Kent. Its missionaries worked among the Northumbrians, and when it met the northward

*The ruins of Iona, as seen by Thomas Pennant in the 18th century before their later restoration.*

movement of the Roman Church through England it withdrew upon itself, sensitive to criticism, to accusations of schism and disobedience. It could not conform to Roman law, since to do so would be a denial of the saintliness of many of its founders. At its heart was passion and love, and a human tolerance. Its clergy were not called upon to be celibate, and many of its abbots were secular, one of them fathering a line of kings. It had its zealots of course, the Culdees, *Célidé* the Friends of God. In their beginning they emulated the ancient Irish anchorites, living alone in mountain huts with the wolf and the cat, burning with truth in the wilderness of pagan lands. Though in time they too would come together in property-owning monastic colleges, in the early days of the Scots Church they were the hot core of its independence. That independence was challenged when Columban and Roman clergy debated their differences at the Synod of Whitby in 664, summoned by Oswiu, King of Northumbria. Though they argued bitterly over the proper calculation of Easter's movable feast, and the correct form of the tonsure, the true issue between them was the authority of Rome, the acknowledgment of Peter as Keeper of the Keys of Heaven. The young spokesman of the Roman clergy, Wilfrid of Ripon, put that issue clearly to the Columbans. 'Even if your fathers were true saints, surely a small company on a corner of a remote island is not to be preferred to the universal Church of Christ?' Oswiu is said to have smiled when he heard this, and he gave judgment in favour of the Romans.

The Northumbrians' desire for ecclesiastical and political dominion over northern Britain ended in 685, when their king and their army were destroyed by Picts in Angus.

24

But Nechtan, King of the Picts, was converted to Christ, 'by frequent meditations on the ecclesiastical scriptures' said Bede. His taste was for the Roman doctrine, for a stone church, the crown tonsure, and a form of episcopacy. Under pressure from the Pictish Church and Pictish warriors, the Ionans withdrew westward, some of their monks even returning to Ireland. Finally, at some unknown date, they reluctantly submitted to Rome, but they stubbornly clung to many of their practices, the autonomy of their abbacies and their indifference toward celibacy. The bitterness of the last century of struggle between Scot and Pict, between Christian and Christian now, must have been sharpened by the doctrinal dogmas that also separated them. Some time during this confusing period of debate and acrimony, a stranger is said to have brought a parcel of bones to the house of Nechtan. Nobody doubted his claim that they were the true relics of the apostle Andrew, least of all Nechtan, whose recent conversion probably required an act of credulous faith. The stranger was allowed to build a shrine for the bones on the coast of Fife, and Scotland thus acquired its patron saint and the ultimate site for its first university.

A terrible menace from without helped the fragile unification of Church and peoples. The survival of Christianity, both physical and spiritual, under the increasing forays of the Norsemen is perhaps its greatest miracle, of human courage if not of Divine perseverance. The raiders came in waves against the whole coast of Scotland, snatching their shields from the sides of their ships, wading ashore with axe and sword, killing without compassion. To their terrified victims they were the Black Gentiles and the White Gentiles, the one from Denmark and the other from Norway. The loot they took from the isolated religious communities seemed inexhaustible, and the further into the mainland they went the richer it became, silver cups and salvers, golden caskets and crosses, illuminated manuscripts with jewelled bindings, corn, cattle, women and slaves. Where once the raiders had come, they came again, confident that the holy men would rebuild upon the ashes, would replace their sacred treasures, restock barn and byre. Between 795 and 806, Iona was three times wasted, and upon the last occasion every member of the community was slaughtered in a sandy inlet still known as Martyrs Bay. No day was free from fear, from the dread of a seaward sky suddenly full of striped sails, sun-glittered shields, horned helmets and dipping prows of wolf and boar. In time it was realized that there was no security on Columba's isle. Its sacred relics were sent away, some to Kells in Ireland, and others to Dunkeld in Perthshire, where Adamnan had established a monastery, and where Kenneth MacAlpin would soon place his capital. But Iona remained the spiritual heart of the Church, and for a while yet the kings of the Scots would be buried in its earth.

In the ninth and tenth centuries, under such splendidly named leaders as Harold Fair Hair and Ketil Flatnose, the Gentiles established their great settlements. Norwegian jarls ruled in Shetland, Orkney and Caithness. When Harold Fair Hair sent Flatnose to subdue rebellious Vikings in the Hebrides, Ketil abandoned his allegiance and made himself king of the islands instead. Along the Solway Firth, and in the hills of Galloway, the invaders intermarried with earlier settlers, creating a fiery and quarrelsome people of Gallgaels. Three kings of the Scots died in hopeless battles against the southern flood of the White Gentiles, and when this reached its high-water mark outside Dunkeld their successors were glad to make peace. The Norsemen held what they had taken in the north and the Isles, but they were split by dynastic and envious quarrels. They lacked the central organization and logistic skills to fight a prolonged campaign. Their feet were still webbed, their hearts still held in sea-mists, and the service they gave in arms to their leaders was reckoned in 'ships' and 'oars'. They could not subdue the whole country, even had this been their intention, but they remained, the fifth of Scotland's founding people, their blood to be mixed with Scot and Pict, Briton and Angle.

Kenneth MacAlpin was carried to his grave on Iona in 860, followed within forty years by his brother and the two sons who succeeded him. Not much is known of the kingdom they ruled, the land between the old Antonine Wall and the northern territories of the Norse, its provinces of Angus and Atholl and Strathearn, Fife, Mar, Moray and Caithness, each the contested territory of Pictish and Dalriadic chiefs. They governed as *mormaers*, as stewards of the High King, and kinship with him and each other was less the cement of loyalty than a rich soil upon which envy, ambition and murder flourished. The ebb, or the containment, of the Norse invasion was no end to the wearying years of war. The northward pressure of the Angles turned that part of Northumbria beyond the Cheviots into a bloody Flanders. Athelstan, grandson of Alfred, was perhaps the first English king to claim sovereignty over Scotland, and it was a claim with some substance if the *Anglo-Saxon Chronicle* can be believed. In 921 at

*Viking raiders in their longships were the terrible Gentiles of the early Christian chronicles. The Gotland Stone depicts the ferocity of their invasions, in which few escaped pillage or slaughter.*

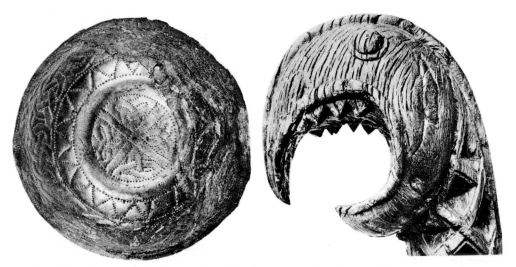

*A silver bowl with a cross on the base found in Shetland on St Ninian's Isle. Loot such as this brought the Norsemen back, again and again.* Right *The prow of a raiding longship was designed to terrify those who attempted to defend themselves against it.*

Bakewell in Derbyshire, King Constantine II of the Scots, with the kings of Strathclyde and Northumbria, and the leaders of all the peoples in all their dominions, had solemnly accepted Athelstan's father as their 'father and lord', his right and the right of his successors to be known as King of all Britain. When Constantine broke this compact by giving asylum to Athelstan's rebellious sons, a punitive English army landed on the east coast of Scotland and raided deep into the Mearns. Constantine hastily allied himself with his old enemies, with Britons of Strathclyde, Danes from Ireland and Northumbria, and marched south toward Cumbria. The English met him on the Solway, on a flat-topped volcanic hill one thousand feet high, and there destroyed his army. Constantine humbled himself and admitted himself Athelstan's vassal. He endured this indignity for a year or two, then resigned his throne to his cousin Malcolm, and retired to the monastery of St Andrews.

Malcolm was the eighth king of Alpin's line since that murderous banquet at Scone. Eight kings in a century, including one short-lived usurper with a hopeless claim to both Alba and Strathclyde, and most of them died in the dreadful clashings of wars, or at the hands of a nephew or cousin who then mounted the sandstone slab. Success gave sanction to murder. Tweedledum followed Tweedledee, their armies exhorted to slaughter by appeals to their heroic ancestry and their prodigious skill at arms. Malcolm was a 'valiant prince and a good justicer' according to tradition, and he was also more fortunate than his predecessors, receiving from Edmund of England the lease of Strathclyde on both sides of the Solway. The gift was not unconditional, since he had first to acknowledge himself England's vassal, and then hold the province against resurgent raids of Norsemen. The wishes of the lords of Strathclyde were not considered, and any objections they may have had were effectively silenced by Edmund. He rode through their lands with fire and sword, and left the defence of burning towns and a terrorized people to his subject Malcolm. The Scot had little time to enjoy his new possession, for he was soon carried in mourning to Iona, dead from poison paid for by his successor. Thus twice in a quarter of a century had Scottish kings surrendered their independence to England, a bitter precedent set, and a cause made for six hundred years of ambitious wars. The superiority of the English crown was further emphasized at Chester in 973 when Edgar, son of Edmund, held council with the King of Scots and seven princes of Strathclyde, Cumbria and Wales. Their talk over, he took the helm of a boat on the river, and they bent at its oars.

This king of Scots was Kenneth II, remembered for the day he hanged five hundred thieves, for his defeat of a Danish assault on Angus, for his love of falconry, and for his poisoner, the murderer of Malcolm. His humble service at an oar on the River Dee was bought with the gift of Lothian, the rolling land between Forth and Tweed, for although Edgar insisted upon his sovereignty over all in Britain, he believed that an alliance well bought was preferable to a battle hard won. The borders of Scotland now stood more or less where they are today, and freed from a fear of the English, Kenneth turned upon the Norsemen and mormaers who had made Speyside a bloody arena for their quarrels. He may or may not have quietened their ferocious passions (the records are not clear), and twenty years after he had expanded his kingdom and surrendered its independence, he too was murdered. Killed, it was said, by a brass image sent to him by a lady. When he took an apple from the hands of the image, a tiny arrow was released and pierced his heart.

Murder and battle killed the next two kings who held Scotland in a swirl of blood. With Malcolm II, their successor, the picture steadies. The Irish *Annals* say that he was honoured among all men in western Europe, and it is difficult to see why, unless it was for his ability to survive. He reigned for twenty-nine years, by ruthless severity, guile, and cunning diplomacy. He married one daughter to the secular Abbot of Dunkeld, and another to Sigurd, the Christian Earl of Orkney. When the Norseman died on the Irish field of Clontarf, wrapped in the raven banner that should have protected him, his lands in Scotland were divided between the Mormaer of Moray and his son by Malcolm's daughter. His rear thus safe in the keeping of his grandson and his steward, Malcolm turned upon the English, believing them to be too much involved with the Danes to withstand the army he took across the Tweed. But they defeated him at Durham, and decorated its palisades with the heads of his spearmen, their dead faces washed, their beards neatly combed.

Thirteen years later, Malcolm allied himself with the King of Strathclyde – over which Scots dominion had long since wasted – and together they burnt all Northumbria between the Tweed and the Tees. The Strathclyde king then died, and before his vacant throne could be occupied by one of his own kin, Malcolm filled it with his grandson Duncan, son of the Abbot of Dunkeld, styling him King of all Cumbria. An Anglo-Danish army came north to answer this impertinence, led by Canute and seizing Lothian from its timorous earl without a battle. Before Malcolm could retake it, he was murdered at Glamis by some of his nobles. As they rode in escape across a frozen loch, the ice broke beneath them and they were drowned 'in the righteous judgement of God'. Or that, at least, was how men told the story.

It is probable that the conspiracy was the result of Malcolm's decision to break the Pictish pattern of inheritance that had determined kingship since the union, and to name his grandson Duncan as his successor. On the genealogical line of the first fifteen kings of Alba the succession darts from side to side like a lightning flash, from brother to brother, to nephew, to cousin, to brother. Now, with some violent exceptions made

*A page from the Annals of Tigernach. Tighearnach O'Braein (d. 1088) was an Irish abbot who recorded events in his own and other countries.*

by usurping assassins, it follows the vertical fall of primogeniture. There were claimants to contest Duncan's accession, but one was murdered the day before the investiture, a second died after it, and a third called Lulach was allowed to live, being a child and simple-minded. Nor were these all. There was a son by the daughter whom Malcolm had diplomatically married to Finlech, Mormaer of Moray. This man stands out clearly from the mist of murder and battle, if more in his Shakespearean image than in fact. Macbeth of Moray was a resolute, ambitious, and self-confident man, untroubled by dreams or by the nagging of his wife. That wife, to strengthen his claim further, was the widowed mother of Lulach.

Duncan reigned for six uneasy years before Macbeth and the Earl of Orkney took the throne from him, killing him in battle near Elgin, or murdering him after it. The legends say that witches and sorcerers turned Macbeth from a valiant prince and a just man into a cruel tyrant, but for seventeen years he held his title with success against Orcadians in the north and Duncan's outraged sons in Strathclyde. One of these sons, Malcolm, with the sympathy of Edward the Confessor and the armed help of Siward Earl of Northumbria, invaded Scotland in 1057, brought Macbeth to battle in Aberdeen-shire and there killed him, far from Birnam Wood and Dunsinane. Malcolm the third of his name, surnamed Canmore the Great Head, was king. For a brief while, among the old adherents to Pictish tradition, there were men willing to fight for Lulach the Fool, but they died with him in Strathbogie, and his body was taken with his stepfather's to the crowded graveyard on Iona. Though the union of races had begun with Kenneth the Hardy in 843, it is with Malcolm Canmore that Scotland steps from the dark ages. It would not abandon murder and treachery, its political, social and religious development would still be orchestrated in the music of war, but the coming of the sixth and last of its founding peoples would give it the strength and discipline of final unification.

The people have been dimly seen behind their warring kings, the braided hair, saffron robes, shining weapons of prince and mormaer. Their way of life can have changed little from century to century. The land was harsh and forbidding. Where it was not granite, sandstone or heathered moor, it was blanketed with forests, impenetrable across mire and fen, its habitable slopes and valleys patched with farms of primitive husbandry. In the early years, after the departure of the legions, the people of the Lowlands lived by the waters of many lochs long since drained, in lake-houses high on timber piles or anchored to foundations of brushwood and stone. With the ebb and flow of war they built defensive, palisaded settlements on hill-tops. Their artifacts were made of bone and iron and bronze, their clothes rough-spun or tailored from hide and fur. In the northern mountains they occupied the brochs when threatened, protected their wattle huts and pens with stakes and ditches. Mud huts, dry-stone walls, and sod-roofed sheds huddled about the early houses of the monasteries, where the air was sweetened by the endless music of bells, handbells of gold, bronze bells calling from riverside towers. Life was a cycle of starvation and gluttony, uneasy peace and wasteful war, drought and flood, sunless summers and winters that were sickly warm or frozen in ice. Religion was an expedient mixture of pagan myth, Scots or Pictish or Brythonic, with the essential truths and parable teachings of Christianity. There was feasting in the light of fire and tallow, the music of the harp and the singing of psalms, the neighing of many horses and the lowing of cattle.

In these days were born, or were imaginatively invented, the heroes and creatures of Picto-Gaelic mythology, giants in caves, unconquerable swordsmen and unbeatable bowmen, immortal bards whose voices are silent, snow maidens and blind seers, water-horses and loch-monsters, speaking stones and singing trees. In their mountain graves between Loch Linnhe and Breadalbane slept the warriors of the Feinn, followers of Fionn MacCumhail awaiting his rousing horn. From the beginning the Christian monks exploited, or perhaps shared, the superstitions of the people, curing the sick with magic, out-tricking their pagan rivals. When a mountain Druid milked a bull, Columba turned the milk to blood, restoring the logic of nature and affirming the supremacy of Christ. We know more of the religious communities than we do of the people. They lived in wattle huts by their stone or timber churches, worked in forges or at the carpenter's bench, wore smocks and hoods of natural wool, and protected their homes with ditches and sharpened stakes. On Iona there was a fine garden, and a man brought from Ireland to tend it. Richer, self-indulgent clergy in the monastery towns had butlers, horses, chariots, and women to solace them at night. Saintlier men in lonelier cells worked on illuminated manuscripts, travelling as far as Northumbria and Saxon England to find particular colours, binding their work in leather and gold from which it was inevitably torn by the terrible Gentiles.

Of the social groupings of the people much is suppositional. The early townships, grouped in the south and scattered in the mountains where fertile earth was sparse, shared communal grazing and cultivated land. The householder was a freeman, for want of an exact word, exacting obedience from his servants and giving it to the leader of the township. His value to the earl of his province, and to the High King, was carefully determined in cattle, in the number of his spearmen, in the area of his grazing. In Alba the structure of society was tribal and familiar, a clan system in formation, where the *gilfine*, the head of five households, was the literal father of his *clann*, his children, though he might be Pict by descent and they Scots. Upon his death his successor was nominated by council from his sons or his kinsmen. Law and justice began and ended in the community with him, mote-hill justice dispensed without appeal in the open. Compared with the mean lives of their followers, such men lived splendidly in houses of wood, two storeys with bedchambers above, walls lined with skins, shields, swords, spears and the grinning heads of the animals they chose for their family totems. Their dignity was supported by the long swords, the wide spears and bull-hide shields of their children, and their loyalty to each other, to mormaer and to king, was knitted from a troublesome skein of consanguinity.

By the year of Malcolm Canmore's accession all Alba probably spoke a coalescence of Gaelic and Pictish, with the former largely predominating, and it was slowly replacing the original tongue of the Scandinavian settlers in the north and the isles. It was spoken in Strathclyde too, among the Gallgaels and Alban settlers, to be fused with Cumbrian Welsh and surviving into the last century as a philologist's curiosity. But the Northumbrian rulers of Lothian, the settlers of the eastern Lowlands, spoke an English that would soon become the language of Scotland and its kings. Gaelic would be left to the mountain people, a barrier between them and the south, jealously preserved for as long as they inhabited their hills. The Scots of Dalriada gave the land its name and its kings, the spirit of its history and the substance of its dreams, but their language would die with them.

ET FV

VE R TERVNT ANGLI

# PART II

# The Norman Invasion

*'Strike their long spears with a staff,*
*and you disarm the Scots'*

The coming of the Normans. Details from the Bayeux Tapestry, showing
the last stand of the English at Hastings, and their final rout.

The royal house of Canmore lasted for two hundred and thirty years. In its beginning it was a Celtic monarchy, rooted in the line of Gabhran the son of Erc, but it ended as the apex of a feudal Norman ascendancy from which the Celtic people of the *Gaidhealtachd*, the mountains and the isles, were slowly isolated by language, custom and tradition. The history of Scotland may now be seen as part of a larger story, the Norman conquest and colonization of Britain, and its wars for independence as civil wars within that framework. Although the sixth and last of the founding peoples were the most influential, they were numerically the smallest. They came as land-seekers, as lords and clerics, becoming king-makers and kings. They also came by invitation.

The progenitor of the house of Canmore, Malcolm III,[1] reigned for thirty-six years, a savage man and intemperate in war, a brute beast when seen beside the devout and saintly figure of his second wife, Margaret. There is truth in the claim that the end of Celtic independence began with this remarkable woman, that her soft hands opened the door to mailed and gowned incomers, that the treacherous ambitions of the next two and a half centuries were made possible by her high-minded influence over her husband and his kingdom. She was English, a daughter of Alfred's house, and she came to Scotland in 1068 with her Hungarian mother, her sister, and her brother Edgar Atheling, the King-Elect of England. Like many others whom Margaret encouraged to settle in Lothian, they were refugees from Duke William's conquest. Her marriage to the King of Scots was perhaps the only sagacious achievement of her feckless brother, although Malcolm needed no encouragement to fight Normans or invade England. Five years before the Conquest he had burnt Northumbria, and after 1066 both he and William turned that unhappy province into a slaughter-house where the dead rotted without burial. When Malcolm then invaded Cumbria, the rape of it was so fierce, said Simeon of Durham, that there was scarcely a Scottish household without an English slave thereafter. But this Malcolm did for his own pleasure and ambition. He had little interest in his brother-in-law's desire for the English throne.

The southern boundaries of both Cumbria and Lothian were undefinable, and no one could say whether they were provinces of the King of Scotland or might reasonably be claimed by William. Certainly they could not be left a burning desert, a bloody arena of contention between Scot, Englishman, Dane and Norman, and in 1072 William came north on one of the most brilliant campaigns of his life. An army of horsemen, in hauberk and helm, advanced through Lothian to the ford at Stirling, crossed it and rode on to the Tay, where they were joined by a great fleet. Scotland had not been so resolutely invaded since the legions left, and Malcolm's reaction was understandably prompt. He agreed to treat with William. They met at Abernethy within sight of the Norman ships. Here, where Iron Age men had built a timber fort, the Romans a camp, and the Picts a capital, Malcolm paid homage and declared himself the Conqueror's man. As hostage for his good behaviour he surrendered Duncan, his eldest son by his first wife. This act of submission would bedevil Anglo-Scots relations for centuries. It is not clear, and perhaps was not clear then, whether Malcolm was paying homage as King of Scotland or as the Lord of Cumbria and Lothian, whether he was surrendering

[1] His title of Great Head referred to his rank, and not to his appearance or his wits. Canmore derived from the Gaelic *ceann*, a chief or leader, and *mor*, great or important.

*The oldest building in Edinburgh, this chapel was built on Castle Rock for St Margaret, queen of Malcolm Canmore.*

the independence of Scotland, as his ancestors had twice done, or acknowledging his title in fief of territories outside his kingdom.

Whatever his thoughts, his promise to 'do right' to William was briefly kept. Seven years later his spearmen and shaggy horsemen were again burning Northumbrian villages along the Tyne. They came again when the Conqueror died, to be driven out by William Rufus, whose Anglo-Norman knights then began the colonization of all Cumbria south of the Solway and Northumbria south of the Tweed, nippling the round hills with their timber keeps.

The savagery of invasion and counter-invasion was almost an irrelevance. The Normanization of Scotland had already begun under Margaret's gentle encouragement. Though English, her tastes and her pleasures, emotionally and intellectually, were for things Norman. Her biography was written by her confessor Turgot, the Saxon Bishop of St Andrews, and although it is heavy with pieties and homilies she emerges from it as a human and compassionate woman. She would rather have been a nun than a queen, but she liked rich clothes and colourful tapestries, spiced meats, gold and silver plate, balladry and dancing, and she encouraged the Scots to like them too. Her generosity to the poor was extravagant, giving them what she had and what she could part from her besotted husband. When he saw her kneeling to wash the feet of a beggar he was so astonished and so awestruck that he knelt to join her. He was also silenced by her scholarship, and would solemnly kiss her books of devotion, or steal them from her chamber, returning them bound in gold and jewels. He tolerated the English and the Norman-English who filled her court, and he spoke her language in preference to his own Gaelic. When three Benedictine monks came from Canterbury at her invitation, to debate the state of the Scottish Church with its Celtic clergy, he acted as her interpreter, ready 'both to say and do whatever she might direct'.

According to Turgot, this debate lasted for three days, and Margaret took a leading part in it, contending 'with the sword of the Spirit, which is the Word of God, against the defenders of perverted custom'. To her the Celtic Church was primitive in form and odious in custom, untidy in organization and sterile in ritual. Its bishops were ineffectual and its hereditary abbots a blasphemy. As far as she could, she worked to bring it in line with the doctrine and formula, the imaginative and inspired framework of Rome, encouraging the clergy to accept both poverty and celibacy, to allow their lusts to be sublimated into the creation of wondrous churches, great and selfless monastic orders.

35

Where she could not direct, she set an example of piety and self-denial, making no secret of her contempt for priests who lived like husbandmen, with farms and cottages in the shadow of their churches. Her love of richly-endowed shrines balanced her insistence upon the self-deprivation of those who served them. She built a church at Dunfermline, where she had married Malcolm, and filled it with rich and beautiful ornaments. Her own tiny chapel was constructed high on the castle rock of Edinburgh, and she restored the scattered monks to the distant isle of Iona. She was benefactor of the church of St Andrews on the Fife coast, giving it an 'elegant crucifix' said Turgot, and encouraging pilgrims from Lothian to visit it by the establishment of a ferry between the south and north shores of the Forth.

Her influence over the indulgent Malcolm was deep and strong, and his tolerance endless, even when she gave to the poor his gifts to her, or opened his chests to find more jewels and more ornaments for her endowments. She persuaded him to share the pleasures of her English court, to drink French wine instead of ale, and to give English, Biblical or classical names to their six sons. It may have been upon her advice that he accepted an invitation to talk with William Rufus after the Scots had been driven north of the Solway and the Tweed. They were to have met at Gloucester, but when Malcolm arrived there William churlishly refused to see him. The Scot went home in a rage, gathered an army and led it joyously into Northumbria. He was killed outside Alnwick, by treachery it was said. As he leant from the saddle to take the keys of the castle from the lance of its keeper, the point was thrust into his eye.

His son Edgar brought the news of his death to Margaret in Edinburgh, and found her mortally ill. As the young man stuttered an account of the skirmish, in which his brother Edward had also died, the Queen did not weep. She gave thanks in prayer for her grief, saying that it purified her soul in the last moments of her life. She died three days later, and her body lay in her chapel on the rock until it could be carried secretly to her ferry and her church at Dunfermline. A fear that some outrage might be committed on the saintly corpse was well grounded. Out of the mists of the Hebrides, upon the news of Alnwick, had come Malcolm's brother Donald Bane. He appealed to the hatred of an anglicized Church, of English clerics, courtiers, singers, knights and traders. He recalled the old Pictish tradition of lateral succession, and declared his right to the throne. And then, said the Anglo-Saxon Chronicle, 'the Scots drove out all the English who were with King Malcolm before.' Of the King's sons one only, Edmund, did not join the flight to the south. For reasons that were probably more psychological than political, he swore to support his uncle, and was given Lothian to rule as his reward.

At the court of William Rufus was Duncan, the hostage given at Abernethy twenty years before, his life surprisingly spared and more Anglo-Norman now than Scots. He went to William, said the Chronicle, 'and did such fealty as the King would have of him, and so went to Scotland with what aid he could get of English and French, and deprived his kinsman Donald of the kingdom and was received as King'. He was a simple, trusting man, for once king he agreed to dismiss the southerners whose arms and horse had brought him the kingdom, promising that he would 'no more introduce into Scotland either English or Normans, or allow them to give him military service'. Once they were gone he was murdered, upon orders from his half-brother Edmund it was said, and Donald Bane came out of the mountains to reign again. He was over sixty, and would have been wise to stay at home, content with strong Celtic support, but he madly joined a Northumbrian rebellion against William Rufus, and in the disasters

*St Andrews Cathedral, from the St Regulus Tower.*

*Alnwick Castle, Northumberland, the scene of many conflicts between Scots and English. Malcolm Canmore was killed here in 1093, the victim of an English lance.*

that followed he was unseated by his nephew Edgar, second son of Malcolm and Margaret. This young man had no doubts about his victory, for when his army was encamped at Durham he had seen St Cuthbert in a vision and been promised guidance and protection. Such a heavenly and productive alliance may have softened his vengeance, for he spared his uncle's life. He put out the old man's eyes and left him to rot in prison. Edmund was allowed to enter a monastery, where he died in remorse and was buried in chains at his own request. Edgar was king.

In this violent flurry of arms, murder and coronation, the law of primogeniture was conveniently set aside. Duncan, first son of the first wife of Malcolm, himself left an heir, but the boy was a minor and the marriage of his parents, it was soon said, was invalid, having been within forbidden degrees and without dispensation.

Donald Bane was the last Celtic King of Scotland. Edgar and the two brothers who succeeded him, Alexander and David, were Scots by half their parentage, but Anglo-Norman in mind and character. They preferred Lothian and its hills, the high rock of Edinburgh, to the mountains of the Pictish heartland, English speech and English dress to the language and habit of the Celt. All three died peacefully, the first two child-less, and the mildness of their departure is a refreshing change from the slaughter-house deaths of their predecessors. They built abbeys, monasteries and churches, inheriting some of their mother's excessive piety, or at least realizing that in a nascent feudal society a strong Church was buttress to a strong Crown. The years they had spent in England, the friendships made, and the debt owed to Anglo-Normans for their inheri-tance, gave them a deeper emotional attachment to the south than to their own kingdom, a conditional loyalty that was further strengthened by a dozen marriages into the Norman royal house, their own and their kinsmen's. The Normanization of Scotland, which had begun under their gentle mother, increased in their successive reigns. The changes it brought were irrevocable and decisive, though not quite what Andrew Lang meant

*The Benedictine Abbey of Dunfermline, the shrine of Margaret. The body of Bruce lies under the choir.* Right *The Augustinian Priory of Restenneth, Angus. Probably founded by David I, it was certainly burnt by Edward I.*

when he wrote 'The long process began by which English brewers, soap-boilers and upholsterers sit in the seats of MacDonells and MacPhersons.' The responsibility for that calamity, if calamity it is, must rest upon the MacPhersons and MacDonells themselves, seven centuries later.

It was the first of the brothers, Edgar, who abandoned the Dunfermline home of their parents and established his on the castle rock of Edinburgh, which David would in his turn make the nodal capital of Scotland. Geography and politics justified the choice. It was impregnable, close to the sea and the south, a hinge between those subjects whom Edgar always addressed as 'Scots and English'. The impression of unity given by the phrase is deceptive, however. Celtic hopes of independence had not been extinguished with the eyes of Donald Bane, and in provinces like Moray, for example, the heirs of Lulach the Fool were jealously ready for revolt. They gave Edgar no trouble. That came from Magnus Bare Leg, King of Norway. When the Gaels of the Isles rose against his semi-autonomous lieutenants, he ruthlessly suppressed them, and having come this far had ambitions of going further. Under threat of invading the mainland, he bullied Edgar into ceding to him the whole of the Hebrides and the peninsula of Kintyre. Though the Isles were lost to Scotland, they did not long remain the docile property of the Norwegians. The half-Norse, half-Celtic chiefs who ruled them soon developed a fierce and passionate independence, subject to no one and nothing but their own pride and ambition.

With England, however, there was peace, cemented by the marriage of a Canmore sister to Henry I, and by the wedding of his illegitimate daughter to Alexander. Peace brought more Anglo-Normans to Scotland, not only clerics finding high office in the Church, or traders profit from its growing commerce, but knights and cadet sons greedy for land and rank they might not expect in England. They brought with them the pattern of Norman feudalism, the interdependence of peasant, knight, baron and king, the obligation of military service and the chivalry that softened its brutishness, the holding of land in feu and upon written charter, the rights of primogeniture in succession and inheritance, French wine and French music, the love of chain-mail and gaudy clothes, arrogant power, solemn humility and wanton dalliance. They came slowly, first taking land across the Solway and the Tweed, then deeper into Lothian, across the Forth and Tay. By the reign of the third Canmore son, they and the Celtic earls who adopted their manners and customs were a steel loop about the mountains from the south-west to the north-east.

Before Edgar's death he made a sapient division of his kingdom between his brothers, although there is no evidence of hostility between them. Alexander was to inherit the throne, but the young David would hold Lothian and Strathclyde as his lieutenant. Alexander was a devout and scholarly man, humble and polite before the monks whose company he enjoyed. To the rest of his subjects, according to Abbot Ailred of Rievaulx, he was 'beyond measure terrible, a man of great heart, applying himself in all things beyond his strength'. The division of the kingdom by his brother was probably to his taste, for it gave him time to bring the Celtic mormaers of the north to a proper under-standing of what was now required of them in a feudal kingdom. It was not done without blood. When the men of Moray and the Mearns, pulling one of Lulach's descendants from obscurity, rebelled against this unwelcome Normanization, the King suppressed them so violently that thereafter they called him Alexander the Fierce. More peacefully, and following the example of his mother, he brought the Church closer to Rome. He appointed her biographer, Turgot, to the see of St Andrews, long vacant since the death of Scotland's last Celtic bishop. When Turgot died, Alexander applied to Canterbury for a successor, and although the Englishman who came soon decided that life in Scot-land was not worth a bishopric, another was found to serve Rome and deal sternly with the Culdees. Anxious as he was to bring his people in line with Roman Christianity, filling the monastic houses he established with Anglo-Norman monks, Alexander was stubborn in defence of the Scottish Church and resisted English attempts to place it under the authority of the archbishops of York. The Scots clergy would in time repay the debt, becoming passionate supporters of the nation's independence.

David, who succeeded Alexander in 1124, was the most English of the brothers, bred and educated by the Normans. During his governorship of Lothian and Strath-clyde he had, by choice, spent most of his time across the Solway, and when he came to Edinburgh he brought with him the Norman-English companions who had delighted him there, giving them land, rank and privilege. Over the next half century they, and others who followed, established almost all of the great families of Scotland, in the Lowlands and the Highlands. They were the ancestors of the Sinclairs, Frasers, Chisholms and Boswells, Montgomeries, Lindsays, Maxwells and Melvilles, Cummings and Gordons, Giffords and Oliphants, Crichtons and Setons. And more. Among David's friends were three who could not have foreseen the ultimate realization of their am-bitions. The first was Bernard de Bailleul, son of a Picardy knight whose service at Hastings had won him estates in Yorkshire. The second was Robert de Brus, whose Norman father had also fought at Hastings, and whom David made Lord of Annandale. The third was Walter FitzAlan, the son of a Breton with rich estates in Shropshire and Norfolk. In love and trust, David made him Hereditary Steward of Scotland. A Balliol, a Bruce, and a Stewart would in their turn rule the nation as kings.

For comfort and security, to protect themselves against each other and the people

*A Viking armlet from an Orkney hoard. The Hunterston Brooch, 8th century. A Highland brooch, c. 1650. Queen Joan's gold ring, 1424. The Kames Brooch, 14th century. A gold ring, c. 1300, found at Holyrood. A Celtic brooch, 2nd century. Overleaf The Cistercian Abbey of Melrose. Founded by David I in 1136, it was frequently burnt and in 1544 finally destroyed by the English.*

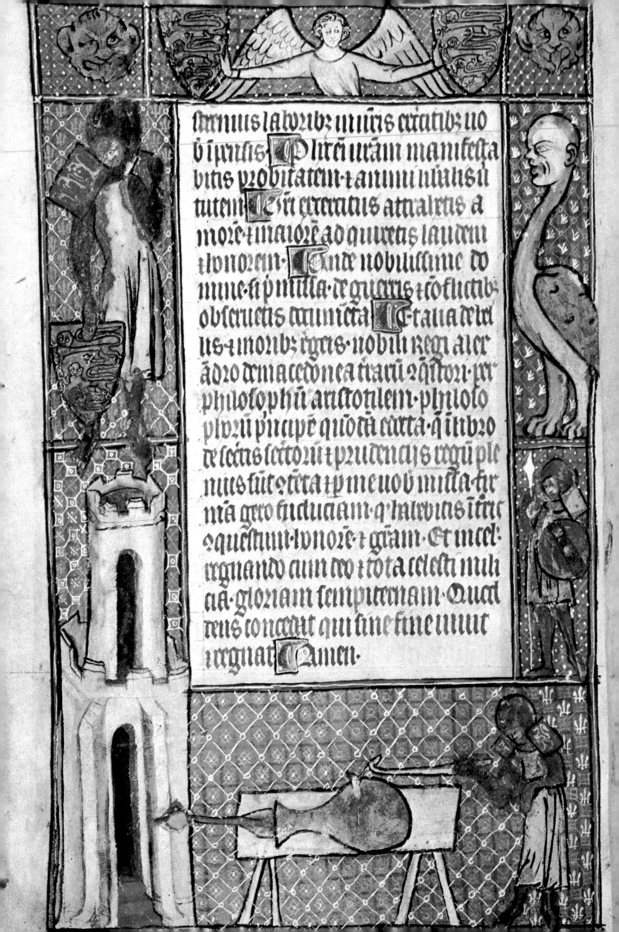

strenuis laboribz in uiris exreatibz uo
bi i puatis. Q lucei uram manifesta
bitis probitatem · 7 animi inuailis ui
tutem. Et in exreatitis attualreris a
more · 7 maioze ad qurreras laudem
7 honorem. Unde nobilissime do
mine · si p missla · de gurreris 7 conflictibz
observeris rerum iecta. Et alia deta
lis · 7 monibz egeneris · nobili regi alex
ando dem macedonica trarum 2 historon · pr
philosophii aristotilem · philoso
plozum principem quondam cartta · q i libro
de secreris secrorum 7 prudencia is regum ple
nius suit 7 tecta · 7 p me uob missla · fir
mia gero fiduciam · q haluruis i terre
e questimur · honore 7 gram. Et in cel
regnando cum deo 7 tota celesti mili
cia · gloriam sempiternam. Qual
terus concedit qui sine fine uiuit
regnat. Amen.

over whom they had been placed, the Normans built fortresses, timber towers palisaded upon a hill and curtained with a ditch. At first these keeps were thickly clustered in Strathclyde and Lothian, but before the century was half run they had spread north beyond the Mounth, the Dee, the Don and the Spey, across the Grampians to Moray. Held by the curl of a river, or on a man-made mound if rock or hill were not available, these castles were quickly and inexpensively built. The stone donjons already rising in England would not appear in Scotland yet, but timber and earth, tower, palisade and ditch were powerful enough. Within the bailey-wall were stables and workshops, bakeries and barns, a great hall across an inner ditch where the lord walked over rush floors in a trailing tunic, dined at a rough table, choked in the smoke of a central fire, admired his meagre tapestries and the gleam of his weapons, bred heirs and marriageable daughters, and envied his neighbours.

These feudal castles, more than anything else perhaps, impressed the native peoples of Scotland with the strength and permanence of their new rulers. In the towns there were more subtle manifestations: English clerks and monks, courtiers and traders, strange ships on the Firth of Forth, churches and monasteries building, all making David the most powerful king the country had yet had. 'The whole barbarity of his nation was softened,' said Ailred, 'and immediately submitted itself to a king of so great benevolence and humility; as if forgetting their natural fierceness, they submitted their necks to the laws which royal gentleness dictated.' But Celtic necks were not so easily bent, or Celtic ferocity soothed by a king's humility. They were subdued by the grey divisions of his feudal cavalry, by faceless men in conical helmets, by long swords, kite-shaped shields and lowered lances. The revolt came, as before, from the men of Moray. Five thousand of them rose behind Angus and Malcolm, grandsons of Lulach, setting their leather shields and their contempt for body-armour against the plunging roar of a Norman charge. Absent in England, as he usually was, David left the suppression of the revolt to his Constable, who met the men of Moray when they reached the North Esk. Earl Angus died in the hopeless fight, and Malcolm was betrayed by his own followers. As Norman horsemen forayed and burnt in the Moray glens, the earldom was placed in forfeit, a title and a favour to be given at will by later kings, and the broken lands of Lulach's children were parcelled out among the Normans.

Invincible though they were against the Celts, David's friends were less successful when they rode with him against England in 1138. The death there of Henry I had been followed by civil war, by the anarchic reign of Stephen and the claims of Henry's daughter Matilda. Tied by blood and emotion to both, David resolved his confused loyalties by supporting first one and then the other. He rode into Northumbria with Norman horse, Lothian men-at-arms, and Galloway kerns, and even, it is said, some mercenary Gaels from the Isles, all marshalled by his lieutenants De Brus and De Bailleul. David's ambitions had gone beyond the profit to be got from the quarrels of his English kin, the return to Scotland of its lost provinces beyond the Solway. Among his banners was the Dragon of Wessex, his mother's house, proclaiming his right to the kingdom he was invading.

Thurstan, the courageous Archbishop of York, declared a holy war against the advancing army, calling upon peasant and baron in the name of God. The response was spectacular, and villages were emptied of men and boys, marching to the gathering behind their priests. The news of this, and of Thurstan's call, made many of David's lords uneasy, though they were less moved by the exhortation than by the remembrance

*A 14th-century pot-de-fer. From an MS. on the duties of a king by Edward III's tutor, William de Milemete.*

*The treasures of a resplendent Church under David I are recalled by this enamelled crucifix found in Fife. Right By a silver coinage such as these pieces, minted in the Royal Burgh of Berwick, he attracted profitable trade with merchants from abroad.*

that they held large estates on both sides of the border. Their feudal oaths bound them to both England and Scotland, and whichever way the battle went, they would lose. De Brus argued with David, saying that the King was more Norman than Scot. As the leaders who opposed them were more Norman than English, where was the quarrel between them? When David stubbornly refused to be deflected, De Brus renounced his fealty and left for the English camp. Before he went, however, he ordered his affairs with the discretion and foresight Scots lairds were frequently to show in their wars and rebellions. He left one of his sons with David, giving the young man all his lands in Annandale. Other friends of David's youth, De Bailleul, Walter Espec and more, also abandoned the King for the enemy, making the same cautious disposition of their sons and their estates. And thus in August, 1138, David was defeated by the men who deserted him, by the friends and companions of his youth.

The Battle of the Standard was fought at Cowton Moor near Northallerton. The Holy Army – Norman horse and archers, English spearmen and billmen – was gathered about a mound of holy relics and a great ship-mast from which floated the banner of the Sacred Host, the flags of St Peter, St John and St Wilfrid. The hot summer sun shimmered on lance, sword, axe and mail, on a kite-shield wall, and above the neighing of horses rose the chant of a psalm. As the Scots army advanced Walter Espec, lately a member of it, looked at it and was fierce in his derision. According to the Abbot Ailred he declared that this was a war of men against beasts. 'Before *them* go jugglers and dancers, before us the Cross of Christ and the relics of his saints.'

Whether or not David's men were led by capering entertainers, they were undisciplined and contentious. Jealous of the Norman lords among them, the Galloway men demanded the right to lead the assault, and before it was given went forward in a screaming storm. Few reached the spear-ring, but fell beneath the dropping arrows and lay 'like a hedgehog with quills' said Ailred. David and his son Henry came up in support with the Lothian men and their Norman knights, many of whom sent away their horses that they might not be tempted to flee. They broke the spear-ring as if it were a spider's web, said Ailred, and the English would have run had not one of them held up a severed head on his spear, shouting that it was David's. The Galloway men, already demoralized by the arrows, fell back, followed by the Lothian spearmen who lost their taste for battle with the death of their leader. In the confusion, David decided to die where he had dismounted, but his knights forced him into the saddle and took him away with his standard.

Walter Espec, if Ailred can be believed, did more talking than fighting that day, but what he said clearly expressed the contempt which the Norman overlords of Scotland felt for its native peoples. Not yet would they think of themselves as Scots, and accept the title with pride.

> Who would not laugh rather than fear when the wretched bare-breeched Scots come up against such adversaries? What are these naked men to steel-clad Normans, their leather shields to our lances, their recklessness of death to our reasonable valour? Strike their long spears with a staff, and you disarm the Scots.

At Carlisle, having achieved nothing by his invasion but the loss of friends and the loss of lives, David held a family conference, and by negotiation secured more than a battle might have won, if less than he desired. Northumberland and Cumbria were given to his son, and he returned to Edinburgh with the border of his kingdom now running from Derwentwater to the mouth of the Tyne, and this was held while the English civil war dragged on for another ten years. Stephen could not push the border back, and David gave his unswerving support to Matilda, content with a promise from her son, Henry of Anjou, that when he became King of England the northern counties would become part of the kingdom of Scotland for ever. The promise was not kept.

*English coins of the 12th century, showing Stephen and Matilda. David I involved himself in their quarrels, first with one and then the other, but at last in unswerving support of Matilda.*

In later years men sometimes thought of David's reign as a warm sunrise after a dark, cold night. The Aberdeen priest, John of Fordun, wrote that the King 'enriched the ports of his kingdom with foreign merchandise, and to the wealth of his own land added the riches and luxuries of foreign nations, changing its coarse stuffs for precious vestments, and covering its ancient nakedness with purple and fine linen'. Flemish weavers came at his invitation, settling in large numbers along the east coast, in the four burghs between the Tweed and the Forth, and the six northward to Inverness. They brought new cloths and new skills, new manners and new customs, a confidence based upon profit and influence that would in time grow into a sturdy political flower. They are remembered in two enduring surnames, their own and Taylor. David granted the Flemings liberal privileges, as he did other merchants from England and France, giving them monopolies and the right to choose their own magistrates. He directed the skills and arts of the monastic houses toward commerce, encouraging them to become traders and bankers by the gift of revenues or the freedom from customs dues on their shiploads.

Feudal law and feudal privilege, burghal rights and monopolies, all based upon English precedents, were the bones of the nation, and the Church was its heart. To the glory of that Church, and to enable it to serve commerce as well as it served God, were raised great monuments of black, red and grey-white stone, towers and splendid halls standing against timbered hills and stagnant marshes. Churches that looked like fortresses, as if the Word and the Spirit were under constant threat of attack. The old Culdee communities, remembering their lost independence of muddy gown and ear-to-ear tonsure, were replaced by vigorous, eager men in white and black, Norman-nosed and round-tonsured, singing responses and psalms in unfamiliar accents. Alexander had first brought the Augustinians, and more came from Beauvais when David offered them a settlement at Jedburgh, placing the neighbourhood Culdees under their rule. He welcomed Benedictines from Canterbury, building them an abbey at Dunfermline about his mother's grave and her church of Holy Trinity. Monks from Tiron were given an abbey at Kelso that became the finest on the Borders until it crumbled in the wasting of wars. David was particularly generous to the ascetic Cistercians, with abbeys at Newbattle and Kinloss, and at Melrose, where he settled monks from Rievaulx in Yorkshire, appointing his step-son, Waltheof of Northumbria, as their abbot. Most favoured of all were the Augustinians. A legend says that as David hunted one day by Edinburgh Castle, he narrowly escaped death from the antlers of a stag. In gratitude, and as a penance for sporting on a holy day, he built an abbey on the spot and named it Holyrood, for his mother's cross of ivory, ebony and silver which he placed in its keeping. Some Augustinian canons, then installed in the Castle, were given the abbey and the right to build a trading burgh beside it.[1]

Never again would there be such a building of abbeys and monasteries. All were lavishly endowed, spiritually and materially, with the gift of sacred relics and the granting of royal tithes, fishing rights, pasturage rights, the right to cut peat, to draw rents from the villages within their bounds, and for some the right to administer

[1] The burgh of Canongate. At this time David also founded the city of Edinburgh, giving his friends and retainers strips of land on either side of its wedge of rock. French and Flemish traders largely occupied the Augustinian burgh at its foot.

baronial justice. Built on Crown lands and from the royal purse, they were free of all secular dues, the King's creation from whom he expected prayers for the protection of his kingdom and government, and by which he hoped for heavenly salvation. Such ecclesiastical powers and preference, sharing and supporting the feudal structure of government, were new to Scotland. The Celtic men of God, in the tradition of the Ionans, had largely been simple priests, teachers, advisers, unworldly men dedicated to lives of worship and evangelism. In the anarchy of war and invasion they had sometimes become civil administrators on behalf of their mormaer kinsmen, as they were sometimes compelled to take arms to defend their own ditches, but the Church had walked beside Man in his suffering, offering a hand, a crook in support. The saints of the earlier communities had practised a simple democracy in the choice and election of their leaders and parish priests. Now feudal rights were observed, Norman lords made their own nominations for the parishes on their lands, and the King made the abbots. Monks had themselves once built their wattle chapels. Now the royal purse paid for masons and carvers, goldsmiths and tilers. For all their self-denial and dedication the new brothers – foreigners for the most part, until they found novices among the Scots — were set apart from the people by the magnificence of the buildings in which they worked and prayed. Their greatest influence upon the nation, beyond their growing power as landowners and traders, was the example they set in order and law and discipline, in the management of estates and tenants, in the acknowledgment of God as the omnipotent feudal lord.

*A 13th-century gilt and enamel coffer-hasp found in Dumfries. The chest it once hinged contained the wealth of noble or burgess.*

Seven times daily, seven times seven a week, the sweet music of abbey bells called the monks to prayer. Where their churches served a parish, the people were allowed no closer to God than the nave, cut off by a rood-screen upon which the Cross of Christ was raised before vulgar eyes. From behind this wondrous barrier of stone or carved wood the priest appeared for Mass, in the glittering beauty of rich vestments, a servant of the Almighty and a glimpse of His aweful majesty. To the south of the church were the monastery buildings, cloistered about a square of which two sides were made by the south transept and nave. Here were lodgings for lay brethren, a rest-house for travellers, kitchens and bakehouses, wine-cellars and storerooms, refectory, chapter-house and parlour above which the monks slept austerely in an apiary of cells. A bell awoke them at midnight, and they started their day with prayer before the night was half run, rustling to work in sandals and gown. They were keepers of the greatest palaces in the land, hoteliers, clerks, masons, farmers and cooks. There was food to be prepared for beggars and the poor, advice to be given to farmers and sheep-herders, orchards and herb-gardens to be tended, cattle to be slaughtered, salt to be panned and bread to be baked, parishes to be visited and rents in kind to be gathered from wide estates. In the evening, in the parlour after vespers, there was a brief hour for gossip, for gentle argument, the rest of bones and spirit.

This David gave to Scotland. Along with the churchmen he brought from abroad came Norman and Anglo-Norman clerks and tradesmen, tenants from his English estates to teach by precept and example. In the twenty-nine years of his reign he imposed and encouraged a feudal organization that moulded what could be changed and slowly extinguished that which could not. Its basis was the system of land-tenure brought from the south, the holding of land in feu, and the creation of class strata working it and owning it, from the *nativi*, serfs born unfree and native to the land where they were born, to the baron himself. The new class structure absorbed much that was there already, the old thanes became barons, the free householders *husbandi*, and the carls *nativi*. Land being the basis of rank and wealth, freedom or servitude, new measurements were found for it, that no man might cheat another – furrow-long and ploughgate, oxgate and bovgate, all based upon the simple, earth-turning tool without which man could not survive.

The old Celtic society was largely tribal, with kinship between leader and led, though always distant in time and sometimes imaginary. In the Lowlands, none of it survived the first half of the twelfth century, except in remote parts of Galloway. It survived in the Highlands, becoming stronger if anything with the development of the clan system, and would obstinately survive for another six centuries until it was blown to pieces by cannon and buried under writs of eviction. In the Lowlands the Normans brought a new concept of leadership and loyalty, the one enforced by iron and the other given as a vassal. The possession of rank and property was first justified by the power to take and hold them in the King's favour, and then by the exclusive blood of the holder. The old laws of the Britons and the Scots, such as we know them, defined a man's status and value by what compensation should be paid for taking his life. A thousand cows for the killing of a king, a hundred and fifty for the murder of his son, a hundred for an earl, and sixteen for the loss of a carl. Land was the measure of a Norman's rank, confirmed by charter for him, and for his inheritors once they had paid a year's rent to the King. So many acres, so many ploughgates determined the cost of an armed horseman, of an archer, a spearman. The fruit of the land bought chain-mail and horses, wine, weapons and cloth. But the land was not the lord's. He was the King's tenant-in-chief, and held the land for the King, with the obligation to keep the peace upon it and to serve the King in war. Such service and support the lord in his turn demanded from his vassals. They knelt before him as he had knelt before the King, placing their hands between his and swearing to be his man in peace and war. In this way had Malcolm Canmore paid homage to the Conqueror.

The laws of the Celts had been unwritten, preserved in the breast of the *brehon*, the wise man of the community. Now an emerging nation of rank and privilege, commerce and justice, fief and vassalage, needed written laws and a government to create and impose them. The Normans and the Northumbrians brought with them the idea of a council of great men, giving advice on the rule of the kingdom. David had seen such a body at work in the court of Henry I of England, a meeting of tenants-in-chief who gave aid and counsel when the King felt inclined or obliged to consult them. Though the

*Henry I of England, who broke his promise to give the northern counties to Scotland for ever. But the remorseful nightmare he is here enduring, in the Chronicle of John of Worcester, was caused by his own subjects.*

proposal was not new in Scotland, and had been considered by Alexander, the first Royal Council, a *Curia Regis*,[1] was established by David, drawn from his bishops, earls and barons, and with it was laid the foundation-stone of the Parliament of Scotland.

3

Grief embittered the last months of David's life. His son, Henry, died in 1152, and within a year he too was dead. Looking at his tomb in Dunfermline, one of his descendants said that his generous patronage of the Church had made him a 'sair saint to the Crown', but the Church gave him no place in the Calendar with his mother. His love for the brave son who had fought by his side at Cowton Moor was shared by all who knew Henry. Ailred said that the prince was a pride to the young, a joy to the old, and the glory of all knights. 'We grew up from boyhood together. As a youth I knew him, a youth himself, whom I left in the body that I might serve Christ, but never left in loving memory.' He married an Anglo-Norman, Ada de Warenne, by whom he had three sons, two of whom would become kings and the third the sire of kings. Despite these, his death left a problem of succession, for the law of primogeniture had not yet been followed from father to son, and it was still challenged by the wild claimants of Moray. David sent the first of his grandsons, Malcolm, on a progress through the kingdom, declaring that he should be welcomed as King-Designate. The second boy, William, he took to Newcastle, there to receive between his small hands the homage of the Northumbrians.

[1] This title, however, was first used in the reign of David's grandson, William I.

Child monarchs were a recurring visitation upon Scotland, as if Providence despaired of the institution and the nation. Time and again the weak body of a boy or a girl, the majesty it feebly represented, became a prize for which men killed and betrayed each other. Malcolm IV, the last Scottish king with a Celtic name, had scarcely taken his grandfather's seat when the Gaels rose under the pretender Donald MacHeth, one of Lulach's ubiquitous descendants. His father-in-law Somerled, Under-King of Argyll and Lord of the Hebrides, raided Clydeside as far as Glasgow before Walter FitzAlan drove him back to his ships. The revolt in Moray lasted longer, and it was three years before MacHeth and his father were locked in a Roxburgh dungeon. War was incessant during the twelve years of Malcolm's reign. Nicknamed the Maiden, for his gentleness or his celibate life, he was thought by one English chronicler to be an angel on earth, but he had a brave spirit and an anxious ambition to honour his father's warrior glory. He fought the Galloway men so resolutely and relentlessly that one of their leaders surprised everybody by giving some of his lands to the Abbey of Holyrood, and by entering the Augustinian order himself. Malcolm also fought the French, under the standard of Henry of England. This was selfless service, though demanded by his feudal obligations as an English landowner, for Henry had renounced the promise to surrender Cumbria and Northumberland, arrogantly appealing to the 'authority of might'. Malcolm did not argue. He let the provinces go, contenting himself with an English knighthood and his father's earldom of Huntingdon. Never well, and always exerting himself beyond his strength, he died at Jedburgh in 1165, aged twenty-five, his passing foretold by a great storm and the terrible movement of comets.

The crown went to William, and the Huntingdon title to the third brother, David. Called the Lion from the rearing beast on his standard, William was of a different mould. Red-haired and robust, energetic, self-indulgent and ambitious, he limited the requirements of piety to one monastic endowment and gave his attention to the recovery of the lost provinces in England. Having failed, on a visit to France, to persuade Henry to part with them, he then joined the Plantagenet's sons in rebellion. He sent David to help the English barons at Leicester, where the unfortunate boy was quickly a prisoner, and himself led an army of Norman-Scots, Celts and Galloway men into Northumbria. According to an English chronicler (whose prose was so compelling that later writers would use the stories he told, when they described the behaviour of Wallace's men), his wild kerns slaughtered children, ripped open pregnant women, and cut down priests at the altar. The scarlet lion on its yellow field, soon to be Scotland's own standard, was set up outside Carlisle Castle, but the constable kept the gates shut, and William's horsemen raided manors on both sides of Hadrian's Wall, burning huts and cornfields, killing with the dedicated ferocity of knightly valour. Before Alnwick Castle, which he also besieged, and where the treacherous point of a lance had finished his great-grandfather's life, William's leonine career came to an end. Seeing a body of knights in the July mist, he thought them to be his own and rode toward them. When he saw that they were English he was not afraid, but couched his lance and shouted 'Now it will appear who knows how to be a knight!' If the words were truly his, they suggest that there had been some doubt about it, and even here the question was unresolved. A spear brought down his horse, and with his feet bound beneath the belly of another he was carried prisoner to Henry II at Northampton.

The English King had recently scourged his own body in penance for the murder of Becket. Purified and elated by this, he accepted William's capture as a gift from God and the dead archbishop. Since there was thus no need for mercy, he sent the Scots king to Falaise and an avenging army to Scotland, where it took the castles of Berwick, Roxburgh, Jedburgh and Edinburgh, wasting or taxing the country about. In bitter exile, the Lion became a sheep. He was unmarried, his brother was also a prisoner, and the line of Canmore faced extinction, or at least expulsion, if both endured their imprisonment until death. By the Treaty of Falaise, five months after his capture in July, 1174, William knelt before Henry in homage, swearing to hold Scotland as a vassal. He kept his word for fifteen years.

Although other Scottish kings had paid homage to the English Crown before this, it could not be argued here that it was for William's English estates and not the kingdom of Scotland. Much more than his liberty had been lost when he charged through the mist at Alnwick. The oath he swore made vassals of himself, his brother, his lords and churchmen and all their dependants. Every man, woman and child in Scotland was a feudal servant of the King of England. Twenty-one Scots barons were held hostage until all the terms of the Treaty were met, and English garrisons held the castles they had taken in the name of their master. The degradation continued throughout those fifteen years. If Henry demanded William's attendance, in England or in France, to hear his decision on this or that, then William went dutifully like any other vassal. Only the clergy of the Scottish Church boldly challenged and defied the terms of the Treaty. At a conference in Northampton, their representatives denied that they were subject to Canterbury. The Treaty contains the first recorded reference to an *Ecclesia Scoticana*, a Church of Scotland, and the corporate independence implied by the phrase was stubbornly defended by bishops who until now had been treated with individually. The debates lasted fourteen years until Celestine III, by his bull of 1192, declared *Ecclesia Scoticana* the special daughter of the apostolic see and subject to the pontiff only.

William's humiliation was never more ugly than when he wished to subdue a Galloway rebellion, but had first to ask permission from his liege-lord Henry. He captured a brutal ruffian called Gilbert, who had blinded and murdered his own brother, but could not punish the man. As vassalage demanded, Gilbert was sent to Henry, who fined him, exacted an oath of loyalty, and returned him to Galloway, which he promptly cleared of William's garrisons. Permission was again asked to suppress a Donald Ban MacWilliam who had raised the men of Moray, claiming the throne by right of descent from Malcolm Canmore's first wife. The reasonable justice of MacWilliam's claim was extinguished by his death in battle outside Inverness, and his brother was hanged above the dead, thus saving William from the indignity of another episode like Gilbert of Galloway.

Relief came only with the death of Henry. His successor, Richard Lionheart, was more interested in the Holy Land than in Scotland, and for ten thousand merks of silver (needed to buy arms and ships) he released William from the Treaty of Falaise, and returned to him all the castles the English Crown still claimed in Scotland. In this atmosphere of cordial bargaining, William offered another fifteen thousand merks for Northumberland, which Richard was willing to sell, provided he could keep the castles there. Since the province was useless without these fortresses, William withdrew the offer. In any case, it is hard to see where he could have found the money, having only now paid the ransom of ten thousand merks demanded of him by the Treaty of Falaise.

At the age of fifty-three he at last fathered an heir by his wife Ermengarde de

Beaumont, the illegitimate granddaughter of Henry I whom the English had forced upon him. As an indication of the affection between them, they had been married thirteen years before their son, Alexander, was born.

The death of Richard, by an arrow below the walls of Chaluz, ended the amiable peace between the kingdoms. Bored with the life of indifferent piety he had followed since martial glory escaped him, William thought he could now exert his right to Northumberland over John of England. A skirmish war burnt along the Border, but at the last moment William decided against an invasion, persuaded, it was said, by a Divine warning that appeared to him as he lay asleep by his great-grandmother's tomb at Dunfermline. More probably he was forestalled by John, who crossed the Border himself, demanding compensation of fifteen thousand merks for the damage done to his dignity and his tenants. There were councils and conflicts, stakes laid and passed across the gaming-table of the Cheviots, a manor burnt, an apology made, the gift of a bright-eyed falcon to John, barrelled lampreys to soothe the queasy stomach of William. It was a strange war, in which the dependants were more eager to fight than the principals. Two of William's daughters were sent south so that John might find husbands for them, and until he did they were the pets of his court, dressed in green and fed with costly figs. And the war, if war it was, ended in a weary alliance, with the payment of fifteen thousand merks in dowries.

Old and senile, William died in 1214, his hopes of expanding his kingdom long since abandoned, though he did invest Alexander with his own estates in England. Nobly named, he was a futile warrior at the best, but he left the defiant beast of his banner for the inspiration of his people. In law and government he had followed the example of his father, and the single triumph of his long reign had been one for which he could take no credit, the stubborn and rewarded independence of the Church.

The percentage of Celtic blood in Alexander II was minimal. He was sixteen, and the ceremony of his accession was hurriedly performed before his father's body was cold. There was need for haste. The MacWilliam and MacHeth pretenders, almost wholly Celts, were again in revolt, but their heads were soon brought before the boy-king by his ferocious Earl of Ross. The north secure for the moment, Alexander turned toward the south in his family's old desire for Northumbria. He gave his sympathy to the barons of Runnymede, but instead of their support there came an army sent by John with orders to 'hunt the red fox-cub from his lair'. Though his soldiers burnt Berwick, and reduced most of the castles along the Border, John was too engaged with civil war at home and invading French from without to reinforce them. And then he was dead at Newark, from poison it was believed. More a politician than a warrior, Alexander set aside his claim to Northumbria at the moment he might best have won it. He married John's daughter Joanna, hoping perhaps that her brother Henry III would give him the province along with her hand. The gift was not made, the claim was ignored, and in the years of uneasy peace and spluttering war that followed Pope Gregory – on Henry's instigation, no doubt – ordered Alexander to renew the Treaty of Falaise. The Legate he sent was told by the King: 'Untamed and wild men dwell in my land, they thirst for human blood, and if they should attack you I cannot restrain them.' The Legate's response went unrecorded, but he does not seem to have pressed the order from the Holy Father.

The dragging quarrel was at last ended by a council held at York in 1237. The treaty agreed set down Alexander's grievances, his claim to Northumbria, and his willingness to relinquish it in return for lands valued at two hundred pounds a year. The Border once more ran between the Solway and the Tweed, with three marches on either side, each governed by a warden sworn and bound to keep the peace, if possible, among the hot-tempered reivers of both nations. The peace established was long-lasting, broken only by the summer storms of sudden affrays. When it ended, it would not be in a struggle for a province but for the independence of Scotland itself.

Alexander died in 1249, on an expedition to wrest the Hebrides from the tenuous control of Norway. He was tired and sick. He had just suppressed two rebellions in Galloway, and he had no strength for a sea-borne campaign against the distant isles. He died on his galley by the rock and green island of Kerrera, while his waiting fleet lay at anchor about him in the Firth of Lorne. He was, said the generous encomiums of the chronicles, a father to his people and a second Peter to the Church of Christ.

*The seal of Alexander II, showing him enthroned and mounted. In the saddle he wears hauberk and helm, and his shield and horse-furniture are emblazoned with the Lion of Scotland.*

Once again a child was king, Alexander III, a boy of eight seated in solemn consecration on the Stone of Scone, while a Celtic bard recited in Gaelic his descent from Fergus, first King of the Scots in Albainn. This echo of old ways and old kings, however, meant less than the presence at the boy's side of Walter Comyn, Earl of Menteith, who with his half-brother Alexander, Earl of Buchan, controlled the kingdom for the first six years of the young man's reign, never forgetting their own royal descent from Duncan I. In his infancy, Alexander had been betrothed to Princess Margaret of England, and within eighteen months of his accession the Comyns took him to York for his marriage. The English chronicler Matthew Paris said that Henry III asked why he should not pay homage, and that the boy replied he had come in peace, not to answer difficult questions. He had probably been schooled in the response by the Comyns, as in his further plea: 'I am a King, and by your goodness a knight, but I am a child, without aid of knowledge.' Henry did not press the point against such subtle innocence. There were other ways to control Scotland.

Among the lords who had land or kin on both sides of the Border there was already a party sympathetic to England, led by Alan Durward, Justiciar of Scotland, and by Robert de Bruce, descendant of the deserter at Cowton Moor. By his marriage to Alexander's aunt, de Bruce had a claim on the throne for his heirs, though no one yet would have allowed it much substance. The Comyns kept this English party from the King's person for as long as they could and by a spear's-length if necessary. In 1255 they were ousted from the regency, replaced by a council of fifteen lords each of them carefully chosen by the King of England. When he was eighteen Alexander was no doubt glad to be free of the noisy arguments of both factions, and at twenty-two he was fired with a desire to complete the work his father had left unfinished on the Isle of Kerrera. He sent emissaries to Bergen, offering to buy the Hebrides. King Hakon of Norway thought this amusing. He had money enough, he said, and then realized that what could not be bought might well be taken, particularly since he could put little trust in Hebridean lieutenants who were now more Gael than Norse. Hearing that the bloody Earl of Ross was already harrying Skye (the report had the usual account of children spitted on Scottish spears), he gathered an army and launched a fleet to chastise Alexander.

The Battle of Largs is an epic conflict of Scottish legend, wherein single corpses are counted as tens, and a ragged seashore skirmish is transformed into a struggle of giants. The weather, which wins more battles than generals admit, won this engagement before it was truly begun. In July, 1263, old Hakon's fleet left Kirkwall in Orkney and sailed north about the cap of Scotland to the Sound of Skye. There he was joined by Magnus, King of Man, and by a few Norse and Celtic chiefs who could not avoid their obligations, or who hoped to turn them to personal profit. The Lord of Argyll, from whom Hakon expected much, prudently stayed at home in his sea-loch, though some of his Islay followers gladly raided Loch Long. As the fleet moved on toward the Firth of Clyde, slowly against increasingly adverse weather, Alexander tried to blunt the edge of Hakon's hostility with negotiation. He sent Dominican monks, and they dragged on the discussions from day to day, encouraged by every contrary wind that gave him time to gather an army. Even so, by late September the fleet was well into the Firth and moving northward. Forty ships had been left in Loch Long with the Islay men, and others got far enough up the Clyde, it was said, to send hungry raiders to the Stirling plain. On the last day of the month a great gale tore Hakon's mighty vessel from the strands of its eight anchors, and drove ten provision-ships ashore by Largs on the Ayrshire coast. Their crews were attacked by Scottish archers, a confused, witless exchange of whistling arrows, quickly ended by nightfall. In the morning Hakon brought his drifting ship under control and inshore, landing more men. They were suddenly faced by the main body of Alexander's army, now drawn up on a ridge. Still there was no great battle, a clumsy charge of horse along the beach, a counter-charge, and then the Scots fell back to the escarpment, where they watched as the Norwegians waded out to their ships and sailed away. From this, later chroniclers would create a 'dangerous and cruel battle' in which sixteen thousand Norsemen and five thousand Scots were slain, and all but four of Hakon's ships destroyed. As an afterthought almost, God was given credit for orchestrating the slaughter with a storm.

Yet it was decisive. Though he reassembled his fleet, Hakon retired to Kirkwall, where death and the next bitter winter took the surrender of his aged body. Three years later, by the Treaty of Perth, his successor released Man and the Western Isles to Scotland for four thousand merks of refined silver and an annual payment of one hundred more.

If this annuity was ever paid, no record has been found of it. The long threat of the Norsemen was over, and the kingdom of Scotland stretched from the North Sea to the furthest shore of the Atlantic. The Treaty meant nothing to the Islesmen, however. The chiefs of Clan Dougall and their eager rivals of Clan Donald, both claiming descent from Somerled, were too busy with dynastic arguments to care much about the transfer of an external authority which neither of them acknowledged.

Alexander was still only twenty-five, and already loved by his people, the chroniclers said, because he was 'righteous, holy, wise and kind, mild and merciful'. The twenty years of life left to him would be scarred with sorrow as death winnowed his family. The child-wife placed in his bed by the English died in 1275, and the three children she bore him also died. For ten years he would not marry, but he was old for the time, and he needed an heir. In 1285 he married Yolande, daughter of the Comte de Dreux. He loved her and could not bear to be parted from her for an hour longer than was necessary, and this devotion was responsible for his death within a year of their marriage.

4

If David's reign could have been seen as the sunrise of promise, that of Alexander III was glorious noon. Troubled and dispirited men in the next century looked back to it with wistful longing. A few jingling lines, said to be the earliest scrap of Scots verse, sing of an age when there was law and peace, ale and bread in abundance, happiness and glee, and wine bright in the flame of good candles. The quarter of a century between Largs and the death of Alexander was probably not so rich, not so abundant and secure as the anonymous rhymester remembered, but he and others needed reassurance in the darkness of the great struggle against England, in the pain and bloodshed and treachery of a war for independence. Our gold has been changed to lead, he cried. Christ born in virginity, succour a land once so happy and now so desperate!

In the last years of Alexander's reign it was possible to accept the almost incredible proposition that peace was an alternative to war, not a hasty interval for the dressing of wounds and sharpening of swords. The King, said that old verse, had 'Scotlande lede in lauche and le', had ruled by law and in peace, and during the brief respite of his reign the great changes that had been taking place over a hundred years were given time to take root, to strengthen the country for the bitter century to follow. The feudal rule of the provinces below the mountain line, the common framework of one law, one Church and one tongue, encouraged the separate peoples there to think of themselves as one nation. They were Scots. The word implied no kinship or sympathy with the real Scots, the Gaelic tribes now known as *bruti* and contained in their hills as much as possible, but was given to them and accepted by them because the inherited title of their feudal superior was King of the Scots. The paradox did not escape a percipient Englishman of the thirteenth century, who wrote that the kings of Scotland prided themselves on being French in race, manner and speech and culture, and had reduced the Scots to slavery. The same could have been said of the Normans who were vassals of those kings, and who, by the end of the century, were calling themselves Scots. At first this was no more than a geographical distinction of feudal holdings, and Norman-Scots and Norman-English fought each other in territorial rivalries, not national wars. The reasonable conflict of loyalties which made Robert de Brus change his coat before the Battle of the Standard would also influence his descendant Robert Bruce and others at the beginning of the War of Independence, but the continuation of the struggle would call for a deeper purpose than feudal interest, a fierce patriotism to inspire both baron and peasant. The wars of the interregnum would still be civil wars between Norman rivals, but after Wallace's fight at Stirling Bridge the cause would be seen as national, and in the Declaration of Arbroath the liberty of 'this Scottish nation' would be maintained by barons and freeholders whose pride lay not in the Norman ancestry of most of them, but in the ancient independence of Alba and its kings.

Beyond that fragment of melancholy verse there is no surviving literature to illuminate Alexander's age, and there was none to survive, perhaps. There was a Thomas of Erceldoune in Berwick, a poet and seer also known as the Rhymer, but the authorship of the work credited to him is questionable, the language English, the spirit Norman, and it tells nothing of Scotland. The poet-historian of Scottish nationalism, John Barbour, was yet to be born, and his passionate cry that 'Freedom is a noble thing!' would be made long after his countrymen had proved it in blood. The enduring evidence of the age is more tangible, the ruins of great abbeys, of the stone castles that were now replacing the timber towers first built by the Normans. The castle was the hub of the feudal wheel. The palisade of stakes that had once surrounded it had now become a stone wall, like an apron spreading down the slope on which it stood, a towered, corbelled and battlemented wall that could be fifteen feet thick and forty or more in height. The ladder-entry to the high door of the old keep had become a gate-house in this wall, a castle in itself, with a portcullis and a drawbridge of wood and iron. The wooden huts that once crouched at the foot of the keep were taken within the wall, stables and storehouses about court and forecourt, buttery, brew-house and bakery, a dovecot for eggs and cushioning feathers, and safe housing for the master's falcons – merlins for his lady, hobbies for his sons, and peregrines for himself. A great square donjon rose from the wall at its highest point, above earth, rock and punishment pit. Within it was the big hall, floored with reeds and quarrelling dogs, swept by winds through its open windows. Here servants and guests slept on heather or straw, here the lord dined, entertained and dispensed justice, nobly elevated by the luxury of the chair on which he sat and the dais on which it was placed. The kitchens that adjoined the hall had great ovens, and spits large enough to take the carcass of an ox, racks for salting fish, butts of wine and barrels of ale, pantries for bread, and larders for preserving meats in their own fat. What was stale was given to the poor, what was still edible was made more so with pepper and cloves, cinnamon and nutmeg. Over the hall, reached by winding stairs, were the lord's chambers, their bleakness softened by tapestries gaudy with heraldic arrogance, great beds and chests, a discreet privy above a falling chute that carried his ordure to the stagnant moat below.

Year by year the castle would become more complex, with outer and inner walls, more towers and ditches, a labyrinth of defences, for although powerful it was never unconquerable. Determined and expendable men might reach it across a moat filled with faggots, protected from arrows and stones by a roof of wooden shields. They could break its walls with siege-engines, climb them by ladders, or leap down upon them from wooden towers of their own construction, calling upon God and the saints for courage. Understandably, such direct assaults were rare, and succeeded only when the besieged were weak from hunger, disease or despair. It was easier to bribe the lord, or threaten to hang a kinsman held as hostage.

*Scotland's kings and their Norman barons were accused of being more French than Scots. This 13th-century gemellion from Limoges is an indication that their taste in ornaments was indeed sometimes more Gallic than Gaelic.*

Behind their precinct walls the abbeys and monasteries were as impressively remote as the castle, the spiritual heart of feudalism as the keep was its muscle. They stood like white and red islands in a green sea of orchards and fields, and since David's day they had increased. Ten dioceses, under the favour of King and nobles, grew richer on grants of land, fisheries, sheep-walks and customs dues. Power and wealth, a cloistered life, set the religious orders apart from the people. Vows of poverty and humility, individually taken, were meaningless within corporate luxury and indulgence, and service to God was perhaps an irony when it was dependent upon the generosity of King and barons. At the beginning of the thirteenth century successive popes had given their special blessing to new orders of wandering friars who, unlike the monks, made the world their religious house, supplementing the work of parish priests, preaching in the open and tending the sick in a hovel, walking with the vulgarity in odorous streets, and owning nothing but dusty sandals and a worn gown. Even so, in time these mendicant grey, white and black friars had their stone palaces, flocks and gardens, accepting endowments of land for easing the soul of a rich man past the terrible judgment of God. The monastic orders gave the Church its leaders, and what concern they felt for the moral probity of its servants was not so much exercised upon abbey or monastery as upon the unfortunate parish priest. Though he was usually appointed by the feudal lord, and lived close to temptation, criticisms of his behaviour at the end of the century may also illustrate the laxity of discipline inside the religious houses themselves, screened from common view. By a series of thunderous orders from his ecclesiastical superiors he was told to be discreet and modest in his appearance, to wear no jewels or clothes of striped colours, to live continently and banish concubines from his house. He was to shun all lusts of the spirit or the flesh, pride, gluttony and drunkenness, and to avoid taverns except when his travels brought him to them for shelter. For the glory of God and the respect of men, his church was to be kept roofed, its windows glazed, its chalice to be of silver and not of wood, its altar-cloth white and its vestments clean, for what was unbecoming in profane things was filthiness in things sacred.

The frailty of man corrupts the organizations he creates as much as it does his own nature, even when their purpose is to struggle against his weaknesses. But his courage to destroy what he has created is noble, and his faith in re-creation is enduring. Two hundred years after the gentle example of Queen Margaret and the pious foundations of her son, the germ of corruption was working in the Scottish Church. Another hundred years would pass before it would burn a heretic for denouncing the growing plant, and one hundred and fifty more before reformers would tear out the flower by its root.

The trading burghs of Scotland, third in the trinity of feudal power, were the heart of a mercantile and agricultural economy that had replaced the pastoral tribalism of the past. A revolution had passed across Europe, bringing trade between nations as well as war, and it reached Scotland last of all. Berwick and Roxburgh, the first of the commercial towns, were created by David, and by the reign of Alexander III there were many more. They had once been forts, or fortified villages standing upon an estuary, a river-ford, a junction of rough roads, convenient centres for the exchange of local produce. David's encouragement of foreign trade, and the minting of a silver coinage, attracted merchants and craftsmen from beyond Scotland, Flemings principally, but also Normans, Norman-English, and Anglo-Danes. They were the first burgesses, not native Scots, their rights and duties defined in the charters granted them by King, Church or barons. With good reason, they were obliged to maintain the towns as fortresses, for they were a greater temptation to an invader than a wooden Border keep. First timbered and palisaded, in time they became towns of stone, walled, gated and towered. Each burgess was bound to build his fortified house within a year of the granting of his charter, and in such a way that it joined with the houses of his neighbours to form a defensive honeycomb, its walls hopefully secure in a countryside of omnipresent menace. In the years that followed these merchant forts gave Scotland its characteristic domestic architecture, turreted walls and arrow-slit windows.

King, abbot and baron drew rent from their burghs,[1] *burgage* rent on land held by the burgesses, money from tolls, revenues, taxes on wool, hide and cloth, flesh, fish and grain. The King's Chamberlain presided over the royal burghs, controlling them through sheriffs who were usually local lords, and who soon made their office hereditary. Almost from the granting of their charters, the burgesses worked to extend their privileges, to escape from the frequently rapacious control of the sheriff, and to deal directly with the King's Exchequer. Though David endowed many abbeys, churches, and barons with the right to establish their own burghs, and to enjoy some of the revenues therefrom, they remained for a long time regional markets only, and the royal burghs north and south of the Forth were the important international trading centres.

The greatest contribution to the nation made by the burghs – beyond the increasing prosperity they brought – was their sense of community based on common interest rather than tribal loyalty, their interdependence in rights and liberties, the brotherhood of their gilds, and their stubbornness in mutual defence. And there, perhaps, may be some explanation for the passionate nationalism of the Scottish people at the beginning of the fourteenth century. The burgess was not yet rich, his importance was less apparent than that of the baron whose castle dominated his town, but the security of the nation was vital to him, and the collective power of his gild a stronger example of unity than the bannerets and bonds of contentious knights. Like the trading burgh itself, the idea of a gild, a fraternal society for mutual protection and advancement, was borrowed from England and from Europe, its name derived from *geld*, from *gilde*, a payment made by each toward the common purpose of all. Its temple was a fine hall built in the centre of the town, a court-house and a council-house properly enriched with furniture and hangings. There privilege and pride were carefully maintained, discipline and order imposed. The ancient sanctuary of the church for a criminal fugitive was surpassed by the burgh's right to grant a man freedom from vassalage, could he manage to live unchallenged in the town for a year and a day. As the charters of establishment became more comprehensive, the burgesses buying liberties and rights with the same cunning they used in trade, many of the burghs became self-governing, electing their own civil officers and determining, to a degree, their own financial responsibilities. Since their laws differed from those of the kingdom outside their walls, they had what was in effect their own parliament, the Court of the Four Burghs,[2] presided over by the royal Chamberlain and hearing dispute and appeal.

Behind their gated walls the burgh towns were colourful and noisy, with garden enclaves and narrow streets, a wide market full of stalls on feast days, the swirl of rich

---

[1] Burgh is the Scots form of borough, derived from the Old English *burg* or *burh*, and earlier European words for a fortified civil community. Not all Scots towns with the suffix *burgh* were trading towns. In some cases it is a derivation of *broch*, in others it recalls the fort or castle that was its central origin. But the idea of a fortified place is common to all.

[2] Berwick, Edinburgh, Roxburgh and Stirling.

*Dunstaffnage Castle, Argyll. Here was once a fortress of the Dalriadic kings, housing the Coronation Stone before its removal to Scone. The present castle was built in the 13th century. Right 'For the glory of God and the respect of men . . .' The 13th-century Norman church at Leuchars, Fife.*

cloth, the odour of raw flesh, ale and new bread, the sight of ship-masts beyond the roofs, and the sound of half a dozen European tongues. Though there were rarely more than a thousand people in the largest burghs, and fewer than four hundred houses in Edinburgh, their size was relative, and there had been nothing like them before. As he walked in solemn procession to his gild-hall, or cleaned his weapons at home, the burgess could take pride in the liberties that both maintained. He could travel when and where he wished, and claim the special protection and jurisdiction of his own courts. He held his house and garden in freehold after the payment of one year's rent. He could marry, as could his children, without permission from a feudal lord, and without payment of dues. No tax was levied upon his estate at death, and his own burgh decided the wardship of his children in their minority. He took an oath of loyalty to the King and to the community of his town, and expected each to honour him as he did them. Freedom, as Barbour would say, was a noble thing, and the burgess had shown it to be practicable, profitable and pleasurable before the standard of revolt was raised against the English.

Over all men there was law and justice, of the King and the barons, the Church and the burghs. The King was the supreme judge, and in his name two Justiciars rode through the north and the south, ensuring that his sheriffs were his proper and dutiful servants in civil and criminal administration. Alexander III knew that his Justiciars could be lax or indifferent, his sheriffs corrupt and oppressive, and he sometimes travelled with the former on their rides, listening to cases, hearing appeals, and pronouncing sentences. At the summit of government, law and justice, the *Curia Regis* had now cohered into a council of officers privy to the King: his Chancellor most intimate of all and keeper of his seal, a Chamberlain who managed his exchequer and collected his rents, the Justiciars who were his law officers, a Marischal to keep order in his house, and a Constable to protect his person. Below these, the King could demand the presence of any of his tenants-in-chief for their aid and counsel. He was under no compulsion to take their advice, and not for a hundred years yet would they oppose his decision.[1] Since the law of the kingdom was feudal law and determined by the King, this talking-assembly of officers and tenants who advised him became a court of law, a *parliamentum*, the word a bastard offspring of Anglo-French and Latin parents. The first recorded reference to the King's High Court of Parliament occurs in 1293, six years after the death of Alexander.

The punishment of offenders against the law was harsh and inexorable, its ultimate horror the pit or the gallows. The gibbet stood outside burgh and keep, its rotting fruit a punishment and a warning. The pit was an airless hole far below the great hall of the castle, silent but for the scratch of rats, the drip of water, and the cries of the condemned who were lowered into it. The conical shaft beneath the ecclesiastical castle of St Andrews was thirty feet in depth, twenty-seven in diameter at the bottom and seven at the top. Innocence was sometimes hard to prove, except by twenty-four witnesses, and these were worthless if twenty-four more were ready to testify to guilt. Then there could be a desperate appeal to God's judgment, in combat with the accuser, by grasping the cherry-red end of a heated bar, by immersion in a pool. Innocence was established by a dead opponent, by an unburnt hand, by drowning. The law demanded blood for blood, a hand pierced by the same knife that had wounded another, iron nails driven through the ears, a slit tongue, broken limbs, mutilation until death. Though crime was savage and brutal, punishment was its master in ingenuity.

Of the people little is known with certainty. Like rock strata, earth layers, they were pressed down by each other's weight, Pict, Scot, Briton and Angle, the subsoil of a nation. They lived close to the earth and the beasts upon it, believing in the magical influence of the sun and the planets, in the charms of their pagan past, in imps and monsters and the crucifixion of their Saviour. The struggle to live after birth frequently killed all but the strong, and since man was born to labour, there was perhaps as much relief as grief in prayers for the departing souls of puny infants. The sick could die from the cure and not the illness, and lepers were driven out with sticks and stones upon the orders of the parish priest. Drought and flood, frost and pestilence, were constant enemies, and ennobled man a relentless master. The survivors lived well when they could, on peas and beans, milk and cheese, the flesh of animals in good times. Their love-play was brief and bawdy, their marriages determined by their superiors. Their games propitiated half-forgotten gods or trained them for war. Their rough clothes covered rough skins, and both a rough and hardy spirit.

All men, the free and the bonded, were obliged to defend what was theirs or what they worked for others, and by that obligation to defend what was the King's, for there was nothing that was not his. The Scots soldier was a mounted man, made so by William the Lion, who ordered that all who possessed land or movable property should keep at least one horse for use in public service. Though he fought on foot in battle, the Scot was carried to it on a shaggy horse, no more than a pony bred in the Highlands by the Gaels and driven down for sale in Stirling or Berwick. Foreigners wrote with awe and admiration of this northern centaur, long-legged on a crude saddle, with padded coat,

---

[1] And it would be later still before they could demand and secure the right to sit in parliamentary council. From this the next step was election to it by their peers.

iron hat, wooden shield and swaying spear. On foot, the spearmen fought in bristling schiltrons, compact and disciplined bodies that were irresistible in offence, and for a time unbreakable when attacked. The feudal obligation upon all to bear arms, and to be skilful in their use, was maintained by the English custom of *wapinschaw*, a weapon-show twice a year when every male between sixteen and sixty displayed his arms for inspection. The commonalty of the field were required to show a bow and quiver at least, a forester his crossbow and spear. A man whose lands were valued at less than forty shillings needed dagger and hand-axe, and he whose land was worth no more than a hundred must arm himself with bow, quiver, dagger and short sword. From these, in war, were trained companies of archers, spearmen, and mounted men-at-arms. Over them all was the knight or the lord, who stepped down from the saddle only to die defiantly where he stood. He was armed with lance, sword, axe or mace, and he covered his head with a steel cap and his body with a hauberk of mail much as his ancestors had done at Hastings. War-harness of plate armour, cunningly hinged and strapped, would be later bought at great price from Germany or Italy, and few but the great could afford it. Contrary to the belief of sceptical men in later centuries, plate armour was neither over-heavy nor cumbersome, and probably weighed no more than the full-pack, side-pack, steel helmet, arms and ammunition of a foot-soldier in World War One.

Pleasures for rich and poor were few and crude. There was a little mummery before King and court of which no record remains but an entry in the Exchequer Accounts for the 'King's charge in play'. Rougher pleasures, and more dramatic, were the tourneys which William had introduced, perhaps to quieten the memory of a lance witlessly couched before Alnwick Castle. These courts of chivalry were watched by King and people, and punctiliously arranged by Constable and Marischal, a noisy clangour of blunted weapons, and sometimes warm fountains of blood when honour was defended to the death. The pleasures of scholarship had scarcely made a beginning outside the religious orders. The monks of Dunfermline had established schools at Perth and Stirling in 1173, and throughout the following century other orders set up more, teaching choirs and the reading of music. Parish priests were sometimes masters of small schools for the sons of barons and freeholders, but their pupils were few, and those destined for the Church no doubt.

There was the land, and the delight of the chase across it. Though men were bringing order to their own lives, husbandry, trade and government, they had scarcely altered the face of a country largely dominated by wood, bog and rock. A great forest washed over the Stirling plain to West Lothian, and the wolf that snarled on the burgh seal of Stirling was a reminder of his flitting presence among the trees. The land teemed with wild beasts, outnumbering man and hunted by him with ferocity and joy. Noisy clouds of wildfowl hung above the lakes and the coasts, and boar rooted in the forests about Berwick, Haddington and the towns of Fife. There were wild herds of white cattle, with flowing manes like lions it was said, beautiful and black-muzzled, and bold when attacked. Red deer were pursued in herds, driven into natural pounds and slain with axe and sword. Walter FitzAlan, King David's Steward, gave the monks on his land a tithe of the skins from the deer he killed, and the gift was generous. Falconry, hawking, was an exquisite sport, and one of the oldest, its birds given mounting precedence from the kestrel of a servant to the gerfalcon of a king. Alexander prized the gerfalcons and tercels he kept at Forres and Dunipace, and by his decree the trees in which wild birds nested were protected until the young had flown. The killing of animal and fowl went on with no perceptible effect upon their numbers, for nature still held a balance against man's self-indulgence. The sea was silver with schools of fish. There was a great harvesting of herring, salmon and lamprey, sturgeon, eel and trout, and here at least the law protected loch, river and inlet to encourage their growth.

Below the mountains, where Celtic bards were the custodians and creators of heroic verse, feudal Scotland in the thirteenth century had no great *chansons de geste*, chanted by jongleurs in the market-place or the great hall of the castle. Or none that has survived. The stuff of such epics was perhaps yet to come, and of the past there was only a melancholy memory.

> Quhen Alexander our kynge was dede,
>     That Scotlande lede in lauche and le,
> Away was sons of alle and brede,
>     Of wyne and wax, of gamyn and gle.
> Our golde was changit in to lede.
>     Crist, borne in virgynyte,
> Soccoure Scotlande, and ramede,
>     That is stade in perplexite.[1]

---

[1] This version is from the *Oxford Book of Scottish Verse*, 1966. *Lauche*: law. *Le*: peace, quiet. *Sons*: abundance. *Alle* and *brede*: ale and bread. *Gamyn*: amusement. *Stade*: placed.

Edwardus.

# PART III

# The War of Independence

*'For freedom alone, which no honest man gives up*
*but with life itself'*

Edward I of England, the great Plantagenet who was also Scotland's noblest and most relentless enemy,
and 'by the force of his enmity one of the creators of that country's will for independence'.

On the day following the feast of St Agnes in 1284, said the *Chronicle of Lanercost*, Prince Alexander of Scotland was 'taken from the world, being only twenty years of age, dying on his birthday,[1] changing the rejoicing for his birth into lamentation for his death'. He died from a lingering illness that had unhinged his brain, but in the moments before he departed the clarity of his thoughts returned, and he was gifted with prophecy. The sun of Scotland, he said, would set with the morrow's sunrise, and his uncle Edward of England would fight three battles. 'Twice will he conquer, in the third he will be overthrown.' These words were repeated to the chronicler by a knight, a tutor, and a priest who heard them.

The younger of the King's sons was already dead, and less than a year before his only daughter Margaret, Queen of Norway, had died in labour. Alexander III was childless and without a male heir, but the chronicler had no sympathy for him. Such calamities were the just punishment of God, sent to bring him to a proper spirit of penitence. Succession rather than repentance, however, was uppermost in the King's mind, and within a week of the death of his prophetic son he called a Great Council of his magnates. They agreed with him that should he have no other issue, the throne would go to the infant granddaughter whose birth had killed her mother. Her name was also Margaret, and she was nearly three when Alexander married Yolande de Dreux. There was no issue from that winter coupling, and six months later the King too was dead.

On a snow-whippèd Monday in mid-March, 1286, he sat in the Maiden Castle of Edinburgh with his lords, considering what steps might be taken to secure the release of a Galloway baron from an English prison. A decision made or deferred, they supped late on fresh lampreys, the King calling upon one of the company to be merry, for who knew but this might be Judgment Day. Let it be, said the lord in the same spirit, we shall meet it with full bellies. When supper was over, and despite the gale now blowing up the Forth, Alexander left to join his wife across the water at Kinghorn. By Queensferry the boatman at first refused to sail and then, being accused of cowardice, stoutly told the King that it would be a 'great honour to share the fate of your father's son'. The keeper of the royal salt-pans at Inverkeithing, when Alexander reached the north shore, also failed to persuade him to wait out the night in comfort and security. Eager to be with his young wife, he rode ahead of his guides, fell from his stumbling horse and was killed in the darkness. The heat of wine as much as love probably brought him to that, but both are human and sociable weaknesses. He was one of the most likeable of Scotland's kings, and did not deserve a chronicler's comment that those who knew him best wept the least at his death.

When he was entombed in the south aisle of Dunfermline church there was no enthusiasm for the little Maid of Norway, or at least for a kingdom under a child-queen and jealous regents. On behalf of all present that day in the abbey, the bishops of Glasgow and St Andrews, Robert Wishart and William Fraser, sent two priests to her great-uncle in England, asking for guidance and favour. Edward can have expected no less, for in his opinion he was Lord Paramount of Scotland, so acknowledged by an oath of fealty which the Earl of Annandale had sworn on Alexander's behalf in 1278. Being messengers only, the priests would not have debated the point, or argued that the oath

---

[1] In fact, seven days later. The *Chronicle* also gives the year inaccurately as 1283.

*At Edinburgh Castle (shown here as it was in the 18th century) Edward I lodged in 1298, and fed and calmed his mutinous army before leading it against Wallace at Falkirk.*

had been for their king's English estates only. Nor did Edward press the matter now, perhaps because he had just spent a bloody decade bringing the Welsh to such an acceptance of his suzerainty. At this moment he appeared briefly on a stage he would dominate so terribly for the next twenty years, Scotland's noblest and most relentless enemy, and by the force of his enmity one of the creators of that country's will for independence. He was not yet fifty, the first of his name and the greatest of the Plantagenets, a lover of music, poetry and chess, crusader, hunter, wrestler and master in the lists, the envy and delight of European chivalry. Tall and splendid afoot, he was a giant in the saddle of his black destrier, his pale yellow hair flowing over the polished plate of his armour. Scotland would need a Bruce to cast a longer shadow.

While the emissary priests were still in England, a nervous council of Scots lords and clergy appointed six Guardians to govern the realm in Margaret's name. Three were to rule the land north of the Forth: Bishop Fraser, Duncan MacDuff, Earl of Fife, and Alexander Comyn, Earl of Buchan and the head of his ambitious family. In the south: Bishop Wishart, James the High Steward, and John the Black, the Comyn Lord of Badenoch. All but Fife[1] were of Norman descent, and between the prelates only can there have been a deep and common interest, the continued freedom of the Scottish Church. The excluded Bruces had little respect for the Guardians, or their own promise earlier to accept Margaret, and they were soon rattling spears throughout Annandale in

---

[1] He was the ninth earl. The MacDuffs claimed descent from a son of Eochaid the Fair, a seventh-century king of the Picts, and ruled their province as a kingdom until the beginning of the twelfth century. The 'Kingdom of Fife' lingers emotively in Scottish memory, and the distinction is defended with pride if not always with accuracy.

support of their claim to the throne and their feud with the Comyns. Alarmed by this, and anxious for his daughter's future, King Eric of Norway sent an ambassador to England in May, 1289, asking for Edward's protection and, if possible, a suitable husband. The thought had not been overlooked by the English king, and he was already securing the Pope's dispensation for a marriage with his son Edward of Caernarvon. This prince was Margaret's uncle, and by his late birth to middle-aged parents was also a year her junior. At Salisbury in November a treaty was concluded between Scots, English and Norwegians, so hedged with qualifications that while none opposed the match, none was heartily in favour of it. Scots and English met again the following summer, at Birgham where the soldiers of Malcolm II had turned the Tweed red with the blood of Anglo-Danes, and this time the Scots were less concerned with the marriage than with how much of their independence would be included in the dowry. Upon their insistence, the treaty declared that Scotland was separate and divided from England, that its rights, laws, liberties and customs were 'wholly and inviolably preserved' for all time. Should Edward and Margaret die childless, then her kingdom would pass to her nearest heir 'wholly, freely, absolutely, and without any subjection'.

Possibly the Scots were too tired, too weak to object when Edward turned these rights upon their head by the addition of one phrase: 'Saving always the right of our lord king, and of any other whomsoever, that has pertained to him . . . before the time of the present agreement, or which in any just way ought to pertain to him in the future'. With Edward's authority as Lord Paramount thus obliquely stated, the Bishop of Durham came to Scotland, to demand the surrender of its castles to his master, to sit with the Guardians, and to have a casting vote among them. They tolerated his domineering presence at their councils, but they kept the castles locked against his lieutenants. Before the Birgham meeting an English ship had left Yarmouth to bring Margaret to her great-uncle's court, loaded with sentimental presents of sugar-loaves, gingerbread, figs and raisins. It returned empty and without her, Eric having more faith in one of his own vessels, and Edward angrily sent it back. The Maid sailed in September, but in what ship is not known. Autumnal gales drove it among the isles of Orkney, where she died, from sea-sickness it is believed.

Scotland's throne was now open to a dozen contenders, and the land menaced by civil war. In the south-west the Bruces put a small army on the march for Perth. In the north, where the lords of Mar and Atholl were gathering their vassals, it was said that the Seven Earls of ancient Pictish tradition had the right to elect a new king, though their duties were probably no more than inaugural. Of the twelve claimants six were descended from bastards, five from William the Lion and one from Alexander II, and nobody but themselves had much hope for them. Black John Comyn, Lord of Badenoch, had a right by descent from Duncan I, and the remaining five by descent from the sisters and youngest brother of Malcolm IV. For some years the strongest contender of these had been the most bizarre. Count Florence of Holland said that the brother, David of Huntingdon, had relinquished his rights to one of the sisters, the Count's ancestress. He now abandoned the claim, leaving the principal struggle to the two men who might have been excluded by it, had it been true: Huntingdon's descendants Robert Bruce of Annandale and John Balliol. The old Earl of Annandale had never surrendered his belief that the throne should be his, and had long been known as the Competitor. He was suspected of having entered into a bond with Florence by which they would share the kingdom, whichever way a decision went between them. His mother had been

Huntingdon's daughter Isabella, and the fact that Balliol had undoubted precedence through an elder daughter was of no consequence to the Bruces. Their confidence was confirmed by the Seven Earls, who ignored the Pictish arithmetic that should have made the Black Comyn their choice, and declared that Alexander III had appointed Annandale as his heir.

> Said they, the heir by the nearest male
> Was Robert the Bruce, of Annandale,
> The Earl of Carrick; he alone
> Was rightful claimant to the throne.[1]

Other men were less eager to help a Bruce on to the Stone of Destiny. As soon as a rumour of the Maid's death reached Perth, Bishop Fraser had written to Edward, asking him to come to the Border and there choose a claimant who would take his counsel and be his man. Fraser did not say who this should be, but he told the King that if John Balliol should come before him it would be to Edward's honour and advantage to treat him well. Fraser was honestly concerned to avoid a civil war, but by this letter he opened the door to half a century of savage bloodshed. On the other hand, without it Edward would not have abandoned the union of the kingdoms he had hoped to achieve peacefully with the marriage of the Maid. In the early summer of 1291 he came to Norham on Tweed with all his northern levies, his standards and his chivalry. The Scots who had come to hear his adjudication were told that they must first acknowledge him as the Superior and Lord Paramount of Scotland. Someone asked why they should throw away their freedom, and was given less of an answer than a threat. 'By Saint Edward whose crown I wear,' said the King, 'I will maintain my just right or die in the cause!' The boldness of the question and the arrogance of the retort stiffened the Scots, and with two exceptions they rejected Edward's demand. The exceptions, however, were decisive – Annandale and Balliol. With seven other claimants later, they put their seals to an acknowledgment of Edward's feudal sovereignty, promising to accept his choice in the matter of the throne, and granting him the castles he demanded. 'Ah, foolish folk,' said Barbour, 'how blind ye were . . .'

> For had ye thought with greater care
> What perils to you soon might grow,
> Ye would not have arranged it so.

Even then Edward did not choose between the final contenders, Annandale and Balliol, and the horsemen and councillors dispersed from Norham. Seventeen months passed, increasing the hostility between the Comyns and the Bruces, for John Comyn was Balliol's man and married to the claimant's sister, and the hatred now growing between the two families would survive an uneasy alliance and mature in murder at the Greyfriars monastery of Dumfries.[2] Scottish support for Annandale was strong, but when the troublesome matter was at last settled in November, 1292, by a court of a

---

[1] This and following quotations from John Barbour's epic poem *The Bruce* are taken from the version published in 1964 by William MacLellan & Co. Ltd, translated by Archibald A. H. Douglas. Grateful acknowledgment is here made to the translator and the publishers for permission to use these quotations.

[2] The Comyns's claim, which they did not press, was based on the marriage of their Norman ancestor to a great-granddaughter of Duncan I. More immediately, Annandale's case was that the King's Great Council in 1238 had declared him the senior *male* heir by Huntingdon's daughters. This, however, had been nullified by the birth of Alexander III and Balliol.

hundred and four auditors sitting in Berwick with Edward as judge, the decision fell upon Balliol. Each claimant had nominated forty of the auditors, the remaining twenty-four were the King's men, and the choice was clearly his. It cannot be faulted by the rules, and the correctness of it should not be obscured by the monument of emotion upon which the greatest of the Bruces has since been elevated.

Three days later, Balliol swore fealty to Edward. He then left in haste for Scone, where he was installed on St Andrew's Day. At Christmas he was across the Border again in Newcastle, kneeling in homage before his superior lord, the King of England.

Above *and* opposite *John Balliol's seal.* Toom Tabard, *though reluctant to enter into armed combat, is seen here in the hauberk and helm of a medieval warrior.*

King John, whom historians find it difficult to call anything but Balliol, has been rightly regarded as a puppet or a lamb among wolves. He was in his early forties, simple-minded and weak-willed. The founding of a Scots college at Oxford by his parents suggests that he may have been something of a scholar himself, but he needed courage and cunning more than learning. He was never well, foolishly haughty in manner, and craven when he should have been bold. He soon felt and answered the pull of feudal strings in Edward's hands, going meekly to England like any baron when summoned there in a dispute over a territorial inheritance of the MacDuffs, though it was a matter he was entitled to deal with himself in Scotland. He was told that the Treaty of Birgham was no longer valid, and appears to have made no great protest when the Sheriff of Northumberland ordered him to appear in London upon a charge that he had not paid the wine bills of Alexander III. Edward's treatment of the wretched man was brutally humiliating, and it may be that he wished to provoke some defiance in Scotland that would permit him to suppress the mounting hostility to Balliol and himself.

If so, it soon came when Balliol was told to muster men and money for a war against Philip of France, whose claims of feudal superiority Edward was resisting as arrogantly as he imposed his own upon Scotland. Meeting at Scone in July, 1295, a Committee of Twelve – four bishops, four earls and four barons – persuaded their timorous king to break from Edward's grasp and to conclude an alliance with Philip.[1] Encouraged by the resistance of his barons, and by the unnatural fever of his own defiance, Balliol declared that his homage and his promises had been given under threat of violence, and when Edward seized his estates in England he expelled all English landowners from

*John, created King of Scotland and vassal of England by Edward I, here sits on a throne the power of which he could not wield.*

Scotland, the ambivalent Bruces among them. Old Annandale the Competitor was recently dead, his lifelong hopes unrealized, but his claim to the throne and a taste for intrigue were vigorously alive in his son and grandson. Being still more Norman in loyalty than Scots, they offered their swords to Edward once they were across the Border, confident that he would return to them the lands of Annandale which John Comyn had now taken.

At war with France in Gascony, embroiled in yet another Welsh rebellion, his own country restless, Edward Plantagenet came north upon Scotland like an outraged lion. The Border was already in bloody confusion, English merchants were being murdered in the royal burghs of Berwick and Roxburgh, and John Comyn was besieging the Bruces

---

[1] The first formal treaty of many between Scotland and France, although there had been earlier links between the two countries. It is regarded as the beginning of the 'Auld Alliance', remembered with more emotion and sentiment by the Scots than it ever was by the French.

*The gateway to Scotland, Berwick today is peaceful, but warring armies of English and Scots fought for it century by century, and what had once been a Royal Burgh became at last an English border town.*

in Carlisle. Edward wasted no time in raising this siege, but led his army to Berwick at the end of March, 1296. Its castle was held by Sir William Douglas the Hardy, the first of his name to be noted in history, a ruffian by all accounts who had ejected the magistrates of Berwick, beheaded one prisoner and thrown another into the pit. The presence of such a man can be encouraging in war, however, and the people of the burgh outside his gates jeered at Edward across their timber wall and shallow ditch.

> Waune thou havest Berwick, pike thee
> Waune thou havest geten, dike thee.

But there was more strength in their lungs than in their defences. Englishmen in bowl-like helmets poured over the palisades at the first assault, and it was said that the Scots were so astonished that none could lift a sword or thumb an arrow. The town was taken in a few minutes, but the killing went on in the thin afternoon sunshine until Edward, looking down at a child that clung to the bloody skirts of its mother, called *'Laissez! Laissez!'* Among the last to die were thirty noble Flemings who fought on in their burning hostel until its roof fell upon them. The castle surrendered at dusk, and Douglas was granted his life, by knightly custom perhaps, or because his support for John Balliol had been lacklustre at its best.

Edward's chief lieutenant was John de Warenne, Earl of Surrey, a hard and hot-tempered old man whose warrant for his feudal rights, he said, was the rusty sword his ancestor had used at Hastings. With the finest English chivalry, northern levies and Welsh bowmen, he was sent north to take Dunbar, while Edward indulged his taste for military engineering by turning Berwick into a fortress base, directing a thousand impressed labourers in the rebuilding of its muddy walls. At Dunbar, in their castle above the sea, the Scots were as courageous and as foolhardy as the burgesses of Berwick.

74

They too waved flags and shouted insults, and since it was common knowledge that all Englishmen had tails they promised to dock every one they captured. Surrey turned aside from these taunts and advanced upon John Comyn's disorderly army, where it was gathered on the heights. As the English broke formation to cross a gully, the Scots left their own position and charged down with braying horns. Welsh arrows hummed among them, and Surrey's knights and men-at-arms rode into the confusion with lance, sword, axe and mace. Ten thousand Scots, they boasted, died under their sacred weapons, and those who ran were pursued as far as the Forest of Ettrick. John Comyn was captured, with three earls and a hundred of Balliol's barons, and the defenders of Dunbar hid their flags, closed their mouths, and opened their gates.

Scotland was disarmed and paralysed. James the Steward surrendered Roxburgh at the first blast of a herald's trumpet, and others quickly followed his example. In the south-west young Robert Bruce, Earl of Carrick since his grandfather's death, crossed the Solway with English soldiers and took back the lands of Annandale in the name of his father. Edward came to Edinburgh in June, to lodge with the Augustinians at Holyrood, and to watch his beloved siege-engines as they hammered at the wall of the Maiden Castle. He accepted the submission of its constable after eight noisy days, and rode on in triumph to receive Linlithgow, Stirling and Perth.

> Castle and town throughout the land
> Ere long were in Sir Edward's hand;
> And all were stuffed with Englishmen.

They were villainous, wicked, covetous Englishmen, said Barbour, haughty and merciless. They hanged chivalrous knights by the neck-bone. They violated the wives

*Weapons such as this medieval siege-engine, the stone-throwing precursor of artillery, formed part of the great train which Edward I brought against Scotland in 1305.*

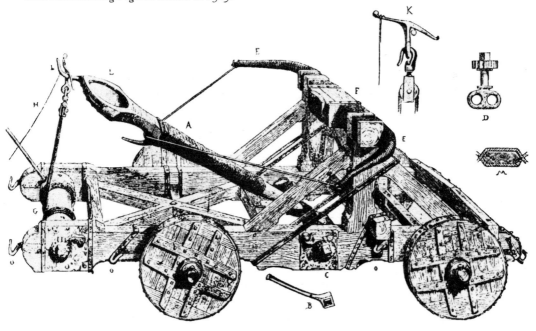

and daughters of good men, stole their purses, horses and hounds, even the knives from their tables. 'What miseries are worse than those?' There was probably nothing that Barbour recorded from the fireside tales of old men that did not happen. Medieval war was as savage as any before or since, and the Scots had behaved no better when raiding Northumberland while the English were burning Berwick.

On July 2 at Perth, Edward received a miserable letter from Balliol, praying for forgiveness and peace and kindness, blaming his disobedience upon evil counsellors and his own simplicity. When he walked into the hall of Brechin Castle a week later, and surrendered to Bishop Antony Bek of Durham, the red and gold arms of his humbled kingdom were ripped from his tunic. From that day he was known by the derisive nickname of Toom Tabard, the empty coat. It was sadly more truthful than any of the braggart titles given to other Scottish kings.

As he was sent to comfortable captivity in England with his son, his victor marched triumphantly on to the Moray Firth before turning back in a forgotten valley between mountain walls. The rape of Scotland's dignity lasted twenty-one weeks, and it was thorough. The Stone of Destiny, the Black Rood of saintly Margaret with its fragment of the true Cross, were carried to Westminster, joining the sacred plunder Edward had taken from Wales twelve years before. He stripped the nation's archives of their records, having as great a love for documents as he had for siege-towers and scaling-forks. His lieutenants, however, hanged Scots for stealing books, as they hanged them for taking beer and candles, for concealing a horse, for vagrancy and insolence. At Berwick in October, while Edward halted on his homeward way, he stole the kingdom's freedom, an act of larceny in which he had the active cooperation of its principal leaders. Two thousand earls, barons, churchmen, burgesses and freeholders swore fealty to him, putting their names to what came to be known as the Ragman Rolls, from the tangle of ribbons that hung from their seals.

Edward departed from Scotland with a flourish of gross contempt. It eased a man, he said, to be rid of filth, and he left the ordure to the governorship of the Earl of Surrey. He would have been wiser to choose a more subtle, less provocative man than the mailed and obdurate John de Warenne, as it would have been more sensible to appoint a tax-collector less corrupt than his wife's fat and lazy steward, Hugh de Cressingham. There was immediate resistance to both, flash-fires of protest about which we know little but significant references in the records, orders against travelling abroad, against the carrying of letters, demands for reinforcements. The first name that appears is not a Bruce or a Comyn, a Douglas or a Stewart. The man who did arise may not have been all that love and legend have since made of him, but he came when there was a need, and by his martyrdom gave the Scots an oriflamme which even the following banner of Bruce would not obscure.

## 2

William Wallace of Elderslie steps fully grown into history, a tall young man of great strength and courage. Little is known of his life but the last bitter month of it, and a glorious year when he was twenty-six and the leader of his country. The rest is legend or myth, of which the spirit if not the substance is true. He was the second son of a small landowner by Paisley, of Norman descent, or perhaps Strathclyde British, for his name was sometimes spelt Walays or Walyes, and that was the usual English term for a

*Part of the text of the Ragman Rolls shows, among others, the name of John Balliol. Two thousand Scots put their seals to this document, swearing fealty to Edward I.*

Celt or a Welshman. In the earlier records of the Edwardian occupation there is a reference to 'William le Waleys, a thief' who escaped arrest after stealing beer from a Perth tavern. Whether this was he or not, his appearance in May, 1297, was unquestionable and decisive. In the words of the chronicler John of Fordun, he 'lifted up his head' and slew William Hazelrig, the English sheriff of Clydesdale.

He did not begin a revolt against the English, but responded to one already begun. In the west Bishop Wishart and James the Steward were gathering some of the Galloway lords in arms, but these 'malefactors and disturbers of the peace' did not alarm Edward or excite much enthusiasm among the Scots. A spark was needed, a bold act from which there could be no retreat. According to the *Lanercost Chronicle*, Wishart and the Steward 'caused a certain bloody man, William Wallace, who had formerly been a chief of brigands in Scotland, to revolt against the King and assemble the people in his support'. A fifteenth-century minstrel, Blind Harry, from whose fanciful poem *Wallace* most of the legends come, said that he was an outlaw, hiding in a priest's gown, and that he killed Hazelrig as a reprisal for the murder of his own wife by English soldiers. But whatever the motives or causes, the War of Independence properly began that May in the streets of Lanark, over the dead bodies of an English sheriff and his garrison.

The effect upon the subjugated Scots was electric. 'The reviving malice of that perfidious race,' said the Lanercost chronicler, 'excited their minds to fresh sedition.' Wallace found himself the commander of a small army, and his opinion of the Galloway lords is shown by the fact that he did not march to them, but went northward into the mountains where Andrew de Moray was raising an army of Gaels. Toward the end of the month, Wallace came out of the hills and fell upon Scone, where the English justiciar, William de Ormesby, was holding court, outlawing those who would not take an oath of fealty to his king. Escaping capture, he rode wildly to Edinburgh with the news. Surrey was away on his English estates, but Hugh de Cressingham awoke from his complacent indolence, pulled his gigantic body into the saddle, and went to war under his churchman's banner. Not against Wallace or De Moray, or any of the local risings that were burning across his province, but against the confederation of lords in the south-west, James the Steward, Robert Bruce of Carrick, and Sir William Douglas among them. He surrounded them at Irvine on the Ayrshire coast, where they surrendered ignobly, as if glad to be quit of their own quarrels. They asked only that they should not be sent to fight for Edward in France, and offered hostages for their good

*Urquhart Castle, Inverness-shire, was built in the 12th century on what may have been the site of a Celtic fort. It was later held by the Comyns and in Bruce's wars it changed hands four times.*

behaviour. Douglas failed to produce his, and was thrown into prison at Berwick, where he had put better men, and where he was said to be 'very savage and very abusive'. He died two years later in the Tower of London, contrite at last, but his son James would not forget.

Wallace and De Moray, who had still not met, now held most of the garrisons north of the Tay, and by frightened report were hanging 'English knaves' on every tree. Hugh de Cressingham was worried about taxes, and petulantly told his master that not a penny would be raised until Surrey stirred himself and returned to his duty. De Warenne was already riding north before Edward read this dispatch, or a later and more confident assurance from the clerical tax-collector that 'as for the people on the other side of the Scottish sea, we hope soon to have them at our pleasure'. Beyond that sea, the Firth of Forth, Wallace's ragged army of outlaws, peasants and hedge-knights was besieging Dundee, while Andrew de Moray, having taken Inverness and Castle Urquhart in the Great Glen, was now marching in triumph through Aberdeenshire. The two young men met in friendship at Perth, where, it was said, their followers elected them 'leaders of the army of the Kingdom of Scotland'. They fought for King John Balliol, they said, declaring his abdication to be invalid and exacted under duress.

The army of the realm of Scotland, which now lifted the siege of Dundee and marched south to fight Surrey, was drawn from the middle folk, the low folk, from Lothian and Galloway, Gaels from Badenoch and Moray, Picts from Fife, commanded by small knights and clan chiefs. The great lords of Scotland stood aside, or took their swords into John de Warenne's camp, where chivalry was better served and honoured. Wallace's men were foot-soldiers whom he had hastily drilled to fight in the oval spear-ring of the schiltron. They had made many of their weapons themselves, the long, twelve-foot spear, axes and knives, and few wore plate or helmet above their tunics of rough hide and homespun cloth. They lived frugally on oats and lentils which they carried in a bag behind them, and at the beginning of September, 1297, they came down from the Ochil hills to the Stirling plain and met the mailed cavalry of England.

On the eleventh day of the month, from the southern slope of Abbey Craig, they looked across the Forth to a great army, Welsh and Gascon and Sherwood bowmen, mounted men-at-arms with swinging spears, massed English knights in shining helms, the skirted harness of great war-horses, bannered lances and emblazoned shields. They were invincible, or so James the Steward and the Earl of Lennox thought, as they rode from Surrey's camp to mediate with Wallace. He sent them back. 'Tell your people we have not come here to gain peace, but for battle to avenge and deliver our country. Let them come up when they like and they will find us ready to meet them to their beards.' He ordered his spearmen to hold their ground until they heard his horn, and then to charge.

Most battles have a theatrical point of decision for which men will fight with crazed desperation, a hill, a ford, a bloody ditch. At Stirling here, below the sheer rock of the watching castle and where the river snaked in lazy bends across the flat carse, it was a wooden bridge so narrow that no more than two or three horses could ride over it abreast. James the Steward told Surrey that such a hazardous frontal attack was unnecessary – he knew of a ford further down the river where fifty horsemen might cross in line. Hugh de Cressingham, ever the careful treasurer, asked why Edward's money should be wasted in prolonging the war. With Surrey's permission, he led the van of the English knights across the bridge, and on to an unexpected meadow-marsh. As they struggled to bring their horses into line, a horn brayed, and the schiltrons came down the slope upon them.

The brutish fight lasted for an hour, and Surrey could only watch, unable to cross the deep river or a bridge soon blocked by dead and screaming wounded. Hemmed in by the spears, their throats cut under the rim of their bascinets when they fell from their hamstrung horses, the English knights did not yield. Whatever his faults, Cressingham knew that he was to die and was determined to do so with knightly courage. Armoured on a great horse, his fat body rode into the spear-ring with a killing sword until he was plucked from the saddle and destroyed.

Surrey drew back from the far bank, turned and fled, butchering his horse with spurs until he reached Berwick. He left Stirling to surrender, and his army to be slaughtered by the pursuing Scots. The great carcass of Cressingham was stripped of its plate and linen, and its skin flayed. The *Lanercost Chronicle* said that Wallace ordered some of it to be made into a baldrick for his sword, and other stories claimed that it was cut into saddle-girths for his horsemen, or small pieces that were sent throughout the country in triumph. The Scots followed the English down through the Lowlands, to the Border and beyond. In October they were riding their shaggy ponies across the northern shires of England, 'wasting all the land, committing arson, pillage, and murder'. For three weeks, it was said, the worship of God stopped in every church and monastery between Newcastle and Carlisle, and only the intervention of Wallace prevented the murder of monks at their altars. Without siege-engines they could take no castles, and Robert Bruce's father kept the gates of Carlisle closed against them. When a storm of snow and an army gathered by the Bishop of Durham barred their crossing of the Tyne, they came joyously home to Scotland on St Cecilia's day.

In November the gay and gallant Andrew de Moray died of the terrible wounds he had received at Stirling Bridge, and Wallace now styled himself Guardian of Scotland, holding it still for Toom Tabard, who may have wished in far captivity that he had a less embarrassing supporter. While Moray lived, both he and Wallace had written to the merchants of Hamburg and Lübeck, inviting them to come again in trade 'because the kingdom of Scotland, thanks be to God, has been recovered by war from the power of the English'. Except for Edinburgh, Dunbar, Roxburgh and Berwick, all the castles of the land were in the hands of the Scots, and James the Steward and the Earl of Lennox, changing their coats again, offered Wallace their support. Most of the Scottish lords stood apart, however, jealous and contemptuous, unable to serve under a man who was no more than a small landed laird. Nor could Robert Bruce, while the cause was still Balliol's, come from Carrick in friendship.

Wallace's leadership had eight months yet to run, and few if any men have had so remarkable an influence in so short a time. His example was inspirational, his courage infectious, and his victory at Stirling Bridge a hinge upon which the door of the future turned. It is clear that he saw himself as a patriot, though the word had as yet no meaning. The sense of unity, of nationhood, that had been growing in the reign of Alexander III, flowered first in him. Love of his country, which changed him from an outlaw to a national leader in a few weeks, was stiffened by a hatred of the English. Stories of his relentless lack of mercy toward some of his captives were long disbelieved. They did not fit the conventional pattern of a hero. But the age had little mercy for all men, and this century has shown that those who resist a powerful and inexorable occupation cannot afford its luxury. Wallace's determination to destroy the enemy, wherever and whenever he met it, never to bargain with it, was the greatness of his strength. Such a man had been dreamt of, and by his coming inspired love, unity and sacrifice.

*St Andrews Cathedral, Fife, the heart of the Old Faith. Begun in 1161, completed in 1318 and destroyed in 1559, it was used as a source of building materials until 1826.*

Arma virum que cano
Troye qui primus ab

In the beginning of 1298 the hope of sympathy and support from France ended bitterly in peace between Philip and Edward, and the Plantagenet came home from Gascony to deal with the Scots. He moved the seat of his government to York, and on July 3 he crossed the Tweed by Coldstream with twelve thousand five hundred foot and two thousand horse, veterans of his campaigns in France and Wales. Eight earls, two of them his kinsmen and one a Scot of Angus, rode behind him with their knights and tenants. Bishop Bek of Durham, armed for a cause that was surely God's, commanded thirty-two bannered knights, all his liege-vassals. The dust of a great baggage-train, wheels, feet and hooves, hung above the forest lances leafed with pennons, and the summer sun struck bright sparks from helm and shield. Above them all the tall figure of Edward on a black horse, his yellow hair now white, his ageing back held straight in its cuirass of steel. As this mighty force moved northward by Roxburgh and Lauderdale, skirting Edinburgh toward the Stirling plain, swallowing lonely castles and digesting their burnt stones, it was less powerful than it might have seemed to the watching Scots on the hills. It was hungry. The fleet that should have provisioned it had been delayed by weather. It was undisciplined. Welsh archers quarrelled viciously with Gascons, and both with English men-at-arms. It was diseased. The summer heat and dust, plague and sickness raddled its splendid chivalry. At Kirkliston, near Linlithgow, Edward decided to fall back on Edinburgh, where he might calm and feed his mutinous men.

As he was making this decision, two Scots lords sent him word that he would find Wallace's army in the great forest by Falkirk. 'God be praised!' he said. 'They shall have no need to follow me, for I shall go to meet them and on this very day.' He marched, and that night he did not sleep, but rode among his sleeping soldiers. In the flurry of a false alarm he was thrown from his horse, breaking two ribs, but he hid this from his army and rode with it again in the pre-dawn mist of Mary Magdalene's Day, July 22. Within an hour or two they came upon the Scots, four bristling schiltrons on a slope east of Falkirk, their flanks covered by Ettrick archers and a few horse.

Wallace had never before faced such an army, or fought a battle without a natural defence. Here was no river, no narrow bridge to halt an armoured charge, and he may have sensed that this was the end, for he made no great exhortation, but spoke simply and bluntly to his spearmen. 'I have brought you to the ring, dance if you can.' Behind a fragile barrier of stakes and ropes, a strip of bog that would slow but not stop a charge, the schiltrons made ready, the front ranks kneeling, the inner ranks standing, their long spears lowered. They were ready, and the stubborn, bloody dance began before the English archers came within range, and before Edward rode to the van with his standard. Bishop Bek's young knights, impatient with his call for caution, told him to go to Mass, and charged upon the schiltrons. Held by the steady spears, they drove off the flanking horse and slaughtered the Ettrick archers about the body of their commander. Turning again on the schiltrons, they were once more held, but thrust and hacked at the hedge until Edward called them back. He brought up his Welsh bowmen, and they stood calmly before the defenceless Scots, quiver to bow, arrow by arrow in a rustling rain, until the spear-rings were opened by lanes of dead and dying. This time when the English knights charged, they were not held.

Wallace escaped, riding northward to Callander and the mountains. The dead of his valiant army cannot be estimated, although the Lanercost chronicler recorded a preposterous figure of sixty thousand, many times the total number of men engaged. 'Nor was there slain on the English side any nobleman except the Master of the Templars, with

*A misericord from Carlisle Cathedral, where in 1307 Edward I gave his sick-bed to God in thanks, and rode on to his death at Burgh-on-Sands.*

five or six esquires who charged the schiltrons of the Scots too hotly and rashly.' More English horses were killed than men, and Edward paid compensation for more than a hundred lost by his knights. England exult! cried the chronicler,

> Berwick, Dunbar and Falkirk too,
> Show all that traitor Scots can do.
> England exult! Thy Prince is peerless,
> Where thee he leadeth, follow fearless.

The Guardianship of Scotland was now taken from Wallace, or resigned by him, and in his place the Scots accepted an uneasy triumvirate of Bishop William Lamberton of St Andrews, young Robert Bruce of Carrick, and John Comyn the Red, now Lord of Badenoch since the death of his father in England. There is a darkness over Bruce's activities during Wallace's brief Guardianship, and the romantic notion that he fought with the Scots at Falkirk is scarcely credible. His father held Carlisle for Edward, their lands in England had been distrained for debts owed to the King, and three weeks before the battle Bruce asked protection for some of his men travelling on Edward's service. After Falkirk, however, the English drove him from his lands and burnt them.

The arrows of his bowmen had won Edward little. When he reached Stirling he found it a ruin, and the country wasted. He replied by burning St Andrews, and then retired upon Edinburgh with aching ribs and a hungry and clamorous army. Only in his widely scattered garrisons was an Englishman safe. Between them was a hostile country, black fields and steadings. Edward went home, promising the governors he left that he would come again in the spring to punish the Scots and 'put down their disobedience and malice'. But he did not come north again for three years, and in this bitter time

Scotland had two governments, the English and the Guardians. The flimsy alliance of the latter was soon broken. One of Edward's agents reported that when they met at Peebles, in August, 1299, Bruce and Comyn quarrelled fiercely over some property left by Wallace, and that in his anger the Red Comyn took Bruce by the throat. Lamberton and Wallace's elder brother, Malcolm, persuaded them to put duty before dignity, but neither forgot the incident. Within a year they quarrelled again, and this time Bruce resigned in disgust. A parliament of lords, meeting in the royal burgh of Rutherglen, replaced him with Ingram de Umfraville, the turncoat Angus earl who had fought for Edward at Berwick and Falkirk. His elastic conscience and dubious motives were perhaps too much for all to stomach, for later there appears to have been one Guardian only, the Liddesdale knight Sir John de Soules.

In May, 1300, Edward at last came north, invigorated in his seventh decade by marriage to a young princess of France. He brought with him his son, Edward of Caernarvon, and this time he crossed the Solway not the Tweed, determined to destroy the Galloway lords. A great fleet provisioned his army at Carlisle. 'Mountain and valley,' it was said, 'were filled with carts and sumpter-horses, stores and baggage, tents and pavilions.' But once across the Solway the campaign spluttered ineffectively, with no great battle drawn. De Soules and de Umfraville snapped at the English flanks but were easily driven away. The Red Comyn was worsted in a skirmish near Kirkcudbright, and the English sat down before Caerlaverock Castle at the mouth of the Nith, covering the gentle hills with their sylvan huts and coloured tents. The castle fell after a week, and then Edward withdrew to England. He came again the next year, angered by a letter from Rome telling him that Scotland was a papal fief. 'By God's blood!' he swore, 'I will not be at rest, but with all my strength I will defend my right.' But this campaign was no more effective, and though he wintered at Linlithgow with his young queen until 1302 he was not so much defeated by battle as by the lack of one. 'As none of the Scots would resist,' said an English chronicler, 'nothing glorious or even worthy of praise was achieved.' Deserted by Pope Boniface and Philip of France, who found sympathy for Scotland a tedious complication of the quarrel between them, the Scots were dispirited and without direction. In this year Robert Bruce of Carrick submitted and swore fealty to Edward, persuaded by his dying father perhaps, and certainly by the Guardian's continued allegiance to Toom Tabard. If he hoped that Edward would support the Bruce claim to the throne, and destroy both the Balliol and Comyn factions, he received no promise of it.

The King went back to warmer lodgings in Westminster, but was drawn north again the following year when his viceroy and a body of mounted spearmen were routed at Roslin by the Red Comyn and Simon Fraser of Tweeddale. This time his rage was violent. He marched north to Dunfermline, where the bishops of Glasgow and St Andrews, the Red Comyn and Sir John de Soules came before him in fear, accepting their lives and freedom in return for an oath of allegiance. With invisible halters about their necks, the Scots lords met in parliament at St Andrews in March, 1304, under the direction of Edward, and until a permanent constitution could be established Robert Bruce of Carrick and Bishop Wishart were appointed Guardians of the realm, with the English baron John Mowbray. Eighteen months later, guided by Wishart, Edward framed his 'Ordinances for the Establishment of the Land of Scotland', proposing a government of twenty Englishmen and ten elected representatives of the Scottish estates. It was a wise and statesmanlike plan, if somewhat premature in its vision of a united kingdom and government, but it was based upon the premise that Scotland was justly an English province, a feudal barony and not a people intent upon liberty.

That was being defended in Stirling Castle, where Sir William Oliphant and fifty men still held out boldly. In May, 1305, Edward accepted the challenge with avid delight. Great crowds of Scots and English watched the siege, and in Stirling town a window was cut into the wall of a house so that the English queen and her ladies could be entertained without discomfort. In August the walls at last fell to Edward's great engines War-Wolf and All-the-World, and Oliphant and his men were led before the King to kneel in supplication, naked but for their smocks.

That month Wallace returned, if indeed he had ever left Scotland, though there is

*An early map of Kirkcudbrightshire. This was part of Galloway, of the land of the Gallgaels, of the MacDowall lords, bitterly contested in the wars of independence.*

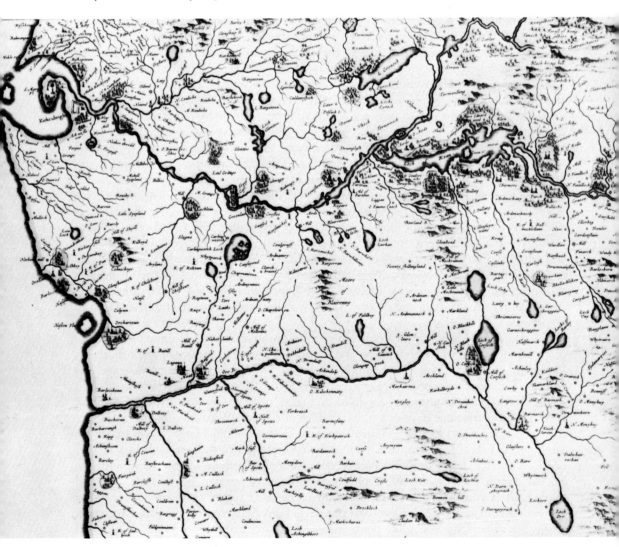

*Stirling Castle above the cockpit of Scotland was the prize for which Englishman struggled with Scot, and Scots fought among themselves for nearly a thousand years.*

some evidence that he went to France to secure the support of Philip and the Pope. It is strange that he gathered no army in these years, and this may suggest that Falkirk had had a traumatic effect on his self-confidence, that Andrew de Moray rather than he had been the principal organizer and commander of resistance. Perhaps, too, he was jealously thwarted by certain lords with whom, according to documents found upon him at his capture, he was in confederation. But he had remained an example to men like Oliphant, refusing the advice of those who would have him submit. 'I and my companions who are willing to cleave to me,' he said, 'will stand for the liberty of Scotland.' And he had yet to make his greatest inspirational contribution to that cause. On August 5 he was betrayed near Glasgow by the Scots knight Sir John de Menteith, who was said to have turned over a bannock on a tavern table, a sign to the English that the brigand was among them.

He was paraded through the streets of London, behind its mayor and sheriffs, and on August 23 he stood trial in Westminster Hall as a traitor, charged with breaking his oath of fealty. That he had never taken such an oath was of no consequence, and the charge was derisory. His crime was his challenge to Edward, the unity of the Scottish people, and the victory of Stirling Bridge. He was charged with the illegal assumption of the Guardianship, with the murder of Hazelrig, the invasion of England, the burning of monasteries and the murder of nuns. His death was an obscene spectacle and allowed him little dignity. He was dragged on a hurdle from Westminster, four miles to the Tower, and from thence to a copse of elms at Smithfield. He was hanged, drawn, and emasculated, his entrails burnt before his dying eyes. His head was piked above London Bridge. One quarter of his mutilated body was exposed by the open sewer of Newcastle, another at Berwick, a third at Perth, and the fourth at Aberdeen. Justice demanded no less, said the Lanercost chronicler.

> Butcher of thousands, threefold death be thine,
> So shall the English from thee gain relief.
> Scotland, be wise, and choose a nobler chief.

Seven months later, Scotland did. Or rather, that nobler chief chose himself.

## 3

In February, 1306, Robert Bruce rode to the church of the Minorite friars in Dumfries for a council with his enemy John Comyn the Red. He was thirty-one, and since the death of his father two years before he had been the head of his family and its claimant to the throne. Three times he had risen against Edward, and three times knelt in humble submission, and he had commanded the great engines which broke down Oliphant's walls at Stirling. His father's debts to the English Crown had been set in abeyance, his own estates had been returned to him, and when he took his seat at the Westminster parliament he had asked for, and been given, the forfeited lands of his neighbour Ingram de Umfraville. He was the King's bought man and the joint Guardian of Scotland, but his loyalty was to personal and family ambitions alone, and even as he battered at the stones of Stirling Castle for his English masters, he and William Lamberton had been joined in a 'treasonable band' against them. Edward may have heard of this, for toward the end of 1305 he took away the Umfraville lands and gave them back to Ingram, removed Bruce from the guardianship, and once more demanded payment of those questionable debts. It was a time for caution or boldness, and which the devious and cunning Earl of Carrick chose may explain his bloody meeting with Comyn, or make it totally incomprehensible.

Barbour said that Bruce and his few followers came to Dumfries 'intent that he should speedily avenge the other's treachery', but the suggestion seems ridiculous. No man deciding upon the removal of a rival would be insane enough to select a church for the murder. On the other hand, the mistrust between the two men was so great that only in church together would each feel safe, and only there might one be easily betrayed. Exonerated by his death, the Comyn's intentions have never been examined. Barbour said that Carrick had already secured his support for the band with Lamberton, and that the Badenoch lord revealed it to Edward, which is of course possible. More probably the meeting in the Greyfriars' church was to explain the band to Comyn and command his support. Whatever the murky reasons, the outcome was more decisive than anything Bruce might have imagined.

There was an angry quarrel as they stood alone, a dagger drawn and thrust into Comyn's body. Bruce came out of the church and told his men that he thought he had slain the Red Comyn. 'You think?' asked his friend Roger de Kirkpatrick, 'then I'll make sure', and went into the church with others. Some of Comyn's men may also have been outside the door (it is hard to believe he would have come alone), for it is said that his uncle at once drew a sword, and was quickly killed when it glanced from the armour beneath Bruce's cloak. Inside the church, Kirkpatrick's men drove away the friars who had carried Comyn to the altar, and dispatched the wounded man with their daggers.

There were many partisan accounts of the murder, Scots and English, and if the Minorite friars saw and heard what truly happened their mouths were perhaps stopped by Bruce's generous patronage later. As Barbour said,

> Howsoever the quarrel fell,
> He died thereby, I know full well.

And soon all Europe would know. The crime was abominable, and sacrilege detestable. For most men, perhaps all men but Bruce at that moment, it would have meant an end to ambition, to life itself if it could not be sustained in an outlaw's miserable and excommunicated existence. There was a brief moment only for decision as he stood outside the church door, listening to the clanking of armour inside, the outraged cries of the Franciscans. His one powerful rival was dying. There was his secret band with Lamberton, but he could not know what effect the murder would have upon the bishop. The speed with which he acted makes a strong case for premeditation, or perhaps shows a desperate spirit breaking from its dissembling past and grasping the future by the throat. Bruce did not become a patriot above the body of Red Comyn. The liberty of Scotland was now the only cause that might preserve his own.

Upon his orders, his brothers and his men seized Dumfries Castle, unseating the English justices in session, and as they then moved north against other fortresses in Clydesdale he rode straight to Glasgow, falling upon his knees before Bishop Wishart, asking for absolution. With the amoral acumen Wishart relied upon in moments of crisis, he readily gave it, and followed it with a rousing sermon of support from his pulpit. On Palm Sunday, five weeks after Comyn's murder, Bruce was in Scone and king. The sacred Stone upon which he should have sat was in Westminster Abbey, but a circlet of gold was placed on his head by Isabel, Countess of Buchan. Her husband, whose horses she had stolen to reach Scone, was the Red Comyn's nearest kinsman, but she was a MacDuff, and marital loyalty came second to her family's hereditary right to crown the kings of Alba. Her brother the Earl of Fife, who should have performed the ceremony, was probably still in one of Edward's prisons with his sons. The crowning was watched by three bishops, including Lamberton, and by Atholl and Lennox, two of the Seven Earls and scarcely enough for a quorum. Bruce's four brilliant and mercurial brothers were also there – Edward, Nigel, Alexander and Thomas, who had been taking castles and raising the country for him, and who were now, by this hurried ceremony, elevated to princes of the kingdom of Scotland. The encouragement in all their faces was perhaps more hopeful than reassuring. 'It seems to me,' said Bruce's wife Elizabeth de Burgh, daughter of the Earl of Ulster, 'that we are but a summer King and Queen whom the children crown in their sport.'

The sport had yet to begin. Bruce knew, said Barbour, that he 'would have a bitter fight against the King of England's might'. Edward was hunting in the New Forest when he heard the news, and it embittered a spirit already soured by ill health. He ordered the immediate mobilization of his northern levies, and was carried to his parliament at Westminster upon a litter. His commander in Scotland, and its Guardian since the removal of Mowbray, was Aymer de Valence, Earl of Pembroke and married to the murdered Comyn's sister, and before the Cliffords and the Percies came over the Border with their levies he had begun to organize an army against Bruce. At the feast of Pentecost that early summer, Edward knighted the Prince of Wales and three hundred squires, distributing gold and fine linen among them before sending them north to de Valence. Dead or alive, he said, he would enter Scotland and avenge Comyn's murder. Two swans clothed in gold were brought before him, and he swore upon them and by God that he would take no rest 'until the Lord has given me victory over the crowned traitor and perjured nation'. The murderers of Dumfries, all those found in arms, were to die as Wallace had died, with their estates forfeit, and Bruce's lands were to be given to English border lords like Henry Percy. Following such orders of fire and threat, the old king was carried slowly and painfully northward on his last campaign.

Before de Valence and the Prince of Wales moved against him, Bruce had been subduing hostile MacDowalls in Galloway, and Comyn revolts elsewhere. He now retreated

to Perth with a small army, mostly spearmen and little knights from his own lands. Since the heady days of Comyn's murder, only a few weeks before, there had been fading support for the lion banner of Scotland which Wishart had carefully brought to the coronation. Many lords had drawn back, afraid of Edward's approaching shadow, many more had joined the Comyns with de Valence, and in the Argyll hills John MacDougall of Lorn[1] was gathering an army of Gaels to make what profit he could from Scotland's adversity. Bruce abandoned Perth to de Valence, and then returned to challenge it, but his men were surprised and routed at Methven. He fought for a while in nothing but his shirt, and then ran with them, a fugitive.

He rode westward toward Argyll with what men he could regather, though he knew Lorn was out against him. His wife, his brother Nigel, his daughter Marjorie by his first wife, and a northern earl or two rode with him. In early August, at Dalrigh in the dark hills south of Rannoch, the MacDougalls came upon him and scattered his little army still further. Bruce sent his wife and daughter away westward with Nigel and the Earl of Atholl, to the great donjon of Kildrummy near Aberdeen, high above a ravine and the valley of the Don. There they were safe only until Pembroke and the Comyns came up in a cloud of steel and banners. The women fled further north, beyond the Moray Firth to Tain, where a Balliol earl made them his prisoner. At Kildrummy, the keeper prudently surrendered it and his remaining guests to Pembroke.

Robert Bruce disappeared into the West and the Isles, where loyal help and treacherous friends were always awaiting the fugitive princes of Scotland. He went south to the long peninsula of Kintyre, Clan Donald lands, confident that Angus Og of Islay would help a man so recently abused by his enemies the MacDougalls. Where he spent that winter cannot be certainly known, and it is unlikely that he had time for the study of arachnids. Barbour said that he went on to the small isle of Rathlin off the Irish coast, but it would have been more of a prison than a refuge, though he may have hoped for help from his father-in-law in Ulster. Wherever he was, before he reappeared in Arran in February, 1307, he secured from Clan Donald a promise of help that would in time put him securely on the throne he had taken with a dagger-stroke.

The stories of his wandering lived for centuries in the twisted folk-memory of the Gael, like the brooch that was said to have been torn from his shoulder at Dalrigh and was kept thereafter with pride by MacDougall chiefs. He and his few men, said Barbour, lived as ragged outlaws, their clothes torn, their shoes of raw hide, and there is a curious and romantic similarity between some of the stories told and the adventures of his descendant four centuries later after Culloden, except that his were a prelude to triumph and the other's an epilogue to disaster.[2]

In October Edward reached the Lanercost priory outside Carlisle, borne there, said its chronicler, 'in a litter on the backs of horses because of his age and infirmity'. There he would stay for nine months, growing weaker with each, in body if not in spirit, for the news he received from his lieutenants and son in Scotland was joy to his revengeful temper. The old Earl of Atholl, taken at Kildrummy, was soon hanged, but since he was

---

[1] Descended, like the MacDonald chiefs, from Somerled, first Lord of Argyll. The once great power of the MacDougalls declined after their opposition to Bruce, and passed to Clan Donald. The MacDowalls of Galloway in the south-west of Scotland were members of the MacDougall clan.

[2] The historical and traditional evidence for the belief that Bruce spent some time in Orkney, under the protection of Hakon of Norway, is discussed in *The Scottish War of Independence* by Evan Macleod Barron.

*The tomb, in Westminster Abbey, of Aymer de Valence, Earl of Pembroke and Guardian of Scotland.*
*He was the only English leader, apart from Edward II, to escape from Bannockburn.*

*Decorative brooches such as these held a valued place among the ornaments produced for both sexes by Scottish craftsmen of the 14th and 15th centuries.*

a man of rank his gallows was raised thirty feet above the ground. Nigel Bruce was hanged too, his entrails burnt before him, and then he was beheaded. The head of Simon Fraser of Tweeddale was impaled on London Bridge beside the skull of Wallace, whose younger brother, John, was also barbarously dispatched by rope, knife and axe. Wishart and Lamberton were imprisoned in chains, Bruce's queen was locked in an English manor house, his young daughter was sent to the Tower and then to a nunnery, and his sister Mary and Isabel of Buchan were exposed in lattice cages at Roxburgh and Berwick. Against great men and lesser men, whose allegiance to Bruce was real or suspected, the Plantagenet's vengeance was implacable: 'Burn down all his manors and houses, destroy all his lands and goods, and strip all his gardens so that nothing is left. . . .' Lock and chain, rope and axe, evisceration and fire were the answer to traitorous rebellion. The reasonable clemency which Edward had once shown to all but Wallace was now abandoned, as if close to death he wished to climb heavenwards on a stairway of skulls.

Bruce came out of his misty hiding to Kintyre in February, 1307, with his brothers Thomas and Alexander, and a band of Islesmen and Irish who though small in number were still enough to be divided into two divisions. While he sailed with one to his lands in Carrick across the wide Firth of Clyde, his brothers took the other further south, landing in narrow Loch Ryan on the Galloway coast. They were quickly captured by a MacDowall chief and taken to Lanercost, where Edward as quickly dispatched them. Alexander, the brilliant scholar of Cambridge, was hanged. The boy Thomas was also lifted upon a gibbet, but before this he was dragged through Carlisle by a team of horses.

Twenty miles north of Loch Ryan, Robert Bruce and his tall, olive-skinned captain James Douglas took the first division against the coastal keep of Turnberry, once the King's boyhood home. A signal fire, which a spy was to light if it were safe to land, was lit in error or by treachery, and the countryside was full of hostile patrols. Nonetheless, before dawn the wild Islesmen raided a village of huts outside the castle, and where most of its garrison was sleeping, killing without remorse, said Barbour, 'like men that had a right good will'. They also made so much noise about it that Henry Percy had time to close the castle gates against them. They stayed below the walls for three days, sharing Percy's silver and horses, and then withdrew to the hills in a guerrilla war upon Edward's forces between Galloway and the Clyde. The net about them was small-meshed, drawn in the north, east and south by Lorn, de Valence and MacDowall, but even so Douglas led a few men through it on a northward foray into Lanark and his family's lands. The example of this lisping young man, it was said, could turn the worst coward into a leopard, as effectively, perhaps, as legend later turned him from a pathological terrorist into a chivalrous knight. He surprised and killed most of the English garrison of Douglas castle while they were at Mass. The rest were supping in the castle, and with a blood-thirsty zeal that would have delighted his savage father he threw their bodies and their meat and their meal into the cellar, and burnt the castle above them in a grisly fat-spitting barbecue that was from thereon called the Douglas Larder.

The closing net soon held Bruce in the lovely tableland of hills and lochs that is now the National Forest Park of Glen Trool, country which he and the people who had joined his Gaels must have known well. They used this knowledge to ambush and defeat a small body of horse under John Mowbray, and then exploited the victorious skirmish by breaking out northward into Ayr. Encouraged by the spearmen who came to his standard, Bruce felt strong enough for a chivalrous encounter on an open field and in a knightly way. On May 10 he challenged de Valence at Loudon Hill, a lonely cone of heather and rock above the valley and east of Kilmarnock. He placed his men, less than a thousand perhaps, on the slope and between mossy grounds, their flanks further protected by shallow ditches. De Valence probably had far fewer than the three thousand armoured horsemen given him by Barbour, but they outnumbered the Scottish spearmen.

> Coats of armour all aglow,
> And hauberks gleaming white as snow,
> Were glittering in the morning air
> Like heavenly angels, shining fair.

De Valence led these steel angels, visor down and lance couched behind a shield emblazoned with ten red martlets. They came up the side of a small burn in a heavy, vainglorious charge that became slower and slower as the slope rose. Stopped by the flanking ditches and the groundless moss, the brightly coloured knights were gaffed like salmon by the Scottish spears, 'till from their wounds the red blood ran'. Unable to break Bruce's schiltron with sword or lance, the survivors turned into the dusk and ran with de Valence. It was Bruce's first real victory, but he could make little profit by it. He defeated another body of horse three days later and boldly laid siege to Ayr, until de Valence came up with reinforcements and drove him back to another fugitive existence in the Galloway hills.

The irritating news of Loudon Hill was brought to the sinking King of England at Lanercost, but Edward would not relinquish life while 'King Hobb', as he called Bruce, still enjoyed it. There was some small cheer in a report that James Douglas wished to submit, and if this were true it indicates how even Bruce's most loyal friends were losing their taste for a heather war. At last Edward decided to enter Scotland himself, believing that old and dying he could still do what his captains could not. On Whit Sunday, as he lay on his litter and watched the gathering of his army, four hundred young knights rode gaily past him, their lances and their helmets dripping with fresh spring leaves. His spirits and his strength lifted by the sight, he arose and said that he would ride into Scotland. He gave the litter to God in thanks at Carlisle Cathedral, mounted his black destrier and rode at the head of his army.

*Durham Cathedral, where the captured standard of Scotland and the Holy Rood of Saint Margaret were exhibited after the disastrous defeat of the Scots at Neville's Cross in October, 1346.*

He travelled seven miles only, to Burgh-on-Sands. Weak from exhaustion and dysentery, he was lifted from his saddle. He died there in a mean town on the Solway shore, three miles of tide-water from Scotland, and at the age of sixty-eight. He was the most resolute and most inexorable enemy Scotland had known and would ever know, and perhaps the wisest. It would be three hundred years before the kingdoms would be united as he hoped, and four centuries before the government proposed by his Ordinances would be given some reality. Even then, perhaps, it would be premature, for before the independence of a nation can be safely surrendered it must first flourish and its roots be preserved.

It was said that he asked for his heart to be carried to the Holy Land by a hundred knights, and his bones to be taken into Scotland by his son, borne against the Scots wherever they were found in battle. The young man sent both to Westminster Abbey for burial.

94

## 4

As if the shrinking of the great Plantagenet's heart had contracted the limbs of his kingdom, the English armies were withdrawn from Scotland. The new King Edward was no hammer of the Scots but an amiable and frivolous young man, happier in the company of his Gascon favourite, Piers Gaveston, than with the life of dust, blood and steel which his father had imposed upon him. Aymer de Valence was called home with his knights and earls, and the defence of the south and west was left to Ingram de Umfraville and the MacDowall lords of Galloway. By English blandishments and Comyn threats, many Scots who had once supported the Balliol cause and later Bruce were persuaded to take up arms against him. Among them were Stirling's gallant commander Oliphant and the young Thomas Randolph, Bruce's nephew and a witness of his coronation. Bitter or benign imprisonment helped some lords to change their allegiance, and under the watchful eye of the Comyn clan they were now Edward II's lieutenants, charged with the extirpation of Bruce. These wayward Scots and the remaining English held every major stronghold, and could not be subdued without siege-trains. The first phase of the struggle for independence had ended at Burgh-on-Sands, and it now became a civil war, fought on the open and suffering land between impregnable studs of stone.

Bruce went north with three thousand men, many of them Ettrick archers and spearmen lately in arms against him. He marched beyond the Tay and the Moray Firth, and without a battle he brought the Celtic Earl of Ross to a truce, and then to love and comradeship. He turned southward again, to face John Comyn of Buchan, who had raised an army to end their blood-feud. Sick from exhaustion, from a strain that had not relaxed since his dagger was drawn in Dumfries two years before, Bruce could no longer sit in the saddle. Like the old English king, he was carried on a litter at the head of his army, his brother Edward riding by his side. His weakness drained the strength of his men and many deserted, believing him about to die. But of the thousand or fewer who remained, said Barbour, there was not one who would not have accepted the death of a brother in return for the life of the King. Too sick at last to be moved, even by litter, Bruce halted at Slivoch to the north-west of Inverurie in the valley of the Don.

When Buchan heard of the King's illness, and the wasting of his army, he advanced boldly upon Inverurie. It was Martinmas, and November snow fell upon the wood where Bruce's starving men had taken their stand, and upon Buchan's cold and dispirited army beyond it. For three days rival archers skirmished among the white and leafless trees, while the Comyn's forces grew in number, and then the King's men came out of the woods, led by Edward Bruce and grouped about the royal litter. So defiant was their impudence, and so bold their bearing, that Buchan did not attack, and they carried their king northward to the hills of Strathbogie. The necessary battle came at Christmas, however, when Bruce heard that his enemies were boasting of the slaughter of one of his patrols. Like Edward again, he rose from his litter, saying 'Their boast has made me hale and sound.' With seven hundred men he moved quickly eastward across the snow to Old Meldrum, where Buchan was camped by Barra Hill. The Comyn's men had time enough to stand to arms, but when Bruce's spears pressed upon them, said Barbour, 'they quickly turned their backs to go, and fled and scattered far and wide'.

Buchan was plainly a bad general, if not a coward, and his flight eventually took him two hundred miles from Barra Hill to England. Bruce marched upon his unprotected province, the flat and bleak shoulder of Scotland. To the King the terrible rape that followed, the 'Herschip of Buchan', was a strategic necessity, the subjection of castles and the liquidation of garrisons, but to his hungry and ragged men it was a joyful opportunity for rich loot and savage revenge.

> His men through Buchan did he send
> To burn and slay from end to end.
> He ravaged it in such a way
> That fifty years beyond that day
> The Rape of Buchan still was grieved.

The terror and the burning, by which great forests were left as black and monumental stumps, were effective. By bright midsummer all the north-eastern castles, with the exception of Banff, were in Bruce's hands, and lords who had fought for Edward and Comyn now knelt before him in allegiance. In July he led an army against the MacDougalls, and found them on a brae-side at the head of Loch Awe, in some of the wildest and most beautiful country of the western Highlands. John of Lorn was ready to fight the battle from a distance, from his galley on Loch Etive, but his kerns were placed for ambush in the narrow Pass of Brander where the River Awe rushes by the feet of Ben Cruachan. The trap was sprung against the MacDougalls by James Douglas, who took his archers over the summit of Cruachan to their rear. As Bruce led his army into the Pass and a cloud of arrows, Douglas came down the steep brown slopes of the brae. It was a bitter desperate battle, fought on so narrow a field, said Barbour, that two horsemen could not ride together. When the men of Lorn finally broke and ran they were drowned and slaughtered as they fought with each other to cross a bridge over the Awe. The galley of John MacDougall took him safely away.

In the south-west a fierce and reckless campaign by Edward Bruce had driven Ingram de Umfraville and the Galloway lords from the field and into the safety of their keeps. He captured his nephew Thomas Randolph, who still had spirit enough to taunt the Bruces, saying they fought with cowardice and deceit. He was sent to prison for reflection, and was soon brought to an understanding of military guile and to the offer of his sword in his uncle's service. In March, 1309, success persuaded the King to call a parliament at St Andrews, where his newly loyal lords could formally acknowledge his authority and convey that fact to the Pope by way of Philip of France. The composition of this parliament shows the ethnic texture of his supporters at this time. Apart from some like the Douglases, the Keiths and the Boyds, they were largely Highlanders, Celtic families attracted to his banner by the strong pull of blood-feud and ancient myths. Some months later the clergy of Scotland also gave their support to the crowned and excommunicated murderer.

The response of Edward to the unpleasant reversal of power in his northern province was weak and vacillating. The lieutenants he sent to Carlisle and Berwick in the autumn of 1309 were reluctant to cross the Border while the Gascon mountebank was whispering in their king's ear. The following summer he came himself, reinforcing his garrison at Perth with a large fleet, but the army he took across the Tweed in September, 1310, trudged sullenly about the Lowlands without fighting a battle, weary from mud, wind and rain. Bruce withdrew before it, and wasting the country behind him. Edward reached Linlithgow, quarrelled with his barons, retired to Berwick, came back half-heartedly and retired again. He offered to treat with Bruce, broke his word or had it broken for him by Robert, and sent the unhappy Gaveston to reinforce Perth with two hundred men. He then went back to London, where his jealous lords and parliament were demanding the banishment of his ennobled Gascon pet. As England hung on the edge of civil war, Bruce ignored another papal excommunication for his 'damnable perseverance' in sin and crossed the Border on a whirlwind, burning Haltwhistle, Gilsland and the valley of the Tyne in eight days, driving home great herds of cattle. He came back for another two weeks of bloody sport, defying the English wardens of the marches and so frightening the lords and merchants of Northumberland that they gladly bought a truce for two thousand pounds.

It lasted no longer than February, 1312. Then the raids began again under Edward Bruce and James Douglas, the burning of towns and the levying of blackmail, the driving of cattle and the ransoming of prisoners. Chester-le-Street was seized, Durham and Hartlepool sacked, and more money taken for the brief respite of truce. Edward offered peace, and was refused, but could not turn to angry war. His rebellious barons hated Gaveston more than Bruce at this moment. The Gascon was foolish or foolhardy enough to leave Berwick and come south to his king's aid at Scarborough, where they had a short and anguished reunion before Edward left to fight the barons. They avoided him, starved Gaveston out of his castle, and paid two Irishmen to hack his handsome head from his body. One principal cause of dissension was thus brutally gone, but the struggle between Edward and his lords dragged on until the end of the year, when he was forced to stifle his grief and longing with an amnesty for Gaveston's murderers. His father would have arranged it differently.

The year had begun well and continued well for Bruce. Before his terrible raids upon England he had taken the walled and moated town of Perth from its commander, William Oliphant. For nearly two months it had held out against him, sustained by English ships and garrisoned by stubborn men who jeered at him from their walls. He marched his army away for a week and thought of what he had seen of the defences, remembering where the water of the moat might reach no higher than a tall man's throat. He came back with a few men on a moonless night in early January, and was the first into the water, wearing full armour and carrying a ladder and a spear like the others. The Scots were on the wall before its hired watchman awoke and gave the alarm, and once there they soon took the town with spear and sword. 'Next day,' said the Lanercost chronicler, 'Robert caused all the citizens of the better class who were of the Scottish nation to be killed, but the English were allowed to go free.'[1] William Oliphant was not killed, but was 'bound and sent far away to the Isles', his noble defence of Stirling for-gotten in this confusion of treacherous loyalties, or perhaps remembered by the man who had besieged him there too, and then in England's name. Upon Bruce's orders, Perth was destroyed, its moat filled with its walls.

By the end of 1313, a year of spectacular triumph in which Robert proved that his genius for war lay in mobility and surprise, in the skills of guerrilla fighting applied to field campaigns, the English and their Scottish partisans had lost all but a hand's-span of the strongholds they held at its beginning. Edward Bruce had taken thirteen of them in the south and west, though most were timber keeps and not garrisons of stone, and in the summer he had persuaded the constable of Stirling to surrender his great donjon within a

---

[1] Bruce's clemency or cruelty at Perth has been successfully clouded by the chroniclers, which is why, perhaps, the pen is mightier than the sword. Barbour said he was merciful to all the citizens, and John of Fordun said he killed all traitors, Scots and English.

year if he were not relieved before. Such victories, the violent raids into England, a sea-borne conquest of the Isle of Man, and a truce finally forced from Edward by the threat of another invasion of his northern counties, were fragile triumphs, however, and would be of value only if they gave Scotland the time, the unity and the strength to face the powerful English army which Edward must bring to the relief of Stirling and the re-conquest of all that had been lost. Berwick was still his, the key of the Border lock and more English now than Scots, arrogantly proud of having thrown back an assault by Bruce, though its citizens should have given more credit to a barking dog that first sounded an alarm.

In Lent, 1314, Linlithgow was taken from the English by a ruse, when a farmer filled his hay-cart with armed men and halted it beneath a falling portcullis. Edinburgh's castle fell soon after. This rock-heart of the country was taken by Thomas Randolph, his thoughtful transference of loyalty to his uncle having been recently rewarded with the earldom of Moray and the possession of Man. With thirty men he climbed the north face of the cliff, by a path that was inevitably given his name, rather than that of William Francis who suggested it, and who had used it when he was in the castle for a discreet descent to his nightly wenching. Once inside the castle, Randolph opened the gates to the rest of his men, and took possession more easily, perhaps, than Barbour imagined sixty years later.

> A mighty struggle there was seen,
> With sundry weapons stout and keen
> They laid about with all their might,
> Till swords that had been fair and bright
> With blood were covered to the hilt.
> And many of them there were killed.

It was the year of Bannockburn. In less than a decade Robert Bruce's ambition had changed him from a self-serving claimant to a desperate murderer and an excommunicated fugitive, from a heather king to the general of armies and the master of a wide province, and now, by the irresistible compulsions of these metamorphoses and in one climactic battle, he was to become the founder of a nation's independence.

## 5

In the late afternoon of Midsummer Eve, 1314, Bruce looked southward across the shallow run of the Bannock. He was a small figure on a small grey horse. He wore a coat of mail and his face was unguarded, his reddish hair covered by a leather cap and a simple bascinet surmounted by his circlet crown. Beyond the burn he saw steel and banners, tall lances and glittering dust, and he heard the noise of a great army. Edward II had come to relieve Stirling, to honour his inheritance, and to destroy 'Robert de Brus who calls himself king of Scotland'.

The English king had crossed the Border in early June, and marched by way of Lauderdale to Edinburgh, there meeting the fleet that brought him provisions and supplies. Though he had healed the quarrel with his lords, with the help of the Pope and by the birth of a son, three great earls only had come with him: Humphrey de Bohun of Hereford, Gilbert de Clare of Gloucester, and of course Aymer de Valence of Pembroke. Since the beginning of the year, when his summons had gone through his kingdom, he had been mobilizing the most puissant army England had ever put to the field, though it was far fewer than the hundred thousand Barbour would wildly claim. If sickness and desertion, garrison and guard are allowed their winnowing, he had between two and three thousand mounted knights and fifteen thousand archers and spearmen. His cavalry – hauberked, helmed and greaved – was the hammer-head of his army, his infantry a shaft. Victory depended upon the weight, the speed, the moment and the shortness of a charge. Once launched it was soon exhausted, and was regrouped with difficulty. Once moving it could see what lay ahead only, and little of that. The terror it could inspire was the strongest of its weapons, the unnerving approach of faceless men, heads covered with slit-eyed helmets, coloured surcoats on black mail, the lowered points of pennoned

*Left  Chain mail, traditionally believed to have been brought in the 14th century to Scotland from Italy. Right  An Italian visored bascinet, c. 1380, with chain mail covering the neck. Bottom  Gauntlets of gilt latten, a mixed yellow metal resembling brass, made in the 14th century.*

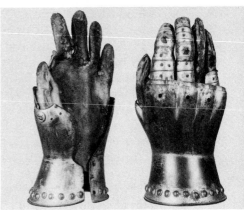

lances, the beat of hooves and the clanking of iron shields. Its objective was rarely men similarly mounted and armed, though these might be singly engaged in knightly encounters. Its victims were the expendable cattle of warfare, bowmen and spearmen in leather coats or quilted tunics, but with courage they could sometimes make an abattoir of its noisy and expensive chivalry.

The Scots were heavily outnumbered. Barbour said there were thirty thousand, as ridiculous an exaggeration as his estimate of the English, though the odds were perhaps the same. There were no more than five hundred light-horsed riders, a few score Ettrick archers, and five thousand spearmen or less, grouped in four divisions. War had been their way of life since boyhood.

Six and a half centuries have changed the field, and men still argue about the site of the battle, disputing its proper position by yards. It is now lost under the urban spread of Stirling, under roads, railway, farms, houses and pit-head, drainage schemes and timber clearance. Little is as it was when Edward's army came north from Falkirk that dry midsummer season, choked with dust and sweating with heat. To the south of the castle rock, four hundred feet above the Stirling plain, the land shelved down to the hunting forest of New Park, low and timbered hills held in a serpentine curl of the Bannock. Further south was the rock outcrop and scattered trees of Torwood. The road from Falkirk, first made a thousand years before by the Romans, ran northward from Torwood, over the burn and through the Park, past St Ninian's church to the castle gates. Bruce had decided to fight here, before Stirling, rather than anywhere else in his kingdom, and having made the choice had picked his ground with cunning and skill. Arriving from Torwood on Saturday, June 22, he placed his four schiltrons along the road through the New Park, facing eastward, screened by trees, and with the advantage of higher ground above the plain. The left flank division, by St Ninian's, was led by Thomas Randolph. The next schiltron was commanded by Walter the Steward, though because he was young and inexperienced its effective leader was his lieutenant James Douglas. Then Edward Bruce's division, entrusted with the lion and yellow standard of his brother. The King himself led the right flank schiltron, upon the southern edge of the Park and the bank of the Bannock. A supply camp at Cambuskenneth, north of the Forth, was commanded by Sir John Airth.

In this, the most decisive battle of its history, Scotland's army was strongly Celtic. There were Lothian men and borderers with Edward Bruce and the Steward, but there were also Gallgaels from Galloway, Scoto-Picts from Fife, and Randolph's spearmen were from Moray and Ross. With his own Carrick levies, Robert's division included Islesmen, mountain men from Argyll, Gaels brought by Angus Og of Clan Donald, honouring an old promise and expecting rich rewards. 'My hope,' Bruce told him, 'is constant in thee', and that hope was reciprocated. The lands of the chief of Clan Donald had been forfeited since his support for Balliol, and his younger brother Angus Og might this day win them for himself, as well as those of the MacDougalls.

To the natural protection of the New Park, Bruce had added a further defence. On Saturday evening the men of his division dug a screen of holes between the trees and the water of the burn, each a foot wide and three deep, covered with brush. A honeycomb, Barbour called them, and with the Bannock they protected the right flank of the army from a charge of horse. After Mass on Sunday morning, Bruce rode to inspect the pits and was pleased by what he saw, sending word that his men, then breaking their fast with bread and water, should 'busk them on their best manner', should arm and stand ready for the day. If any man was poor in heart, unwilling to take what God might send, he could go now without molestation. Commanders had made such offers before, and would make them many times again, and history has yet to record an army that accepted so generous a release from imminent slaughter. In the nervous tension before battle, when men are cunningly told that they may stay or go, they stiffen their self-respect by choosing the former. Bruce's army answered as he had expected, with a single cry, said Barbour, that none was afraid.

*The seal of Robert Bruce, a cast from the original in the Bibliothèque Nationale. The equestrian statue in his honour at Bannockburn is based on this likeness.*

A skirmish line of Ettrick archers now ringed the borders of the New Park, and within it the schiltrons had moved a few yards from the road to better ground. Some of Randolph's men were forward with the archers, the main body standing by St Ninian's. Edward Bruce had also advanced eastward from the road, and his brother was facing south across the pot-holes and the burn. The camp-followers, the 'small folk and pover-ale' of the Scots army, waggoners, victuallers, yeomen, boys and women, were sent to the low top of Coxet Hill in the heart of the Park and behind the Steward's schiltron, still formed along the road. If the day went ill, the small folk would be butchered. If it went well, they would be its grisly scavengers. At noon Bruce waited before his division for the return of Douglas and Sir Robert Keith, whom he had sent south to Torwood to watch the advance of the English. They were astonished by what they saw, a great column of horse and foot, two miles long in the summer heat and approaching on either side of the road.

> Their shields were shining dazzlingly,
> Their bascinets were burnished bright,
> Reflecting back the sun's great light.
> Embroidered banners floated high,
> And spears and pennants could they spy,
> And countless knights upon their steeds,
> All brilliant in their coloured weeds.

The bravest host in Christendom, said Barbour, would have been dismayed by such a multitude. As the King's Marischal, master of his five hundred light horse, Keith was probably more than dismayed. He and Douglas rode back and told Bruce that the English 'covered all the earth', and were ordered to keep what they had seen to themselves, to spread instead a story that the enemy was advancing in disorder. It was a bold lie, of which the English were soon to make some truth.

As his van marched out of the Torwood, Edward already knew how the Scots were placed to meet him. This was war, but it was also a noble game of chivalry, in which one armoured boy was to touch an agreed spot within an appointed time, and another was to prevent it if he could. That morning Bruce had allowed the Governor of Stirling, Sir Philip de Mowbray, to ride out to meet Edward, perhaps in the hope that he would tell the English that they had come too late and could not relieve the castle by Midsummer Day. What de Mowbray did say was that the Scots had blocked the road through the New Park, but since Edward had arrived within the appointed time he had won the game, and a hard battle could be avoided with honour.

It had already begun. Edward may have sent orders to Hereford and Gloucester, in the van with his young knights, to halt on the south side of the burn, but they had marched too far in this stifling heat to stop now, and each was the jealous rival of the other. As soon as they saw the Scots skirmish line retreating into the Park, they ordered their trumpets to sound and led their eager young men forward at a gallop, over the burn and slowly up a rise toward the trees. One Scot alone seemed to be waiting for them, on a grey Highland pony and war-axe in hand. Hereford's nephew, Henry de Bohun, recognized him, and spurred ahead of the others on a vainglorious charge into history. Bruce did not move until the Englishman's lance-point was feet away. Then he pulled the little horse aside, like a deer starting, his axe cutting down through de Bohun's helmet and skull from crest to chin. He rode back to his division, and when he was reproached for the risks he had taken he looked sadly at the splintered haft of his weapon and said 'I have broken the haft of my good battle-axe.' Gloucester and Hereford and the bold young knights were now among the pot-holes and the spiked iron balls that had been scattered about them in the grass. As the English horses stumbled, reared and screamed, the spears of Bruce's men came forward, and the trumpets that had brayed an advance now called an urgent retreat.

Bruce's encounter with de Bohun was the stuff of heroic legend and has been so honoured in schoolrooms ever since, but in an age sceptical of human motives he can appear more artful than valiant, and much safer than his reckless opponent. Once committed to his tilt, head down and lance couched, de Bohun relied upon weight and not manoeuvre, and against an enemy similarly committed victory would have been decided by brute impact. But here a cool-headed, lightly armed and lightly horsed man ignored the nice obligations of chivalry, side-stepped a rider who could not be halted and slew him like an ox as he passed. Outnumbered three to one, the Scots should have seen the lesson, which was perhaps what Bruce intended.

As Hereford and Gloucester fell back across the burn, three hundred other knights under Sir Robert Clifford were riding across the Carse of Stirling, the meadow-land between New Park and the Forth. Edward had ordered this flanking movement to the east, as a reconnaissance of the Scots position, or to escort Philip de Mowbray back to his corner in the castle, where he should properly have been by the rules of the game. Before they reached the castle, or upon their return, Thomas Randolph's division came out of the Park and attacked them, its commander angered by Bruce's taunt that he had let a rose fall from his king's chaplet in allowing Clifford to pass. The sloping ground was broken, and Clifford drew back to bring the scattered attack further into the open, but when he finally charged the spearmen they came together like iron dust to a magnet.

There was a bloody mêlée about the barbed and unbreakable schiltron, unsaddled knights, skewered horses and masking dust. As the Scots advanced, slow pace by pace, the circling riders hurled their lances and swords against the schiltron in impotent fury, and then broke off the fight, some riding to the castle and others back across the carse. By the loss of one man only, it was said, Randolph had restored the rose to Bruce's crown.

*The Monymusk Reliquary, a casket that originally contained relics of Columba, was traditionally borne before the Scots in battle. The Abbot of Arbroath carried it at Bannockburn.*

It was the only major action of a day now dying in a sultry summer dusk. Before nightfall the English army began to move on to the carse, making camp three miles or less from the New Park on narrow ground between the Bannock and a bend of the Forth. Edward needed water for his parched men and horses, but it was an insane choice, almost an island, the Forth to its right and rear and the deep-sided burn on its left. The earth was marshy, veined by tiny streams and each a hazard to heavy cavalry. That night, according to their own chroniclers, many of the English foot-soldiers were drunk, but others made fascines of wood and brush to fill the brooks in the morning. On their front to the south-west, the dark rise of the New Park was pricked by Scottish camp-fires. During the dark hours before dawn Airth and his men at Cambuskenneth were attacked and killed by the Earl of Atholl, who thought this a favourable moment to gratify his family's quarrel with Bruce.

The English chronicler, Sir Thomas Gray, said that Bruce was doubtful of the next day's fight and talked of retiring southward, over the Campsie Fells and into the strong ground of Lennox. He decided to stay after he had spoken with a deserter from Edward's camp. This man was a Scottish knight, Sir Alexander Seton, who sweetened his shameful arrival with news that although the English were demoralized they could not believe

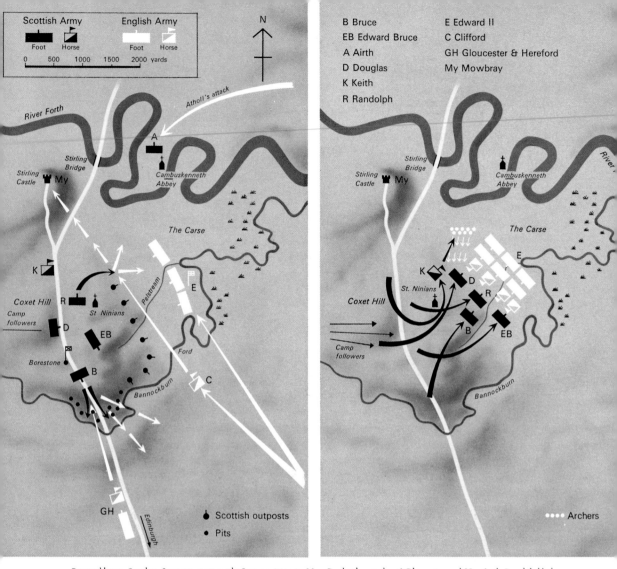

*Bannockburn, Sunday, June 23, 1314: the Scots position in New Park, the repulse of Gloucester and Hereford, Randolph's defeat of Clifford. Right Monday: the Scots move out of New Park to attack, the front followed by Bruce and the Highlanders.*

that Bruce would leave the Park against them. He offered his head if this were not so. 'If you attack them in the morning you will defeat them easily and without loss.'[1]

Monday, the Feast of St John the Baptist, was another day of heat and sun. The Scots rose early for Mass and a lesson on a text from Isaiah, 'Comfort ye, comfort ye, my people . . .', and then piously broke their fast again on bread and water. When Bruce had knighted the Steward, James Douglas, and others, he ordered his army forward on to the carse. Edward Bruce's division led the advance, followed on his left by Randolph and the Steward, with Bruce and his Gaels closely in the rear. A staggered line, scarcely a mile across, approaching the narrow neck of marshy ground where the English stood

[1] Gray's *Scalachronica*. He heard the story from his father, who was taken prisoner in Clifford's fight. No other chronicler mentions it. Seton's arrival was probably true, and Moray McLaren (*If Freedom Fail*) reasonably suggests that Bruce had already decided to attack, and that what Gray's father overheard was a discussion on a possible line of retreat in the event of disaster.

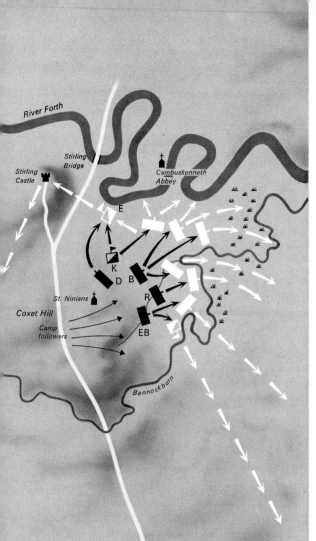

*Bannockburn, Monday: Bruce sends in the Highlanders and the English break. Right The Augustinian Abbey of Cambuskenneth, where Bruce's supplies were kept before Bannockburn and where his Parliament met in 1326.*

between Forth and burn. Four dull-coloured divisions with banners and steady spears, marching upon armoured cavalry. Edward was rightly astonished. 'Will they fight?' he asked. 'They will fight' said Ingram de Umfraville, once the Guardian of Scotland and now its enemy. The King could not believe it, and was soon sure the Scots were yielding. Some distance across the carse they halted, to tighten their formation probably, and in good discipline they crouched or knelt with spears thrust into the earth to take a sudden charge. 'They kneel!' said Edward. 'They ask for mercy!' Not from you, he was told. 'To God they pray, for them it's death or victory.' So be it then, said the King, and ordered his trumpets to sound.[1]

[1] Barbour started the unlikely story that the Scots knelt to pray halfway across the carse, and it was believed by later generations who liked to think that the courage of their ancestors had been well laced with piety. Bruce's men had made their peace with God at Mass, and to make it again at this moment would have been dangerous as well as superfluous.

But Hereford had left the advance guard, where he had been disputing the right to command with Gloucester, and was now bringing their petulant quarrel to Edward. Gloucester heard the trumpets, lowered his lance, and spurred upon Edward Bruce's division. Without his emblazoned surcoat the young man's leadership was at first unrecognized, and the charge that followed him was loose and disordered. Even so it was heavy with the iron weight of horse and rider, bending the line of Lowland men. Gloucester died at once, thrust from the chair of his saddle, and his vengeful knights splintered the Scottish spears with their eager bodies, 'till through their armour burst the blood, And streamed to the earth in growing flood'. In the clashing of metal, the terrible cries from dust-dry throats, Randolph and the Steward came up on the left to support Edward Bruce, and the English van withdrew for a brief and sweating respite. The Scots line did not halt. Bridging the neck of land between river and burn, it marched slowly on with lowered spears. Edward's army was contained where it could not deploy, his fifteen thousand infantry held uselessly behind the wall of his cavalry. And upon that soggy, contracting ground a great charge was no longer possible. When the spear-hedge reached them, the knights threw their lances like javelins and drew their swords.

> A mighty struggle then was seen,
> And many fighters bold and keen
> With spears, with maces, and with knives,
> And other weapons, braved their lives,
> And many of them there fell dead.
> With blood the grass became all red.

It was horrible to see and hear, said Barbour, seeing it and hearing it years later in the fireside tales of old men. 'For men of valour and of might did many deeds of courage.' Too late Edward tried to use the archers whose whispering arrows and long white bows had won Falkirk for his father. A company or two slipped along the bank of the Forth and thumbed their cloth-yards into the dense flank of the Steward's division, before they were driven off by Keith's horsemen. When Bruce saw this he loosed the High-landers from reserve, with a cry – or so said Barbour – of 'Be cheerful and act valiantly!' Cheerful enough, they screamed into the English knights with long sword and axe, over dead men and horses in the wrack, 'giving and taking wounds full wide'. Somewhere in this bloody scramble a Scots sword or spear killed Edward's ally John Comyn of Badenoch, his father's murder still unavenged.

All four divisions were now in line, in an arc pressing upon the retreating knights, and beyond them, in the ox-bow of Forth and burn, the English foot at last broke. They ran past their king's standard to the river, or eastward where the Ettrick archers were waiting among the mossy streams. Now that the ground was free behind them, some of the knights turned their horses about, and the exultant schiltrons cried 'On them! On them! They fail!'

The cry was heard by the poor folk on Coxet Hill, and they saw the running men. They made banners from strips of cloth tied to the branches of trees, elected a captain bold, and came out of the New Park behind him, shouting 'Upon them now! They shall all die!' Some ran with their knives toward the burn, now choked with cloth-yard dead, some in pursuit of the fugitive foot, and others to the rear of the schiltrons. Barbour said that the English believed them to be reinforcements, and lost all heart for further fight, but it is unlikely that they could have been seen beyond the dust, the moving

*James III, from the altar-piece of Trinity College Church, Edinburgh.*
*The standing figure is St Andrew, and the third is perhaps one of the King's brothers.*

spears and banners. The English were already demoralized and already running, to the Forth, to Stirling and to Torwood, to drown and to die, to find miraculous safety.

> The lads and servants and the rabble
> Seeing them overwhelmed in battle,
> Among them ran and many slew.

Men and horses passed dry-foot over streams bridged with dead, and killed without compassion. The impossible had become a triumphant reality. Mailed horse had been defeated by a sturdy advance of foot, six thousand men had routed three times their number. English lords and knights stood bareheaded, naked and disarmed, saved now by the value of their noble blood. But their valueless servants were butchered on the bloody earth before them. In Edward's camp the loot was magnificent, armour and weapons, silver and gold plate, a siege-train, pay-chests, church vestments that were to have been worn at a victory Mass, meal, meat and wine, trinkets that would be treasured in Scots households for another three centuries. And in the wild joy of the victors, in the arrogant pride of generations to come, it would be forgotten that the English had fought with courage and honour.

Five hundred knights, led by de Valence, closed about Edward when the battle was lost, cut a way through the Steward's men and rode to the gates of Stirling. Sir Philip de Mowbray refused to open them, saying that the King would not be safe here, but he may well have decided that by the rules of the agreement Edward had no right of entry. Upon his advice the King rode south to Linlithgow, where his pursuer James Douglas, who had begged permission from Bruce and sixty horsemen from Keith, finally lost him. At Dunbar a ship took Edward away, and his knights were left to find their own way across the Border.

It was an evil, a miserable and a calamitous day for the English, said the melancholy chronicler of Lanercost, and the name of Bannockburn would stick in men's throats for many years. More than this. 'Robert de Brus was commonly called King of Scotland by all men because he had acquired Scotland by force of arms.'

Following the sweetness of victory came warmer pleasures. Bruce's wife and daughter came home from England, part of a bargain by which the Earl of Hereford, captured in flight, was exchanged for fifteen Scots in English hands. Among them too was Bishop Lamberton, and old Robert Wishart, now blind from his long imprisonment. The defences of Stirling Castle, surrendered by de Mowbray, were destroyed, and for the rest of the summer across Lothian and the Lowland shires English and Welsh soldiers were hounded from their fugitive holes and murdered by the country folk. A parliament met at Cambuskenneth, in an abbey founded by David and two miles from the still stinking battlefield, and it passed a sentence of forfeiture upon all Scots who had fought for the English that Midsummer Day and in the years before, upon all who would not now 'stand forth' and declare their allegiance to Robert King of the Scots.

Now that Bruce had made himself secure it was time to determine his succession. He had no son, and although there was his daughter Marjorie by his first wife he had too much sense of history, past and recent, to entrust the crown to a woman. A national assembly of clergy, earls and barons, meeting at Ayr, decided with her consent that should the King die without a son the throne would go to his brother Edward, and his male heirs. This was the side-slip of succession peculiar to Pictish tradition, and it may

*A breathtaking but fanciful fresco showing Aeneas Sylvius Piccolomini at the Court of James I.*

have pleased his northern earls more than it did Marjorie and her young husband, Walter the Steward.

The Bruces had paid bitterly for this triumph, in conscience and in blood. Three brothers brutally dead, ten years of war, treachery, and hardship. Nor had the two days' battle on the Bannock burn ended that war. Edward recognized neither Scotland's independence nor her king, but the advantage and the initative were now with the Scots. The northern counties of England were again raided and burnt, Edward Bruce and Douglas going over the Border like riotous schoolboys year by year, driving cattle and levying blackmail, and although they could take no great castles they kept the country between in a state of bewildered terror. From their bloodthirsty behaviour, and the equally brutish response of English knights, Walter Scott would later weave his romantic verse.

Such a life fired Edward Bruce's rash ambition for greater achievements. When the titular King of Tyrone, whose power to make the offer is in doubt, invited him to take the throne of Ireland he gladly accepted, and sailed across with Thomas Randolph and Robert's indulgent permission. Some of the people rose for him, not so much in love as from a natural desire to be rid of the English and the Anglo-Irish. The O'Briens, the O'Tooles, O'Carrols and other Ulster clans carried him to Dublin on the wave of their fierce victories, and there crowned him High King of Ireland. Since even the native Irish could not agree upon his right to the title, Robert arrived with a large army to persuade them, and soon taught them that there was perhaps little difference between an English and a Scots overlord. When Edward Bruce was killed in battle near Dundalk there was small regret among his disillusioned subjects, and one of their annalists was of the opinion that from the beginning of the world Ireland had never been more blessed than by his death.

His dying, without lawful issue, also left the throne without a successor. Marjorie Bruce was dead, two years before in childbirth. In December, 1318, a parliament at Scone declared that the King would be succeeded by his grandson Robert, born to her and Walter the Steward. Thus far had the Norman families of de Brus and FitzAlan risen, from landless men to the Crown of Scotland.

6

Fortune is a fickle jade, said Barbour, smiling upon a man today and turning against him tomorrow. Fortune is a wheel, with one man atop and another below, 'for on a wheel, as ye can see, Two opposites may balanced be'. He was jeering at Edward's flight from Bannockburn, which the English called the Battle of the Pools, though that could not have been any easier in their throats. After the death of his last and vainglorious brother, Bruce frequently saw the back of the jade's head and felt the downward dip of the wheel. He held his kingdom eleven years more and until death, but under almost constant opposition and assault from without. He held it by the consent of the mass of its people and the majority of its barons. Four years before Bannockburn the Scots clergy at Dundee had declared that the nation would live and die with a king who, 'possessing the right of blood and endowed with the other cardinal virtues, is fitted to rule and worthy of the name of King and the honour of the Kingdom'. By the sword, they said, had Robert restored the realm. Success was all, the throne was his and doubt was buried with the dead of Bannockburn.

He would then have preferred peace, but Edward was stubborn in defeat and the Scots reckless in victory. A Border war continued fretfully across the Solway and the Tweed, the ill-protected and ill-supported northern shires of England resisting when they dared, or buying peace when they could not. On either side of that arbitrary frontier men of the same racial ancestry built their tall black towers, thumbed their noses at each other, and plunged into a reiving way of life that was to last for three centuries. Scots armies went south like bandits, intent on blood and plunder, but Bruce's tactics in carrying the war to the land of his opponent were wise not spiteful. England might survive the bleeding of its northern counties, for its arteries flowed from the south, but the heart of Scotland was within reach of the Border and bled from every raid across it.

*Pope John XXII, to whom the Declaration of Arbroath was addressed, in 1329 finally acknowledged Bruce as King of Scotland. In this 15th-century miniature he is receiving emissaries from the Greek Church.*

The Holy Father, John XXII, disapproved of Bruce as strongly as his predecessor, but when he was elected to the office he tried to put some gristle into the truce that had been proposed by Clement V. He sent four cardinals to Britain, two to Westminster and two to Edinburgh, ordering his dear sons in Christ to behave themselves and live in peace. Bruce received the cardinals with courtesy, but refused to accept letters that addressed him as *regnum Scotiae gubernantem*, as a noble man governing Scotland and not as its king. 'All my people call me king, and foreign princes address me under that title. . . . I will listen to no bulls until I am treated as King of Scotland and have made myself master of Berwick.' He was once more excommunicated, but the cardinals could find no Scots cleric willing to deliver the papers as custom demanded, and they left Scotland with outraged dignity.

Berwick fell in the spring of 1318 after an eleven weeks' siege, not by assault but by money paid to its gatekeeper Peter Spalding, who thus joined a long list of men whom history remembers for the one fact that they took a bribe. Edward went north to retake the town from Walter the Steward, with a monstrous engine of war called the Sow and an assurance from the Pope that he could pay his soldiers with a tithe previously promised to a crusade. He had got no further than York when Randolph and Douglas rode over the Border on a wild diversionary raid. There was little resistance to this terrible foray. England had not yet recovered from two years of famine during which starving men had eaten their horses and dogs, thieves in prison had devoured their weaker companions, swords had been drawn in parliament, and the bitter knights of Bannockburn had turned to banditry to keep themselves alive. Despite that generous tithe, Edward's army was unpaid and mutinous, his lieutenants inactive in their deafening quarrels. Free to do as they wished, the Scots burnt Northallerton and Boroughbridge, Knaresborough and Skipton, and would have burnt Ripon too had not its people, besieged for three days in their holy minster, bought its immunity for a thousand merks. The Scots then went home by way of Wharfedale, still burning and looting. 'They made men and women captive,' said the Lanercost chronicler, 'making the poor folks drive the cattle, carrying them off to Scotland without any opposition.'

In June the next year the English army at last reached Berwick, filled the creaking belly of the Sow with a storming-party and advanced it against the walls. But a Flemish engineer employed by the Steward had devised an ingenious stone-thrower, and this, said the ribald defenders, soon caused the sow to farrow. Douglas was again sent across the Tweed on a fierce diversion, riding deep into Yorkshire down the valley of the Swale. Edward's queen and judges fled from York with his exchequer when the Scots sat down to sup twelve miles from the city's gates. As they calmly ate their oaten cakes beside their hobbled horses they saw a great mob of desperate country-folk approaching in arms, led by an archbishop and a bishop and by white-robed Cistercians. The Scots rose from their supper, formed their spear-ring and shouted in defiance, so terrifying the peasants, said the chronicler, that they turned at once and ran.

> Then the Scots, breaking up their schiltron, mounted their horses and pursued the English, killing both clergy and laymen, so that about four thousand were slain, among whom fell the mayor of the town, and about one thousand, it was said, were drowned in the water of the Swale. Had not night come on, hardly a single Englishman would have escaped. Also many were taken alive, carried off to Scotland and ransomed at a heavy price.

Embittered and disillusioned, Edward lifted the siege of Berwick and abandoned the war. Three days before Christmas he agreed to a truce for two years, but still he would not, could not acknowledge Bruce's sovereignty or Scotland's independence. He and the Pope encouraged each other in their mutual hatred, and in January, 1320, John ordered Bruce and his principal bishops to appear before a papal court at Avignon. Once again the King was addressed as Governor, and once again he angrily refused to accept the letters. When the bull of excommunication against him and the bishops was renewed – some papal clerk must now have known it by heart – an assembly of lords at Arbroath Abbey replied with a defiant and dignified remonstrance. Though it followed a tradition of such direct appeals to the Holy Father, it was and has been unequalled in its eloquent plea for the liberty of man. From the darkness of medieval minds it shone a torch upon future struggles which its signatories could not have foreseen or understood.

The author of this noble Latin address is unknown, though it is assumed to have

*Arbroath Abbey, Angus, was originally a priory and contains the tomb of its founder, William I. Here, in 1320, an assembly of Scottish lords put their seals to a resounding declaration of faith and purpose, affirming their independence.*

been composed by Bernard de Linton, Abbot of Arbroath and Chancellor of Scotland. Above the seals of eight earls and forty-five barons, it asked for the Pope's dispassionate intervention in the bloody quarrel between the Scots and the English, and so that he might understand the difference between the two its preamble gave him a brief history of the former. Few of the barons, aware of their own Norman ancestry, can have believed it rightly described them, or did so believe it in noble self-delusion. Twenty-five years of war had created a new nation of Scots, justifying their continued struggle for independence by identifying themselves with the minority of Scotland's founding peoples, and it was proper for that minority to be represented among those ribboned seals by a Cameron and a Campbell, a MacDuff, Fergusson and a Murray. With dubious authenticity the preamble said that the Scots had journeyed from Greater Scythia by way of the Tyrrhenian Sea and the Pillars of Hercules, and after many years among the savage tribes of Spain had come to this land. They had driven out the Britons, destroyed the Picts, resisted Norsemen, Angle and Dane, and thereafter lived under 'one hundred and thirteen kings of their own royal stock, the line unbroken by a single foreigner'. The laughable fiction of this is irrelevant. What is important is the passionate sincerity of the men who believed it, who were placing a new and heady nationalism above the feudal obligations that had divided their loyalties less than a quarter of a century before. Blessed by Christ and protected by St Andrew, said the preamble, the Scots had enjoyed their freedom in peace until it was stolen from them by the English. Then neither age nor sex, religion nor rank, monk nor nun, had been safe from cruelty, massacre, violence, pillage and arson, outrages which 'no one could describe nor fully imagine unless he had seen them with his own eyes'. From such evils Scotland had been delivered at last by its tireless Prince and King, the Lord Robert.

> Yet if he should give up what he has begun, and agree to make us or our kingdom subject to the King of England or the English, we should exert ourselves at once to drive him out as our enemy and a subverter of his own rights and ours, and make some other man who was well able to defend us our

King; for, as long as but a hundred of us remain alive, never will we on any conditions be brought under English rule. It is in truth not for glory, nor riches, nor honours that we are fighting, but for freedom – for that alone, which no honest man gives up but with life itself.[1]

Let the Pope urge the King of England to 'leave us Scots in peace, who live in this poor little Scotland . . . and covet nothing but our own'. If he did not, if he lent too credulous an ear to the English, then he must take responsibility for the 'slaughter of bodies, the perdition of souls, and all the other misfortunes that will follow'.

In its mixture of defiance and supplication, nonsensical history and noble thought, two things make the Declaration of Arbroath the most important document in Scottish history. Firstly it set the will and the wishes of the people above the King. Though they were bound to him 'both by law and by his merits' it was so that their freedom might be maintained. If he betrayed them he would be removed and replaced. This remarkable obligation placed upon a feudal monarch by his feudal subjects may be explained in part by the fact that Bruce was still a heather king to many of them, still a wild claimant ruling upon sufferance and success. But the roots of his kingship were Celtic, and a Celtic tradition was here invoked, the memory of the Seven Earls, the Seven Sons of Cruithne the Pict in whom, it was believed, had rested the ancient right of tanistry, the elevation of kings by selection. This unique relationship of king and people would influence their history henceforward, and would reach its climax in the Reformation and the century following, when a people's Church would declare and maintain its superiority over earthly crowns.

Secondly, the manifesto affirmed the nation's independence in a way no battle could, and justified it with a truth that is beyond nation and race. Man has a right to freedom and a duty to defend it with his life. The natural qualifications put upon this by a medieval baron are irrelevant, as are the reservations which slave-owning Americans placed upon their declaration of independence. The truth once spoken cannot be checked, the seed once planted controls its own growth, and the liberty which men secure for themselves must be given by them to others, or it will be taken as they took it. Freedom is a hardy plant and must flower in equality and brotherhood.

The spirit and language of the petition persuaded Pope John that the Scots were an extraordinary and obstinate people, and now that his enthusiasm for Edward was blowing cool he advised the King to make peace with them. But Scots money, Edward believed, was buying the sympathy of his uncle Thomas of Lancaster, and when he had removed this treason with the earl's head at Pontefract he mustered an army to cross the Border. The Scots had expected no less. They invaded England while Edward was still gathering his soldiers at Newcastle, plundered Lancashire and returned home. When the cumbersome and ill-provisioned English army crossed the Tweed Bruce retreated before it, burning the land behind him, leaving neither meat nor meal, byre nor harvest, nothing but ashes and a blackened earth. 'Thus the English were compelled to evacuate Scottish ground,' said the Lanercost chronicler, 'before the Nativity of the Glorious Virgin, owing as much to want of provender as to pestilence in the army, for famine killed as many soldiers as did dysentery.' They retired from Edinburgh in a mutinous humour, sacking the abbeys of Holyrood and Melrose, and burning Dryburgh, slaying priests and desecrating altars like Norsemen. They were followed to the Border by Douglas and

---

[1] This version is taken from *The Declaration of Arbroath 1320 – Facsimile and Translation* (H.M.S.O.). Reproduced by permission of H.M. Stationery Office.

his horsemen, and in the autumn of that year, 1322, Bruce crossed the Solway and the Pennines, ravaged the North Riding and almost captured Edward at Rievaulx Abbey. Ever chicken-hearted and luckless in war, said the chronicler, the English king fled in fear, leaving his silver plate and treasure to the Scots.

Unable to defend his kingdom, or prevent its northern counties from making their own peace with Bruce, Edward sent an envoy to Berwick in the spring of the next year, agreeing to a truce for thirteen years and promising to place no obstacle in the way of Bruce's efforts to secure papal recognition. Randolph was sent to Avignon, and proved himself as cunning a diplomat as he was a bold reiver. He told the Pope that his king was eager to lead a crusade against the paynim under the banner of the Holy Church, and could do so more effectively if the Pontiff acknowledged his right to the throne and his country's independence. John accepted the good sense of this, and formally recognized Bruce as king, but he would not yet lift the bull of excommunication. He courteously explained his change of mind to Edward, who was infuriated by it, and by the treaty of mutual assistance which Randolph later negotiated between Scotland and France.

The truce brought an unnatural peace to Scotland, and men told each other with surprise that their towns had not been burnt for a year or more. Their warrior king now had a son, a boy David born in March, 1324, and this too could have been seen as a miracle, God's blessing on a marriage barren for so long. Two years later in the abbey of Cambuskenneth, the Parliament of Scotland was attended for the first time by representatives from the King's burghs, and with the earls, barons and freeholders they

*The ruined Augustinian abbey of Holyrood, Edinburgh, was founded by David I in penance, it is said, for sporting on a holy day. Repeatedly the target of the invading English, it was finally sacked by the Scots in 1688.*

agreed to pay him a tenth of their revenues to fill his emptied exchequer, and to maintain him in a royal state now recognized by all but the King of England.

Edward II died in 1327, having lived his miserably unsuccessful life in the suffocating shadow of his father. He was first deposed by his unloving queen Isabella and her paramour Roger Mortimer, and then forced by them to abdicate in favour of his son. He wept like a fretful child, and was carried from dungeon to dungeon, each worse than the last, sometimes exposed to the jeering mob with a crown of straw upon his head. One night in September his agonized screams were heard from the cesspit cell where he was held in Berkeley Castle. In the morning he was dead, with no mark on his body, though it was later said that a red-hot iron, thrust into his anus, had helped him into everlasting life. He was buried in Gloucester, 'among the monks and not in London among the other kings, because he was deposed'.

The new king was fifteen, and his mother and her lover ruled his country for him. Uneasy and uncertain in power, they endeavoured to make the northern Border safe at least, but in reaffirming the truce they foolishly spoke of 'Robert and his adherents'. Since they were also entertaining John Balliol's claimant son, with too much respect and ceremony for Bruce's pride to stomach, Douglas was sent into Northumbria on a salutary raid. The wasting war began again.

The boy-king Edward III was given nominal command of the army assembled at Newcastle in April, 1327, levies from the shires, mercenaries from Germany, Flanders, Artois and Bohemia, and some strange bottle-shaped tubes that discharged great arrows of iron when flame was put to them. Edward was perhaps delighted by the fascinating toys. His tutor had recently given him an illuminated Latin manuscript on the duties of a king, an unconscious irony since his father the King was at that moment a prisoner of his mother the Queen, and among its happy illustrations was a painting of this early and dangerous *pot-de-fer*. The effectiveness of artillery, however primitive, requires the cooperative presence of an enemy, and the clouds of Scottish horsemen would fight no set battle as the English army lumbered into Northumbria, but harassed its flanks like flies and burnt the land about it. They ignored all the rules of chivalry, but they were superb light cavalry, shaggy and resolute men with spears slung, their feet hanging below the bellies of their Highland ponies. John Froissart, who saw them when he came to Scotland forty years later, found them a 'bold, hardy race, and much inured to war'.

> When they invaded England they brought no carriages, neither did they encumber themselves with any provision. Under the flap of his saddle, each man carries a broad plate of metal; behind the saddle a little bag of oatmeal. When they have eaten too much sodden flesh, and their stomach appears weak and empty, they place this plate over the fire, mix water with their oatmeal, and when the plate is heated, they put a little of the paste upon it, and make a thin cake, like a cracknel or biscuit, which they eat to warm their stomachs: it is therefore no wonder that they perform a longer day's march than other soldiers.

Like a water-beast stranded upon earth, the English army pulled itself in pursuit of these agile tormentors. The knights of Hainault and Flanders, in desperate imitation of their enemies, tied loaves behind their saddles and then could not eat the bread, for it was soon sour with horse-sweat. The land, they said, was savage and wild, full of deserts and mountains, fit for beasts only. Their night-camps were raided by wild men crying 'You are all dead!', and when taken prisoner they were left to die with their legs broken. And it rained, it rained for a week without stopping. Edward wept in boyish shame.

Bruce was now fifty-four, prematurely aged, sick and slowly dying from what may have been leprosy. Even so, when Douglas crossed the Tweed he had gone to Ulster in the hope of lighting a rebellion there. The plan was ill-conceived, and further marred by his increasingly violent temper. Had he controlled himself, said Barbour, 'all of Ireland's pleasant land might well have fallen into his hand'. But when he came home there was happy news from Northumbria. Douglas and Randolph were still bleeding the province and exhausting the demoralized army that was trying to protect it. The Scots left a ribald verse on the door of a church, mocking the heartless, witless, graceless, thriftless English, and when they had burnt enough and killed enough they decided to go home. By uncommon good luck Edward blocked the ford across the Tyne, and offered knighthood and lands to any man who could bring him news of the Scots. An English squire found them snugly camped in Weardale, or more correctly was found by them, and was sent back to Edward with a message that they were eager to fight. He marched to them and found them waiting on high ground south of the Wear. He sent them heralds, inviting them to cross to level ground and chivalrous battle, but they said that they were content where they were. For three days the armies faced each other, sounding trumpets against the sky, and at dawn on the fourth day the Scots were gone, to another hill two miles away. Their bellies were empty, but they stood boldly to arms, protected by a wood and a marsh. In the night Douglas rode upon the English camp with two hundred spearmen and almost captured Edward. 'We have drawn blood,' he said when he returned.

Another day, another night the Scottish fires burnt brightly, but at dawn the hill was bare. The Scots were again gone, this time homeward through the marsh.

Once more Edward wept in shame, and took his dispirited army to York, where it was disbanded. In a yellow autumn Douglas raided Durham and then joined Randolph at the siege of Alnwick, while Bruce, in war-harness for the last time, brought an army about the English castle of Norham-on-Tweed. It was September, and while the wretched prisoner of Berkeley was dying his son's parliament sat at Lincoln to consider how the mercenaries might be paid and the war continued, but Mortimer persuaded it to sue for peace and to offer Bruce a marriage between his son and Edward's sister Joan. When Robert received the offer he lifted the siege of Norham and went home to Edinburgh. That winter, rotting sick in his chamber at Holyrood, he listened to emissaries from England, and considered an answer that was later written for him by Bishop Lamberton.

In February one hundred Scottish knights brought it to Edward and his parliament at York, riding on safe-conduct where they had recently passed no less freely in war. There could be peace, said the terms they brought, there could be a marriage, but only if England fully and unreservedly recognized the Lord Robert as King of Scotland. The condition was met, and in May the English parliament ratified the treaty, agreeing to a final and perpetual peace qualified only by Scotland's alliance with France. Though both parties set their seals as equals, the English were bitterly aware that they were surrendering, and they would soon call it the 'Shameful Peace', taking Mortimer's head in savage revenge. Edward renounced all claims of sovereignty, and declared that his most dear friend and ally, the Lord Robert, was 'by the grace of God illustrious King of Scots'. He agreed to return all documents relating to Scotland's freedom or subjection, all those that could be found, that is, and this promise was duly fulfilled, six hundred years later by his descendant. Margaret's holy relic, the Black Rood with its fragment of the True Cross, came back to the abbey by Edinburgh, but the Stone of Destiny was not returned, nor was it mentioned in the treaty, a curious and intriguing omission. Scottish legend, unwilling to think this slab of sandstone meant so little to Bruce, believes that Edward agreed to restore it but was prevented by the citizens of London.[1] For their part, the Scots agreed to pay the English an indemnity of twenty thousand pounds in yearly instalments, and in a treaty more distinguished by the terms that were broken than by those that were kept, it is encouraging to know that this one was honoured.

The children David and Joan were married at Berwick in July. He was five and she was seven, and their innocent nuptial joys were noisily celebrated by a bruising tournament between English and Scottish knights. In the circumstances, it was the only possible consummation.

In October the Pope, accepting the advice the English were bound by the treaty to give him, lifted the ban of excommunication from his 'dearest son Robert'. A year later he issued another bull authorizing the crowning and anointing of Bruce and his successors as Kings of Scotland. Before the news of this reached Robert, indeed a week before the bull was dated, the old fighter died in his castle palace of Cardross above the Clyde. He had come there to die, to be solaced by his hawks and his caged lion, by his garden and the painted walls of his chamber, by the company of his jester Patrick. His life had been relentlessly hard, punishing his body and his conscience, but it had been a triumph, and had brought success to his family's ambitions and independence to his country, though which gave him the greater satisfaction it would be hard to say. He was Scotland's greatest king, perhaps the only great one. He would not recognize the bronze image of the Patriot King which later centuries would cast from his mould, and it may be proper that the Wallace Monument, however execrable in taste, towers above his in the cockpit of Scotland, but it is what a nation does in the name of its immortal heroes that matters, not the fact that they were mortal men.

The drama of his life was carried beyond death. A gate was sawn in the cage of his body, and his heart was taken out and placed in a silver casket. The corpse was then embalmed and borne slowly to a tomb in Dunfermline Abbey church. Before his death he had asked his friend Sir James Douglas – that tall, broad, terrible raider – to carry his heart upon a crusade against the paynim and to bury it by the Sepulchre in the Holy Land. The love he had so miraculously inspired among diverse men was loyal to his memory, and a body of dedicated knights followed Douglas to the nearest fight, against the Moors of Granada. They died with him in battle, surrounded by Saracens and abandoned by their Spanish comrades. Douglas threw the heart of Bruce deep into the enemy, telling it to go first as it had always done, and then plunged after it with his knights, shouting the name of his house.

It is said that the heart was brought back to Scotland, and it may be the mummified organ, enclosed in lead, that lies under the floor of Melrose Abbey, by the water of the Tweed and the three green crowns of the Eildon hills.

---

[1] To be fair to the myth, English records suggest that when Isabella came to her daughter's wedding she promised to return the Stone (William Croft Dickinson, *Scotland from the Earliest Times to 1603*), but there seems to be no record of a Scots request for it at this time.

## 7

Robert Bruce had eclipsed the sun, blinding men with the aureola of light about his helmet. When he was gone his shadow no longer hid a poor and wasted country, a tired and demoralized people scarcely begun on a faltering recovery from the wars that had brought them independence. The two men whom he had entrusted with the guardianship of the child-king might have sustained that independence, but they were dead too within three years. Douglas died as if he were enacting the last stanza of a *chanson de geste* specially composed for him. Less spectacularly, but with equal and disastrous finality, Thomas Randolph expired at Musselburgh from a sudden and mysterious sickness which the English naturally put down to poison.

The regency passed by election to another of Bruce's nephews, Donald, Earl of Mar, an anglicized Scot who had once been sympathetic to the Balliol cause. Toom Tabard had been dead for nearly twenty years, but his son Edward was now hot for regaining the throne, encouraged by the secret sympathy of Edward III and by the thought, perhaps, that Mar would offer no serious resistance. In the summer of 1332 he sailed from the Humber with eighty-eight ships, English archers and spearmen, English lords hungry for land grants in the north, and a number of Scots barons whom Bruce had exiled and who were nobly known as the Disinherited. They landed on the Fife coast in August and marched toward Perth. Mar met them on Dupplin Moor near the River Earn in a bloody fight that started at sunrise and lasted until high noon. At first the English assaults were held, but when the cloth-yard began its whistling song the schiltrons were destroyed. 'One most marvellous thing happened,' said the Lanercost chronicler, 'the pile of dead was greater in height from the earth toward the sky than one whole spear length.' In this reeking shambles lay the body of Regent Mar, and with him Bruce's bastard son, Randolph's gay young heir, and many more.

Six weeks later Balliol was crowned Edward, King of Scots, at Scone, attended by men who had once been Bruce's staunch supporters. One was William Sinclair, the warrior Bishop of Dunkeld, and another was of course Duncan MacDuff, Earl of Fife, following a family tradition of being present at all coronations, whoever the principal might be.

Balliol rode southward then to the Lowlands, as if drawn in fear and uncertainty to the English border, promising Edward III land and homage, and offering to marry Joan if her union with the boy-king David could be dissolved. Behind him the Scots loyalists gathered under another Randolph and another Douglas, and they fell upon him one December night in Annan, driving him out of his kingdom, half-dressed and astride an unsaddled horse. Archibald Douglas, younger brother of the crusading James, was elected Regent.

Edward's secret sympathy for Balliol now became open support. Declaring that the Treaty of Northampton had been broken by Thomas Randolph's encouragement of border reiving, he brought an army to take the town and castle of Berwick.

The Scots who met him at Halidon Hill on July 19, 1333, had learnt nothing from the lesson of Dupplin Moor. They clung to a belief in the invincibility of the schiltron which Wallace had created and which Bruce had begun to discard. But the young Edward who had wept for shame in Northumbria was already the future victor of Crécy, and the weapon that was to win him that and other battles had a triumphant rehearsal two miles north-west of Berwick. His army held the northern slope of Halidon

Hill in three divisions, each with a salient of archers, lithe young men in deerskin jackets and iron helmets. Their white bows were six feet long, cunningly made from yew, ash or elm, and strung with hemp, flax or silk. Their deep quivers were full of cloth-yard arrows of oak, tipped with burnished steel and winged with feathers of goose and swan. Between the projecting companies of archers were narrowing funnels, tempting the foolish Scots toward a line of spearmen, the banners and shining arms of Edward's cavalry. The schiltrons floundered through the marshy ground at the foot of the hill and slowly climbed the slope with spears lowered. The humming volleys of steady arrows dropped upon them as soon as they came within range, and it was said that the Scots turned their faces away as if they were marching into a storm of sleet. The spear-rings were soon broken, the grass slope strewn with quilled bodies, but the survivors clawed their way upward into the trap set for them. When they reached the waiting lances they were weak and breathless, and the English knights rode down to butcher them with sword, axe and mace. The last schiltron of Scots were Highlandmen from Ross, Strathearn and Sutherland, and these ran first said the Lanercost chronicler, 'making use of their heels, but the English pursued them on horseback, felling the wretches with iron-shod maces'.

In a millennium of Scottish defeats, this was among the worst. The regent Douglas was mortally wounded and died a prisoner. Sherwood arrow and iron mace killed six earls of Scotland, seventy barons, five hundred knights and squires, and spearmen uncountable. The English, it was said, lost no more than fourteen men, a dozen of them archers.

Balliol was restored and Berwick surrendered, to be English thenceforward except for one brief period. The wind of arrows at Dupplin Moor and Halidon Hill blew away Scotland's independence, and almost a century would pass before it was truly recovered. Balliol was his father's son, and gave Edward III all that was desired by that sensual and ambitious man, land, castles, homage, and the title of Lord Paramount of Scotland. The Disinherited came home, if home is the proper word, and the southern counties of Scotland from Haddington to Dumfries were given to the crown of England, their castles once more stuffed with Englishmen as they had been forty years before. It was no worse than some Scots had expected. Before Halidon Hill a Scottish monk had begged his countrymen to turn back, 'For I behold in the air the crucified Christ coming against you from Berwick, brandishing a spear!'

Only children in their games, it was said, dared to call David Bruce king. With his queen and his two sisters, he had been sent to France by those barons whose quick wits and faster horses had carried them from Halidon Hill. Philip VI of France gave them asylum at the Château Gaillard, where the boy grew into a gay, sweet-voiced and self-indulgent young man, learning the art of chivalry from fireside tales and illuminated parchment, and dreaming of a triumphant return to his kingdom on the armed shoulders of France. For twelve years that kingdom was in a state of anarchic civil war as successive regents challenged Balliol's rule, riding boldly across the land between his isolated castles. John Randolph, the last male of his name and third Earl of Moray since his brother's death at Dupplin Moor, almost liberated the country with Bruce's grandson, Robert the Steward. But the English took him on the Border and told his fiery sister Black Agnes, Countess of Dunbar, that they would kill him if she did not surrender her castle. Let them, she said, for then she would inherit the earldom of Moray. For six months she successfully held the castle against the Earl of Salisbury, standing boldly on

*Edward III of England gave up his claim to Scotland in 1328 but later supported Edward Balliol and the Disinherited. At Halidon Hill he gave the Scots one of their worst defeats.*

its battlements with her women, watching the battering-ram below and dusting her fine gown with a linen napkin. It was all the stuff of balladry, wherein Lord Salisbury cried 'Came I early, came I late, I found Agnes at the gate.'

When Edward III turned against France, leaving Balliol to hold Scotland as best he could, Philip VI sent the exile of Château Gaillard back to his own country in the hope of a diversion. Balliol fled at once to England and David entered Edinburgh in triumph, responding to the emotional press of its citizens by unlooping a mace from his saddle-bow. 'Stand still,' he yelled, 'or the most forward of you will get one with this!' He was eager to fill his father's shoes, and be taller by an inch. He was also suspicious of his nephew Robert the Steward, his senior by eight years and once the legal heir to the kingdom. Uneasily united, both men invaded England in October, 1346, with an army of Gaels and Lowland spears, too late to help Philip of Valois. Two months before at Crécy, English arrows had destroyed fifteen hundred of his knights and ten thousand of his men-at-arms.

At Neville's Cross near Durham the white bow and the goose-feather were again triumphant. Twelve thousand Scots were met by an army of northern lords and outraged churchmen whom David contemptuously dismissed as 'miserable monks and pig-drivers'. Halidon Hill was forgotten and the schiltrons were again withered by arrows, and when they broke in stumbling, bloody confusion the English knights raised a great crucifix and began the butchery. Praise be to the Most High, said the Lanercost chronicler, 'with trumpets blaring, shields clashing, arrows flying, lances thrusting, wounded men yelling, and troops shouting, the conflict ended about the hour of vespers'. Robert the Steward rode away before the battle was half begun, or so said the English, but David fought with desperate courage and with two arrows in his body. He was seized by an English squire, whose teeth he knocked out with his dagger hilt, but he was overwhelmed and dragged away a miserable prisoner. The flower of Scotland,

*At Château Gaillard David II and his queen and sisters were given asylum by Philip VI of France after the battle of Halidon Hill in July, 1333.*

said the chronicler, 'by the just award of God, fell into the pit which they themselves had dug'. In that pit the English found the lion standard of Scotland and Margaret's Black Rood, and they laid both before St Cuthbert's shrine at Durham.

David was taken to gentle captivity in the Tower of London and he remained in England for eleven years, most of which his subjects spent in fruitless bargaining over the ransom that should be paid for his return. England's failure to exploit the victory of Neville's Cross, to find the men and the will to garrison Scotland and enforce a ransom, has been ascribed to the terrible wasting scourge of the Black Death.[1] The horrible egg-sized pustules in armpit and groin, the black spots, rotting flesh, choking lungs and bloody urine that are the most mentionable manifestations of the plague, first appeared in Dorset toward the end of 1348, and within a year they had reached the Highlands of Scotland. A third of England's population probably died in this ghastly visitation, and the Scots at first rejoiced to hear it, relying on God, St Ninian, and St Andrew to protect them. There was no immunity, and like others in Europe they died by their fires, at the plough or in a roadside ditch, so bloated and so stinking that even those who loved them left them to die alone. For a while the cold Scots winter held the pestilence in check, but in the sickly spring of 1350 it raged again, and although it may have killed less than it did in England its effect was disastrous upon a people and an economy already weakened by war. Nothing like it, said John of Fordun, had been known since the beginning of the world.

Great men saved themselves where they could inside their castles, trusting in fragrant herbs, in vinegar, rose-water and prayers, but most of all in gates tightly locked against the poor. When the air no longer smelt of death, they turned again to the release of their king. The quarantine of the Tower had kept him alive, although thirty thousand are believed to have perished outside its walls, and now he offered Edward his homage, his crown if he died childless, in exchange for liberty. He is said to have visited Scotland in 1352, upon his honour to return, so that he might persuade his parliament and Robert the Steward to accept this shameful exchange. It was rejected, and the French, hard-pressed again by the English, sent gold and knights to ignite the Border. They captured Berwick and held it for a while, but were soon asked to leave by the Scots, who always liked the spirit and never the substance of the Auld Alliance. In any case, this Gallic intervention brought Scotland nothing but ill. Edward invaded it and ravaged it from the Tweed to the Forth, a winter campaign of flame that was called the Burnt Candlemas because it was begun on the Feast of the Purification of the Virgin, and the tallest candle that his archers lit was the Abbey church of Haddington. A year later the Scots submitted, accepting worse terms than they had been offered three years before. David was released in exchange for one hundred thousand merks, payable in ten yearly instalments during which there was to be a truce between the kingdoms. The first instalment was punctually paid, the second late, and others later still. When Edward III died in 1377, twenty years after David's release, a quarter of the ransom was still owing and was never paid.

Nearly half of David's life, and almost all of his formative years, were spent outside the country of his birth. He had little sympathy for it, and although it placed itself in pawn for him he increased its miserable poverty by squandering some of the ransom money upon his self-indulgent fancies. His suspicion of his nephew became a patho-

[1] Philip Ziegler, *The Black Death*, 1969.

Castrum Royale Londinense   vulgo   the TOWER

*The Tower of London, England's great fortress, palace, and prison. David I was held here in 'gentle captivity' for eleven years after his defeat at Neville's Cross in 1346.*

logical hatred, and the feelings of Robert the Steward were probably reciprocal. Widowed in 1362, and still childless, David had no wish to leave his crown to his kinsman, and he took another wife. Though handsome, she had survived four husbands without issue, and as if he realized that only a miracle would produce fruit from this union he rode to London, and offered to leave his crown to Edward if the ransom were lifted. When he returned to secure his parliament's agreement he was bluntly told that it was 'in no way willing to comply with, nor in any wise willing to assent'. Such bold defiance encouraged Robert the Steward, and he raised a revolt against his uncle, but was as quick to abandon his followers as he had been to recruit them, and at the first show of force against him he humbly swore an oath of fealty to David. He was imprisoned in Loch Leven Castle with his hot-tempered son Alexander.

The last years of David's life were spent in extravagant pleasures and frustrated longing for the luxuries of France and England. He loved theatrical tourneys, bright passages of arms, red and blue velvet embroidered with white roses. He was brave, he had been brave at Neville's Cross, and for this and the memory of his father he was tolerated. His barons and his people nobly endured him and the burden of his ransom to keep their independence. He died at Edinburgh Castle in February, 1371, dreaming of a crusade, of a divorce, and of remarriage to the daughter of Black Agnes of Dunbar.

From his weakness, from his indifference to power except where it brought him pleasure, his parliament drew a paradoxical strength. Government devolved more and more upon the *tres communitates*, the Three Estates who now appear in the records for the first time, prelates, barons and burgesses. Upon them rested responsibility for imposing taxes, controlling expenditure, administering justice, and treating with other nations, subject to the King. They provided two instrumental committees, administrative and judicial, selected to maintain the essential duties of parliament while the rest of its members were dismissed. The King's councillors, by feudal right and in his name, appointed these committees, but the legislative body of a true parliament was taking root, and with a growing consciousness of its power. Though they were junior members of the Estates, the importance of the burgesses lay in the fact that they above all in the kingdom were expected to provide the crown with money. Despite war and pestilence, the burghs were slowly prospering. Edinburgh, Dundee and Aberdeen were already great ports, the source of revenues, and when the obligation to find much of the King's ransom was placed upon his burghs they cannily secured valuable monopolies in return. The burgesses were still excluded from the King's General Council, this privilege being confined to his spiritual and temporal lords, but they held the purse-strings of the nation and by that a greater potential power than any iron mace and emblazoned shield.

The common people, Barbour's 'Scottish men, good men throughout the land', are still seen dimly, and most frequently behind the twelve-foot shaft of a schiltron spear. Feudal law still bound man to man, to civil lord and Church lord, and human stock as well as livestock passed from one to another by grant and charter. The Scots peasantry probably never heard the words of the Arbroath declaration, nor would have been able to relate its defiant faith in liberty to their own way of life, but a silent and strangely undramatic revolution had taken place, unmarked and almost unrecorded. Between Bannockburn and the middle of the century, serfdom as a legal state fell into desuetude. The men who had died in battle from Stirling Bridge to Neville's Cross had won that small freedom from servility. The Black Death destroyed much of the old relationship between lord and servant, but long before that traumatic experience the appeal of the national war had been made across feudal divisions. The peasant or small landowner often broke with his lord when he went to fight with Wallace or Bruce, and the throat he cut in the name of Scotland might well have been that of his master. When he returned to the wasted land, the ties of feudal obligation had been slackened. The lord needed money more than service, for his castle and his retainers, and although the tenant lost some of his security thereby, the rent he paid freed him from the worst of servility and increased his stature as a man.

The war for independence also gave the Scots commonalty a robust self-respect, a contempt for arrogant chivalry. The French who were sent to Scotland to fight for it against England were shocked by the impudence of Lowland countryfolk. When they protested against the outrageous prices they were charged for meal and forage, they were told that it was small repayment for the fields destroyed by their knightly games. They were also disgusted by Scotland, by its stark poverty and mean comforts. According to Froissart,

> When these barons and knights of France, who had been used to handsome hotels, ornamented apart-
> ments and castles, with good soft beds to repose on, saw themselves in such poverty, they began to
> laugh, and to say 'What could have brought us hither? We have never known till now what was meant
> by poverty and hard living. We now have found the truth of what our fathers and mothers were used to
> tell us when they said, Go, go, thou shalt have in thy time hard beds and poor lodgings.'

There were two peoples in Scotland, said John of Fordun, and those of the seaboard and the plains were civilized and urbane, patient, affable and peaceful, 'yet always prone to resist a wrong at the hands of their enemies'. The Highlanders and Islesmen, however, were savage and untamed men, exceedingly cruel and hostile, preferring the hunt to honest toil. But they too would as soon die as be enslaved. It is this, not handsome hotels and ornamented apartments, that makes a nation.

# THE ROIAIL PROGENEI OF OUR MOST SACRED KING IAMES BY THE

grace of God King of E.S.F & I. &c. Decended from ye victorius King Hy 7 & Elizabeth his wife wherin ye 2 deuided famlies ware vnited together.

HONI SOIT QVI MAL Y PENSE

James King of England Scot land France and Ireland

Anna Daughter to Frederik a King of Denmak

Francis the second King of France

Mary Queene of Scotland maried furst

Secondly Henry Lo: Darley D of Albany K of Scotland

James the fift King of Scotland

Mary sister to ye D of Guise & Duchis of Longevill

Margret mar Mathew Steward Earl of Lennox

Mathew Steward Earl of Lenox

furst Iames the fourth King of Scotland

Margret eldest daughter to K Henry ye 7 maried

Secondly to Archbold Don deld Earle of Angwish

The familie of Lancaster.

The familie of Yorke.

Henry the 7 are of the family of Lancaster

Elizabeth eldest daughter to K E ye 4 are of York

Beniamin Wright sculp

Comp Holland excu Lon 1619

# PART IV

# The Steward's House

'Families at strife with one another make bequest
of hatred to their children . . .'

Scotland's first Stewart king was tall and handsome, though the beauty of his face was marred by his bloodshot eyes. There were more defects in his character, and he was as weak as many of his line who followed, a timid and hesitant man, too tender-hearted to be bold. The problem of his successor was immediate upon his coronation, but unlike his uncle David II he had no lack of heirs. He was fifty-five and had been twice married. His first wife, Elizabeth Mure of Rowallan, had borne him four sons and six daughters before their clearly happy union was solemnized by marriage. He was now married to Euphemia, daughter of the Earl of Ross, and she had given him another quiver of sons and daughters. Beyond these he sired at least eight bastard sons. One of the few resolute decisions made by Robert the Steward, outside his bedchamber, was the choice of an heir from this teeming brood.

The problem was complex and dangerous. The degree of consanguinity between Robert and Elizabeth was well within that forbidden by the Church.[1] A papal dispensation for their marriage had removed that objection in 1347, and had further legitimized the 'multitude of children of both sexes' who had preceded it, but when it came to the matter of the royal succession there were many who questioned the dispensation, and doubted whether a child born out of incest should become king.

On March 27, 1371, the day following his coronation, Robert II cut through the hedge of debate and secured from his prelates, barons and officers a declaration that the heir to the throne was his eldest son by Elizabeth – John, Earl of Carrick and Steward of Scotland. If possible, this sickly, limping man was a weaker vessel than his father, and the King's Council might have been wiser to look beyond the prodigality of the first marriage-bed to the abundance of the second. Two years later at Scone, a parliament reaffirmed the King's choice, to avoid the 'uncertainty of the succession', and stood logic upon its head by stating that the crown, which had come to Robert through his mother, should not pass to a woman until all his male descendants were extinct, a possibility that is almost beyond imagination.

The spirit of the Bruce had been weakly inherited by his son David. It scarcely existed at all in his grandson who 'would rather remain at home than march to the field', and there was soon marching to be done when a renewed alliance with France broke the truce with England. The Scots barons were eager for war, and even had he wished Robert could not have controlled them. They had little respect for him. He was an old man who had come to the throne by accident, a man whose father would have been of no great consequence but for a fortunate marriage. He let them have their war, as he left the rule of the Highlands to his third son Alexander, Earl of Buchan. This ruffianly paranoiac, rightly called the Wolf of Badenoch, made a shambles of the glens during his viceroyalty, and when reproved by the Bishop of Moray for deserting his wife, he plundered Elgin and burnt its hospices, churches and cathedral. In energy at least, he was a Bruce.

The war with England started with the usual overture and beginners at Berwick, which the Scots at first took and then quickly lost. The fighting soon became a bloody border feud between the house of Douglas on one side and the Percy clan on the other. William, Earl of Douglas, had opposed the King's choice of a successor, but had been

---

[1] Their exact relationship is obscure.

bought off with the justiciary of all Scotland south of the Forth and a marriage alliance with the royal family, and he now behaved as if it were his own kingdom he was defending. He and Percy were twice brought to a sullen truce between 1381 and 1384 by John of Gaunt, who on the second occasion found it necessary to occupy Edinburgh. He was the first Englishman to express a liking for the place, and when he left he tolerantly restrained his soldiers from burning it according to their custom.

The French refused to allow the Scots to slip from their obligations under the alliance. In May, 1385, Jean de Vienne, Admiral of France, arrived in the Forth with ships of war, arms and plate armour, fifty thousand francs and 'all the flower of chivalry'. His knights were coldly received, forbidden to enter any castle, and billeted in wretched hamlets from Dunbar to Dunfermline. Why, they asked their admiral, had he brought them to such a country, where they were likely to be murdered in their beds before they met the English? They were cheated every time they parted with a franc, forced to pay sixty florins for a horse worth no more than ten, and then could buy no harness for it. Scots farmers had no belief in the right to forage at will, and in one month they murdered a hundred Frenchmen they found making free of their fields and byres.

*A Douglas tomb in Lanarkshire. Thomas Pennant's caption here is at odds with the text of his* Tour, *and this is probably the effigy of the fifth Earl of Douglas, son of the Tineman, who brought James I home from England.*

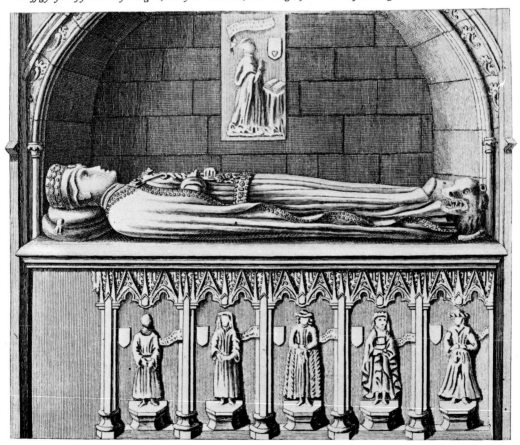

At least the King, a strange man with eyes that seemed to be lined with scarlet cloth, understood their knightly purpose, and gave them leave to invade England with his own army. When the Scots played their old war-game of raiding and retreating, the French were disgusted. Unable to fight on their own, they fell back too, and watched the smoke of burning abbeys on the southern horizon. When the English retired, Douglas followed them into Teviotdale, exhorting the French to do their part as he was doing his. De Vienne looked at the two thousand lances in the Franco-Scots army, its thirty thousand ragged spearmen, and remembered that Richard II was said to have twice that number of archers alone. He decided that a battle would be foolish and inglorious, and raided Cumberland instead, while the English burnt the beautiful abbeys of Melrose, Dryburgh and Newbattle, 'sparing nothing, saving nothing, and having no mercy on age or religion'.

When de Vienne decided to take his demoralized knights back to France he was presented with a bill for their debts and for the damage they were said to have done, and was himself kept in pawn until the money was paid. Thus, said Froissart, 'many knights and squires obtained passage to France, and returned through Flanders, or wherever they could land, famished, and without arms or horses, cursing Scotland and the hour they had set foot there.' They wished their king would make a truce with England for two or three years, 'and then march to Scotland and utterly destroy it, for never had they seen such wicked people, nor such ignorant hypocrites and traitors'. Such was the usual spirit of the Auld Alliance.

The Scots continued their war alone, and in 1388 a new Earl of Douglas, James, took an army into the Percy earldom of Northumberland, burning all he could before retiring triumphantly with the captured standard of Shakespeare's Hotspur, young Henry Percy. Swearing that his pennon would never leave England, Hotspur pursued the Scots and came up with them in an August dusk below the Roman wall at Otterburn. They fought throughout the night, on the slope of a hill and the soggy earth of a marsh, a macabre moonlit riot of steel and blood. English and Scots were so inextricably mixed, hacking and hewing with sword and axe, that the yew-bow which had won so many battles could not be used. Douglas and Percy fought each other until they were blinded with sweat and blood, and when they fell apart Douglas was thrust down by lance-points in his shoulder, breast and thigh. As his chaplain fought above him with an axe, he called for his sister's son Sir Hugh Montgomery.

> 'My nephew good,' the Douglas said,
>   'What recks the death of ane?
> Last night I dreamed a dreary dream,
>   And I ken the day's thy ain.
>
> 'My wound is deep, I am fain to sleep,
>   Take thou the vaward of me,
> And hide me by the bracken bush
>   Grows on yon lilye-lee.'

To those who carried him to the rear, and asked how he was, he said 'Right evil, but thank God few of my fathers died in their beds.' He told them to take his banner back into the fight, to cry 'Douglas!', and let no one know that he was dead. When Montgomery and Percy faced each other toward dawn, and surely too weary to fight more, Hotspur was asked to yield. If he must, then he would, but to whom?

'Thou shalt not yield to lord nor loon,
    Nor yet shalt thou to me,
But yield thee to the bracken bush
    Grows on yon lilye-lee.'

Not to brush nor briar, he said, but to the one he did. 'Earl Douglas was buried at the bracken bush, and the Percy led captive away.' The anonymous *Ballad of Otterburn* is the most evocative of all Border verse, and its noble and imaginative rhythms come closer than reality to the spirit of these savage opponents. Two centuries later, Sir Philip Sidney said that the old song of Percy and Douglas moved his heart more than a trumpet-call, and close to death Walter Scott was said to have murmured 'My wound is deep, I am fain to sleep . . .' In an age of more complex and more remote brutishness, it answers a longing for the simple courage by which men once ennobled their foolish savagery.

Robert II died two years later in Ayr. He was seventy-four, he had reigned for nineteen years, and at least one of his contemporaries remembered him with kindness. 'A tenderer heart might no man have.' His son John, of the bastard birth, was advised by his Council to take the name of Robert also, his own having too unpleasant an echo of an English king, a Scots puppet and a French pope. As timid and as tender as his father, he was also as inactive, though the reason may have been more physical than psychological. Lame from an injury received in a youthful tournament, he was unable to ride a horse, and could not have led an army to battle even had he wished. Had his strength of will been equal to his kind heart and his love of justice, he might have been able to rule in fact as well as name, but for most of his reign there was no rule at all. The war with England was quiescent, but conflict was a cancer from which it seemed Scotland must bleed, and its people fought among themselves. Without strong government, the law was ignored, the powerful oppressed the weak, and the whole kingdom, said a chronicler, was a den of thieves. The years were full of 'horrible destructions, burnings and slaughters', all of which went unpunished because justice itself was outlawed.

In the Highlands, bloodshed and brutality increased beyond their normal heroic limits, or were repressed with greater ferocity by the Wolf of Badenoch. In 1396 there was an extraordinary attempt to bring the tangled quarrels of the Gaels within the law. To settle a feud between Clan Chattan and Clan Kay, its cause now forgotten, each was ordered to pick thirty of its warriors to fight to the death in judicial combat. This Homeric contest took place on the North Inch of Perth, a flat meadow by the River Tay, in a gladiatorial enclosure of wood and iron that cost the Royal Exchequer fourteen pounds two shillings and eleven pence. It was watched by a great crowd, including Robert III and his court, and the most remarkable thing about it is not that the crown should order it, but that the clans were happy to obey. When the grisly struggle was over, and while the air stank of warm blood, the King's heralds declared Clan Chattan to be the victors. There can have been no doubt of it. Bow and sword, axe and dagger, slaughtered all but one of Clan Kay's warriors, it was said, and he wisely escaped by climbing the enclosure and swimming the Tay.

The King's brawling brothers were a microcosm of the kingdom. Alexander the Wolf was at odds with all, and all resented the eldest, Robert, Duke of Albany, a hard and ambitious man who held the keys of Stirling Castle and the royal purse as Chamberlain. He had been made Governor of the realm two years before their senile father died, and he kept the office when his brother succeeded. Now the King boldly took these powers of government from him, but mishandled affairs with such pathetic ineptitude that the

*Richard II of England, in whose perplexed reign the war with Scotland began again, was deposed by his successor, Henry IV, who continued the fight more resolutely. His archers destroyed the schiltrons at Homildon Hill and he held Prince James captive in the Tower.*

General Council removed them from his feeble grasp in 1399, and gave them to his son and heir David, Duke of Rothesay, with 'full power and commission of the King' for a period of three years. The Council's motives were wise, but its judgment poor, for Rothesay was dissolute and foolish, twice betrothed and twice repudiating the unions, turning the noble fathers of both women into sullen enemies of the Stewarts. He died in 1402, and although legend said that Albany starved him to death in Falkland Castle, a parliamentary inquiry said that he had departed by divine Providence and no other cause. It did not say what method Providence had chosen. Albany once more became Lieutenant and Governor of the realm, and between him and the crown there was only a boy of seven, Robert's second son James.

The war with England began again and dragged its bloody tail along the Border. The Earl of March, father of one of Rothesay's rejected brides, abandoned his castle at the eastern gate to Scotland and went to the English court. Henry IV sent him back with an army under Hotspur, but before it reached the Tweed it was met by the Scots near Wooler in Northumberland. They were led by Albany's son Murdoch, and by Archibald fourth Earl of Douglas. In the meshed relationships of the time, Douglas was not only married to a daughter of Robert III but was also the brother of Rothesay's second betrothed, and was believed to have helped Providence with that wretched man's departure. He was known as the Tineman, the Loser, and today at Homildon Hill was no exception to the reputation. When his schiltrons were bleeding and disorganized by cloth-yard volleys, he ordered them down the slope against the English. They ran instead, and Douglas was taken prisoner with the barbs of five arrows in his body. It was then that he made his compact with Percy, to aid Glendower against Henry IV. Once more Douglas was the Loser, this time at Shrewsbury fight, but as a body to be ransomed he was luckier than Percy who was quartered and impaled.

In 1406 Robert made an effort to save his son from Albany's ambition. He sent the boy to France, but east of Flamborough Head the ship was taken by the English. The news was brought to the King on the Isle of Bute, and he died in terrible grief. In his last years he had become an ironically majestic old man with a white and patriarchal beard, a foolish old man who had done no wrong, said the ballads, who had broken no laws and spilt no blood. Human virtues these, but none of them proper qualification for a medieval king. The valedictory prayers spoken above his grave are forgotten, but the epitaph he composed for himself endures: 'Here lies the worst of kings and the most miserable of men.' Once more the throne passed to a child, and he a prisoner of his enemies.

Albany was appointed Governor and Regent by a General Council at Perth, and with or without its authority he lived and ruled as a king, striking his own seal and granting charters in his name and not that of his absent nephew. He governed firmly when he could, and by intrigue when he could not. He was careful not to force the resentful barons into open revolt, buying their silence or support with gifts of crown lands, and pensions from the royal revenues. He was a cynical and dissembling man, but the strongest of his father's addled brood, and without him the kingdom might well have collapsed further into barbaric anarchy. Even so, he could not or would not entirely check the banditry of the barons, and entered into a band of mutual support with the most powerful, the triumphant house of Douglas. This band contains the only light the records throw upon his ultimate ambition. Though kindness and friendship were to last for all time between the parties, their agreement and their equal fellowship would end should Albany 'come to the estate of King'.

In the uneasy peace of his regency Scotland recovered some of its nerve, harvests were good and the burghs once more prospered, scars healed and the people breathed an air that was for a while free from the stench of blood. Scotland's loyalty to Benedict XIII in the papal schism had barred its students from satisfactory colleges in Europe, and now his bulls granted them the right to found a university of their own at St Andrews. Questing doubt, stirred by that schism and by John Wyclif's assault on prelacy in England, reached Scotland and was given its first martyr by the burning of a heretic at Perth. Scots soldiers went abroad to fight the Goddams with France, and only in the Highlands was the sword still loose in the sheath.

The sun of Clan Donald had been rising from the mists of the Isles since the western lands were surrendered by Norway. Never wholly subdued by the kings of Scotland, giving their support in the wars for independence in return for the territories of their enemies, claiming the lordship of the Isles by right of descent from Somerled, the chiefs of this proud tribe considered themselves independent of all authority, the proper leaders of what remained of Dalriada and the Celtic heart of Scotland. In the words of their seventeenth-century poetess, they were the 'race of Colla of vast armies and many tributes'. In 1411, Donald of the Isles claimed the earldom of Ross in the name of his wife. By the standards of the time he was a civilized man, more so than the opponent he was soon to meet at Harlaw, and he had been welcome at the English court. His mother was a daughter of Robert II, and to the arrogant boast of his Gaelic ancestry he could thus add a pride in the blood of Bruce, with whom his grandfather had fought

*Scotland's oldest university, St Andrews, began teaching in 1411. Papal confirmation of the foundation came from Pope Benedict XIII in 1413.*

at Bannockburn. What right his wife had to Ross may have been superseded by a nun, Albany's granddaughter, and she had surrendered it to the duke's son, but Donald resolved this confusion in the old way. He brought an army to the mainland, and gathered to it other clans with grievances to soothe. Armed with bows and axes, knives and swords, there were said to have been ten thousand men under his banner, and if so it was the largest Highland army ever raised. By galley and on foot, Donald took them up the Great Glen to Inverness and the land of Ross. There he defeated Angus Dubh Mackay, who foolishly disputed both the claims and the presence of Clan Donald, and then marched to the south-east, promising his wild Islesmen the plunder and the freedom of Aberdeen. On the way he burnt and harried the lands of Alexander, Earl of Mar, the son of the now dead Wolf of Badenoch. By the village of Harlaw in Aberdeenshire, above the water of the Ury, the clans were met by Mar and an army of local knights and burgesses.

The Red Harlaw was the bloodiest battle fought by the Gaels, a family quarrel on a monstrous scale between Clan Donald and the House of Stewart. As harsh and brutal as his lupine father, Mar was also an able general, and although outnumbered by the clans he drew his knights and spearmen into a knot and held the red ground on which they stood from early afternoon until a July dusk. Ill-armed against spear and lance, the Highlanders fought with savage courage. Their losses were disastrous, nine hundred dead it was said, including two chiefs, but in dying they killed almost as many of Mar's men. When night fell and they withdrew, neither side could call this slaughter-house a victory, although the bards and the historians of Clan Donald would do so, and remember it in their heroic songs. The earldom of Ross went to Albany's son.

The Regent died in 1420. He was eighty-three, and there is no evidence that premature senility, the curse of his family so far, had affected him. In some way, and by some authority unknown, he persuaded the General Council to accept his son Murdoch as Regent and Governor, and the choice was calamitous. Lawlessness increased again, the Border barons rode their raids, terrorized the burghs, and pursed the crown's revenues. In the second year of Murdoch's regency less than four per cent of the customs due from Edinburgh reached the royal exchequer, and in other towns this bold thieving was almost as bad. The unrest and discontent of the people and the small lairds had come close to open revolt when James came home from his eighteen years' exile, released by a treaty which Murdoch soon regretted, and upon promise of sixty thousand merks which the English said had been the cost of maintaining their prisoner in a proper state.

'If God gives me but a dog's life,' said James when he saw and heard what had happened to his country, 'I will make the key keep the castle and the bracken bush keep the cow through all Scotland.' In the week of his coronation a parliament at Perth declared that peace would be enforced throughout the realm, and 'if any man presume to make war against another he shall suffer the full penalties of the law'. Rents would be paid, loyalty and service demanded from all, and rebellion punished by death and forfeiture. Within a year James had broken the power of his cousins the Albany Stewarts and seized their estates. Upon some real or contrived charge of treason, Murdoch and his two sons, with the aged father-in-law of one of them, were first imprisoned and then taken to the heading-block at Stirling.

There were men who mourned their death, believing them friends of the poor and the victims of a tyrant. The romantic and frequently misguided attachment to the unsuccessful members of the House of Stewart has deep roots in Scotland's history.

2

He was thirty when he came back to Scotland, of medium height but large-boned and thickset, quick in his movements like a fox. He was an athlete, rider and wrestler, skilled with bow and spear, and proud of the strength in his broad chest and muscled arms. His darting and inquisitive mind was as fascinated by the machinery of war,

Left *James I of Scotland spent most of his childhood a prisoner of the English before his countrymen agreed to his ransom.* Right *While a captive he wrote 'The Kingis Quair', a melancholy, yet sensitive lyric poem. It was discovered and printed in 1783 by Lord Woodhouselee.*

gunnery in particular, as it was intrigued by the management of men. All this could be said of his great-great-grandfather the Bruce, but James I was also something his ancestor could never have been. He was a poet and a musician, and almost unique in the contradictory powers of tranquil reflection and uncompromising action. Beyond firm government perhaps, the greatest gift he brought his bleak country was the first of its lyrical verse.

Idle in England he had read all he could, and his long poem *The Kingis Quair*, inspired by Chaucer's translation of a French allegory, is a soft voice speaking with a love of evocative words, melancholy in spirit but rich with the feeling and longing of a sensitive exile. There is a sweetness and a clarity in its imagery, and the weight of silken chains on a forgotten prisoner.

> The bird, the beste, the fisch eke in the see,
>   They lyve in fredome everich in his kynd;
> And I a man, and lakkith libertee;
>   Quhat schall I seyne, quhat resoun may I fynd,
>   That fortune suld do so? thus in my mynd
> My folk I wold argewe, bot all for noght:
> Was non that myght, that on my peynes rought.
>
> Than wold I say, 'Gif God me had devisit
>   To lyve my lyf in thraldome thus and pyne,
> Quaht was the caus that he me more comprisit
>   Than othir folk to lyve in swich ruyne?
>   I suffer allone amang the figuris nyne,
> Ane wofull wrecche that to no wight may spede,
> And yit of every lyvis help hath nede.'

It was not a woeful wretch who came home to Scotland, but the first real king the country had had since the death of Robert Bruce. He brought with him a bride Joan Beaufort, a niece of Henry IV, and a sixth of his ransom had been obligingly remitted as her dowry. It was not only a marriage of dynastic arrangement, and it is pleasing to believe she was the girl he saw from his prison tower, and fell in love with as she walked among the hawthorn hedges and the nightingale's song.

> And therewith kest I doun my eye ageyne,
>   Quhare as I sawe, walking under the tour,
> Full secretly new cummyn hir to pleyne,
>   The fairest or the freschest yong floure
>   That ever I sawe, me thoght, before that houre,
> For quhich sodayn abate, non astert
> The blude of all my body to my hert.

From James I, perhaps, comes that legendary Stewart charm, more disastrous to Scotland than an Albany's corrupt rule. In a crude and unhandsome portrait there is still an instant appeal, a melancholy sensitivity and tragic loneliness. Upon his return to Scotland, however, he needed determination more than sensitivity, and a persuasion stronger than charm. The man who had sighed for love at a garden window in London, was merciless and resolute on a throne. His concern for law and order, while it was primarily needed to secure his crown, also had roots in a poet's sense of justice, but he did not respond like a poet. When he had exterminated his cousins, with a speed that quietened his rapacious barons more effectively than the enactments of his parliament, he turned upon the Highlands. He was the first of his family to treat the clans like cattle, showing that contempt most of them had for the Gaelic people, and making the Highlanders' ultimate self-sacrifice for the House of Stewart as pointless as it was heroic.

In 1428, forty and more chiefs of the mountains were summoned before James and his parliament at Inverness, including Alexander of the Isles, the son of Donald of Harlaw. If they came in arrogance, each with his wild tail of bard, gillies and sword-bearer, they were greeted as thugs. As each appeared before the throne he was seized by men-at-arms and thrown into the dungeon-pit. One by one, the chiefs of Clan Donald, Mackay, Mackenzie, Campbell and all the tribes of the north, while their poet king amused his parliament with a witty Latin squib on their certain hempen departure. Three only were in fact hanged, and the rest released after a short but salutary imprisonment. Clemency was wasted upon Alexander of the Isles. He remembered the treachery that had preceded it, and when King and parliament were gone he came back and burnt the burgh of Inverness to the ground, one of seven bonfires which the MacDonalds lit upon that ground in their clan's riotous history. James marched into Lochaber, isolated Alexander from his allies, and forced him to come to Edinburgh in submission. Wearing shirt and drawers only, holding his claymore by the blade, he knelt before the high altar of Holyrood and humbly offered the hilt of the weapon to the King. James would have hanged him, it is said, but for the intercession of the Queen, and he was sent to a Lothian castle in the keeping of a Douglas earl.

Had the sword and rope, merry Latin rhymes and the marching of mailed men been all there was to the King's rule, his kingdom would have benefited little from his reign. In thirteen years he strengthened the machinery of government and justice, replacing the baron's law with the King's law, and restoring the crown to a respect it had not received since Bruce's heart was taken from his rib-cage. The enactments of parliament were properly recorded in the King's Register, and copies distributed among all sheriffs so that no man might claim ignorance of the law. Justice was to be available to all, poor and rich 'without fraud and favour', and since this principle was easier to enact than to enforce, the King himself chose a special court from the Three Estates to consider complaints and abuses. He also set up a committee of wise and discreet men to examine the laws at intervals, and to advise upon their amendment if necessary. The court of complaints was concerned with civil justice, and it is probable (the records are lost) that James also strengthened the power and responsibility of the courts of criminal justice. In these things and others, his efforts were to regulate both government and administration, and he clearly wished to establish a parliament such as he had seen at work in England. He insisted that the members of the Estates should attend in person, and not by deputies unless with good reason. When this was amended later, and small barons and freeholders were allowed to choose 'wise men' to represent them, as commissioners of the shires, the seed of an elected parliament had been planted.[1]

All these changes and more were enacted within four years of his return, the creative explosion of a mind that had long been restless and inactive, aching for employment.

> Bewailing in my chamber thus allone,
> Despeired of all joys and remedye,
> Fortirit of my thoght and wo begone . . .

Though orthodox in faith and sincere in piety, he was a rough opponent of Rome

[1] A brilliant and concise account of the changes made by James in government and administration is given in *Scotland from the Earliest Times to 1603* by William Croft Dickinson.

when he thought it threatened his own and his country's independence. He denied the Pope's power of provision, the right to appoint bishops to vacant sees in Scotland, and thus have influence over one of the estates in its parliament. It had become the King's right to approve a bishop-elect before consecration and papal promotion, and he stopped his churchmen from bargaining with Rome for these benefices, arguing with some justice that the traffic was impoverishing his kingdom. When his parliament declared this 'barratry' illegal, taxed the export of gold and silver, and forbade the clerics to travel abroad without royal licence, the Pope demanded the repeal of the acts. The King's haughty response was to acknowledge the authority of the Council of Basle, which had attempted to reform such papal powers of provision. In his concern for the true duties of churchmen, however, he was hard and exacting, ordering Augustinians and Benedictines to set their houses in order, lest the crown regret its past generosity in endowments. Monastic religion, he said, was defamed in Scotland and held in contempt, and so that they might have an object lesson he later invited some Grey Friars of the strict Observance to found a colony in his kingdom. He was dead before they came, but the citizens of Edinburgh gave them a rich house near the Grassmarket. One of the few things he had in common with the regent Albany, beside blood and name, was a detestation of the Lollards. Scotland burnt its first heretic during the regency, and in 1433 it burnt a second, Paul Crawar, a reasonable fellow by the sound of him, a Bohemian graduate of medicine and the arts who came to St Andrews University as an emissary of the Hussites. He was also said to have preached free love and socialism, that enduring combination of human desires. The candle that was lit from the faggots at his feet burnt longer than his judges could have imagined.

No king had done so much for Scotland, outside of war, since Alexander III, and few had made so many enemies. The work he set himself was too great for one man, and in his efforts to break the power of the barons he was frequently foolish. He alienated the Douglases by imprisoning their earl, and deprived the Earl of March of his title and estates because of his father's desertion to the English thirty years before. Four-fifths of his ransom were yet to be paid and many of the lords had kinsmen still held hostage in England, and bitterly resented the King's indifference to them. His custom of appropriating estates to the crown when there was doubt about an heir may have been good housekeeping or feudal custom, but most men considered it robbery. His large family of first and distant cousins was patterned like marble with jealousy, spite, envy and greed, and it was perhaps inevitable that this Stewart king should die by a Stewart plot.

He himself made it possible by weakening his prestige with a half-hearted war. On her way to marry the Dauphin his daughter Margaret narrowly escaped a piratical attack by an English ship, and in what seems like pique but may have been the ready acceptance of an excuse, James besieged the castle of Roxburgh, which had been in English hands for a hundred years. He abandoned it without assault, for what reason is not clearly known, though his wife is said to have warned him of plots against him. There was a plot, within his family and his household, and the unpopularity of the King's withdrawal from a chivalrous field gave it courage. At its veiled centre was the Earl of Atholl, 'that old servant of many evil days', a son of Robert II's second marriage and by his own reckoning the rightful king. His son, Sir Robert Stewart, was the King's Chamberlain, and it was he who found a willing assassin in Sir Robert Graham, a man with his own festering grudge and a scarred memory of imprisonment and banishment.

At the end of 1436 James went to keep Christmas with the Dominican friars at Perth.

As he crossed the Forth a Highland woman warned him that he would never return alive, a common warning in Scots history and just as commonly ignored. She followed him to Perth, it was said, repeating her tedious warnings, and she was present on the night of February 20 when Robert Stewart opened the door of the convent where the King was staying, and admitted the Graham.

James was in his wife's chamber, talking to her and her ladies, relaxed in his dressing-gown, amused by the Highland woman's last warning and telling stories of omens and premonitions. When he heard the noise of heavy feet, clanking armour, his quick mind sensed what they meant. He wrenched up the planking of the floor and dropped into a vault or drain below, hoping to escape into a court beyond but forgetting that its mouth had recently been closed to prevent his tennis-balls from rolling into it. Graham and his eight confederates broke into the room, dragged out the fighting King, and butchered him with twenty-eight dagger-strokes.

The Queen was wounded in her efforts to save her husband, and it might have been better for Graham had he killed her too. This 'freshest and fairest flower' of the King's youth became a tigress in revenge. Atholl and Robert Stewart, Graham and his hired cutthroats were soon taken, and suffered long and appalling torture until the Queen's grief was satisfied and they were sent to the merciful headsman.

## 3

Once more a child . . . His mother took him quickly to the safety of Edinburgh Castle, and within five weeks of his father's murder James II was crowned and anointed in the Abbey church of Holyrood. He was six years of age, and the flaming birthmark that disfigured his innocent face was an ominous forecast of what was to happen to the uneasy kingdom he inherited.

The ceremony at Holyrood broke the hallowed tradition of a coronation at Scone, and this too may be seen as an omen. Tortured beyond imagination, Robert Graham had died in the belief that he had slain a tyrant. Some men agreed with him, a few were ready to profit by the assassination, and many feared what would now happen. Since the death of Bruce, in the following reigns of supine or absent kings, the power of the barons had been increasing, and James I had been able to keep them in check only. Most of them were interrelated, and through many ran the red thread of Stewart blood. The great Douglas clan had become the most powerful, pre-eminent in ambition, pride, greed, treachery and valour. It was probably Celtic in origin, taking its name from *dhu glaise*, a dark stream in Lanarkshire where it first held land, and its progenitor had been Sir William Douglas the Hardy, who defended Berwick against Edward I in 1296, and who died a broken penitent in the Tower of London. It was now divided into two loose families, of which the Black earls of Douglas were the stronger, descended from a natural son of 'Good Sir James', Robert Bruce's heart-bearer. The Red Douglases, earls of Angus, had a similar bastard origin in a half-brother of the hero of Otterburn, and both Black and Red had married daughters of Robert III. Between them and their eager cadet houses they controlled wide lands across the south, many castles and a great army of shaggy riders. In their ambition they looked beyond their battlements to the throne itself.

Despite this, Archibald the fifth and present Earl of Douglas was an indolent man. He had brought James I home from captivity, and a quarrel with the King later, a chastening term of imprisonment, seem to have exhausted his talent for intrigue and his inherited ambition. He now became Lieutenant-Governor of the kingdom, with Bishop John Cameron of Glasgow as Chancellor, but neither of them was able or willing to control the feuds and factions of contending families. Small lairds and great lords formed bands for mutual defence. Boyds of Kilmarnock and Stewarts of Darnley murdered each other by stealth, or fought theatrical battles according to the rules of chivalry, pausing for breath, and resuming at the call of a herald's trumpet. In the Highlands, Keiths and Mackays fought in the glens of Sutherland and Caithness, and the Macleans came out of the west to ravage the Stirling plain. The Earl of Douglas took his pay as Regent, and let the world do as it wished. When he died, in June, 1439, there was a savage and bloody struggle for the power he relinquished.

The keepers of Stirling and Edinburgh castles, Sir Alexander Livingstone and Sir William Crichton, first fought between themselves. Crichton had some advantage in the quarrel by holding the boy-king, but by means unknown Livingstone kidnapped James and carried him to Stirling. With motives that can well be understood, the Queen Mother sought some safety for herself, and perhaps a protector for her child, by marrying Sir James Stewart, the Black Knight of Lorne, but Livingstone violently abducted them both, and held them until the Three Estates – with noble and unexpected courage – demanded their release. In this stalemate the bandit knights agreed to an alliance, and turned their murderous attentions upon the family they feared most, the Black Douglases.

William, the sixth Earl of Douglas, was only sixteen, a rash and ingenuous young man who was affectionately fond of James, and was in his turn admired by the King. Such a warm attachment, backed by five thousand knights and spearmen who would ride from the Earl's lands at his call, made him a potential menace to Livingstone and Crichton. They first accused him of treason, of desiring the throne for himself, and then invited him and his only brother to dine with them and the King at Edinburgh Castle, where their differences might be amicably resolved. The young men went in foolish trust, and 'banquetted royally with all delicates which could be got'. There then seems to have been a hasty mockery of a trial, after which the Douglases were dragged outside to a courtyard and there beheaded. The helpless King wept for his friends, and the murder was immortalized in rhyme.

> Edinburgh Castle, toun and toure
> God grant thou sink for sinne!
> And that even for the black dinner
> Earl Douglas gat therein.

There was no rallying cry of 'Douglas!' The clan's blood was thick, but family envies were strong, and unexpected good fortune was welcome from whatever source it came. The successor to the earldom was James the Gross, great-uncle of the dead, and he may have been party to the conspiracy, for he took no revenge. When he died three years later his son William, although married to a sister of the murdered youths, joined with Livingstone in an alliance against Crichton, and the country suffered under a banditry that cannot be dignified by the name of civil war. For eight years Douglases and Hepburns, Stewarts, Ruthvens and Crawfords, Kennedys and Ogilvies fought with or against each other on both sides of the Forth. When the brutal brawl was halted, it was not by exhaustion or good sense but by the end of a truce with England. An invading English army burnt Dunbar and Dumfries, and within a month William Douglas, with his brother the Earl of Ormond and his cousin the Earl of Angus, destroyed Alnwick and Warkworth in Northumberland. In October, 1449, the houses of Percy and Douglas met in battle by the water of Sark near Gretna, and the English were routed. Livingstone was still Regent, for want of a better title, but William Douglas was the most powerful man in the kingdom, a giant whose estates straddled the Lowlands from the Clyde to Galloway and the Forth to the Border. His three brothers, of Moray, Ormond and Balvany were strong in the north and north-east, and the Red Douglases of Angus no less. As if land, armies and kin were not enough, William allied himself with Alexander Lindsay, the Tiger Earl of Crawford, and with John MacDonald the Lord of the Isles.

Against this menacing confederation, and almost overlooked by history until now, was James of the Fiery Face. In his nineteenth year the King stepped from the wings to his marriage with the Burgundian Mary of Gueldres, and almost immediately demonstrated that he had become a man. Behind his crimsoned features was a ruthless and determined character, moulded by terror, by the murder of his father and his friends, by lonely isolation and night-riding dreams. His valiant English mother was now dead, and his only followers were the doubtful Crichtons, a border-bandit Hepburn, James Kennedy the Bishop of St Andrews, and a stepfather whom he had recalled from exile. He had also the inherited courage of his mother and the cunning resourcefulness of his father. He drove out the Livingstones, imprisoned a few and beheaded others where they had killed the Douglas boys, and for the moment immobilized Earl William by giving him some of their forfeited estates. When the Douglas went abroad, parading his magnificent train before the Pope and spending a suspiciously long time at the English court, the King made an attempt to weaken his power. How this was done, and for what

*Warkworth Castle, Northumberland, was destroyed by the Douglas Earls of Angus and Ormond in 1449 as a reprisal for the burning of Dunbar and Dumfries. The war at this time was largely a feud between Douglas and Percy.*

expressed reason, is not clear, but Douglas was alarmed enough to hurry back and make a formal submission before Parliament. The King and he were publicly reconciled, and all good Scots, it was said, 'were right blithe of that accordance'. A sigh of relief is sometimes clearly heard across the centuries.

But the ambition of a Douglas was not so easily humbled, and the Earl was soon conspiring with Lindsay of Crawford and John of the Isles, and perhaps even with the English. James had received good schooling in duplicity and treachery, however, and exercised both upon William Douglas in a manner that placed him high above his barons in perfidy. At supper one Tuesday evening in Stirling Castle, to which he had come on the King's safe-conduct, Douglas was ordered to break his band with his confederates. He replied that he could not and would not, whereupon James stabbed him in the neck and the body, screaming 'Since you will not, I shall!' As the Earl fell, a courtier crushed his skull with a pole-axe, and others pushed forward to stab and thrust at the lifeless body. Wine and passion probably explain the disgusting murder. They could not excuse it. As for the part played by the King's followers, it might be charitably assumed that they, like Bruce's men at Dumfries perhaps, wished to relieve their master of some of the odious responsibility for the crime.

The Tiger Earl of Crawford reacted to this supper-time entertainment by raising his people, and James took shelter in Perth with a small army. The new Earl of Douglas, James, led six hundred men to Stirling, nailed his brother's safe-conduct to a board, and dragged it through the streets at the tail of a winded horse. He then plundered and burnt the town, renouncing his homage to James and offering it to England. The King was alarmed by this tumult and anger, and but for Bishop Kennedy would have fled to France. When his parliament loyally exonerated him, and Crawford's army was dispersed at Brechin, he came down upon the Douglas lands with such feverish savagery that the Earl James quickly submitted. Murderous in passion, the King was foolish in guilt, and he not only accepted the Earl's fealty but secured for him a papal dispensation to marry his brother's widow, a union that was more of a property conveyance, for she was herself a Douglas. Through her mother she was also descended from Robert II, and by her children, if any, the Douglas clan would regain the Stewart blood it had lost with the youths whom Livingstone had murdered. What the Earl thought of his king's clemency was not recorded, but he made the best use of it. When he was sent with a peace commission to London in April, 1453, he secured the release from prison there of his wife's uncle Malise Graham, Earl of Strathearn. This Graham was the nephew of James I's murderer, and to those who regarded Robert II's first marriage as incestuous and invalid he was the proper occupant of the throne. The King awoke late, but not too late, to the witless error of his judgment. By bribery and by threat he neutralized the Earl's allies, and then marched upon the Douglas lands. The Earl of Moray was killed in battle, Balvany was driven into exile, and Ormond was kindly allowed to recover from his wounds before he was sent to the heading-block. The absent Earl of Douglas was attainted and his estates forfeited to the Crown.

James II was twenty-five years of age, and for the last five now left to him he governed his country in peace. His success was remarkable. Out of anarchy and banditry he created order and rule, first by the destruction of Douglas power and then by the strengthening of his own, continuing the work his father had begun. He cunningly used the rivalries and irresolution of his barons to increase their dependence upon him, and even succeeded in alienating the Red Douglases of Angus from their Black cousins. In the Estates he

*James II, from the Diary of Georg von Ehingen, c. 1450, a crude portrait with a suggestion of the disfiguring birthmark that gave the King his nickname, 'James of the Fiery Face'.*

created a royal party of peers of his own elevation, and married his sisters to others with a shopkeeper's skill. He had his father's fascinated interest in artillery, though in his case it was more political than scientific, a realization that his brass bombards made him the master of his barons' castles. His enthusiasm was too strong, and it destroyed him.

In 1460 he involved himself in the English civil war, favouring the Lancastrian cause and using it as an excuse to recover Roxburgh, that castle tooth by which England still held the claim of feudal superiority. He brought his cannon and an army of Islesmen to its walls, and as he stood by a great, hooped gun called 'the Lion', it exploded and killed him.

Of his three sons, the eldest was only nine.

With Bishop Kennedy the Queen Mother governed in the name of James III, and when she was dead in 1463 the honest and humane old cleric kept the country at peace for another eighteen months, until he was carried to the extravagant tomb he had designed for himself. The relative stability of this period had been broken only by Clan Donald's raids on behalf of Edward IV of England, but now the clock slipped back thirty years, and the Boyds of Kilmarnock boldly followed the example of Livingstone and Crichton. In July 1466 the young King was lifted from Linlithgow and carried to Edinburgh Castle by Sir Alexander Boyd, whose brother Robert, Lord Boyd of Kilmarnock, was its governor. There were others in the plot – Flemings and Kers, Hepburns, Lindsays and more – and after three months in the custody of this mailed and obdurate gang the boy appeared before parliament and gravely declared that they had acted with his approval. Lord Boyd, that 'mirror of chivalry' who had been the King's instructor in military duties, now became his Guardian and Chamberlain.

The Boyds were audacious and charming ruffians, and in them their family made a brief appearance at the front of the stage before stepping back into obscurity. They were less rapacious than Crichton or Livingstone, and they did not over-fatten their pride with rank. Influence intrigued them, and the exercise of power, and what titles there were to be got went to Kilmarnock's son Thomas. He was married to the King's sister Mary, created Earl and Sheriff of Arran, and Steward of Kirkcudbright. He had an excess of the Boyd charm and was subtle and wise withal, adroitly making himself the first man in the kingdom, even above his father. He negotiated a marriage between the King and Princess Margaret of Denmark, with a dowry of sixty thousand florins, but he made a mistake in going to fetch the young woman. The mistake was repeated by his father, who left with an embassy to England. In their absence their enemies worked upon the unhappy King's doubts and fears, and when Arran arrived at Leith he was met aboard ship by his wife, who told him that her brother had 'conceived great hatred against him'. Accepting the end of his brief good fortune, Arran sailed back to Denmark, where he was joined by his father. Their estates were forfeited, and Sir Alexander Boyd lost his head. Arran's wife prudently deserted and divorced him, marrying one of the Hamiltons, who, though once allies of the Boyds, now rose higher on their ruin.

With his marriage, the minority of James III came to an end, and like his father and his grandfather he began to impose his will upon the country, but without their strength and character. For a while he seemed successful. When the King of Denmark admitted that his exchequer contained no more than two of the sixty thousand he had promised as a dowry, James took the islands of Orkney and Shetland as a pledge, and then persuaded their overlords to part with them entirely. He also concluded a treaty with Edward IV, by which England abandoned its interest in John of the Isles and the exiled

Earl of Douglas, and when that was done James fell upon Clan Donald by sea and land and forced John to submit and to surrender the earldom of Ross.

Yet he was no soldier. It was said that he loved a solitary life best, and his parliament repeatedly and unsuccessfully reminded him that his duty was to govern. His barons were contemptuous of the 'masons and fiddlers', the musicians and architects whose company he enjoyed, together with a tailor, a shoemaker and a goldsmith, astrologers and alchemists who helped him in his search for the philosopher's stone. It was too early for such catholic tastes to be admired, and public favour and private loyalty went to his brothers Alexander, Duke of Albany, and John, Earl of Mar, both of whom were masculine young men from a familiar mould. Albany was a great horseman with large eyes and a 'very awful countenance', and Mar was tall and handsome, a fine archer and a splendid huntsman. Robert Cochrane, the King's favoured architect, is believed to have persuaded James that they were conspiring against him, and that Mar was using magical arts, conjuring his death by melting waxen images in his likeness. Both brothers were imprisoned in Edinburgh Castle, where Mar died from over-zealous bleeding during a fever. Albany killed his gaolers, slipped down the rock-face with his page on a rope of sheets, and walked away to Leith, carrying the boy whose legs had been broken by the

*'There was always the sound of voices, of creaking leather, of harness . . . the harp of an Irish minstrel . . .' A 15th-century harp such as that used in the Highlands for another two hundred years. Right Edward IV of England, who sent Richard of Gloucester to depose James III in 1482.*

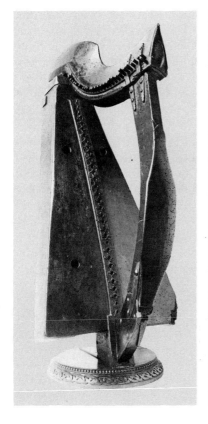

last drop to the bottom of the cliff. From Leith he went to France. And Cochrane became Earl of Mar.

Kings who are despised by their contemporaries frequently have more vision and wisdom than their admired predecessors. James III was believed to be a mean man, unstable and treacherous, and this may have been true, but his artistic tastes and sensitive pleasures enabled some of his subjects to lift their eyes from the filth of bestial conflict. In his reign music was clearly heard above the sound of arms. He sent musicians abroad to learn their art, and encouraged collegiate churches to make choirs and instruments an inspiring part of their services. He had an intense, if sometimes superstitious, interest in the sciences, in medicine and surgery, astrology and astronomy, in the industry of book-binding and the ennobling art of poetry. The singing voice of the Dunfermline poet and schoolmaster, Robert Henryson, survives the clanging noises that drowned it while he lived, and upon which he turned his scholar's back.

> I mend the fyre and beikit me about,
> Than tuik ane drink my spreitis to comfort,
> And armit me weill fra the cauld thairout:
> To cut the winter nicht and mak it short,
> I tuik ane Quair, and left all uther sport,
> Writtin be worthie Chaucer glorious,
> Of fair Creisseid and worthie Troylus.

Artistic tastes do not preclude stupidity. The gift of an organ to a church, the sending of a lute-player to France, the patronage of an architect, are no alternative to kingly guile. James antagonized his barons by barring them from his Secret Council, the little committee of intimates who helped him shape his policies. Bad harvests, famine, the plague and rising prices angered a restless people who believed their king did nothing but sit at Stirling with his masons and fiddlers, counting his gold. In this hostile atmosphere, James went reluctantly to war with England. His brother Albany was there, marching northward to seize the throne, with an English army under Richard of Gloucester, loaned to him by Edward IV in return for his promise of homage, land and castles. The barons whom James gathered at Lauder in Berwickshire, in the summer of 1482, were in no humour to fight for a king who went to war with a council of low-born favourites. They were particularly hostile to Cochrane, whom they unfairly blamed for the debasing of coinage, and who offended their dignity with his gold ornaments and black velvet clothes. According to legend, they sat in Lauder Kirk exchanging doubts and fears, each unwilling to face the King, until the young Earl of Angus, Archibald Douglas, said 'I'll bell the cat!', and went to the royal tent. When James refused to dismiss his favourites, the enraged barons seized six of them and hanged them from a bridge above the Leader Water. Cochrane died with splendid arrogance, unsuccessfully demanding that he be throttled with a silken cord, not with 'ane tow of hemp, like ane thief'.

The lords ignored the approaching English and took their king back to Edinburgh, a prisoner, closing the castle gates upon him as Albany and Gloucester arrived at the foot of the rock. Some peculiar agreement was then reached between Albany and the barons, by which they were to accept him as Regent and he was to persuade Gloucester to withdraw. This the Englishman did, no doubt confused by devious ambitions that outmatched his own, but he held Berwick and made it forever English. Albany trusted the barons no more than they trusted him, and with the aid of the citizens of Edinburgh he

*Edinburgh Castle today. After their revolt at Lauder in 1482, the Scots barons held James III a prisoner here until his brother, Albany, deserted the English and released him.*

released his brother and restored him to the throne. Their shabby reconciliation, expressed in public manifestations of love and kindliness, was soon threadbare, and when Albany discovered that the King knew of his continued desire for the crown, and his hope of English support, he crossed the Border while he could. He came madly back the next year with a company of horsemen and the long-exiled Earl of Douglas, fording the Solway and riding into Lochmaben at fair time. There he was stoutly attacked by its citizens and some of the local bonnet lairds. He escaped their loyal fury, riding hard to England and a ship for France, where he died vaingloriously in a tournament a year later. But James Douglas was captured, and expecting no less than death he would say nothing when he was brought before the King. He was not sent to the headsman but to Lindores Abbey, and there at last he spoke: 'He that may no better be, must be a monk.' For a Douglas, that was perhaps worse than death.

The old pleasures and surviving favourites to whom the King again turned may have solaced his mind, but they were of little use in the iron government which was now more than ever demanded of him. The death of his queen in 1486 drove him further into retirement, to the rooms Cochrane had designed at Stirling Castle, to the richly bound books of his physician William Scheves, to the conversation of William Elphinstone who was the wisest of his favourites, a brilliant jurist whom he had raised from lowly church office to the bishopric of Aberdeen. In his pathological irresolution, the King's only positive thought seems to have been a determination to increase the wealth of the crown. This consuming avarice brought him to the last crisis of his reign and eventually to his lonely death. When he insisted upon the revenues of Coldingham Priory he was challenged by the border Homes, who claimed the rich dues for themselves. The dispute grew into revolt, the Homes first securing the support of the Hepburns, then the Bishop of Glasgow, the Red Douglases, the Campbells of Argyll and more. Coldingham Priory was forgotten in older, itching grievances. It is said that James went to Lindores Abbey and offered James Douglas his freedom in return for his support. 'Sir,' he was told, 'you have left me in your black coffer too long.'

With the support of the earls of Huntly and Crawford, James met the rebels at Blackness on the Firth of Forth. There was no battle, perhaps because his eldest son was with his enemies, as a prisoner or an ally, and in the peace that was agreed the tired King disbanded his army and went to Edinburgh. The rebels mustered again, and he came out to meet them. At Sauchieburn on the Stirling plain, near the site of Bruce's great battle and in the same summer month, he watched as his Highlanders and burghal levies were slaughtered by border lances and Douglas spears. He turned and fled, but was thrown from his horse near Beaton's Mill. He asked a cottage-wife to find him a priest. She brought him one, or at least a man who said he was a priest, and when James asked for absolution this stranger drew a knife and killed him.

At Sauchieburn, it was said, the King had worn the sword of Robert the Bruce.

## 4

Brutality and humanity are eternal. Between one century and another there is a difference in degree not kind, and no age may except itself from the judgment it passes upon others. A Graham murdering his king, a king stabbing his guest, a mob of nobles hanging their rivals from a bridge, churchmen burning the substance of a man to save his suppositional soul, are all timeless and vary in costume only. Humanity survives by a brave faith in its ultimate triumph over brutality, although like light and shade they must coexist to be defined. Part of that slow victory is that whereas the savage incidents of history quickly seem remote, their passion unnatural and their motives unsympathetic, man has an enduring empathy with the ordinary life of his nameless predecessors, and is reassured by the recognition of common hope and experience. At such moments the drama of history moves from the stage and into the audience.

The records of Scotland in the fifteenth century contain for the first time a realistic picture of its people. Aeneas Sylvius Piccolomini, the lively and sensual Italian who became Pope Pius II, visited the kingdom in the reign of James I, whom he described as a robust and excessively fat man. He did not like the country, and blamed his subsequent rheumatism on its miserable climate, but he tried to be fair to its coarse inhabitants. 'They eat flesh and fish to repletion, and bread only as a dainty. The men are small in stature, bold and forward in temper; the women fair in complexion, comely and pleasing, but not distinguished for their chastity, giving their kisses more readily than Italian women their hands.' Their greatest conversational pleasure was to abuse the English, and they boldly inspected Aeneas 'as in Italy people stare at an Ethiopian or an Indian'.

He was never sure that he was safe among them, and he was frightened by their stories of the wild and northern Scots 'who live in the wooded region, speak a language of their own, and sometimes use the bark of trees for food'. He was genuinely distressed by the poverty of the common people who lived in squalid hovels, with turf for a roof and an ox-hide curtain for a door. 'In this country I saw the poor, who almost in a state of nakedness begged at church doors, depart with joy in their faces on receiving stones as alms. This stone, whether by reason of sulphurous or some other matter which it contains, is burned instead of wood, of which the country is destitute.' He heard of a miraculous tree which dropped fruit in the shape of geese. Those which fell into a river 'immediately assumed life, and swam about under the water, and flew into the air with feathers and wings'. This extraordinary fruit was always to be found in another district, but had he seen it he might have realized that the gannet was no more miraculous than coal.

Aeneas was a subjective observer, and convinced that the northern limit of civilized life was Newcastle. In the statutes of the last half of the century there is a less personal but richer picture of a rough, warm and human society. No man might drink wine, ale, or beer in a tavern after the last stroke of nine, and any who did went to the King's prison until he could pay a shilling for his release. When innkeepers complained to the King that his lieges would not stay at burgh taverns when travelling abroad, preferring the houses of their friends, he ordered them to do so, and fined any burgess who played host. Ferrymen were told to build gangways athwart their boats, so that horses might be carried 'without scathe or hurt'. All freeholders were encouraged to plant trees and hedges, to sow their heaths with broom. No man was to spoil the nests of partridge, plover or wild duck, or molest them during moulting time, but all birds of prey were to be killed. Three times a year between Martinmas and Lammas, wolves were to be hunted and destroyed, and a penny was to be paid for every head brought before a sheriff. No leper might beg in church or churchyard, or enter a burgh except on Monday, Wednesday and Friday, and then only between ten o'clock and two. Every man with a plough and eight oxen was to plant so much wheat, peas and beans. Beggars and idlers who harried the King's poor lieges had their ears nailed to a tree, but all dioceses that maintained hospitals were advised to be diligent in their concern for 'failed and miserable persons'. From the Border hills to Dunbar and Stirling, beacon fires were to be ever ready, and to burn like candles when necessary so that 'all may see them and come to the defence of the land'.

When James II's parliament decided that his kingdom was 'greatly impoverished through sumptuous clothing both of men and women' in the burghs, it forbade all but councillors and their wives from wearing costly clothes of silk, scarlet gowns or trimmings of marten fur. Women were to dress discreetly and according to their estate, to cover their heads with kerchiefs and little hoods as were worn in Flanders and England. No ordinary woman could wear fur except on holidays, or go to church with her face so hidden by her headdress that it could not be seen. No cleric, unless a dignitary of cathedral or college church, could wear scarlet or fur, and common men should dress in grey and white cloth. On holidays, however, labourers and husbandmen could sport in 'light blue or green or red and their wives right so, and kerchiefs of their own making', provided the price of the cloth did not exceed elevenpence an ell.

The Scots peasant, Jock-upon-land, worked the earth as his ancestors had done, though he now held it on a lease for five years or less, depending on his lord's good will for renewal. His wooden plough and heavy oxen furrowed hill-side fields, above valleys that were as waterlogged as they had been in the days of Malcolm Canmore, and he was rarely able to let a field lie fallow before planting it again with oats and barley. He slaughtered and larded his surplus cattle at Martinmas in November, and wintered the rest under his own cottage roof. The insecurity of his tenure did not encourage him to build a house of stone instead of turf, to plant hedges or an orchard. The average size of a holding was thirty acres, and these a man worked in partnership with his own kin, or with three or four neighbours, making a tiny township of their buildings. Before the next century was truly begun, James IV would realize that such men had taken but a half-step from serfdom, and he would encourage his barons to follow his example, to set these farms in feu, to give the land in perpetuity to those who worked it and in return for a fixed annual rent.

The black keep had sometimes grown to a great castle, but more often had been expanded to form a hollow square enclosing a courtyard, still battlemented and gated, still a fortress but also a house. Within the great hall, in the smoke of turf or coal fires, there was a crude elegance that may have amused Aeneas Sylvius but flattered the vanity of a bonnet laird. Young boys brought metal finger-basins to his guests. Stone walls were warmed by coloured cloth. Flemish linen was spread over the long board, and upon it was placed a great salt-cellar, the evidence of wealth and the division of rank. By Scottish custom, men and women ate with their heads covered, and only servants were hatless. The air was thick with the hum of flies, and sour with the stench of discarded food. Torches flamed on pewter and sometimes a single dish of gold, raped from an English castle or church. Fingers scrabbled in wooden cogs, and waiting hounds yawned on a floor of rushes. The courtyard was full of horses, doves, fowl, and ricks of hay and straw. There was always the sound of voices, of creaking leather, of harness and spur and arms, and occasionally the music of a lute, the harp of an Irish minstrel. Scotland exported little but skins, wool and fish, and what luxuries and creature comforts it enjoyed came dearly from abroad – velvets and damasks, silks, spices and wine, figs and almonds, raisins and dates. Company and conversation its people found best among themselves.

The burghs had grown. War and fire seemed to temper and strengthen them, and they were richer, politically potent. The glazed windows of their storeyed houses looked

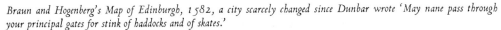

*Braun and Hogenberg's Map of Edinburgh, 1582, a city scarcely changed since Dunbar wrote 'May nane pass through your principal gates for stink of haddocks and of skates.'*

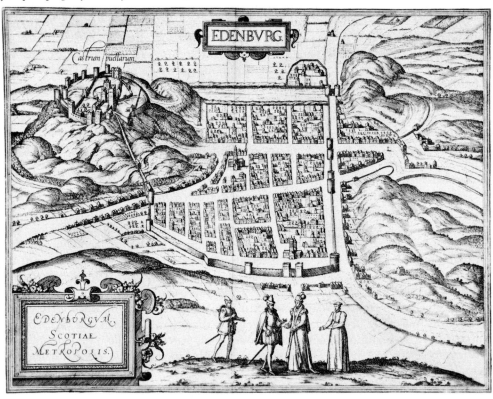

over the burgh-muir, the wet turn of peat and the black furrows of run-rig farms, nets and fishing-boats, white clouds of sheep. They were all of a pattern, and differed only in size, one main market street like a herring-bone with alleys and lanes. Daily life began and ended ritually in the market street, with the marching strut of the burgh piper and drummer. Here were celebrated the feast days of which the year seemed largely composed, when the town minstrels played and Jock-upon-land danced in green or red or blue. Here was the kirk, the tolbooth gaol and court-house, and here the market-cross, the social and political centre of the burgh where the King's law was proclaimed, offenders sat in placarded disgrace, and the dismembered limbs of traitors and criminals were publicly exposed. Here were middens populated with vermin, wandering dogs and swine, a laundering-well, fish-stalls, cloth-stalls, and the bloody work of fleshers' knives. The great burghs were fast becoming cities, not only larger in size but fouler in squalor, stinking ant-heaps, breeding-grounds for the mob that would sway history with a gust of its noisy breath. Greed and profit, said the poet William Dunbar, blinded rich merchants to the disgraceful state of their towns, to the nests of beggars in the dark wynds, to the molestation of honest folk on the market street. Edinburgh was the worst of all.

> May nane pass through your principal gates
> For stink of haddocks and of skates,
> For cries of carlings and debates,
> For fensum flytings of defame:
>     Think ye not shame,
> Before strangers of all estates
> That sic dishonour hurt your name?
>
> At your high Cross, where gold and silk
> Should be, there is but curds and milk:
> And at your Trone but cockle and whelk,
> Pansches,[1] puddings of Jok and Jame,
>     Think ye not shame,
> So little policy to work
> In hurt and slander to your name!

The historian John Major[2] said that with the exception of the citizens of Perth the Scots would not build walled towns, 'and the reason of this may be that they thus get them face to face with the enemy with no delay, and build their cities, as it were, of men'. Though the explanation was more probably a matter of simple economy (rebuilding walls was expensive in years of incessant war), the spirit was true enough. The people could be called to arms within twelve hours of the first beacon flare, each man keeping horse and weapons always ready, 'and whether in order of battle or not in order of battle, rushes on the foe, not seldom bringing destruction to himself as well as on the invader'. If the towns had no walls, the country was studded with fortress keeps. 'There are in Scotland for the most part two strongholds to every league, intended both as a defence against a foreign foe, and to meet the first outbreak of a civil war.' Major refused to repeat old slanders against that foreign foe. 'I am not wont to credit the common Scot

---

[1] *Pansches*: tripe.

[2] Born *c*. 1469 at Gleghornie near North Berwick, and studied at Cambridge and Paris. A renowned preacher in Scotland and in Europe, and prolific writer on theology and philosophy. His *History of Greater Britain* is valued for its shrewd picture of his own country in his own times.

in his vituperation of the English, nor yet the Englishman in his vituperation of the Scot.' He admired his countrymen's stubborn defence of their independence, but seemed to think it a waste of lives. There was no serious wish for peace between the two nations, but since English and Scots had little love for their own monarchs one kingdom might well be made of the two. Moreover, the Scots never had better kings than those born of English mothers.

Of the two nations in Scotland – the Wild Scots of the mountains and the House-holding Scots of the south – Major belonged to and preferred the latter, believing that the wild men may have had more courage but certainly had less intelligence. A quarrel-some and contentious nature was common to both, however, and skill at arms was placed above all else. Burgh merchants, 'accustomed to luxurious eating and drinking and a quiet fashion of life', were unfit for a prolonged struggle, but the little lairds thought of nothing else but fighting.

> The farmers rent their lands from the lords, but cultivate it by means of servants and not with their own hands. They keep a horse and weapons of war, and are ready to take part in his quarrel, be it just or unjust, with any powerful lord, if they only have a liking for him; and with him, if need be, fight to the death. The farmers have further this fault: that they do not bring up their sons to any handicraft. Shoemakers, tailors, and all such craftsmen they reckon as contemptible and unfit for war; and they therefore bring up their children to take service with the great nobles, or with a view to living in the country in the manner of their fathers.

The nobles set the people an example in quarrel and bloodshed, and the feuds of the lord were relentlessly pursued by his family and retainers. Thus had it been in the days of Abraham and Lot, thought Major, when even their shepherds would not keep the peace. 'From the beginning of time families at strife with one another make bequest of hatred to their children; and thus do they cultivate hatred in the place of God.' The fault lay partly in the gentry's refusal to educate their sons. 'They ought to search out men learned in history, upright in character, and to them entrust the education of their children, so that even in tender age these may begin to form right habits.' The Estates were of the same mind, and an Act of 1496 obliged all barons and freeholders of sub-stance to send their sons to school, to learn at least some Latin. If Major is to be believed, few obeyed the statute, but even so it is probable that the freeholders of Scotland were already better educated than their equals in Europe. A second Scots university was founded at Glasgow in 1450, and a third at Aberdeen in 1494, but Major thought this was excessive. 'I look with no favour on this multitude of universities, for just as iron sharpeneth iron, so a large number of students together will sharpen one another's wits.' And then he regretted the thought. 'In consideration of the physical features of the country this number of universities is not to be condemned.'

Scots churchmen were the valiant equals of their parishioners in war, but in spiritual matters they were not worthy of comparison with English priests. Their bishops ordained men who were quite unskilled in music, and who 'ought at least to understand the Gregorian chant'. There was rarely more than one parish church to thirty villages, and five or ten miles might separate a township from its confessor. 'In the neighbouring chapels of the lords, however, they may have a chance to hear divine service, because even the meanest lord keeps one household chaplain, and more, if his wealth and other provision allow it.' That wealth was frequently on the hoof, and a lord could own a thousand cattle and ten thousand horned sheep. There were also herds of horses, brought down from the north for the Lowland spearmen. 'At Dundee a Highland Scot will bring two hundred or three hundred horses, unbroken, that have never been mounted. They are brought up alongside their dams in the forest and the cold, and are thus fitted to stand all the severity of the weather.' Great men rode stable-fed stallions, but the Highland geldings of their followers were pastured, and could thus carry a lightly-armed man further and longer than any other horse, ten or twelve leagues without food.

The French had a proverb, said Major, *Il est fier comme un Ecossais*, and none was more proud than the Wild Scot. Highlander and Lowlander had different tongues, a different way of life, and there was hatred between the two. A Householding Scot himself, one of the 'quiet and civil-living people' who led a decent life, Major wrote of the Gaels as if they were aliens, certainly as a people inferior in manners and morals. 'It is with the householding Scots that the government and direction of the kingdom is to be found, inasmuch as they understand better, or at least less ill than the others, the nature of a civil polity.' This judgment was not peculiar to his century, and four hundred years later Victorian landlords, philanthropists and journalists would use much the same words to justify the eviction of the last of the Highland people. Some of the Wild Scots, said Major, those whose lands and herds were vulnerably close to their southern neighbours, were tractable and easily brought to obedience.

> The other part of these people delight in the chase and a life of indolence; their chiefs eagerly follow bad men if only they may not have the need to labour; taking no pains to earn their own livelihood, they live upon others, and follow their own worthless and savage chief in all evil courses sooner than they will pursue an honest industry. They are full of mutual dissension, and war rather than peace is their normal condition. The Scottish kings have with difficulty been able to withstand the inroads of these men. From the mid-leg to the foot they go uncovered; their dress is, for an over garment, a loose plaid, and a shirt saffron-dyed. They are armed with bows and arrows, a broadsword, and a small halbert. They always carry in their belt a stout dagger, single-edged, but of the sharpest. In time of war they cover the whole body with a coat of mail, made of iron rings, and in it they fight. The common folk among the Wild Scots go out to battle with the whole body clad in a linen garment sewed together in patchwork, well daubed with wax or with pitch, and with an over-coat of deerskin. But the common people among our domestic Scots and the English fight in a woollen garment.

Scotland and its southern people at the close of the century can be seen in the urbane and civilized dispatches of the Spanish ambassador, Don Pedro de Ayala. They were not an industrious race, he thought, and when there was no war to satisfy them, they fought among themselves. He was impressed by their military power, and by their boast that their king could assemble a hundred and twenty thousand men in thirty days, not counting Islesmen, and moreover pay them. Two or three times he had seen, not as many as this, but perhaps forty thousand, and counted more than twelve thousand great and small tents. They took great pride in their arms and equipment, and although much of their artillery was old, they also had some very fine French guns of modern design.

The people – and in this context he probably meant the gentry – were handsome, vain and ostentatious, courageous and strong. 'They like foreigners so much that they dispute with one another as to who shall have and treat a foreigner in his house. They spend all they have to keep up appearances. They are as well dressed as it is possible to be in such a country.' Like other strangers, he was faintly shocked by the boldness of Scotswomen, but they were honest and courteous, graceful and handsome, 'absolute mistresses of their houses, and even of their husbands, in all things concerning the administration of their property, income as well as expenditure'. They were much better dressed than Englishwomen, and the kerchief and veil of their headdress made a finer show than any he had seen.

The land was rich in natural wealth, in fish, wildfowl, deer and fruits, and great flocks of sheep were grazed in the savage parts, but the husbandry of the common people was wasteful and improvident. It was impossible to describe the immense quantities of salmon, herring and stock fish which the Scots exported, but it sufficed for Italy, France, Flanders and England. There were seventy seaports, populous towns and villages, houses of hewn stone, windows of glass, and many chimneys. 'All the furniture that is used in Italy, Spain, and France is to be found in their dwellings. It has not been bought in modern times only, but inherited from preceding ages.' There were two archbishops and eleven bishops, and more than sixty monasteries, rich and magnificent abbeys, all founded by kings. Of the great men owning great estates, fifteen were earls, and thirty-five were barons, with many lesser lords. 'I saw two [of the earls] come to serve the king in the last war with more than thirty thousand men, all picked soldiers and well-armed. And yet they did not bring more than one-half of their men.'

It was a very old and very noble kingdom, said the ambassador, powerful enough to defend itself without fear of God, and it was ruled by a man who possessed great virtues and no defects worth mentioning.

## 5

The Renaissance sun, which burnt so fiercely elsewhere, brought light more than warmth to the kingdom of Scotland. There was little in art and thought and manners to be re-created. Where it was influential, the nation's culture was Celtic not Mediterranean, its traditions martial, its Church political and patriotic. Its meagre wealth was largely spent upon castles and spearmen, and it had no self-indulgent moneyed class to patronize the arts. Its nobles were frequently brutish in their pleasures, and its slowly prospering merchants were intellectually little better than the stall-holders and craftsmen of their burghs. Life was hard, and the struggle to sustain it left few men with the leisure to debate its nature and purpose. The great philosophical and political challenge of the Renaissance was to medieval universalism, to the rule of Pope and Monarch under God, and it produced Machiavelli's Prince, supreme, amoral, unquestionable. It might be said that Scotland had anticipated this challenge nearly two centuries before by the Declaration of Arbroath, and that the later growth of government by King and Estates – with the seed of elected representation already germinating – made it unnecessary and impossible for a Stewart to become a Medici. In the arts Scotland planted a kailyard compared with the Renaissance flower garden of other nations, but unlike most of them it had fought its first battles for the freedom of man, without which all art may seem an insulting frivolity.

Although peripheral, Scotland was none the less susceptible to the breaking of old bonds and to the release of a new spirit. Under a popular, brave and vigorous young king, the country prospered and grew in importance, invigorated by trade and by learning, strengthened by law and justice, and freed for a while from the fear of invasion and civil war. 'There is as great a difference between the Scotland of old time and the Scotland of to-day,' de Ayala wrote in 1498, 'as there is between good and bad.' James IV was twenty-six when that was written, and he had been king for ten years. After the murder of his father – for which he believed himself responsible, and in expiation of which he wore an iron chain about his body – there was a brief period when it seemed as if the old bloody struggle for power was to be repeated. Although the

Homes and the Hepburns profited in rank and power from their rebellion, and Bell-the-Cat Angus ruled shortly as Guardian, they could not hope to dominate a hostile and horrified people. Within a few weeks of Sauchieburn William Elphinstone, Bishop of Aberdeen and the murdered king's principal adviser, was readmitted to Parliament and the Secret Council, and a policy of pardon and appeasement brought most factions together in protective unity, if not in friendship, about the throne. Not the least reason for this surprisingly civilized resolution of their wasteful quarrels was the young occupant of that ancient chair.

James IV was the best loved of all the Stewarts, instinctively inspiring a loyalty that reached its zenith in the Homeric slaughter of Flodden. In the best meaning of the title he was a Renaissance prince, a sunburst after the gloomy cloud of his father's reign. He was intelligent and curious, colourful and high-spirited, warm-hearted and gay, generous and extravagant. He could pull a tooth, apply a leech, and set a broken leg, play a practical joke, couch a lance against the best of his knights, ride far and hard at the hunt, finance an alchemist who hoped to transmute base metal into gold, and encourage the same wretched man in the belief that a pair of artificial wings would transport him safely from the walls of Stirling Castle to the ground. He could discuss clothes with a tailor, ships with a sailor, guns with an artillerist, and music with a minstrel. He filled his palaces with jesters, dancers and gamblers, and what money he did not lose at cards he gave to the leprous and the poor. He rode abroad at the head of a brilliant cavalcade, delighting in fine clothes, fine horses and complaisant women. But he could also feel the iron chain of guilt about his body. He could bend a rebel lord without breaking the man, honour good government, serve justice, and respect his people. Though he listened to his counsellors, said Don Pedro de Ayala, in great matters he acted upon his own judgment, 'and in my opinion he generally makes a right decision'.

He is of noble stature, neither tall nor short, and as handsome in complexion and shape as a man can be. . . . His knowledge of languages is wonderful. He is well read in the Bible and some other devout books. He is a good historian. . . . He never cuts his hair or his beard. It becomes him very well. He fears God, and observes all the precepts of the Church. . . . He says all his prayers. Before transacting any business he hears two masses. After mass he has a cantata sung, during which he sometimes dispatches very urgent business. He gives alms liberally, but is a severe judge, especially in the case of murderers. . . . He is active and works hard. When he is not at war he hunts in the mountains. . . . God has worked a miracle in him, for I have never seen a man so temperate in eating and drinking out of Spain. Indeed, such a thing seems to be superhuman in these countries.

He is courageous, even more so than a king should be. I have seen him often undertake most dangerous things in the last wars. I sometimes clung to his skirts and succeeded in keeping him back. . . . He is not a good captain, because he begins to fight before he has given his orders. He said to me that his subjects serve him with their persons and goods, in just and unjust quarrels, exactly as he likes, and that, therefore, he does not think it right to begin any warlike undertaking without being himself the first in danger. His deeds are as good as his words. For this reason, and because he is a very humane prince, he is much loved.

De Ayala was less approving of the King's passion for women, though he blamed the great men who had unscrupulously encouraged it when James was young. These nobly born paramours were kept in great state, and when love or desire cooled they were married to nobler husbands. 'It may be about a year since he gave up, so at least it is believed, his lovemaking, as well as from fear of God as from fear of scandal in this world, which is thought very much of here.' This afterthought was perhaps more diplomatic than true. Don Pedro wanted Ferdinand and Isabella to marry their third daughter to the King of the Scots. By such a match, he thought, they would not only acquire a faithful ally but also serve God.

The King's loves and lusts were part of the man's hungry zest for life. Knowledge and learning fascinated his questing spirit, and by Scotland's first compulsory education act in 1496 his parliament ordered all barons and freeholders of substance to put their eldest sons to school at the age of eight or nine, first to master Latin and then to receive some teaching in Art and Law. He did not exempt his bastard sons Alexander and James, sending them abroad to study at Padua, and later at Siena and Rome under the scholar and humanist Erasmus. Alexander was a brilliant child, or at least a lucky one, for while he was still a minor his father gave him the see of St Andrews. In this foolishness James was no worse than some of his barons, for their ambitious jobbery packed the ecclesiastical houses with their kin. The King's interest in medicine was not limited to the pulling of teeth, or the alchemistic and aeronautical experiments of his Italian leech Damian. Aberdeen University, created by Elphinstone in 1494, was the first in Britain with a foundation for teaching medicine, and in 1506 James granted a royal charter to a college of surgeons instituted twelve months before by Edinburgh's Town Council.

The King had his great-grandfather's love of poetry, if no talent for it himself, and poets flourished under his patronage. Robert Henryson, the Dunfermline schoolmaster, died an old man early in the sixteenth century, and he belonged to the pre-Renaissance age. The gentle wit and narrative style of his moral tales were Chaucerian, and like Aesop, whose fables he retold in a Scots setting, he exposed the weaknesses and virtues of humanity by the personification of the animal world. He was compassionate and reflective, and sadly longed for a 'simple life without dread'. He was a lark singing high above the carrion crows of war and intrigue, and the final verse of *The Preiching of the Swallow* is the heart-cry of a man tired of the brute wastefulness of his century.

> Pray we thairfoir, quhill we are in this lyfe,
> For four thingis: the first, fra sin remufe;
> The secund is fra all weir and stryfe;
> The thrid is perfite cheritie and lufe;
> The feird thing is, and maist for oure behufe,
> That is in blis with Angellis to be fallow,
> And thus endis the preiching of the Swallow.

The poets who followed Henryson, particularly William Dunbar, shone more brilliantly but with less human sympathy and sincerity. They were small masters of the magic and music of words, and used their talent as an instrument. Once a Franciscan friar, Dunbar was in effect a court poet, granted an annuity of ten pounds, which by greedy complaining he increased to eighty pounds in ten years. He was probably one of a mission sent to London in 1503, to bring back the King's bride Margaret Tudor, and he celebrated their marriage with his first great poem *The Thistle and the Rose*. He was a self-centred man, reserving his sympathy for himself, but he had a sharp eye for the world about him, squalid and magnificent, noble and depraved. Sir, he told his royal master, you have many servants . . .

> Kirkmen, courtmen, and craftismen fyne;
> Doctouris in jure and medicyne;
> Divinouris, rethors and philosophouris,
> Astrologis, artistis and oratouris;
> Men of armes, and vailyeand knychtis,
> And mony other gudlie wichtis. . . .

*James IV, who was perhaps the best loved of Scotland's later kings. A Mytens copy of an earlier painting, now lost.*

 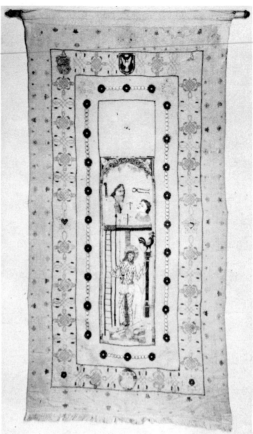

*Margaret Tudor was the wife of James IV and the ancestress of both Mary Queen of Scots and her husband Darnley.* Right
*The Fetternear Banner, with the arms of Bishop Gavin Douglas, poet and prelate, translator of the* Aeneid.

Musicians, minstrels and merrie singers, shipbuilders and masons, glaziers, gold-smiths, printers and potters, and 'all of thair craft cunning'. But also boasters and gossips, fawners and spongers, thieves, rogues and beggars, who preyed upon the King because he was gracious and meek. Dunbar's throat burst with words, imaginative and sweet, bawdy and derisive, and sometimes as rich as brocade and as hard as plate-armour. He mocked lovers and cuckolds, praised his mistress for all the virtues 'except onlie that ye ar mercyles'. He was in love with rhyme, and mourned the loss of the 'makaris', the poets who had preceded him. Noble Chaucer and John Barbour, Blind Harry and Andrew of Wyntoun, John Clerk and James Afflek, good Quintin Shaw and Sandy Traill. Men who are now no more than names. Dunbar's *Lament for the Makaris* was written when he was ill and at the nadir of melancholy, but its morbid despair was as much a part of his creative spirit as joyous ribaldry and satirical scorn.

> Our plesance heir is all vane glory,
> This fals warld is bot transitory,
> The flesche is brukle, the Fend is sle;
> *Timor mortis conturbat me.*

The stait of man dois change and vary,
Now sound, now seik, now blith, now sary,
Now dansand mery, now like to dee;
*Timor mortis conturbat me.*

Though subjective, the gloom is prophetic, as if Dunbar could already hear the challenge of an English trumpet below Flodden Edge. His voice was the strongest of his age, but there were others like Walter Kennedy, who mourned the lusty folly of youth, and gentle John Reid of Stobo, the probable author of *The Three Prestis of Peblis*. There was also Gavin Douglas, bishop of Dunkeld, whose vigorous and inspired translation of the *Aeneid* restores a name dishonoured by his murderous father Bell-the-Cat. The King's encouragement of such men, by patronage or inspiration, was in the pattern of a Renaissance prince, but a greater service to literature and learning was the patent Elphinstone persuaded him to grant to the Edinburgh burgesses Walter Chapman and Andrew Myllar, giving them permission to establish Scotland's first printing press in 1508. Though it was intended that the press should make books of law, ritual and theology, and did indeed produce the beautiful *Aberdeen Breviary* among others, the black type-case in the Southgate shop also served Henryson, Dunbar and Douglas. And in time, a short time, its successors would be employed by the explosive intellects of the Reformation.

About its major towns and below the Highland line, the mood of the kingdom was blithe and gay, noisy with the sound of pageants and games, masons' hammers and ship-wrights' saws, the thunder of new guns in Edinburgh's artillery park, the thump of a football kicked in defiance of the law, the crack of a whip at the burgh pillory, choral

*The devices of Walter Chapman and Andrew Myllar. James IV permitted them to establish Scotland's first printing press.*

music at mass, and a falconer's encouraging cry on the Pentland Hills. After his marriage to Margaret Tudor, peace with England enabled the King to cooperate with the English wardens in the suppression of Border cutthroats of both nations. He once sat in judgment himself at Jedburgh, and with such merciless severity that his summary use of the rope was long remembered as 'Jeddart Justice'. In the Highlands, violence and disorder were less easily controlled. Soon after the King's coronation, MacDonald Islesmen swarmed ashore on the mainland, reclaiming the earldom of Ross for John, Lord of the Isles. They were defeated, and the lordship was abolished, but it took five more punitive campaigns and twelve more years before Clan Donald was quietened. Other chiefs and other clans, not the least the Campbells, rose upon the ruins of the MacDonalds' power, mulching a rich soil of hatred for a future harvest of feud and bloodshed. James visited the West Highlands three times, on progress or campaign, hanging a rogue or two, but more often dividing the chiefs, buying the support of one with what he took from another. Using clan against clan, he set an example which successive kings and governments would profitably follow for the next two hundred and fifty years. His courage and his physical strength, his charm and his knowledge of Gaelic, made him popular with the Highlanders, and even some of the MacDonalds admired him. Though he never wholly succeeded in governing the clans, and though he trusted them no further than the armour he wore beneath a black and scarlet surcoat at their councils, many honoured their promises, and many went with him to Flodden.

By the twenty-fourth year of his reign, and under the wise guidance of Elphinstone, James had strengthened and extended the machinery of government, justice and administration, imposing order by his own authority. He called two parliaments only after 1500 and he chose his own Privy Council, but in the manner of a Renaissance prince he widened it to include new men of learning and of law. He encouraged trade, did his best to establish an honest currency, demanded respect for the law as well as for the force of its application, and built a small but bold navy, the first ship of which was named for his English wife. By his residence in the palace he built next to the abbey walls of Holyrood, Edinburgh became the principal burgh, the capital of the kingdom. Upon its great wedge of rock the tenemented city looked westward, northward and southward upon a country more stable than it had ever been, a prospering country of merchants, poets, surgeons, scholars, artisans and craftsmen, jugglers and dancers, village women who brought their sensual and exciting king scarlet baskets of cherries and strawberries. It was still a rough and crude country, still at the door of enlightenment, but its face was lit by the sun of the Renaissance. All this the King now seemed to throw away, for a turquoise ring and on a point of chivalrous but foolish honour.

The honeymoon peace with England had survived the death of the King's father-in-law in 1509, but it grew progressively uneasy year by year. English Borderers again crossed the Tweed in search of ancient enemies, or more exactly their stock and goods. At sea, English ships attacked and captured two vessels of Scotland's little navy, killing their commander, Sir Andrew Barton, whose bravery so impressed the Englishmen that they sportingly composed a ballad in his honour. Henry VIII did not suppress the border banditry, or restore the prizes his pirates had taken, but it was not this that brought the two nations to war. Europe was moving under changing alliances, and in 1512 Henry joined the Holy League which the Pope and the Emperor Maximilian had formed against France. The French naturally appealed to the Auld Alliance, but Julius II – who had once called James 'Protector of the Christian Religion' – now

*Henry VIII, whose 'Rough Wooing' of Scotland to secure the marriage of his son to the infant Mary devastated the Borders and made a 'jolly fire' of Holyrood.*

threatened to excommunicate him if he broke his solemn treaties with England. James protested that they had already been broken, that Henry was 'slaying, capturing and imprisoning' his subjects, but the protest was unanswered. Elphinstone urged caution and prudence, and for once was tragically ignored. In the early summer of 1513 an envoy brought an appeal for help from Louis XII. He also brought a turquoise ring from the French queen, and a letter naming James her champion, inviting him to step one pace into England, to strike one blow for her.

On August 13 the Lyon King of Arms delivered a defiant ultimatum to Henry VIII at Therouanne in Flanders. He was churlishly dismissed, and three days later the English routed the French in a comic runabout known as the Battle of the Spurs. The war was virtually over, but James was already moving toward the Border with the largest and most glorious army a king of Scotland had ever led, or would ever lead again. Advancing to meet him was an army equally large, twenty thousand men perhaps, under the long-faced and insolent-eyed Earl of Surrey, supported at sea by his son Thomas Howard, the piratical Lord Admiral who had seized those Scottish ships in the Downs.

The armies met in England on a lonely north-eastern spur of the Cheviots, where the grass sings to the wind, and the land weeps from hidden streams. The three hills of Flodden are a formidable natural fortress to the south-west of Norham, and their formation has been well described as a kilted man, seated and facing east.[1] Monylaws Hill is his waist, Flodden Hill and Edge his right thigh and knee, and Branxton Hill his left. The ground between the thighs, the sag of the kilt, slopes down to the little River Till. Though the English were between him and Scotland, three miles away, James had out-manouevered Surrey to set his army upon these hills, and the position seemed unassailable on the morning of Wednesday, September 7, when the Rougecroix herald brought him an insulting challenge. Surrey offered a battle two days hence, on open ground below the hills, a 'good ground for two armies to fight, and therefore I will look for no more of his delays'. James outmatched the insult. He would fight where he stood, and not on ground an English earl had chosen with the aid of witchcraft or sorcery. But Surrey's arrogance had angered him, and anger would make him foolish.

On Thursday the English army, reinforced by Thomas Howard and a thousand men from the fleet, marched up the eastern bank of the Till, turned into battle line and faced the apron of the kilt. When he saw that the Scots would not come down, that the marshy ground across the stream was covered by artillery, Surrey wisely abandoned his position. He retired to the north, crossed the Till by Twizel Bridge, and reformed below Branxton Hill. Had the Scots fallen upon him at the crossing he would have been defeated, but they did not leave their high ground.

On Friday morning the crest of the Flodden massif was obscured by thick smoke as the Scots burnt their camp refuse, and under this deliberate or providential cover James moved the full strength of his army northward to the ridge of Branxton Hill, in four divisions and a reserve. A south wind of stormy rain blew the smoke down the slope, sometimes hiding Scots from English, and English from Scots. It was late afternoon, within two hours of sunset, before Surrey's advancing men formed their battle-line four hundred yards below the ridge, on sloping ground of coarse wet grass, narrow streams and sucking bog. Not once during those waiting hours did the Scots come down upon the confusion of their enemies.

[1] Moray McLaren, *If Freedom Fail*.

The battle began with an artillery duel, a muffled thudding on the heavy air, above the noise of steel and harness, trumpet calls and rallying cries. The Scots guns were either not yet in position, or could not be depressed far enough to do damage, but Surrey's cannoneers worked their pieces with deadly skill, killing Scotland's Master Gunner, Robert Borthwick, and bitterly galling the waiting spearmen. James could have withdrawn his divisions to the other side of the ridge, and held them there until the breathless English reached the top, but he could no longer control his anger and impatience. Too late, and with that foolhardy courage de Ayala had deplored, he led his magnificent army down through the rain and smoke to its destruction. Had he wished to remain where he was, he could not have done so now. His undisciplined left flank of Borderers under Lord Home, Gordons with the Earl of Huntly, had endured the cannonade long enough, and were already away against the nearest English. The silent advance of the Scottish centre, one column led by James and another by the Earl of Crawford, was at first a steady flow of lowered spears, but it soon became a wild slide of barefoot men on a glissade of wet grass. The slide ended in a shallow and unexpected valley, and from this they had now to climb upward, two hundred yards toward the waiting divisions of Surrey and Thomas Howard. Above on the ridge, the Islesmen and Highlanders under the earls of Argyll and Lennox saw no enemy to their front and remained where they were, watching the fight below with professional interest. Further back, and on the southern slope of Branxton Hill, the Earl of Bothwell's reserve saw nothing and did nothing.

The Borderers and Gordons fell furiously upon a smaller division of Cheshire men commanded by Surrey's third son, Edmund Howard, broke them and raced on toward the English camp. They were plundering dead and prisoners when Lord Dacre struck their flank with fifteen hundred horsemen, and after a flurry of spears and lances both sides drew back and watched each other in cautious and useless immobility. Upon the ridge, the watching clansmen were suddenly surprised by Sir Edward Stanley, who had cunningly brought his rearguard up from dead ground on their right. Lightly armoured, and unable to use their one tactical advantage of the charge, the Highlanders fell beneath the familiar rain of English arrows. When Stanley's infantry and horse advanced, they ran, leaving Matthew Stewart of Lennox and Archibald Campbell of Argyll among their bloody dead.

The centre of the field below was a slaughter-house. Dusk was coming, darker still under thickening clouds, and lividly lit by the spark of steel on steel. For the first time in a close engagement the Scottish spear met a superior weapon, and ironically one that was already obsolescent. The English footman was armed with a bill, a short shaft of oak topped with an axe blade and a curving hook. With this he lopped off the head of an advancing spear, and killed its defenceless owner. He worked with the steady, scything sweep of a harvester, and with a belly that had been empty for more than twenty-four hours. When Stanley's men came down from the ridge, the Scots were surrounded, and no quarter was given. One by one, each commander died with his men, Erroll, Crawford and Montrose, earl, baron, knight, churchman and soldier. James rode deep into Surrey's division, and got within a spear's length of the English earl before he fell. His body was full of arrows it was said, one hand hung from a strip of skin, and his neck was severed by the stroke of a bill. His reckless valour impressed the English, although they thought it foolish. 'O what a noble and triumphant courage was this,' said Edward Hall's *Chronicle*, 'for a king to fight in a battle as a mean soldier. But how so ever it happened,

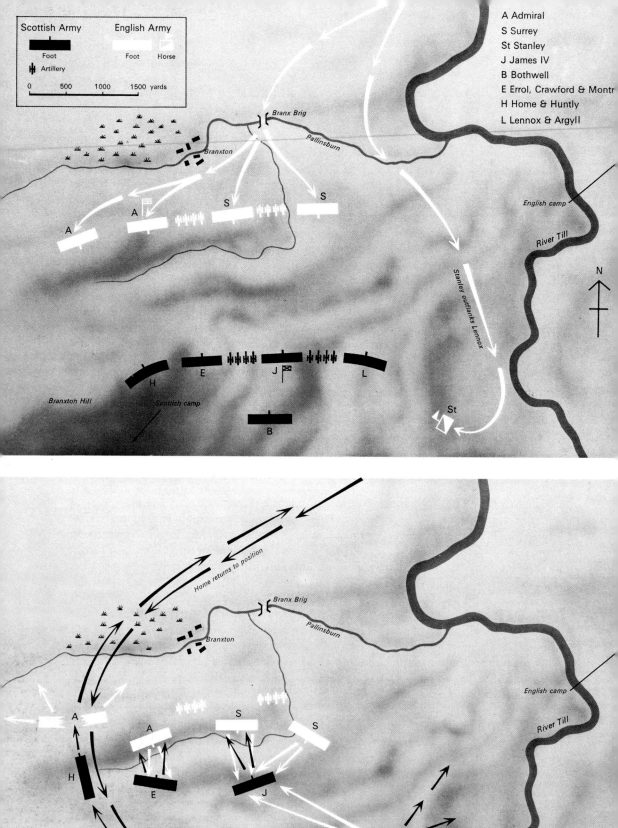

Scottish Army   English Army

Foot          Foot        Horse

Artillery

0   500   1000   1500   yards

A Admiral
S Surrey
St Stanley
J James IV
B Bothwell
E Errol, Crawford & Montr
H Home & Huntly
L Lennox & Argyll

Branx Brig

Pallinsburn

English camp

River Till

N

Stanley outflanks Lennox

A   A   S   S

E   J   L

H

Branxton Hill

Scottish camp

B

St

Branxton

Home returns to position

Branx Brig

Pallinsburn

English camp

River Till

A   A   S   S

H

E   J

L

St

Branxton Hill

Scottish camp

B

God gave the stroke, and he was no more regarded than a poor soldier, for all went one way.'

When he died is unknown, but the fight continued until none was alive inside the English ring. Nor is it known that Bothwell answered a call for his reserves, but he is believed to have been killed on Branxton Hill. Away to the west, Huntly urged Home to ride to the aid of their king, but the Border man had a strong respect for his military duty. 'He does well that does for himself,' he said. 'We have fought our vanguard already, let others do as well as we.' The Gordon went nobly off to the fight, but Home remained until dawn on the high ground he had taken. He then slipped away to Scotland.

An exact accounting of the Scottish dead is impossible. It was probably not less than ten thousand, if not the twelve thousand claimed by the English. They died with extraordinary obstinacy and ferocity, and with terrible wounds. 'Such large and strong men,' said the Bishop of Durham, who hewed at them as vigorously as any layman, 'that they would not fall when four or five bills struck one of them.' The best of Scotland died about James and his bastard son, Alexander, the Bishop of St Andrews. Earls, barons and knights, freeholding lairds, farmers and their labourers. Among the common folk of the burghs and the fields the losses were terrible and bitter. There were other towns like Selkirk, no doubt, that had sent a company of spearmen to the King, and now wept at the return of one man only.

On Saturday morning, Lord Dacre's men dragged a half-naked body from beneath the wet, stinking mound in the centre of the field. It was carried to Berwick, where some who had known James IV identified it as his. Others denied this, because there was no iron chain of expiation about its waist. It was disembowelled and embalmed, said Hall, and 'secretly amongst other stuff conveyed to Newcastle'. From thence it went in a casket of lead to London, where Catherine of Aragon thought of sending it further to her husband Henry in Flanders, but changed her mind because 'our Englishmen's hearts would not suffer it'. She sent the corpse's bloody surcoat instead, and with it her congratulations. The restless body of the Scots king was then sent to the monastery of Sheen in Surrey, where it still remained unburied, and when the house was dissolved, and used as lodgings for the Duke of Suffolk, it was thrown into a lumber room with old timber. John Stow saw it there, and said that workmen sported with it, hacking off its head. This head, still red-haired and bearded, had a sweet and pleasing scent that later intrigued Lancelot Young, master glazier to Elizabeth I. He took it to his home in the City of London, and kept it on display, but he was later persuaded to give it to the sexton of St Michael's in Wood Street. There it was at last buried, in an anonymous grave and with a pile of English bones that had been cleared from the charnel-house of the crypt.

Some Scots refused to believe that the King was dead. Four noble horsemen, they said, had carried him to safety, and this sad legend, longing for the return of hope and happiness, is perhaps more moving than a grieving lament for the flowers of the forest.

*Flodden, Friday, September 9, 1513. James has moved his army to Branxton Hill, and waits as the English assemble to the north below. The battle is begun by Home and Huntly, followed by the downward charge of the main Scots divisions.*

# PART V

# Reformation

*'Many began to call in doubt*
*that which before they had held*
*for certain verity'*

John Knox wrote from the galleys where he was enslaved 'God loveth us because we are His own handiwork.'
The English ambassador said that he believed himself to be a member of God's Privy Council.

This century was the great watershed of Scotland's history, from which some of its national strength still flows. Between Flodden and the union of the kingdoms ninety years later there was both reformation and revolution, and despite an occasional surface stillness, or a contrary eddy, the undercurrent of change was irreversible, and so deep that the source of its power is to some extent inexplicable. A decaying and hierarchical Church was destroyed and another was created, as much by political action as from spiritual need. The new Congregation of Christ was offered a share in its clerical government, and a precedent was set for similar responsibility in temporal affairs. Equality before God would no longer be a solatium for bondage upon earth, and a belief in political liberty would take tender root in the soil of religious freedom. Much that is romantic and dramatic in this century is in fact flotsam only, indicating the current of change, not directing it. The tragedy of Mary Queen of Scots may be seen as such an irrelevance, and her judicial assassination by the English should not now disturb a nation that once murdered its own monarchs by stealth.

The boy who became James V of Scotland as a result of that storm-day on Branxton Hill was less than two years old. His heavy-lidded and sensual English mother, who was carrying a second child, headed a council of government which included Archbishop James Beaton of Glasgow and the contentious earls of Angus, Arran and Huntly, and like the rest of the valiant country none of them considered Flodden a proper end to the war. Preparations went ahead for its resumption with the spring thaws, although the dying King of France was less than enthusiastic for this zealous observance of the Auld Alliance. Because it may have seemed unlikely that Margaret Tudor would be vigorous in a quarrel with her red-haired brother, and because Angus and Arran were more concerned with disputes between their Douglas and Hamilton clans, some discontented barons secretly offered the Governorship of Scotland to the new king's second cousin John Stewart, Duke of Albany. But he was in France, where he preferred to be, and was still there when spring came, and with it the birth of James IV's posthumous child and an unwelcome truce between Henry VIII and Louis XII. There was no war. That autumn, for love, lust or self-protection, Margaret married her witless councillor Angus, grandson of Bell-the-Cat. By the terms of James IV's will her regency was contingent upon her remaining a widow, and the Estates now invited Albany to come to Scotland with all haste.

He came when he was given leave by the new king of France, in May, 1515, and Margaret was driven into England with her Douglas. She left her children behind, and with the death of the posthumous son, Alexander, Albany was named 'second person of the realm', heir to the throne. He was a grandson of James II, a shrewd and intelligent man, equable in temper until he was contradicted, and then he would throw his cap at the fire in a rage. He spoke nothing but French, but he ruled with good sense and firmness, and he was loyal to his infant cousin. With two exceptions he appeased those who had opposed his regency, pardoned Archibald Douglas of Angus, and welcomed Margaret back to Edinburgh upon condition that she behaved like 'ane gud Scottis woman'. The exceptions were Lord Home and his brother, who were beheaded for rebellion, and since Home's behaviour at Flodden had now grown into a belief that he had murdered James IV after the battle, they were mourned by none but their own Borderers.

*Mary Queen of Scots in later life, painted during her long captivity.*
*Overleaf James VI of Scotland and I of Great Britain. Anne of Denmark, wife of James VI.*

MARIA
D G
SCOTIÆ
PIISSIMA REGINA
FRANCIÆ DOTARIA
ANNO
ÆTATISREGNIQ
36
ANGLICÆCAPTIVIT
10
S H
1578

Albany returned to France in 1517, to negotiate a renewal of the Auld Alliance with Francis I at Rouen, but what he had intended to be a visit of four months became an involuntary exile of four years. Upon the insistence of Henry of England, a new ally and one to be carefully placated, Francis refused to give the Regent permission to leave, and by the same compulsion the Treaty of Rouen also remained unratified. In Scotland, a regency council of Angus, Arran, Huntly and Argyll was united in mutual distrust only, and the country once more fell into murderous anarchy. The first victim was an unfortunate Frenchman, the Sieur de la Bastie, whom Albany had made Warden of the East March. The Homes killed him, in revenge for their lord, striking off his head and tying it by the hair to a reiver's saddle-bow. In the Highlands, Sir Donald MacDonald of Lochalsh declared himself Lord of the Isles, and seized a royal castle or two with the help of the Macleans and the Macleods. They were bloodily suppressed by the Earl of Argyll's Campbells, and Maclean of Duart quickly changed his coat, asking leave to 'destroy the wicked blood of the Isles'. Lochalsh went to the scaffold, and as the mountain arm of a southern government Clan Campbell was raised higher still above Clan Donald.

The contest for power between Angus and James Hamilton, Earl of Arran, moved from the council chamber to the street. Their bitter quarrel was also personal. Margaret wished to divorce Angus, for his infidelity it was said, and she was smiling with favour upon Arran, though less carnally, perhaps, than politically. The feud involved other men beside the Douglas and Hamilton families. In support of Angus, the citizens of Edinburgh shut their gates upon their own Provost, Arran, and killed his bastard son forbye. Home of Wedderburn, who had slaughtered de la Bastie, now killed the Prior of Coldingham, it was said, so that a Douglas might fill the emptied office. The Lord Chancellor of Scotland, Archbishop James Beaton, was unable to control the two earls. He was Arran's kinsman and a partisan.

The feud reached its climax in April, 1520, when Arran brought a small army to Edinburgh. On the last day of the month the two factions faced each other in the sloping High Street, and the four hundred Douglas spearmen were outnumbered by the Hamiltons. Before the blood-letting began Gavin Douglas, poet uncle of the earl, went to Beaton's house at the foot of Blackfriars Wynd and appealed for peace and good sense. The Archbishop swore that he knew of no evil intended by his kinsmen, but when he struck his chest to emphasize the honesty of his conscience there was a dull ring of armoured plates beneath his vestments. 'A poor conscience, my lord,' said the poet, 'for I heard them clatter.' He went back and told his nephew to defend himself in arms, he would go to his chamber and pray. The fight began when Arran's bastard brother, Sir Patrick Hamilton, was accused of cowardice by the same earl's bastard son. 'I'll fight where thou darest not be seen!' he shouted, charged the Douglases and was quickly killed by Angus. The brawl swayed up and down the blood-greased cobbles, until Home of Wedderburn and his Border horse clattered through the Netherbow port to the help of their Douglas friends. The Hamiltons ran, between the tall houses and down the narrow wynds. Arran and his son escaped across the Nor' Loch, clinging to a collier's horse, but Beaton was found in Blackfriars Church, where his throat would have been cut had it not been for the intercession of Gavin Douglas.

The citizens of Edinburgh, with their pawky taste for a deflationary phrase, called this noble contest 'Cleanse-the-Causeway'.

Arran fled to a brief exile in France, but Angus won little from the victory, and lost

*Above A miniature believed to be of James Hepburn, 4th Earl of Bothwell and third husband of Mary Queen of Scots. Below The murdered body of James Stewart, 'The Bonnie Earl o' Moray'.*

that a year later. When the sweet rivalry of the Field of Cloth of Gold turned to sour war, Francis sent Albany back to Scotland to harass Henry's northern frontier. Though the Regent raised a large army, with a powerful artillery train, Scots nobles were now afraid of another Flodden and would not invade England. English Borderers rode unchecked across the Tweed until four thousand Frenchmen arrived and drove them out, but still the Scots were laggard. When Parliament asked the French to leave, in 1524, Albany went with them, in disgust no doubt. He never returned.

No one had given much thought to the young King, who had been left to 'correctioun at the schools'. At the age of twelve he was now produced for his Erection in Edinburgh, his public investiture with crown, sceptre and sword, surrounded by two hundred English gentlemen sent by his uncle Henry. Although the Estates were not unanimous, they declared a formal end to Albany's governorship, and Margaret was edged from public affairs by her estranged husband. At thirty-five, the Earl of Angus once more became the dominant man of the realm. He replaced Beaton as Chancellor, filled the offices of the royal household with his Red Douglas kin – from treasurer to master of the larder – and held the King in captivity on the castle rock of Edinburgh. The forgotten boy had somehow developed both courage and strength of will, and his hatred of Angus became irreconcilable after his friend the Earl of Lennox was killed in a hopeless rebellion. The King's escape from Edinburgh in 1528 is still a mystery, the subject of fanciful legends, but in July he was in Stirling with his mother, now divorced from Angus and planning a third marriage to Henry Stewart of Methven. A small army quickly gathered about him, led by the enemies of Angus and by some of his fair-weather friends like the Homes. Put to the horn for treason, the Red Douglas held out in his castle at Tantallon for three weeks before surrendering. He took his life into English exile, but his estates were forfeited.

The sixteen-year-old King who dramatically emerged from the chrysalis of his captivity was strong-minded, energetic and half-educated, but anxious to learn quickly. Like most of the Stewarts he was a complex character, combining an impulsive and quixotic temperament, a warm-hearted love of life, with a brutal and sometimes vindictive determination to assert and maintain his authority. He would be remembered as the Poor Man's King, and he certainly had his father's interest in life beyond a palace wall. He sometimes wandered about the country as a humble tenant farmer, the Goodman of Ballengiech, but appears to have fooled no one. According to an English spy, the true commonalty mockingly cried 'There goes the King of Scotland!' It was an impoverished and disordered country when he took control of it, and the most immediate concern of his council was to restore some of its revenues, and to use them for strengthening the machinery of justice. In 1531, upon his promise to defend the 'seat of Rome and holy kirk', he received the Pope's permission to draw an annuity of ten thousand pounds from the Church for the maintenance of a College of Justice, fifteen salaried clerics and laymen, learned in law and acting as a supreme civil court. The bargaining bishops and abbots offered fourteen hundred pounds instead, with a lump sum of seventy-two thousand, and it was accepted, though little if any of the compounded payment went to the College. The prelates raised the tax by evicting many of their tenants, introducing others at higher rents, and there is an ironic humour in their unhappy situation. The Church needed the King's support against the growth of critical and heretical opposition, but in raising the money to pay for it they only increased that dangerous hostility.

Marriage could also fill the emptied coffers of the Crown. For some years the eligibility of the lusty King was hawked about the courts of Europe, its price increasing with every offer, until he finally accepted a Frenchwoman, the daughter of the Duke of Vendôme. When he saw her discouraging portrait he asked for a pension as well as the proposed dowry of a hundred thousand crowns, and when he went to Paris to marry her, late in 1536, he was so disgusted by the ugly and misshapen woman that he refused to take her. With commendable restraint, or perhaps with artful cunning, Francis I reoffered his own daughter Madeleine, whom the Scots had previously rejected. They were married on New Year's Day, and when the gentle and fragile creature was taken to her husband's land she knelt and kissed its soil. Two months later its climate killed her, and with indecent haste negotiations were begun for a replacement. James remembered the face of Mary of Guise, and when it was known that her husband had conveniently died – and that Henry VIII's offer for her had been refused – she was spoken for, married by proxy, and sent to Scotland with a dowry of a hundred and fifty thousand livres. Thus, by way of the hunchback of one poor girl and the weak constitution of another, was acquired the redoubtable mother of Mary Queen of Scots.

The King's ruthless imposition of order was largely effective throughout his kingdom, but it also made enemies. During his minority the Highland clans had been kept in check by the Campbells of Argyll and the Gordons of Huntly, but by 1531 Clan Donald and the Macleans were in revolt, claiming that the King's Lieutenants, the Earl of Argyll and James Stewart, Earl of Moray, were more concerned with their own aggrandizement than their duty. James took an army north against the clans, but their

*James V was not yet two when his father died at Flodden. 'Child monarchs were a recurring visitation . . . as if Providence despaired of the institution.' Right Mary of Guise was the second queen of James V and the mother of Mary Queen of Scots. John Knox saw God's judgment in the agony of her death.*

bold charm and the evident justice of their claim persuaded him to imprison Argyll instead. MacDonald of Islay was made Lieutenant of the southern Isles, but the King lost the loyalty of the Campbells and the trust of his bastard half-brother Moray. A year before he had been less tolerant of Border ruffians, the troublesome Armstrongs, Kers, Scotts and others, wild lance-slung men in iron caps and leather coats, riding north and south on their little ponies, looking for other men's cattle and as ready to intrigue with the English as they were to rob them. These bonnet lairds were encouraged in their reiving by nobler lords like Maxwell, Home, and Hepburn of Bothwell, all of whom the King imprisoned at one time or another. The most colourful of the Borderers, or one the ballads best remember, was John Armstrong of Gilneckie in Eskdale. He had more courage than good sense, for with only a score or so moss-troopers he rode to meet the King in Teviotdale. The ballads say he went in response to a 'loving letter' and was betrayed, but more probably he had a royal kidnapping in mind. He was outmatched in treachery, and all he and his troopers got from the ride was a moorland gallows-lift, ten miles south-west of Hawick.

At least such merciless killings could be justified by the need for law and order. Other brutalities seem to have been motivated by spiteful revenge or sadistic cruelty. One sister of Angus was burnt for conspiracy, and the husband of another was executed on the equally doubtful charge of plotting to shoot the King. The execution of Sir James Hamilton of Finnart is still inexplicable. He was the bastard son of Arran whose taunt began Cleanse-the-Causeway, and as the favoured royal architect he was responsible for splendid improvements to the palaces of Falkland, Linlithgow, Stirling and Edinburgh. He too died on a charge of intended regicide, but it has been suggested that a covetous king – who threatened childless lords into resigning their lands to the crown – wished to acquire his wealth and estates.

Law was maintained by the King's sword and by his regular circuit courts, but by his own actions he slowly isolated himself from his people and his barons. Few of the latter attended his parliament or his council as he grew older, and he depended upon the advice and support of David Beaton, nephew and successor to the archbishop of St Andrews whose life Gavin Douglas had saved in Blackfriars church. Stories of the King's greed, his scandalous lust for women, filled the reports which spies sent to England. He spent money extravagantly, upon himself, his household, favourites, palaces and regalia, and yet still amassed a fortune. The young gallant of the captivity, the Haroun al-Rashid of the wynds, became 'so sore a dread king, and so ill beloved of his subjects'. Neither King nor nation was prepared in heart or mind for the coming war with England.

Honouring his promise to protect the Holy Kirk, James was ready to take part in a Catholic crusade against England and its excommunicated king, but in 1541 the other partners in the crusade, France and the Empire, were so far lost in their own quarrels that each was asking the help of Henry against the other. With motives that are obscure, James agreed to meet Henry at York, there to discuss their theological and ecclesiastical differences. The Scots Privy Council refused to let James go, mistrusting the Englishman's motives and suspecting him of a design to kidnap their king, who had so far been unable to supply them with a living heir. They were supported by the Scottish clergy, who in their turn mistrusted James, and were worried enough by heresy among the people without encouraging it to sit by the throne. Henry waited at York until it was plain his guest was not coming, and then exploded in anger. He resurrected the ancient claim to superiority over Scotland, sent a fleet to harry its coast and ordered his northern levies over the Border into Teviotdale, where the vigorous Huntly scattered them at Haddonrig.

It was the most unpopular war ever fought against the hereditary enemy, but it was not now the memory of Flodden that made the Scots hang back from the fords across the Tweed. The barons would not fight willingly for a king who excluded them from his councils. Some of them were also sensitive to new winds from abroad, though less from conscience than from greed, and they had seen how their own kind in England were profiting from the dissolution of the monasteries. Men like Argyll and Moray, the Border lords and others, remembered too well the harsh treatment they had received, and not even a burning English reprisal for Haddonrig, in which Roxburgh and Kelso were lit by flames, could spark their courage and loyalty. The war was for France they said, and France would not help them. The first army raised would march no further than Lauder, where it disbanded itself. Another of ten thousand men, hurriedly gathered in three weeks by David Beaton, left Edinburgh in November, 1542, under the command of the King's hated favourite Oliver Sinclair.

It marched uneasily to the south-west and the Solway, and was further demoralized when James left it for Lochmaben, declaring that he would cross the sands to England when the tide ebbed. At Solway Moss on November 24, the Scots were met by three thousand Englishmen under Sir Thomas Wharton, deputy warden of the March. Although outnumbered, he boldly advanced his standards and waited for them to come up. When they were within arrow-shot, he released his horsemen on their right flank and drove them into the dank, black pools of the bog. They were killed by spear and sword, sucked down by the Moss, or drowned in flight across the Esk. Twelve hundred of them were captured, including Oliver Sinclair. The Borderers took a bitter revenge on their king, some surrendering without a fight, it was said, and others delivering his nobles to the English.

'Fie, fled Oliver?' said James, when the news was brought to him, 'Is Oliver taken? All is lost!' Sick in mind and heart, he returned to Edinburgh. He spent a week at Linlithgow, where his wife was in the last days of another pregnancy, and then went alone to his favourite palace of Falkland. There he heard of the birth of his daughter. Two sons had previously died in infancy, and he cannot have believed that this girl would survive. That is one explanation of an old story, that his only comment was that the Stewarts had come with a lass and would go with a lass. He died on December 14, from causes unknown, except a wish for death.

It is easy to think of him as an old man, but he was not yet thirty-one.

2

Patrick Hamilton died at the stake on the last day of February, 1528, outside the university of St Andrews. A winter gale blew the smoke across the faces of those who watched, and the reek of his burning, it was said, infected them all. He was not the first heretic to burn, but he was the first known Scot, a brave and steadfast young man. Born early in the century, he was the son of that bastard knight whose reckless charge began the Causeway cleansing, and was thus a nephew of the Earl of Arran and a great-grandson of James II. When still a boy, his influential kinsmen made him Abbot of Fearn in Ross-shire, but although he drew the revenues of the office he performed no duties and wore no vestments. At fifteen he took his master's degree in Paris, and went from thence to study under Erasmus at Louvain, and under Luther at Wittenberg. While at the new university of Marburg he wrote a number of theses for public debate which became known as 'Patrick's Places', and which, according to their English translator, contained the 'pith of all Divinity'. Returning to his home near Linlithgow, he preached the Lutheran word with such dangerous success that he was summoned to St Andrews for debate and interrogation. One of those ordered to reclaim his soul was Alexander Alesius, Canon of St Andrews and an able opponent of heretical doctrines. Hamilton converted him. Hoping that the young man would see the dangers ahead of him and leave the country, Archbishop James Beaton released him, but he stubbornly stayed, preaching in public until he was brought to trial and burnt.

He had never been concerned with the administrative corruption of the Church, or the scandalous immorality of its servants, but with faith and justification by faith, the heart of reforming dogma and doctrine. 'He that hath faith is just and good. . . .' 'Faith is the gift of God, it is not in our power. . . .' 'Seeing that Christ hath paid thy debt, thou needest not, neither canst thou pay it. . . .' His claim that God and Man existed in an amity by faith was interpreted by the Church to mean that a life of goodness upon earth was of no consequence, and his burning was therefore his only salvation. But his voice was heard more strongly after the February wind had blown away his ashes. John Knox said that men began to ask themselves why he had been burnt. 'And when his Articles were rehearsed . . . many began to call in doubt that which before they held for certain verity.'

At the Feast of Epiphany, twelve years later in the palace of Linlithgow, James V and his court watched the performance of a merry entertainment called *A Pleasant Satire of the Three Estates*, in which churchmen got the worst buffeting from the bladder of ridicule.

> Our Bishops, with their lovely vestments white,
> They flow in riches, royally, and delight,
> Like paradise are their palaces and places,
> And lack no pleasure from the fairest faces.
> Also, these Prelates have great prerogatives,
> For why? they may even leave their wives,
> Without any correction or damnage;
> Then take another wanton, without marriage.
> Without doubt, I would think it a pleasant life,
> Now and then, when I wanted, to part with my wife,
> Then take another of far greater beauty:
> But ever alas! my lords, that may not be.

The speaker is an unhappy character called Pauper, but the thoughts are those of Sir David Lindsay of the Mount, poet and friend of James V, and privileged thereby to be his 'correction boy' as well as his clever King of Arms. If there is a hero of the *Satire*, or one this century would take as such, it is John the Common Weal, robust man of the people, robbed of warm clothes and fair living by Church and State. He speaks out against corruption and hypocrisy, he says, because he has been overlooked, and because government 'gangs all backward'.

> As for our reverend fathers of Spirituality,
> They are led by Covetousness and careless Sensuality.
> And as ye see, Temporality has need of correction,
> Which has long been led by Public Oppression:
> Look! where the loon lies lurking at his back!

> Get up, I hope to see thy neck in a rope crack!
> Look! here is Falsehood and Deceit, well I ken,
> Leaders of the Merchants, and silly craftsmen.
> What marvel that the Three Estates backward gang?
> When such a vile company dwells them among,
> That has ruled this assembly many hard days,
> And robbed John the Common Weal of his warm claes.
> Sir, call them before you, and put them in order,
> Or John the Common Weal may beg on the Border.

The warning is clear. What honest John might beg on the English side of the Tweed would not be charity alone. Lindsay's mockery was privileged, protected by his royal friend and kept within palace walls, but it echoed a wider resentment and anger. The abuses and corruption of the Church were as easily seen by Jock-upon-Land and John the Common Weal as they were by a knightly verse-maker, and they aroused more passion than the simple doctrinal heresies of Patrick Hamilton, who served the Reformation best by becoming its early martyr. With an annual income of nearly half a million pounds, greater than the Crown's, the Church was rich and indolent, indifferent to its moral obligations and its parochial duties. Church offices had become political counters or rich rewards to be shared among the families of contending houses, and those who acquired them were frequently as capable of butchery and treachery as their lay kinsmen. Such men could not satisfy the spiritual hunger of a confused and suffering people, and the cloud of their greed still obscures the selfless dedication of their predecessors. They made treasure-houses and palaces of the wondrous buildings which earlier men had built to the glory of God, and they regarded them and their revenues as legacies to be left to a nephew or a cousin. The corruption percolated down to the lowest level. Neglected by their superiors, or set an example by the same, parish priests exacted payment for services that should have been freely given, as if the compassion of Christ were governed by some celestial price-list. John of the Common Weal groaned under the extortions of 'great fat friars, Augustinians, Carmelites, and Cordeliers . . .'

> And all others that in cowls are clad,
> Who labour not and are well fed,
> I mean, not labouring spiritually,
> Nor, for their living, corporeally:
> Lying in dens like idle dogs,
> I compare them to well-fed hogs.

Great and lesser lords whose bastards or cadet sons had no share in ecclesiastical office, and thus could not enlarge their family's wealth or importance, were encouraged by England's example to look upon the Church as a secular and rival landlord, and one that might be profitably plundered without damnation of the soul. But resentment and envy do not alone explain the Reformation. The hatred of greedy prelates, of excessive privilege and preferment, was the carrier-wave upon which rode the intellectual argument for reform. This was simply that too many men now stood between the poor sinner and his Saviour. The doctrine of justification by faith argued the amity of Man and God, without intermediaries. This was the infectious smoke of Master Hamilton's burning.

The Church tried to reform itself, or was exhorted to do so by James V, who is said to have told the clerics that if they did not change their ways he would send the proudest of them to his uncle of England. This was soon after the court performance of Lindsay's

*Satire*, and could not have been entirely coincidental, for the play ends with an imaginary Reforming Parliament, cleansing Church and State upon the orders of Rex Humanitas. Real parliamentary action, however, was designed to protect and strengthen the old faith against new teaching, prohibiting criticism of the Pope's authority, and banning discussion of the Scriptures, even in private. Rewards were also offered to informers, though they might be proven heretics themselves. Such measures, honouring the Auld Alliance as much as the Holy Church, were too late, if ever they could have been in time. The ground swell of doubt and question increased with the return of young students from the Lutheran schools of Europe, with seamen and merchants, exiles and mercenaries. For a century the Scottish Church had been able to suppress or contain the spread of Wyclif's teaching, first brought across the Border by the Lollard martyr, John Resby. For understandable reasons, the names of early Scots heretics are unknown, though one is believed to have been burnt in Glasgow fifteen years after Resby. The parliaments of James I and his successors frequently legislated against the doctrines of the Hussites and the Lollards, so their presence must have been felt and feared, but little is heard of them until the reign of James IV, when an Ayrshire man, Murdoch Nisbet, translated Wyclif's Bible into Scots. The King was tolerant of the Lollards, and admired their courage. When thirty of them were brought before him, and asked if they would burn their writings as the Archbishop of Glasgow demanded, their leader replied 'Sir, the Bishop if ye will.' Amused, James let them go, but the Governors of the country during his son's minority were less tolerant, and banned the importation of 'books or works of the great heretic Luther'. Restrictive laws are made to be broken, and it has been said that many of the men who fought, or refused to fight, at Solway Moss were Protestants, and that the English cynically released their prisoners to foment the growth of heresy in the south-west.

In the years between Hamilton's death and the Epiphany entertainment at Linlithgow there was a steady passage of young scholars from Scotland to the universities of Germany and Scandinavia. When they returned they were more militant than Hamilton had been, rejecting the Church of Rome, insisting that the old fabric must be shattered and another house of God built upon the ruins. This new Church was envisaged in George Wishart's *Confession of the Faith of the Switzerlands*, acknowledging Christ only as its head, limiting the sacraments to baptism and communion, and arguing that civil authority was obliged to defend the true religion. Wishart was a tiresome but zealous dogmatist, a politician more than a theologian, and a man of great courage. He was the son of an Angus laird, a student of St Andrews who became a teacher in Montrose. Threatened with a charge of heresy in 1535, he went to England, where he worked under Hugh Latimer, and then to Basle and Zürich. He returned to Scotland in 1543 or 1544, a follower of the Swiss Reformers who had been disowned by Luther. For two years he preached to large congregations in Dundee, Ayr and Lothian, supported by the gentry as well as the commonalty, and sometimes protected by a great two-handed sword carried by an ecclesiastical notary called John Knox. It is not clear whether Wishart was involved in a plot to assassinate the Cardinal-Archbishop of St Andrews, David Beaton, but early in 1546 he was taken up on Beaton's orders. He went willingly toward his arrest, elated by the thought of martyrdom, and telling Knox to put aside that sword. 'No, no, return to your bairns, and God bless you. One is enough for sacrifice.' He was first strangled and then burnt before the castle of St Andrews. Beaton watched unmoved, said Knox, even when the strangler asked for forgiveness and was kissed on the cheek by his victim.

*George Wishart had a profound influence on John Knox, who carried a great sword to protect him when he preached. Wishart's burning led to the murder of Cardinal-Archbishop David Beaton (right), the strong voice of Catholicism. Knox said his murder was a 'godly act'.*

Three months later a party of the martyr's supporters, led by Fifeshire lairds whose intent was more political than vengeful, stormed the castle and murdered Beaton in his chamber. He died crying 'I am a priest!', which in the view of some who stabbed at his body was an incitement to murder not an obstacle. Knox said it was a 'godly act', insinuating that Beaton had been the Queen's lover, and that both had poisoned the King after Solway Moss. The murderers and their followers held the castle for a year, alternating between riotous licence and penitent sorrow, making their stronghold a centre for religious discontent and political disaffection. Lindsay of the Mount visited them, from curiosity or for security now that his royal protector was dead, and he probably expressed a general opinion when he said that although Beaton had deserved to die, the deed had been foully done. Knox arrived at Easter in 1547, released from doubt and obscurity by the death of Wishart, set upon his reforming course and preaching in public for the first time. The Pope was the Man of Sin, and the Roman Church was the Synagogue of Satan, the Whore of Babylon, but the true Church now emerging was founded upon the Word of God. He was forty-two and had been reborn in the ashes of Wishart's fire, in the blood of Cardinal Beaton. He encouraged the defenders of the castle to believe that their English companions in faith, who had already sent money and provisions, would soon send an army as well, but what came instead was an attack by a French fleet. Knox's confident prophecies of victory were changed overnight into gloomy forecasts of defeat, and for once he was right. The castle surrendered, and the prophet went to the penal oar of a French galley.

It would be eight years before he returned to Scotland, his body and spirit hardened by imprisonment and exile. Chained to his oar at Rouen, and later in England and Geneva, he became convinced that he was destined for greatness. 'God loveth us,' he wrote from the galleys, 'because we are His own handiwork', and it is difficult to avoid the belief that he regarded himself as cast from an exclusive divine mould. Released from the oar, he went to England, where he became a chaplain to Edward VI, fleeing to Switzerland upon the accession of that 'cursed Jezebel', Mary I. He published six resounding tracts upon the religious controversies of his homeland, and one of them at least, the *First Blast of the Trumpet against the Monstrous Regiment of Women*, invites Freudian analysis. Although it was aimed particularly at Mary Tudor and Mary of Guise it also chilled the sympathy of Elizabeth I, since she could scarcely agree that the rule of a woman was abominable before God.

*The tragic protagonists, granddaughter and great-granddaughter of Henry VII: Elizabeth I as seen by Isaac Oliver, and Mary Queen of Scots by Hieronymus Cock, engraved in 1559 before her return to Scotland.*

Knox was never the leader of his country or its reform movement, and throughout his lifetime was always the centre of argument and dispute. He was a noisy rabble-rouser, advocating war and murder, and exulting in the death of those he hated. Drunk with self-righteous passion, and demented by the influence he had upon the emotions of simple men, he was responsible for much of the blood and bigotry of the Church he helped to create. But revolutions are not made by saints, injustice is frequently over-thrown by unreason, and the man who breaks down a door to the future rarely furnishes the room beyond. A definitive judgment upon this crazed and creative creature is almost impossible, for the records of him are largely of his own writing, and what is reasonable in his voice is drowned by the polemical violence of his words. Yet he influenced the history of Scotland more than any man of his time, perhaps, and by the strength of his defiance gave other and better men the courage of their convictions.

## 3

After the death of the wretched, self-pitying Goodman of Ballengiech there was an inevitable squabble over the royal cradle. Archbishop David Beaton and the Earl of Arran competed for the regency, the one standing for the French alliance and the Church of Rome, the other sympathetic to English interests and the new faith. The hatred between them was deep and personal, and went beyond the real or imagined testament of a dying king. Arran's name headed Beaton's list of heretics, and the Earl once threatened the churchman with a drawn sword. Henry VIII could not ignore such an opportunity, and early in 1543 the Red Douglas of Angus, an exile in England for fifteen years, came home with ten lords who had been taken prisoner at Solway Moss. Their freedom was a favour from the English king, and he had further bribed them to secure an alliance with him and the marriage of their infant queen to his son Edward. The balance of power thus fell to Arran, himself heir presumptive to the throne, and within a fortnight he and the Douglases arrested and imprisoned 'that false trumping carle' Beaton. A March parliament declared Arran to be Governor of Scotland, and by the Treaty of Greenwich in July it was agreed that Mary would marry the Prince of Wales at the end of her tenth year, and that peace between the kingdoms would last until a year after the death of either. The same parliament, despite the protests of its ecclesiastical estate, also granted all men the right to read and possess the Scriptures in English.

But in less than three months the wind changed. Letters from Beaton in prison brought a number of his supporters home from France, to ferment the hostility against the English and Arran. Two of these returning exiles were particularly influential. John Hamilton, Abbot of Paisley and Arran's bastard half-brother, was ambitious and persuasive, and upon Beaton's promise of preferment he convinced Arran that were it not for the English alliance it might be possible to arrange a marriage between the Queen and the Earl's son. The presence of the second man was argument enough. The young Earl of Lennox, Matthew Stewart, was a descendant of James II and the son-in-law of Angus by James IV's much-married widow. There was a doubt about Arran's legitimacy by his father's second marriage, and the Abbot of Paisley no doubt reminded him that if Beaton used his authority to declare it invalid then Lennox would stand next in succession. Against such pressures, and growing rumours that he had sold his queen and the kingdom to the English, Arran wavered and then submitted. A week after the Treaty of Greenwich was ratified, he re-entered the Roman Church and did penance for his apostasy, released Beaton and made him and the Queen Mother members of the regency council. In December, when Beaton became Chancellor, a subservient parliament obediently stood upon its head and annulled the Treaty, restored the French alliance, and renewed the laws against heresy.

Henry could blame his own conceit as much as Arran's weak will for this change in affairs. With bold arrogance he had demanded the custody of the Queen and the crown of Scotland in the event of her death, antagonizing the Scots by this old claim to superiority. His response to the annulment of the Treaty was also in character. In May, 1544, an English armada appeared in the Firth of Forth, and when they saw it from the walls of Edinburgh Castle both Beaton and Arran decided that it was a fishing-fleet home from Iceland. The citizens of Leith were equally naive, and were at their Sunday dinner when the English stormed into their streets under the Earl of Hertford. On the following day the fierce and ambitious Seymour was inside Edinburgh, burning its fine houses from the Cannongate to within arrow-shot of its castle walls. This was the beginning of Henry's 'Rough Wooing', and he had given thorough instructions on how his son's courtship was to be conducted. Edinburgh was to be put to fire and sword, so that there might 'remain for ever a perpetual memory of the vengeance of God lighted upon them for their falsehood and disloyalty'. Where there was resistance, men and women and children were to be killed. The palace of Holyrood was to be sacked and burnt, and the towns and villages of Fife to be destroyed, particularly the cardinal's town of St Andrews, where not one stick or stone was to be left upon another, no creature left alive.

Not all of these loving orders were executed, but while Hertford's troopers were devastating the Stirling plain and making a 'jolly fire' of Holyrood, another English army crossed the Tweed and burnt the wondrous abbey of Jedburgh. The Seymour then went home, but the courtship was reopened with the beginning of another year, although this time the invading English were faced by an unexpected opponent – the Earl of Angus who had been their ally in the previous campaign. He is said to have changed his mind and loyalties when his southern friends desecrated the graves of his family at Melrose, but whatever the cause he now met them and defeated them in a February fog on Ancrum Moor. Another Douglas warned the English king that he could never win Scotland by 'killing women and young children', but he sent Hertford north again in the autumn. Scotsmen once more helped him in the butchery of their country. Clan Donald swore allegiance to him, raised the old claim of the Lordship of the Isles, and would have come in fury from the glens had not the death of Donald Dubh robbed the claim of its principal. Jealous now of Arran and David Beaton, Lennox also became Henry's man, raiding the isles of Bute and Arran, the coast of Argyll, with the help of Macleans and Macleods. Once across the Border, Hertford was even more energetic, and his report to his king reads like the boasting of a demolition contractor. Five market towns destroyed, seven monasteries burned, two hundred and forty-three villages, four abbeys, sixteen keeps, fields, barns, windmills . . . And the unmentioned dead who lay in their ruins.

Such lusty, brutal marriage-broking could win no bride, but it increased Beaton's suppression of heresy, and thereby united all those who yearned for a new faith. Their only support could come from England, and the struggle now moved from the campaign field to secret chambers of conspiracy. George Wishart, that 'notable instrument of God' according to Knox, was believed to be the tool of England as well, and his judicial strangulation was less of a glorious martyrdom than a squalid political execution. The lairds who murdered Beaton three months later may have claimed they did so in revenge for Wishart, to remove an 'obstinate enemy against Christ Jesus', but behind their bloody knives was the royal paymaster of England. The death of Beaton, and of Henry VIII in January, 1547, stimulated the French to action, but the expedition they sent was asked to leave after it had taken the castle of St Andrews from its Protestant defenders. When they were gone, eighteen thousand Englishmen came over the Border under Hertford, now Duke of Somerset and Protector of England by his own making. Six thousand of them were cavalry, and eight hundred of the foot were musketeers. There were fifteen pieces of heavy artillery, a thousand wagons, and an attendant fleet tacking up the coast. The return of an old and terrible enemy brought a brief and defiant unity to the Scots, and even Angus stepped out of character again to fight for his country. Arran was able to muster a larger army than his opponent, and on Black Saturday, September 10, he formed a battle-line of four divisions at Pinkie, six miles to the east of Edinburgh.

When Somerset first saw the Scots they held a strong position on high ground, their glittering spears 'like four great fields of ripe barley'. They had no musketeers, only Highland archers from Argyll, but on their right flank to the south was a marsh, on their left was the Firth of Forth, and to their front was the little River Esk. Somerset is said to have offered to withdraw if the Scots would agree to let their Queen choose her own husband when she was old enough. Or perhaps this was an encouraging lie spread by Arran, for it was proudly refused. Pride was again the greatest enemy of the Scots and would lead them to their own destruction. In five hundred years the number of decisive battles they had won against the English could be counted on one hand, leaving a finger or two to wag in caution. Pride and over-confidence had lost them the rest, and it would be so again.

The fight began when English ships moved in to the mouth of the Esk, and at long range so galled the Scottish left with a cannonade that the Argyll archers scattered from it. Somerset then sent his horse to occupy a ridge on the right, and the Earl of Angus boldly left his position of strength with eight thousand men to secure it first. The Scots lost the race, and in the autumn rain the English cavalry came down the ridge upon them. They formed their ancient spear-rings and held the horsemen for a desperate while, but as the superior bill-hook had destroyed their fathers at Flodden, so they were now cut down by English guns and English musketeers. When Somerset's cavalry charged again, the men of Angus broke. In the crying panic of their retreat, the increased thunder of guns and the advance of English infantry, the Argyll clans turned and ran, soon followed by the rest of Arran's army. They threw away their weapons and their armour, but were overtaken by an exulting enemy. Ten thousand died in the rout, nobles, lairds and common men, drowned in the Esk or slaughtered like sheep in the paralysis of fear. They had marched to battle under the banner of the Holy Church Supplicating Christ. It was dragged from beneath the bodies of the priests who had defended it, and was sent to a sickly boy-king in England.

Somerset occupied Leith, ravaged the abbey of Holyrood again and sent his fleet to bombard Dundee, but he was weakly unable to exploit his victory, or persuade the Scots that he wished only to 'forward the godly purpose of the marriage'. He established garrisons where he could, the most powerful at Haddington sixteen miles to the east of Edinburgh, and then returned to pressing problems in England, not the least being the troublesome behaviour of his fraternal vice-regent Thomas Seymour. Torn by schismatic hatreds, and numbed by the losses of Pinkie, Scotland could not alone drive out the English. From her refuge on the island of Inchmahome in the Lake of Menteith, where she had taken her child, the Queen Mother appealed to France. A formidable response arrived in July, 1548, some seven thousand French, German and Italian veterans, but they came to bargain before they would fight. A Scots army was in camp outside Haddington, ineffectually besieging its English garrison, and there a treaty was signed by which the French promised to fight for Scotland and the Scots agreed to send their queen to Paris, as a bride for the Dauphin when both were old enough. When she arrived, a few weeks later, Henry II capered with happiness and announced that France and Scotland were now one country, which was not quite what the Scots had intended. Nor would they have been pleased to know that some Frenchmen, inspired by the proposed union of these young innocents, described it as the suffocation of the lion of Scotland under a field of lilies. Though overblown, the metaphor was apt. When the marriage took place, ten years later, public promises to preserve the laws and liberties of Scotland obscured a private agreement by which Mary bequeathed her kingdom, and her rights to that of England, to her husband should she die childless.

The war was ended by the Treaty of Boulogne in 1549, and the English withdrew from Scotland, their rough wooing at last abandoned. But the French army remained for another eight years, hated and distrusted but protecting the Catholic party in power, and by that the interests of Henry II. Arran's half-brother John Hamilton, now Archbishop of St Andrews, was more subtle than his murdered predecessor, and by the introduction of a Catechism in Scots tried to reach a disarming compromise with many of the propositions of the new faith, even to meeting in part the Lutheran declarations on justification by faith. As before, such efforts were too late, and his attempts to remove corruption and ignorance among the clergy only emphasized their existence. In 1554, when the distant Queen in her doll's-house court reached her twelfth year, French jurists argued that she had now come of age and could govern Scotland through a delegate of her own choice. The Scots Parliament formally transferred the regency to that inevitable delegate, the Queen Mother. The Earl of Arran, who had already been given the French dukedom of Châtelherault, was now forced by threats and bribes to accept his loss of office with unprotesting grace.

*When Edward Seymour, Duke of Somerset and Protector of England, won a decisive victory over the Scots at Pinkie in 1547, the boy king Edward VI wrote him this letter of thanks.*

Mary of Guise was a courageous and charming woman, and her broken English was pretty to hear. But she was French, the officers of her household were French, and the foreign mercenaries who abused and outraged the citizens of the burghs had been sent by the French. For a while, from good will or because she did not wish to provoke open hostility to her countrymen, the young Regent tolerated members of the new faith, and granted English Protestants a refuge from the Smithfield fires of their new and Catholic monarch, Mary I. Scots exiles also came home from England and Geneva, and by their evangelical zeal the new faith grew stronger in the south-west and east. A revolution gathers impetus from the tolerance of its enemies, it is not braked by conciliation. Many lords and gentlemen now kept preachers openly in their houses, and talked guardedly of their readiness to 'jeopard lives and goods in the forward setting of the glory of God'.

John Knox was permitted to return from Switzerland in the autumn of 1555, and on his way at Berwick he married the strangely colourless Marjory Bowes. His reception in Scotland astonished him, and he was moved by the 'thirst of our brethren, night and day sobbing and groaning for the bread of life'. In Edinburgh he was surrounded by an adoring regiment of women, and he preached to private congregations in great houses, fervently sounding the 'auld trumpet'. He also had less spiritual talks with powerful men like the Earl of Argyll and Lord James Stewart, the bastard son of James V, but he received no reply to the letter of thundering remonstrance he sent to the Queen Mother. When he was summoned to Blackfriars Church to answer charges of heresy, the company of Protestant gentlemen he brought with him so cowed the Catholics that the summons was withdrawn. God's voice called him back to Geneva in July, 1556, and when he was gone his enemies burnt him in effigy.

In the following spring some Scots lords invited him to return, for they were now ready to establish the Glory of God, but at Dieppe a letter from a friend warned him that these gentlemen had lost their courage and would disown him. He stayed where he was, bombarding Scotland with sulphurous epistles and writing his *First Blast of the Trumpet*. He was exalted when he heard that a September mob in Edinburgh had taken the image of St Giles from the cathedral, ducked it in the Nor' Loch and then burnt it.

His friend had been over-cautious perhaps, the political and religious revolt had begun, and in December, 1557, it stepped out of the private chamber of conspiracy. Calling themselves the Congregation of Jesus Christ, five lords signed a covenant binding themselves to 'apply our whole power, substance and very lives to maintain and forward and establish the most blessed Word of God'. By the new year their numbers had increased and they were a powerful political party, inspired by that divine word or by a hunger for the rich lands of the Church. At first moderate, they asked for the Book of Common Prayer to be read on Sundays and saints' days, and for preaching to be allowed in private houses until public services could be legally approved.

Many preachers, however, would not wait for the law, and incited or led their wayside congregations in a riot of image-breaking and priest-baiting. When the Queen Mother ordered the Provost of Perth to restore order in his town, to return its people to the Church, she was told that he 'could make their bodies come to Her Grace, but not their consciences'. The old Earl of Argyll warned Hamilton not to provoke the mob, but the advice was ignored, and in the last week of April, perhaps on the same day that Mary was married to the Dauphin in the cathedral of Notre Dame, a harmless old priest was burnt for heresy at St Andrews. In the summer rioting that followed this spiteful act, many of the preachers were summoned before the Regent at Edinburgh. They came as Knox had come, with an armed guard of Protestant gentry, and one of these lairds boldly told the Queen Mother what they thought of her prelates. 'They oppress us and our tenants for feeding of their idle bellies; they trouble our preachers, and would murder them and us. Shall we suffer this any longer? No, Madam, it shall not be!' She told them to love their neighbours, and let them go. Five weeks later the love of the Edinburgh mob again exploded upon a priestly procession for the Feast of St Giles. There was no bloodshed, but the Bishop of Galloway died of shock, and a new image of the saint, replacing that burnt a year before, was broken on the cobbles.

The Lords of the Congregation deplored the behaviour of the mob, but took advantage of its temper to present the Regent with their grievances, complaining of ungodly and dissolute priests, and asking for the Sacraments to be administered and prayers said in English. If there were tumult and disorder, the responsibility was hers. Toward the end of the year the hearts of the true congregation were uplifted by the death of Mary Tudor. Under her successor, Elizabeth, the Reformation was re-established in England, and the Protestants of Scotland could once more hope for its sympathy and aid.

In the spring of 1559 the Queen Mother abandoned conciliation, and on the probable insistence of France she attempted to crush the new faith, demanding that its preachers appear before her in obedience to the Church. Those who would not submit were to be banished, though they preached as well as St Paul himself. None came, and she outlawed them all. At this moment John Knox returned. 'I see the battle shall be great,' he wrote to one of his women friends, 'for Satan rageth even to the uttermost; and I am come (I praise my God) even in the brunt of the battle.' Proclaimed a rebel with the rest, he fled across the Forth and sounded the old trumpet again to hysterical congregations. His Mosaic appearance and electric voice, his oblique call for armed resistance, were irresistible. While he was preaching against idolatry at Perth, a fatuous but courageous priest went to the altar to celebrate Mass. A boy threw a stone at him, and the riot which followed lasted for two days. Two monasteries and an abbey were gutted, stripped of gold, silver and lead, meat and wine, linen and furniture. Their images were burnt, their trees pulled up, and their brethren threatened with death. With this, the civil war began.

The Queen Mother summoned what forces she could under Argyll, Lord James Stewart and the Hamiltons, and marched toward Perth on May 22. The Lords of the Congregation gathered their army, and instructed Knox to write four letters: to the Regent, the French, the nobility, and the Catholic clergy. The first protested loyalty and asked for religious freedom, but to the clergy, to the 'generation of Anti-Christ, pestilential prelates and their shavelings', Knox bluntly explained what was intended. 'We shall begin that same war which God commanded Israel to execute against the Canaanites, that is, contract of peace shall never be made till ye desist from your open idolatry and cruel persecution of God's children.' To illustrate what was meant, the Army of the Congregation occupied St Andrews and sacked its cathedral.

Argyll and Stewart were more in sympathy with the Congregation than with the Regent, and they first drew their army back and then deserted it. The Queen Mother led it further back to Edinburgh and then to Dunbar, while the Israelites sacked friaries, despoiled churches, and occupied the capital. They held it until the close of the year, boldly deposing the Regent and setting up a Great Council in the name of her daughter,

*Persecution was the weapon of both religious parties. The re-establishment of the Reformation in England under Elizabeth – with the arrest of Catholics as shown here – alarmed their co-religionists in Scotland and heartened the Reformers.*

but although she was slowly and painfully dying of dropsy her courage was greater than their revolutionary zeal. She held Dunbar until reinforcements arrived from France and took the town of Leith, fortifying it and stubbornly withstanding assault. Now the Army of the Congregation discovered the difference between a soldier's life and a pulpit war, and it abandoned Edinburgh Castle to the Regent. Scattered to the west, it would have been destroyed by desertion and despair but for the intervention of the English.

Upon the accession of Elizabeth, the arms of England had been insultingly quartered with those of Mary and the Dauphin in Paris, a none too subtle reference to her alleged bastardy as well as a threat to her throne. Since then English money had been coming across the Border to the Reformers, under the direction of her first minister William Cecil, but she had promised no military aid. The arrival of French reinforcements now made it essential. In January, 1560, an English fleet dropped anchor in the Firth of Forth, blockading the French ships and French garrison at Leith. In February, a treaty of mutual assistance was signed at Berwick between England and the Lords of the Congregation. Knox was to have been an emissary to this meeting, but at the last moment it was realized that his views on the monstrous rule of women might not endear him to the servants of an English queen. He was replaced by William Maitland of Lethington, a bland and devious young man who had once been secretary to the Queen Mother, and whose future nickname of Michael Wily would be a felicitous corruption of Machiavelli. By the terms of the Treaty, an English army entered Scotland in April, joined with the Host of Christ and besieged the garrison of Leith.

The French fought well on their crumbling walls, and in their murderous sallies. On May Day they draped their defences with gallant garlands, and killed a thousand Englishmen in the furious assault that followed. The English did most of the fighting, and like others before them they discovered that the Scots had little charity or liking for allies. 'We are so well-esteemed,' said one bitterly, 'that all our poor hurt men are fain to lie in the streets, and can get no house-room for money.' Most of the Israelites held back from this bloody struggle between Catholic French and Protestant English, and the Duke of Norfolk was forced to ask for money and reinforcements from England. The reinforcements were to replace the desertions among his own men, and the money was to pay the Scots to fight beside them.

Two miles away in Edinburgh Castle, Mary of Guise listened to the sound of gunfire. Her body was now gross and swollen from the dropsy, yet her spirit endured the terrible pain until she died on June 11. John Knox rejoiced to hear the news, wildly declaring that she had exulted over the Protestant dead before Leith, and that thereafter 'began her belly and loathsome legs to swell, and so continued till God did execute His judgement upon her'. His great hatreds were never spoilt by small compassions. The obscene agony of the Regent's death, and the empty cause it left, took the spirit from the garrison of Leith, and even before she died the envoys of France and England were discussing peace at Newcastle. Now there was an armistice, and English and French gentlemen dined together amicably on ground where they had recently fought, though Norfolk's officers may not have accepted the roasted rat and the horse-pie which their guests brought to the dinner.

By the Treaty of Edinburgh in July, 1560, it was agreed that English and French troops should leave Scotland, that there should be peace between the countries, that Mary and Francis should abandon the title and arms of the Crown of England, and that Elizabeth should be recognized as queen. The Auld Alliance came to an end here, in the blood of Leith sands, never to have a reality again. To both partners it had rarely been more than a union of convenience, although for Scotland it was sometimes a matter of bitter survival. To the French it was always a political counter in the interminable wars, and they might have agreed with Shakespeare's arrogant reference to the 'weasel Scot', raiding the nest when the eagle England was in prey. Until 1789 France would be an asylum for Scots refugees of the old faith. The Auld Alliance would be kept alive in Jacobite emotion, and four centuries after the surrender at Leith its ludicrous survival would be seen on the backs of automobiles.

The Army of the Congregation of Christ was triumphant in victory. Lindsay of the Mount was dead, but the Reformation Parliament he had foreseen in his *Satire* became a reality. Meeting at Edinburgh in August, it repudiated the supremacy of the Pope, forbade the celebration of the Latin Mass, and approved a Confession of Faith. There was no compromise like the English Act of Supremacy, by which the Crown assumed privileges and rights previously held by the Pope. The umbilical tie with Rome was cut, and the new Kirk of Scotland was born. Drawn up by ministers and engrossed in the register of parliament, the twenty-five articles of the Confession were a full statement of Protestant doctrine and dogma, following the guide-lines of its Swiss model and defining the true Church as that made manifest by the proper ministry and preaching of the Word of God, the limitation of the Sacraments to Baptism and Communion, and the government of ecclesiastical discipline. Truth was to be found in the Scriptures alone, and understanding of that truth was given by the Spirit of God. 'The doctrine taught in our Kirks is contained in the written word of God . . . in which we affirm that all things necessary to be believed for the salvation of mankind are sufficiently expressed.'

Yet the enactment of the Reformation was less than Knox and other extremists had desired. Priests and prelates of the old Church were left in the benefices, and their revenues were largely untouched. Though Parliament accepted the Confession of Faith it declined the Book of Discipline, a plan for the establishment of the new Kirk and its endowment with the wealth of the old. Sanctioned by the General Assembly of the Kirk in December, 1560, the Book was drafted by Knox and his fellow-ministers, the tablets which they brought down from the mountain of their exultation. Though it was as yet theoretical, and was designed as an ecclesiastical rule-book, it was also a political document of immense potency. Harsh and authoritarian, arbitrary and uncompromising, it was none the less concerned with the dignity of man and his equality before God. Church and people were to be united by mutual consent. Ministers were to be elected by the congregations they served, after exhaustive examination of their fitness and character. To assist them in their work, elders would be annually elected from the congregation, 'men of best knowledge in God's word, of cleanest life, faithful men', together with a deacon for the collection of revenues. There were to be no bishops, only Superintendents, each responsible for one of ten districts which roughly corresponded to the medieval dioceses, but care should be taken in their selection so that they did not resemble 'yon idle Bishops heretofore'. They were to work with ministers and congregations in their districts, and to spend no more than three or four months of the year at home in their principal towns. They too were to be chosen by election, by 'the consent of as many of the people as possible'. These ministers and officers of the Kirk were also to be courts of justice and punishment. The State should deal with the capital crimes of blasphemy, adultery, perjury and murder, but the Kirk must be responsible for punishing fornication and drunkenness, ostentation, brawling, wanton conduct and swearing. Excommunication for persistent offenders was to be harsh, and amounted to complete spiritual and social ostracism.

The Book of Discipline dealt at length with the need for a compulsory education system, designed to give the Kirk its ministers and the nation its officers, as well as making learning and wisdom freely available to all men. In every parish there should be a schoolmaster, able at least to teach Latin and grammar. In small and remote parishes, where such a man might not be available, the minister or reader of the kirk was to give this elementary instruction, and religious teaching was to be the basis of all secular learning. In large towns there should be colleges for Latin and Greek, Logic and Rhetoric. The curricula of the universities were to be revised, and extended to include divinity, law and medicine. Their students should come from all classes, and bursaries should be provided for those in poverty. Every man was to read the Bible, and every householder was to make certain that his family and his dependants were properly instructed in the Scriptures.

Less would come of all this than was hoped, or from a second and more successful Book of Discipline in 1578. Grand though the design was, in its vision of democracy and responsible authority, like all revolutionary manifestoes it also contained the seeds of bigotry and intolerance, which would in time flower in the righteous slaughter of women and children, and the justification of murder by faith.

4

The Queen of Scots came home in August, 1561, brought to Leith by a French galley. She was eighteen and a widow, her husband the King of France having died eight months

*The death of Henry II brought the crown of France to Francis and his wife Mary. In this woodcut of Henry's deathbed the recognizable profile of the girl by the right-hand bedpost clearly supports the belief that it is Mary Queen of Scots.*

before, perishing (said Knox) of a deaf and rotten ear that would never hear the Word of God. By the standards of her time she was beautiful, taller than most men, copper-haired, swan-necked and graceful, and her hazel eyes were heavy-lidded and sensual. The six years of her rule are among the most theatrical in Scotland's history, a Spanish tragedy of blood and passion, but it is also possible to see them as an entr'acte only, a pause between events of greater drama. She came upon her own prompting, and her return was perhaps unwelcome to most of her people, although when they heard of her intention some Catholic lords and bishops advised her to land in the north, where twenty thousand men would march to restore the old Church. No regent had replaced Mary of Guise, and government, such as it was, was in the hands of two principal lords of the Congregation, the Duke of Châtelherault and the Queen's handsome half-brother James Stewart, with Maitland of Lethington as their secretary. Neither lord can have expected or hoped for her return, for one had Hamilton claims to the throne, and the other could not forget that only the thickness of a blanket kept him from it.

Because Mary had refused to ratify the Treaty of Edinburgh she had been allowed no passage through England, and English ships took care that she did not land in the Catholic north of their country. The thick fog which covered the Forth upon her arrival was the frown of God, according to Knox, 'and did manifestly speak what comfort was brought unto this country with her, to wit, sorrow, dolour, darkness and all impiety'. She cannot have been cheered by the five hundred loyal subjects who stood below her window that first night in Holyrood, welcoming her with psalms and ill-tuned fiddles. They presented her with a bible bound in purple velvet, and but for the Earl of Huntly they would have entertained her with the burning of a priest in effigy. When she attended Mass on the following Sunday there was a riot, in which the priest was almost murdered. The Mass, John Knox had said, was more fearful than ten thousand armed enemies, and most people of the Lowlands – those who were noisy about the matter at least – agreed with him. Mary was uninvited, a Catholic, French-bred and scarcely able to speak the language of the country, though her Scots was eventually better than her English. She was too beautiful, too foreign, and if John Knox would not say that she was herself a whore, there was no doubt that she had been educated by whoremongers and incestuous profligates. But the flourish of his canonical sleeves should not hide the fires of joy that were also lit for her arrival, or the amiable crowds who cheered her on the Leith road.

Mary was Queen of Scots but they were not the only subjects she claimed, their palaces were cold ante-rooms in which she must wait until her right to the throne of England was realised. In temperament and looks she was perhaps more Tudor than Stewart, a surname which misspelling or French spelling soon changed for ever into Stuart. To have once been the declared Queen of France, England and Scotland, and to become the queen of one alone, the least gratifying of the three, was distasteful and unacceptable. Catholic England looked to her, its support stronger than what she might expect from a France torn by wars of religion, and both now and for the rest of her life she was a threat to the life and crown of Elizabeth. Her devotion to the old Church was constant, strengthened by a fear of being abandoned by the Catholic princes of Europe, but in the main she did not favour her co-religionists above those of the reformed faith, nor let them unduly influence what she believed to be her royal duty.

The godly were less tolerant of her. Light-footed dancing and merry music at Holyrood were thunderously condemned in St Giles, and that spiritual meteorologist Knox was ready to see divine disapproval in every rain-cloud. She went half-way to meet him, no great a step since he was approaching the throne of his own volition, and they had four wearisome meetings in which his menacing rhetoric was less remarkable than her forbearance. His arguments were as heavy with scriptural justifications as hers were light with cunning innocence, but they spoke across a deep schism and through the smoke of martyrs. Her simple claim for the inviolability of princes, put in the form of a question, was answered ominously.

> If princes exceed their bounds, madam, no doubt they may be resisted, even by power. For no greater power or greater obedience is to be given to kings and princes than God has commanded to be given to father and mother. But the father may be struck with a frenzy in which he would slay his children. Now, madam, if the children arise, join together, apprehend the father, take the sword from him, bind his hands and keep him in prison till the frenzy be over, think you, madam, that the children do any wrong? Even so, madam, it is with princes that would murder the children of God that are subject unto them.

The analogy was monstrous, and she could not answer it directly. She said that her subjects must plainly obey Master Knox and not her. God forbid, he said, but kings should be foster-fathers to the Kirk, and queens nurses to God's people. When she said that she would not nourish his Church, that she would defend the true Church of Rome, his angry answer was full of the gutter-passion of the time.

> Your will, madam, is no reason! Neither doth your thought make that Roman harlot to be the true and immaculate spouse of Jesus Christ. And wonder not, madam, that I call Rome a harlot, for that Church is altogether polluted with all kinds of spiritual fornication.

She wept at their last meeting, and he seems to have been moved by her tears, but he told her that he was willing to endure them rather than 'hurt my conscience or betray my commonwealth through my silence'. It would be wrong to see him only as a violent and pathological old man bullying a beautiful young woman. However intemperate his language, he was speaking for a virile and emergent faith, challenging both spiritual and temporal injustice. He may have thought himself a member of God's Privy Council, as the English ambassador suggested, but the political application of his religious premises is now the substance of democracy, and although the backward-looking eye is more sympathetic to the brave woman who met him on the level of his own dialectic, time has perhaps resolved their long-dead dispute in his favour. The songs remember Mary and her descendants with melancholy regret, but they are sung in schools which the Reformers wished to give to the people.

She ruled with caution in the early years, restrained by her half-brother, now Earl of Moray, and by Maitland, who became her secretary as he had been her mother's. In the naive belief that her own freedom of worship might thereby be unmolested, she was persuaded to meet some of the demands of the Reformers, though she was stubbornly determined to bring Knox to trial for treason if she could. Her Privy Council declared that a third of the revenues from the old benefices would be divided between the Reformed Kirk and the Crown (between God and the Devil, said Knox, correctly prophesying that God would get little of His share), and she also agreed, no doubt with anguish, to the trial of forty-eight clerics who had publicly celebrated Mass. She joined her half-brother in a campaign against the rebellious Gordons of Huntly, the most powerful Catholic family in Scotland, and one that would have fought for her and the faith had she asked it. Dressed in green and silver, she charmed the Highland lairds, flattering them by her wish to have been born a man. The Earl of Huntly died of apoplexy during a hopeless battle, but she watched the clumsy beheading of one of his sons.

The most immediate and important problem was her marriage and the disposition of her body, an attempted assault on which had already cost one of her French followers his life. Protestant and Catholic Europe, fighting their wars of religion from the Low Countries to the Mediterranean, were anxious to find her a second husband, to secure her neutrality or her alliance. With more cunning than generosity, Elizabeth of England offered her discredited favourite Robert Dudley, Earl of Leicester, hinting that she might make Mary her heir if this probable wife-murderer were accepted. He was not, and after a year of diplomatic chess the Queen made her own feminine choice upon infatuated impulse. Late in 1564 she permitted the return from exile of the Catholic Stewarts of Lennox. Elizabeth persuaded Mary to recall them, from motives that are as puzzling as they are conjectural, and however they are interpreted no answer seems favourable to England. Matthew, the earl, had supported the Rough Wooing, for which he had been attainted in Scotland, but he had also been imprisoned in England on suspicion of a Catholic plot. He was descended from James II, and his formidable and ambitious wife, Margaret Douglas, was a daughter of the Earl of Angus and James IV's lustful Tudor widow. These claims upon the thrones of Scotland and England were united in their slender and exquisite son Henry, Lord Darnley. He was nineteen, childish and petulant, vain and stupid, and it is difficult to find anything in his miserably short life that excites much more than pity or distaste. But Mary thought he was the 'lustiest and best proportionit lang man' she had ever seen, and as she nursed him through an attack of measles at Stirling she fell passionately and foolishly in love with him.

*Henry Stewart, Lord Darnley, was at this time seventeen, within three years of his marriage and five of his violent death. The child is his brother Charles, later the sixth Earl of Lennox.*

THES BE THE SONES OF TE RIGHT HONERABLES TERLLE OF LENOXE AD
TE LADY MARGARETZ GRACE COVNTYES OF LENOXE AD ANGWYSE.

1563

CHARLLES STEWARDE          HENRY STEWARDE LORD DAR
HIS BROTHER ÆTATIS 6       LEY AND DOWGLAS ÆTATIS 17

Their propinquity set aside by papal decree, they were married six months later on July 29, 1565, in the chapel at Holyrood. Nobody was enthusiastic, except the young lovers and the groom's family. When the Queen's heralds declared that her husband should be named and styled King, only Lennox cried 'God save his Grace!' The Duke of Châtelherault, who was descended from the same daughter of James II as Lennox, knew that the marriage ended the Hamiltons' hopes of the throne, hopes which had been worn thin three years before when his insane son and James Hepburn, Earl of Bothwell, had plotted to abduct the Queen. Moray and Lethington lost their influence to the Lennoxes, and the union of two great-grandchildren of Henry VII increased the threat to Elizabeth and her throne. The Reformers, unappeased by Mary's promise that she would not molest them, were darkly suspicious of the two young Papists whom Knox compared with Ahab and Jezebel, even though Darnley was as inconstant in religion as he was in all things but self-esteem.

Moray's dislike of the marriage was the surface ruffle of deeper discontent and the persistent frustration of his bastardy. He had once stood guard at the chapel door when his half-sister was at Mass, but now he joined with those lords of the Congregation who had refused to consent to the marriage without more positive assurances to the Kirk. They were ignored, and their consequent rebellion was mismanaged and mistimed, and lacked the support it expected from Elizabeth. Flushed with consummated love, and excited by the challenge, Mary gathered an army, released Huntly's heir from prison, and recalled from exile that robust moss-trooper Bothwell. From the absence of any action but hard riding in foul weather the galloping campaign was called the Chase-About Raid, but it ended with Moray's flight into England. The Queen rode gallantly with her soldiers, a pistol at her side, a steel cap upon her head, and a mail shirt beneath her clothes, but few of those who followed her knew that when the rebellion began she had asked for Spanish help to save the Holy Church in Scotland, or that the papal dispensation for her marriage had been granted upon her promise to defend that Church with all her strength.

From the blood-stirring ride of the Chase-About Raid, the feeling of security given by the warm loyalty of armed men, the course of her life now led downhill to the block at Fotheringhay. The first step was taken over the mangled body of David Riccio, a Piedmontese musician who had come to Edinburgh with the ambassador of Savoy. He first charmed the Queen with his pleasing bass voice, and then held her interest by his clever intellect and flattering tongue. She made him her French secretary and principal adviser, and although his company was undoubtedly more stimulating than any of her Scots lords, the favour she showed him was artless and foolish. In the real or politic belief that he was a papal agent, and in certain hatred of a foreign upstart, they decided to remove him. Darnley had once been the Italian's friend, but his jealous and unsteady emotions needed only a touch to change course, and he was easily persuaded that Riccio was now his rival. There were darker influences in the plot, involving Moray and other fugitive lords beyond the Border, promises that Darnley might be king in his own right should Mary die childless. An act of blood would be needed to make the Queen accept this, and the victim should be Riccio.

On the evening of March 9, in the Lent of 1566, the pregnant Queen was at supper in her private chamber on the second floor of Holyrood, attended by Riccio and two or three others. Darnley made an unexpected and uneasy appearance at the head of the staircase, and was shortly followed by a number of armed lords led by Patrick, Lord

196    *James Douglas, 4th Earl of Morton, Regent of Scotland during the minority of James VI.*
*Overleaf A painted ceiling at Stobhall Castle.*

REX · HISPANIÆ

Ruthven, a grim old spectre with armour beneath his cloak, his face white with a wasting sickness. 'Let it please Your Majesty,' he said, 'that yonder man David come forth of your privy-chamber where he hath been overlong.' The terrified Italian's fingers were torn from the Queen's skirts and he was dragged outside, calling for justice and screaming '*Sauvez ma vie, Madame, sauvez ma vie!*' He was killed with more than fifty dagger-strokes, and Darnley's weapon, used by another, was left in the butchered body. At no other moment in her life, not even its last day, did Mary need more courage, for in their desperate passion the murderers might have destroyed her and the child she was carrying, and she always believed that this was what her husband intended. Alarmed by rumours, by the sight of armed men about the palace, the provost and townsfolk of Edinburgh came to its gates. Darnley was sent to reassure them, and the Queen was told that if she attempted to speak from the window she would be 'cut in collops'. Elsewhere in the palace, the earls of Bothwell, Huntly and Atholl were powerless to help, though Bothwell, with his usual adroit cunning, managed to escape.

A parliament was due to meet on Tuesday, March 12, to declare the forfeiture of Moray and the rebel lords, but Darnley discharged it on Sunday, and that evening the bastard earl and his friends arrived in Edinburgh, riding hard from Newcastle. He came to Holyrood and the imprisoned Queen on Monday, offering sympathy and swearing innocence, and she drank his health, forgiving him with a smile. Behind the mask of the smile was fear, and a sickening hatred of Darnley, but also intelligence and courage. She had wept bitterly for her Italian, but dried her eyes while his blood was still wet outside her chamber, telling her ladies 'No more tears now, I will think upon revenge.' That night she detached her husband from the other murderers, and flattered by her protestations of affection, moved by her apparent dependence upon him, and alarmed by her warning of what might now be said of him abroad, the weak and malleable creature helped her to escape. At midnight they went down the privy staircase, through the kitchens and a graveyard to a gate where horses were waiting. She mounted one behind a young esquire, and they rode eastward until their road was blocked in the dark by a troop of horsemen. She was afraid for the child in her womb, but Darnley, in a hysteria that had gone beyond panic, roughly told her that if she miscarried they could make more children. At dawn, in the safety of Dunbar, she cooked eggs for the troopers who had alarmed her. They were James Hepburn's loyal men.

A week later she entered Edinburgh in triumph, with eight thousand men under Bothwell, Atholl and Huntly. Moray remained in the city, relying upon her forgiveness, but his friends were gone, and the murderers of Riccio were wisely riding for the Border. John Knox, to whom the crime had been a just and providential act, retired to Ayr, where he begged God to 'destroy that whore in her whoredom'. The savaged corpse of the Italian was taken from a common grave and reburied in the Chapel Royal, and his young brother was given the secretaryship he had held. No one can know the thoughts of Bothwell at this moment. In his thirtieth year, a crop-haired womanizer and political gambler, he lived a life of sensual pleasure and ambitious adventure, but he was also honest within the context of the age, and was one of the few Scottish lords who did not take English money for their country's honour. The face in a miniature believed to be his portrait supports the claim, a swarthy face and a broken nose, a lover's mouth and fearless, compelling eyes.

The Queen's child, a son James, was born on June 19 after a long and desperate labour, his face masked by a propitious caul. 'My lord,' Mary told her husband, 'God has given you and me a son, begotten by none but you. . . . Here I protest to God, as I shall answer to Him at the great day of Judgement, this is your son and no other man's.' Darnley kissed the infant, and beyond the windows there were bonfires, the thunder of castle guns. The solemn oath was made less to reassure him than to secure his public acknowledgment of his son, to strengthen her own position and to guarantee the succession.

*Arnold van Brounckhorst painted this portrait of James VI as a boy. 'When he was fourteen his lessons ended, and if his education had been narrow in range, it had been deep and thorough.'*

Her reconciliation with Darnley had been brief, and was virtually over as soon as it had served its purpose at her lying-in. Her contradictory actions during the next seven months, though seemingly natural in a desperate and frightened woman, can also be seen to have some vengeful purpose in further isolating her wretched husband from private support and public favour. She had already forgiven the Chase-About lords, and in December she pardoned and recalled some of Riccio's murderers. They returned with no love for the man who had abandoned them that March night at Holyrood. In the same month, although she gave the Reformed Church fresh promises of her tolerance, and assigned its ministers a definite portion of the Third taken from the revenues of the old benefices, she also restored Archbishop John Hamilton to his consistorial jurisdictions at St Andrews. The birth of her son brought her a wave of popular affection, and the French ambassador said that she had never been so well-beloved and esteemed. Her Privy Council told Darnley that he should thank God for such a wife, advice which may have further confused his quarter-witted mind, for frequently at her side during these months was the dark squat figure of Bothwell. He had been well-rewarded for his loyalty at Dunbar, and was now sheriff of Edinburgh and Haddington, Warden of the

Marches, and keeper of many castles. Later men would see more than friendship in his attendance upon the woman he had brought back to her capital, but what foolishness there was in her behaviour, such as a wild ride along the Cheviots to see him when he was ill, may have been no more than an over-emotional concern for a loyal servant. The ambitions stirred in the Hepburn's mind as a result, the dark purposes he set himself to, are less easily defined, but at their extreme they demanded the removal of the Queen's husband.

And then, like the predictable third act of a violent melodrama, there was plot, counter-plot and murder. The consistorial jurisdiction restored to Archbishop Hamilton was primarily for marriage disputes, and that winter there was talk of an annulment of the royal union. Huntly said that Moray and Lethington first raised the question, placing it before him, Bothwell and Argyll at Craigmillar Castle, and that together they discussed it with Mary. There is no reliable evidence of these talks, or none that is not partisan, but Mary is said to have agreed to a divorce providing it did not prejudice the legitimacy and succession of her son. She also asked that nothing should be done that might dishonour her name or injure her conscience. Strange and unlikely words were credited to the normally cautious Lethington, that men would look through their fingers and keep silent, that means would be found for Mary to be quit of her husband, that she should let them settle the matter among themselves. There were other talks no doubt, of which wise men kept no records, and although no move was made toward securing a divorce there were rumours that Lennox was plotting to remove Mary and make Darnley regent over the infant prince. These stories were strong enough to frighten the Queen, and in January, 1567, she brought the child from Stirling to greater safety at Holyrood.

Darnley was ill in Glasgow, foully sick with what is now believed to have been small-pox, though there have been other diagnoses from scabies to syphilis. Mary came to visit him, flattering the pocked face which his vanity hid behind a taffeta mask, persuading him to return to Edinburgh. She did not bring him to Holyrood, where it was feared his disease might infect their child, but to Kirk o' Field, an old collegiate house just inside the city wall and to the south of the Cowgate. He was lodged there on the last day of January, on the upper floor of the Provost's House nearest the wall. The property belonged to Robert Balfour, Canon of Holyrood, whose brother James was one of Bothwell's associates, a blasphemous, amoral rogue who had been sent to the galleys with Knox and who was said to have neither fear of God nor love of virtue. It was upon his suggestion that Bothwell proposed the house as suitable for Darnley's convalescence. The Queen spent much of her time with the sick man, sitting beside his green and yellow bed, placating his childish moods and soothing his petty jealousies. Her concern for him may have been genuine, but the impression that he was being cajoled into a state of innocent trust is also strong, for he was alone and helpless in a city crowded with hateful enemies.

Mary stayed at Kirk o' Field on the night of Wednesday, February 5, and again on Thursday, sleeping in a room below his. On Sunday evening she left a wedding masque at Holyrood and came again, this time with the earls of Bothwell, Argyll, Huntly and Cassilis. Splendid in carnival costume, the lords diced at a green baize table in Darnley's room, while the Queen talked with her husband, and all of the visitors were pleasantly at ease, showing superhuman self-control if one or more of them were responsible for what was being prepared in the cellars below. When Mary was reminded that the party

*A contemporary sketch of the scene at Kirk o' Field after the murder of Darnley shows his infant son* (top left), *his body and that of his man* (top right) *and the ruins of the house* (left centre). *The sketch was sent to William Cecil in London.*

must return to the masque, Darnley sulked and protested, but she gave him a ring as a token of her affection, and promised him that they would spend the following night together at Holyrood. He was left alone with his valet, and at two o'clock in the morning the building burst open in a red and yellow flower, the roar of the explosion awakening the whole city. On the light snow of the garden earth, beneath a pear-tree and some way from the smoking ruins, were found the bodies of the Queen's husband and his man. Neither was marked by the explosion, and both had been strangled.

Bothwell's creatures had been involved in the storing of the powder beneath the house, and the balance of both suppositional and factual evidence suggests that he was responsible for the murder, yet to believe so argues against common sense. The mystery is complicated by paradoxes and by ridiculous contradictions. All explanations have an initial plausibility – from a belief in Bothwell's guilt, and by association the Queen's also, to the proposition that Darnley intended to destroy his wife and her advisers, or the suggestion that others wished to kill them both and put the blame upon Bothwell – and all have a final doubt. It is possible that there was more than one conspiracy, that each exploited or diverted the other, and that members of a third profited from both, throttling the alarmed victim as he ran from the house in his night-shirt. Kirk o' Field will remain a mystery, the greatest in Scottish history, and without a convincing solution a full understanding of Mary Queen of Scots is perhaps impossible.

The Earl of Lennox called to God for vengeance upon the murderers of a son not yet twenty-one. Great men, like Moray, thought it politic to be out of the capital or the kingdom for a while, but the head Lennox wished to see on a spike was that of Bothwell. Although Mary offered two thousand pounds for information, and a free pardon to any who informed, she made no charges against the Borderer, and confident in her protection he shook the dice-cup for the greatest throw of his life. He stayed in Edinburgh, guarded by fifty moss-troopers, although its walls were soon placarded with his crude portrait and the accusation *Here is the Murderer!* He was at this moment divorcing his wife Jean Gordon, Huntly's sister, and his thoughts were set upon her nobler successor. Demands for an inquiry into the murder, from Protestant lords, from Lennox, and from William Cecil in the name of England, could not be ignored, however, and Mary at last agreed that Bothwell and others should stand trial. When her Privy Councillors met to consider its nature and form, he sat with them, and before the trial began he filled Edinburgh with his men. He was accused of 'art and part of the cruel, odious, treasonable and abominable slaughter', but no one appeared to support the charge, and Lennox had been stopped by Borderers on the road from Linlithgow. Although the jurors included some of Bothwell's open enemies, they were forced to acquit him, and he underlined their verdict by publishing a medieval challenge, offering to fight any man who still maintained that he was guilty. A few days later, on April 19, he carried the sceptre before the Queen as she rode to parliament, and that evening twenty-eight lords and prelates were his supper-guests at Ainslie's Tavern in the Canongate. They were invited to put their names to a document which acknowledged his acquittal, and his eminent qualifications for replacing the man he had been accused of murdering. They signed, promising their support for the marriage, and those in doubt were soon reassured by the sight of his troopers beyond the tavern windows.

With the canny Lethington in attendance, he then rode to the Queen at Seton. According to her story, this was the first time Bothwell paid suit to her, and despite Lethington's advice that it was necessary for the security of her kingdom, she refused the proposal of marriage. She then left to join her son at Stirling. Bothwell may have been surprised by this lacklustre response in a woman who must certainly have known of his intentions, if they were not already lovers, but he was confident that no man in Scotland at this moment had the power to stop him. On April 24, as the Queen was travelling to Edinburgh from Stirling, he met her by the River Almond with eight hundred horsemen. He took her bridle, told her that there was a risk of rebellion, and that she should come with him to the safety of Dunbar Castle. She did not protest, and gently restrained those of her retinue who did. One rode to Edinburgh with an alarm, but all its citizens could do was to fire a cannon as the horsemen rode by.

That she was willingly abducted by some pre-arrangement is possible, but not proven, and to believe it perhaps argues cooler heads than would have been likely in this dark atmosphere of fear and confusion. Much that happens to men comes less from planning than from the acceptance and exploitation of chance. Bothwell was a glorious animal compared to her sluggish and invalid husbands, and he undoubtedly attracted her temperamentally and sexually, but this could make her cautious as much as foolhardy. Taken by apparent force, however, she could submit to desire while retaining the protest of reason, and in his body and his protection find welcome relief from a terrible loneliness. At Dunbar, while Huntly and Lethington quarrelled over what had been done, and while his spearmen held the walls against any threat from beyond, Bothwell used the skill of his tongue and the boldness of his sensual appeal to secure the Queen's consent to marriage. And then, or thus goes the Marian case, came rape. 'So he ceased never,' said Mary later, 'till by persuasion and importunate suit, accompanied not the less with force, he had finally driven us to end the work begun at such time and in such form as he thought might best serve his turn.' Others put this more bluntly. James Melville, one of her followers at Dunbar, wrote that 'the Queen could not but marry him, seeing he had ravished her and lain with her against her will'. Nicholas Throckmorton, the English envoy, was told that she was compelled by fear and force to 'become bedfellow to another wife's husband'. It may be confidently assumed that the incident took place in private, and the reports of others depend upon how the principals chose to describe it later. Whether she was or was not raped must rest upon Mary's oblique account, and that was sent with intent to the French court, which may not have cared to hear of any other explanation for her acceptance of Bothwell.

At the beginning of May, Jean Gordon was given her divorce from the Hepburn on the grounds of his adultery with her sewing-maid, and Archbishop Hamilton reversed a papal dispensation and declared that it had been null from the start. On the sixth of the month the Queen was brought back to Edinburgh by her triumphant captor, whom she shortly created Duke of Orkney and Lord of Shetland. John Craig, parish minister of Edinburgh, refused to proclaim the banns until he saw a writ from the Queen, and even then he denounced Bothwell for rape and collusion. The marriage took place in the great hall of Holyrood on Thursday, May 15, and by Protestant rites. The Bishop of Orkney, who performed the ceremony, made his peace with God and his conscience by announcing that Bothwell had now renounced his former life of wickedness and evil. The Queen wore an old black gown, trimmed with braid.

This miserable alliance, which seems to have been without harmony or happiness, lasted a month only before they were parted for ever. Public opinion, where it was not outraged, was numb with shock. As opposition and rebellion grew, Bothwell took Mary to the black, towered castle of Borthwick, south of Edinburgh. Besieged there, they escaped by night, raised another army, if fewer than a thousand men can be so described, and brought it about the palace of Seton, where they spent their last night together. On the morning of Sunday, June 15, while it was still dark, the army of the confederate lords marched out of Edinburgh, led by the Douglas Earl of Morton who had been one of those who signed the bond at Ainslie's Tavern. The two forces met at Carberry Hill near the field of Pinkie, but there was no fighting. All day emissaries galloped between the lords and the Queen, the rebels declaring that they had no quarrel with her, but she must abandon the man who had murdered her husband. She was angrily loyal to him, or to her own self-respect, telling the lords that 'it was by them that Bothwell had been promoted'. The fruitless wrangling was then followed by medieval challenges to single combat, but the first man to oppose Bothwell was rejected as being too low-born, and the second took off his armour and asked for time to prepare himself. During this tragi-comedy the Queen's soldiers were drifting away, disgusted or dispirited. By dusk, when the rebels reopened the parleying, Bothwell knew that there could be no fight, and he suggested that they retreat to Dunbar with what men were left. Mary would not go, and again her motives are obscure. She may have realized that here

*Loch Leven Castle, Kinross-shire. Mary Queen of Scots was imprisoned here in 1567 after Carberry Hill but she escaped its fortifications a year later.*

was an opportunity to be rid of him forever, or she may have believed that she could trust herself to the lords and that he could raise another army. They embraced, and he rode away on the Dunbar road. He found no more soldiers, but fled north to Orkney and Shetland, and from thence to Norway, where, in a bizarre and macabre anti-climax, he was arrested for breach of promise, on a charge brought by a woman he may have forgotten. He was passed from prison to prison in Denmark, each worse than the last, a pawn of European politics until his value was exhausted. His Queen forgot him, or cared not to think of him, and eleven years later he died a madman, chained to a wall it was said. He was a rogue, but a bold rogue and a brave one, more likeable, or at least more forgivable than many noble Scotsmen who died secure in the titles and estates which they had bought with treason, treachery, and murder.

The lords of the Congregation to whom Mary had confidently surrendered took her a prisoner to Edinburgh, where good citizens in the passion of their own rectitude called her a whore and cried out for her burning. She was sent to an island castle on Loch Leven and compelled to abdicate, naming the Earl of Moray as regent for her son. That month, July, she suffered a bloody and dangerous miscarriage, and if it is true that the stillbirth was recognizable as twins, she must have conceived in the rape or surrender at Dunbar. In May of the following year she escaped from the island with the help of a romantic boy, and a group of horsemen on the lake shore took her to a waiting army of Hamilton supporters and Argyll clansmen. It was commanded by the fifth Earl of Argyll, whose military skill at this moment was said to be hampered by epileptic fits and a treacherous sympathy for his opponent, his brother-in-law the Earl of Moray. The royal army and the Congregation of Christ faced each other at Langside, south of Glasgow, and Moray's horsemen were at first scattered, but his musketeers stubbornly held the village houses, and his guns played from the hill above. When the infantry engaged, the struggle was so fierce that their pikes were shattered, and they fought with stones until the Highlanders broke and the Hamiltons surrendered.

Mary rode to the Solway and crossed into England with sixteen companions only. She asked for an audience with Elizabeth, offering to acquit herself of Darnley's murder, but she was never received. From a fugitive asking for asylum, a woman appealing to a woman, she became the embarrassing prisoner of her most implacable and indeterminate enemy. Her death would remove the greatest menace to Protestant England, yet the prolongation of her life was essential to its security. She was held for nineteen years, saved by Elizabeth's clemency when the plots of her supporters and the anger of the English parliament demanded her death. The famous Casket Letters, allegedly discovered in June, 1567, and betraying her complicity with Bothwell, exist in transcript and translation only. For over three and a half centuries no man is known to have seen the originals or the silver box that contained them. But upon their questionable evidence Mary's reputation was destroyed in her own country and in England. She was judicially killed in February, 1587, the willing victim of a plot that had been cunningly encouraged by Elizabeth's chief of intelligence, Francis Walsingham. Jealous of her own reputation, the English queen insisted that the death warrant should be innocently placed among other papers for her signature, that she should sign it by mistake. Having done so, she jested about it.

When the executioner at Fotheringhay picked up the severed head of the Queen of Scots it fell from the auburn wig in his hands. But that is not how she was remembered. Her dangerous charm would recur in her descendants, and almost two hundred years later men would uselessly die for it.

## 5

For ten years Scotland was once more governed by regents. Four ambitious men, of whom two were murdered and one beheaded by their enemies. With the flight of Mary, Gordons and Hamiltons threatened a new revolt, and those men who were jealous and resentful of the Earl of Moray formed a coalition known as the Queen's Lords, though their wish to bring down the Regent was stronger than a desire for her return. Moray knew that the cunning and turncoat brain behind their plotting was his erstwhile confederate Maitland of Lethington, now the champion of the woman he had frequently betrayed. In the autumn of 1569 the secretary was arrested and held in the Edinburgh house of one of Moray's associates, from which he was soon rescued and taken to the castle by his friend the governor, Sir James Kirkcaldy of Grange. This Protestant Kirkcaldy was one of David Beaton's murderers, and his defiance of Moray can scarcely have been based upon an objective sympathy for a papist queen, but his motives were no more convoluted than other men's. In November there was a witless and unsuccessful attempt by English Catholics to release Mary, and when the Regent had captured some of those who fled over the Border, he turned against the Queen's Lords.

The squalid 'war of religion' which then followed hardly merits the ennobling title, although the survival of the Reformation depended upon the bandit struggle. It began appropriately enough with assassination. On January 23, as Moray rode through Linlithgow he was shot in the stomach by a Hamilton laird, who aimed his musket from an upper window and from behind a line of washing. The Regent walked to his lodgings and died a few hours later with calm courage. He was buried in St Giles's and was remembered as the 'good regent', and in a comparative sense the adjective was deserved. John Knox preached at his funeral, 'He is at rest, O Lord, and we are left in extreme misery . . .', but the old polemicist also reminded the Almighty that the Regent had sinned in his foolish pity for Mary and the murderers of her husband. The house in which the assassin had hidden, the horse on which he had escaped, belonged to Archbishop John Hamilton, and some months later Moray's friends hanged the trembling old man at Stirling without the troublesome formality of a trial.

The next regent was Darnley's father, accepted with reluctance by half the nation under pressure from Elizabeth. The desultory fighting between King's Lords and Queen's Lords had been stimulated by the arrival of an English army to support the former, which it did by destroying the palace, castle and town of Hamilton before withdrawing. In the following year the guns of Edinburgh Castle, still held by Kirkcaldy and Lethington, drove the King's Lords from the city below, and by August, 1571, there were two parliaments in Scotland. That called by Lennox at Stirling had a greater validity in the possession of the King, five years old, in splendid robes, and with a new crown to replace that still held in Edinburgh. Each assembly denounced the other, and issued sentences of death and forfeiture as if they were separated by three hundred miles, not thirty. Five days after the boy had sat with his Estates, four hundred riders broke into Stirling, Gordons and Hamiltons, and with a spatter of muskets they captured King, Regent, and King's Lords. When the burgesses recovered their wits and their courage, they fell upon the invaders and drove them out, but Lennox died from the parting thrust of a Gordon sword.

With neither side strong enough to suppress the other, the weary war continued under the succeeding regent John Erskine, Earl of Mar. He died within a few months, of a broken heart it was understandably believed, and he was replaced by James Douglas, Earl of Morton, vigorous like all his clan and as inconstant, for there was hardly a political or religious bond of the past fifteen years to which he had not put his name. France and England were now his negative and positive allies. News of the Massacre of St Bartholomew's Day frightened many neutral Protestants into a belief that they too would be slaughtered if the Regent's party lost, and they hurriedly pledged their support to Morton. The Queen's men, already disheartened by England's declaration that Mary would never return to Scotland, were further weakened when Elizabeth sent soldiers and guns to help in the siege of their only stronghold, Edinburgh Castle. Its two hundred defenders surrendered in May, 1573, when David's Tower crumbled under bombardment, and English soldiers rose from their trenches at the head of the High Street and assaulted the nearest outworks. The victors said that Elizabeth must decide what should happen to their captives, but upon the bloodthirsty prompting of the city's ministers Morton claimed that they were 'fitter for God than for this world'. Kirkcaldy and his brother, with two goldsmiths who had minted coins for the defenders, were all hanged at the Market Cross and their heads spiked on the 'most eminent places of the castle wall'. Lethington would have been hanged too, but he had always outwitted his enemies, and he did so now by dying, from sickness or his own hand.

Morton was secure in his regency, and for the second time England had preserved the Scottish Reformation. It had faltered in Mary's reign, and after her removal little was done to implement the proposals of the Book of Discipline. Roman clerics still held their livings, although in 1568 it was enacted that when the benefices fell vacant they should be filled by reformed ministers. A General Assembly of the Kirk which met at Leith in January, 1572, was strongly influenced by Morton, whose vision of reform was a reflection of the Church of England. By a concordat with the Privy Council it was agreed that the Crown should henceforth nominate bishops to vacant sees, and that they should take an oath of allegiance to the King as supreme governor of the realm and protector of the Church. Although the bishops were to be subject to the Assembly in matters spiritual, the Concordat was a backward step in the context of 1560 and the Book of Discipline. The system of Crown nomination was cynically abused, and part of the episcopal revenues was inevitably channelled into private purses. Morton filled the bishoprics with men of his own choice and clan, and the people called them *tulchans*, from the calf-skins stuffed with straw which countrymen used to induce their cows to give milk.

John Knox died in November, 1572, crying 'Now it is come!' He had reluctantly approved the Concordat, but he had foreseen its abuses, and without him there was no leading opposition. The gap was filled two years later by the return to Scotland of Andrew Melville, the young scholar who came from exile in Geneva to be principal of Glasgow University. He was more stable in character than Knox, more subtle and polished in intellect, and was a product of the reform movement rather than a founder of it. His influence was creative and inspirational, and years later he would tell James VI that there were two kingdoms in Scotland, and that James was a subject of the realm of Christ Jesus, 'not a king, nor a lord, nor a head, but a member'. He transformed the moribund university with new departments, and later at St Andrews he was principal of a new theological college for the education of dedicated ministers. A second Book of Discipline, acknowledged by the General Assembly in 1578, was largely his work, and was stubbornly resisted by Morton, who would have been happy to hang all those responsible for it. The Book repeated the assertion that it was based upon the Word of God, and that premise, when accepted, made its articles indisputable. It again demanded that the whole patrimony of the Church should be devoted to its ministers, its organization, and its obligations to the poor. It was original in its condemnation of episcopacy, declaring the authority of bishops to be unlawful before God. Such authority and discipline should be maintained by church courts – kirk-session, presbytery, synod, and assembly – involving laymen as well as ministers. The power and government of a presbyterian Church came from God, denying all other faiths, and admitting no superior upon earth. In matters of conscience and religion – which could arguably include all human activity – king, nobility and commons were subject to its guidance, its rewards and punishments. This theocratic claim to instruct men in their civil duty 'according to the Word' placed the General Assembly of the Kirk above Parliament, and created a rival government which would in time become the more powerful and influential of the two.

It was not a benevolent government, rather a *politburo* conducting a revolutionary struggle through the six hundred party branches of its first parishes, the fifty district committees of its presbyteries. In the willing fight against the Antichrist in spiritual and secular form, dogma was reinforced with fear, pain and humiliation were recognizable roads to salvation, and the brotherhood of man was built upon the destruction of individual liberty.

The young men who left Melville's university for the ministry, and others who followed them in the next century, zealously embraced a life of ascetic self-denial. In contrast to the glorious vestments of the old priests, they wore hodden-grey on weekdays and blue serge when they preached. By order of the General Assembly, their wives were prohibited from wearing 'all kinds of light and variant hues in clothing, as red, blue, yellow, and such like', and also silk hats, rings, bracelets, buttons of gold or silver. Since all Roman practices were sinful, their converse must be holy in the sight of God, and parishioners were encouraged to wear their hats in church, to remain seated through the entire service, and to abandon such disgusting acts of reverence as kneeling. The local laird, however, was allowed his privileges. He paid for his own pew, and frequently had a retiring-room where he could lounge if the interminable sermons became unbearable. When he arrived in church the minister bowed to him and his family, a servile and obnoxious custom derided by egalitarian English soldiers in the next century.

Sunday under the Roman Church had been a joyful holiday as well as a spiritual feast, but the Reformation Sabbath seemed designed as a foretaste of Hell, or as a source of revenue from the fines imposed upon those who broke it. It began at six o'clock in the evening of Saturday and lasted for twenty-four hours. During this time there was to be no work done, no unseemly activities, no dancing, no playing of the pipes, no markets, gaming, play-acting, or frequenting of alehouses. Kirk-sessions arraigned women for selling candles and bread on the Sabbath, a poultryman for plucking geese, a miller for grinding corn, a fisherman for casting his nets, and high-spirited young men and women for 'insolence in foot-racing, dancing, and playing Barla Breks'. In 1574 the kirk-session of St Andrews ordered a baillie, elder, two deacons and two halberdiers to police the town every Sunday and to 'apprehend transgressors according to the acts of the kirk'. A parishioner was expected to be in kirk before the minister arrived, to behave with decorum, and to remember that this was not an opportunity for 'styking his nybor upon the haffat in tume of preaching'. Fast-days, called in moments of national humiliation, were as sacred as the Sabbath, as a flesher of St Andrews discovered when the baillie, elders, deacon and halberdiers interrupted his enjoyment of a pot-roast.

Obscene and degrading punishments were imposed in the righteous belief that they were necessary for the salvation of the sinner, and were accepted in the spirit of a people at war who will endure indignities and privations that would be insufferable in peace. In 1578 the kirk-session of Perth ordered John Todd to stand in irons for two hours to expiate a slanderous speech. Other slanderers in Dumfries, who had perhaps done no more than speak in opposition to the Church's teaching, were sent to 'stand at the kirk-stile on the Sabbath, with branks upon their mouths'. The brank was a padlocked helmet of iron, thrusting a triangular tongue into the victim's mouth. For the sins of vituperation, abuse, or scolding, offenders were compelled to kneel in penitence before their own doors, and were banished from the parish if they repeated the offence. A wife could be banished for a nagging tongue or dirty hands, and poor men who cursed and had no money for a fine were 'put in the stocks, jaggs, or imprisoned for the space of four hours'. A banished fornicator risked burning if he returned, and the first Book of Discipline had recommended death for adulterers. Although this punishment was rarely imposed, a parliament of 1563 did order the execution of two unfortunates whose extramarital love had been cursed by the birth of a child. When the minister of Jedburgh, Paul Methven, prostrated himself before the General Assembly, and weepingly admitted to adultery, he escaped execution, but he was ordered to stand in sackcloth before his church, to sit on a penitent's stool within. Among a nobility renowned for its bastards, few lords were charged with fornication or adultery, but lesser men were not excused. Barefooted and wearing paper crowns describing their sin, adulterous baillies and their women walked to their public whipping at the Market Cross. The scourge and the brank, the stocks and the stool of penitence, sackcloth and the ducking-pond, banishment and burning, were all revolutionary weapons of the dictatorship of the presbytery.

The tap-root of sorcery and superstition was deep in the pre-Christian memory. Rome had not destroyed it, nor would the Reformers, though they struck at it ruthlessly. The first statute against it was passed three years after the first Book of Discipline, outlawing all kinds of sorcery 'under the pain of death, as well to be execute against the user, abuser, as the seeker of the response or consultation'. Since sorcerers were believed to have sold body and soul to the Devil, burning was their salvation, the Church's punishment, and the public's entertainment. Thus were three women burnt at Perth, and in the same compassion for their souls others were hung from prison walls with weighted feet until they confessed. Flesh was lacerated, cheeks and tongues pierced, bodies torn apart by horses, and the children of the victims were brought to watch the torture.

Dancing was a form of sorcery. The surrender of mind and will to the sensual movements of the body was a triumph of flesh over spirit, of the Devil over Christ. Mary's lightfooted happiness was thought to be satanic joy in the murder of Protestants in France, and she and her companions were accused by Knox of 'dancing like the Philistines for the pleasure taken in the destruction of God's people'. Although the Reformers punished innocent offenders with the pillory, penitence-stool and banishment, they could never entirely suppress the people's love of music and the dance. It was deep in their past, and when Wallace told his men at Falkirk that he had brought them to the ring, now let them dance, he was using a metaphor they instinctively understood. Since the Middle Ages burgh authorities had maintained musicians at public expense. Twenty native dances are named in a ballad composed early in the fifteenth century, and the poem *Christ's Kirk on the Green*, attributed to James V, records the dancing frolics of country folk.

The old carnivals of feast-days, the Maytime games in honour of Robin Hood, miracle plays, masques of the Passion and allegorical mumming, were all condemned and forbidden. There was a pagan violence and a wild abandon in the people's enjoyment of such things, and even pre-Reformation governments had been alarmed by them, and condemned the rioting and drunkenness that sometimes accompanied them. Mary of Guise banned the licentious Robin Hood games, and so did her daughter, but when an Edinburgh artisan was condemned to death for playing the principal role his fellow-craftsmen destroyed the gallows and rescued him from the Tolbooth. David Lindsay's *Satire* had been a powerful argument for spiritual and temporal reform, but the hierarchy of the Kirk hated play-acting as much as dancing. The General Assembly prohibited the performance of 'comedies and tragedies made of the canonical scriptures, both on the Sabbath and other days', although it reluctantly permitted some that were secular in plot, providing 'no swearing, nor nae scurrility shall be spoken'. The ministers' natural fear of drama, of its potential for dissent and criticism in the sinful form of entertainment, was never relaxed, and late in the century they challenged the King's right to admit a company of English players, declaring them 'unruly and immodest', and threatening the Kirk's censure upon all who went to see them. Bigotry held creative freedom by the throat, the genius of which Lindsay may have been a promise was never allowed to develop, and if Scotland has no great dramatist it may perhaps thank the Kirk's steadfast concern for its immortal soul.

In the same stark spirit, the detestation of the 'smell of Popery' which arose from things of beauty, the ministers at first lived in buildings of turf and timber, no better housed than their parishioners. The great cathedrals and monasteries were abandoned to decay, their images and stained glass destroyed, their tombs rifled, the choir-stalls torn down and burnt, and the roofless halls turned into cattle-byres. New churches, built by statute only, were long and narrow, imperfectly lit and inadequately warmed. The exclusive sacrament of communion, withheld from many under the Roman Church, now came close to a bacchanalian celebration. When Knox administered it at St Giles in 1560, eight and a half gallons of claret were consumed, and in the same church fourteen years later the quantity was nearly ten times as great, although there was admittedly a large communion-roll. Compulsory attendance at the Lord's Table was a public renunciation of Popery, and the communicants sat together in democratic conviviality, enjoying abundant shortcake and wine which, said Knox, remained unchanged in their 'very natural substance and might not be adored'. Though this was a crude replacement of an ancient and subtle ritual, and perhaps filled an entertainment-gap left by the banning of impious pleasures, it involved all men in a robust re-enactment of its Biblical origin.

Land and people still disappointed or depressed the visitor. During the regency of Mary of Guise a French ecclesiastic, Estienne Perlin, said that England was as preferable to Scotland as the centre of Paris was to its suburbs. The Scot was bold and gallant enough, but poor, and the greater part of his country was a desert. It was also very cold. Forty years later Fynes Moryson, a peripatetic English student, was impressed by the industry and energy of Scottish merchants, but dismayed by their failure to apply these virtues at home. Many of them lived abroad in Poland and Scandinavia, 'rather for the poverty of their own kingdom than for any great traffic they exercise there'. This derided poverty was real, and bitterly felt by the peasants who were perhaps three-quarters of the population, at the mercy of weather and war and rarely observed by visitors. Below the nobility was a relatively prosperous merchant class. Although the home of a Scottish burgess was modest by Continental comparison, it was solid and comfortable, its windows glazed and its walls sometimes panelled. He sat at the head of his board like a small laird, in brown doublet and scarlet hose, proud of his napery and salt-cellar, his settle and carving-table, his leather coat and steel helmet, leaning lance and two-handed sword. In his chamber were tapestries and a curtained bed, his wife's spinning-wheel, a sponge-towel and a horn comb hanging by a treasured looking-glass. Within the limits set upon their vanity by the Kirk such men lived well, and ate well, though a little coarsely for Moryson's taste.

> Touching their diet, they eat much red colewort and cabbage, but little fresh meat, using to salt their mutton and geese, which made me wonder that they used to eat their beef without salting. The gentlemen reckon their revenues, not by rents of money, but by cauldrons of victuals, and keep many people in their families, yet living most on corn and roots, not spending any great quantity on flesh.

At a knight's house, servants wearing blue caps brought him a great bowl of broth containing a small piece of sodden meat, and he noticed that diners at the upper table had chicken and prunes in theirs. The Scots had no art in cooking, and little to practise upon if they had. The common people lived on oatcakes, on peas and beans. Bread made from wheat bought from England was a luxury for 'courtiers, gentlemen, and the better sort of citizens'. Hospitality to strangers was still warm and liberal, and in the scarcity of inns was freely offered on the briefest acquaintance, though few visitors liked the beds they were given. 'Cupboards in the wall,' said Moryson, 'with doors to be opened and shut at pleasure.' No man was sent to bed without a sleeping-cup of wine, and despite the Kirk's strictures the Scot had a greater capacity for drink than an Englishman, who was usually regarded as a villainous drunkard. Imported wine was taken without sugar, although on special occasions it was sweetened with *confits* in the French way, but home-brewed ale was the more common drink and powerful enough to 'distemper a stranger's body'. Countryfolk and merchants drank more than courtiers, but even their company was to be avoided by a temperate man. 'Myself being invited by some gentlemen to supper, and being forewarned to fear this excess, would not promise to sup with them but upon condition that my inviter would be my protection from large drinking.'

The prospering burgh towns held the poor cloth of this land together like bright buttons, and its green Border was stitched with black keeps. Most strangers thought little of towns or castles, and described them with condescension or pity, but Edinburgh impressed them all by its commanding position. Seen from a distance, surrounded by green fields and a hundred country houses of the nobility, it was like a great jewel set in smaller stones, although upon closer examination it was still the noisy, stinking wen that had disgusted William Dunbar. The fall of tenement houses and gardens from its

*Hermitage Castle, Roxburghshire, was the lonely keep of the Hepburns. Mary rode here in 1566 to visit the Earl of Bothwell when he was ill from a wound. Right The Church of the Holy Rude, Stirling, where Mary Queen of Scots, aged nine months, was crowned on the thirtieth anniversary of Flodden. Her infant son was also crowned here.*

castle hill had overflowed the old medieval wall and was now held by another, built and paid for by the citizens. Its wide main street was still its pride, its only ornament, thought Moryson, 'the rest of the side streets and alleys being of poor buildings and inhabited with very poor people'.

> The houses are built of unpolished stone, and in the fair street good part of them is of freestone, which in that broad street would make a fair show, but that the outsides of them are faced with wooden galleries, built upon the second storey of the houses; yet these galleries give the owners a fair and pleasant prospect into the said fair and broad street, when they sit or stand in the same.

The doors of these houses were heavy and iron-studded, making a necessary fortress of each at times like the causeway cleansing. Their rooms were sparsely furnished and often floored with aromatic grass, but the rafters were gaily painted and the walls hung with tapestries. The glitter of glass and silver, the glow of bright-coloured clothes, warmed the persistent chill of the climate, the 'thickness of the cloudy air and sea vapours'. Dirt was omnipresent, soap was expensively imported in small quantities, and the public wash-women who splashed and scrubbed in the High Street stood ankle-deep in effluent filth. Over this brawling ant-heap of tall houses, tunnelled wynds and walled gardens, rose the crown-steeple of St Giles's. Since the Reformation the church had become the political as well as the religious heart of the city, more important than the castle above it or the palace below, for both of these were too often held by enemies of the faith. The open space about it was filled with market booths, although the Council insisted that only goldsmiths, watchmakers and booksellers might trade there. It was large and lightsome, said Moryson, but not stately, and without beauty or ornament.

> In this church the King's seat is built some few stairs high of wood, and leaning upon the pillar next to the pulpit, and opposite to the same is another seat very like it, in which the incontinent use to stand and do penance; and some few weeks past, a Gentleman, being a stranger and taking it for a place where men of better quality used to sit, boldly entered the same in sermon time, till he was driven away with the profuse laughter of the common sort, to the disturbance of the whole congregation.

Toward the end of the century the Huguenot Duc de Rohan also thought there was little of merit in Edinburgh but its main street. Its houses were commonplace and without luxury, but 'in compensation they are so stocked with inmates that there can hardly be another town so populous for its size'. He saw no splendid buildings at all in Scotland, no antiquities worthy of mention, but thought this of no consequence when he remembered its people. If the country produced little that was necessary for human existence,

> I also found [it] truly generous in the production of virtuous persons. For, besides the nobility whom I found full of civility and courtesy, the country possesses a multitude of learned men, and a people of such courage and fidelity that our kings of France chose from among them the soldiers who formed the special guard of their person.

This generous encomium should perhaps be set beside the opinions of other Frenchmen, in the days when the Auld Alliance was a reality.

6

The coronation of James VI on July 29, 1567, was almost a non-event. Only five earls and eight lords were present in the parish church of Stirling. The rest were cautiously absent, as they were absent from Edinburgh, where the extremists in the General

Assembly were demanding the execution of Mary. The English ambassador declined an invitation, the regent Moray was away in France, and the coronation oath was taken by the earls of Morton and Home. An infant of thirteen months, the King was unaware of what was happening, and the crown, three and a half pounds of precious stones and metal, was considerately held above his head. Away on the island of Loch Leven the castle guns thundered in celebration, and the deposed queen wept in her room.

When James was twelve, the earls of Argyll and Atholl persuaded him to dispense with the regent Morton, and to rule instead through a Privy Council which naturally included them. The strongest influence upon his character until now had been his tutor George Buchanan, a pale-eyed, grey-bearded scholar and historian, a shrewd political thinker and an entertaining man of letters. He was a short-tempered and gout-ridden man, a poor farm-boy in origin, supported for most of his life by pensions from clerics and noblemen who were insignificant dwarfs in the shadow of his intellect. Despite his great scholarship the flaw that still mars his memory is his obsessive and sadistic hatred of Mary. His account of her reign is a libellous comic-strip, made compulsively readable by its wild and outrageous imagination, and he is believed by some to have been the author of the Casket Letters. He was an adherent of the Lennox Stewarts, Darnley was his betrayed hero, and if he did not entirely corrupt his pupil's mind his intimidating influence must have been largely responsible for the King's strange and cold indifference toward his mother's fate. Buchanan and his youthful assistant, Peter Young, subjected the spindly boy to harsh discipline and long hours of study, giving him a love of knowledge that would make him the most scholarly prince in the history of Britain, and one of the finest in Europe. Hour by hour at Stirling Castle, relieved only by long rides on the Kilsyth Hills, he sat with them in the library that had been assembled for his education, six hundred books in six languages. He spoke Latin well before he was fluent in Scots, and at the age of ten he was able to translate the Latin scriptures into French, and from thence into English. When he was fourteen his lessons ended, and if his education had been narrow in range, limited by the walls of the Old Testament, it had been deep and thorough.

And now he had a friend, someone to love and admire as he might an elder brother. In September, 1579, a distant kinsman of his father arrived from France, Esmé Stuart, Seigneur d'Aubigny. Though he probably came on family business, and upon the prompting of ambition, he was suspected by many of being a papal agent, even after he asked for admission to the Kirk of Scotland. He was thirty-seven, gallant and courtly, a dazzling peacock in this northern world of white ruffs and black doublets. He overwhelmed the gauche young boy with friendship and affection, shrewdly aware of the King's desperate need, and James responded with extravagant generosity. As if he were sharing a chest of treasured toys, he gave D'Aubigny a seat on the Privy Council, the revenues of Arbroath Abbey, the keys of Dumbarton Castle, the earldom and then the dukedom of Lennox. The new duke's friend, James Stewart of Ochiltree, was a returned mercenary of misty ancestry, but the King gave him the earldom of Arran and the consequent leadership of Hamilton power on the strength of his grandmother's kinship with old Châtelherault. From a love of intrigue and an over-indulged ambition, both men then conspired with Morton's enemies to bring the ex-regent to trial for complicity in the murder of Darnley. The stubborn old Douglas went bravely to the block, and for years his skull looked down in protest from a spike above the Tolbooth. Remembering his opposition to the second Book of Discipline, and his fervent wish to hang the best of them, the ministers were happy to see him go, but while he was still awaiting the axe they were encouraging rumours of a popish plot involving the two men who had helped to bring him down. To disperse these suspicions, the young King and his favourites signed a document in January, 1581, condemning Rome and denying all doctrines that did not conform to the Confession of Faith. This 'Negative Confession' was useless, however, for Kirk and Protestant lords were determined upon the removal of Lennox. To isolate the falconer, they decided to steal the hawk.

In August, 1582, when James was hunting near Perth, and separated for once from his friends, he was abducted by the earls of Gowrie, Mar and Glencairn and taken to the Gowrie stronghold of Ruthven Castle. The element of personal treachery in this bold kidnapping was in keeping with noble precedent. William Ruthven, one of Riccio's murderers, had only recently received the earldom of Gowrie from his prisoner. Young John Erskine of Mar had been a childhood companion of the King, who had called him 'Jock o' the Slates' from his diligent application to his lessons. Neither they nor their companions, however, had much sympathy for the boy, and when he wept he was told 'Better bairns weep than bearded men'. Lennox fled for ever to France, Arran was arrested, and for ten months the kidnappers and their confederates ruled Scotland with the approval of the General Assembly. When James escaped in June, 1583, the northern lords of Huntly and Atholl rose to help him, the Ruthven men slipped discreetly into England, and even Andrew Melville thought it wise to leave the country for a while. Only Gowrie remained, confident in his strength until he was tricked into a new conspiracy by Arran, now the King's Chancellor. This time he went to the scaffold.

James was not yet eighteen. Though delicate in frame, constant riding and hunting had given his body a resilient strength. He was nervously restless and loud-voiced, remarkably intelligent and intellectually curious. A French visitor called him an old young man, and from his life so far it is easy to understand why. For the same reason he lacked grace, was uncouth in manner and impatient with the trivialities of court life. The forcing-house of Buchanan's tutorship, D'Aubigny's affection, and Gowrie's abduction had taught him to rely upon himself only. He was discovering kingly craft, deceit and guile, power and the mistrust of power. He would be a 'universal king', he said, and that meant a monarch subordinate to none, not even the Kirk. Staunch though he was in his Protestantism, he saw himself in an Elizabethan mould, and accepted the struggle that would bring with the General Assembly. He had not forgiven that hierarchy for its approval of the Ruthven Raid, and in May, 1584, he had his revenge upon it. A subservient parliament passed a series of statutes which became known as the Black Acts, asserting his temporal and spiritual superiority, forbidding all conventions and assemblies except by his consent, warning pulpit and street against criticism of his person, and giving the episcopate a greater authority over diocese and parish than it had had since 1560.

Within a year, however, the Kirk forced him to retreat. The son of the Earl of Bedford was killed in a Border affray, and Elizabeth demanded the surrender of the man she held responsible, the Earl of Arran. Her motives were cunning and involved. Arran's release and return to the King's favour had made him a dictator under the Crown, and he served his master loyally without preference for Kirk or England. That year he had concluded a treaty with Elizabeth, by which James became her pensioner and she promised to do nothing that might weaken his right to succeed her. She was anxious to secure the King's compliance in the matter of his mother's continued imprisonment and probable execution, and she also wished to strengthen the Protestant league with Scotland. For this it would be necessary for James to placate the Protestant lords with the recall of the Ruthven Raiders, which Arran resolutely opposed. When the King refused to surrender his friend, Elizabeth unleashed the banished men and they came back to powerful support from nobility and Kirk. They besieged Arran and the King at Stirling, and the favourite was bold for a fight until he discovered that the castle was without victuals. He recognized a final and losing throw, and accepted banishment with a gambler's shrug. Ten years later, when he returned as plain Captain Stewart, he was murdered by one of Morton's kinsmen. The Douglas clan had a long and relentless memory.

At Holyrood in May, 1586, the King and the General Assembly reached a limping compromise on the sore question of the episcopate. It was agreed that the bishops chosen by James should now be presented to the Assembly for election, and that each would be subject to a presbytery of ministers within his district, ultimately answerable to the Assembly. What control the King retained by this he virtually lost the following year. His foolish and wasteful extravagance had impoverished the Crown, and upon the advice of John Maitland of Thirlestane, his new Chancellor and younger brother of Lethington, he annexed to himself all the lands and revenues still held by the episcopal benefices. The offices were now worthless, and no ambitious King's man would want one as a reward for his loyalty and service.

King and Church faced each other in sluggish opposition, without trust or sympathy, and each waiting for an opportunity to strengthen itself upon the weakness of the other. James put the preservation of the Crown's supremacy before all else, but although he was skilful in thought he was frequently inept and perverse in action. Much of what he did was eventually used against him, and the chronic sickness of his poverty forced him to measures which may have filled his purse temporarily, but which ultimately weakened his power. Toward the end of the century the small lairds got the parliamentary representation they had been demanding, sitting as commissioners of the shires. The King welcomed them as a balance to the great lords, and he was encouraged to believe that their class would now accept the increasingly heavy taxation his spendthrift habits made necessary. But although these men had sweetened their clamant demand with a gift of forty thousand pounds to the King, once in the Estates they were sturdy in opposition to his greed, and almost all could be influenced by the Kirk.

Elizabeth had assured James that she would not dispute his claim to her throne, but she did not name him as her successor, and he was still excluded by an act of the English parliament. His devouring ambition to unite both kingdoms in himself, to be the anointed head of their Protestant episcopal churches, overrode all other desires, and it explains in part his reaction, or lack of reaction, to his mother's death. The rest of the explanation is psychological, with deep roots in Buchanan's teaching, in the influence of the Lennox Stewarts, and in the bitter hostility to Mary which had surrounded him since infancy. He was sickened by blood and alarmed by a drawn sword, which fanciful minds see as the traumatic result of Riccio's murder, when he was still in Mary's womb, but it is true that such revulsion would not excite an interest in the violence and slaughter of her reign. Though he frequently wrote and spoke of his royal ancestors, he rarely talked of his mother, and after her execution he was principally concerned for its effect upon his honour and reputation in Scotland, and upon his claim to the throne in England. There is no certain account of how he received the news, one says that he rejoiced, and it may be charitable to assume that he grieved a little, but he led no army across the Border as some of his forbears would have done, and as some of his subjects demanded. To expect him or his countrymen to have behaved other than they did is to turn one's back on his brief past and their long history.[1]

Melancholy regret for his mother, if it existed at all, was dissipated two years later by his marriage. Unlike his predecessors, he does not appear to have ever had a mistress, although there has been curious and imaginative speculation about an alternate sexual taste. Marriage and children, however, were dynastic obligations, and after some shuffling through the picture-cards of European houses the choice fell upon Anne of Denmark. She was a tall, fair, well-porportioned woman, with a long nose, a good nature and a trivial mind. She was also a Lutheran, and therefore an unpopular choice with Elizabeth, who had proposed Arabella Stuart, a child of ten and the King's first cousin. Tired of storms that delayed his bride's sailing, James went to Oslo to fetch her in October, 1589. The wedding was celebrated with Viking raids on wine and ale, and he stayed in Denmark until May, drinking, hunting, and arguing with learned men. The fruit of this cold, northern union would be late in coming, but it would be abundant.

James was probably happy to escape from his kingdom for a while, and from its vexatious nobility. In the early spring of 1589, Elizabeth told him that her agents had intercepted letters from some of his Catholic lords, addressed to Philip of Spain, offering sympathy for the failure of the Armada, and suggesting that any future attack on England would find an easy route through Scotland. 'Good Lord,' said Elizabeth tartly, 'no king a week would bear this.' The principal correspondent was young George Gordon, the impetuous Earl of Huntly, and he was accordingly taken up and comfortably imprisoned in Edinburgh Castle, where the King kissed him and swore that he believed in the Earl's innocence. The other confederates were marching upon the city, but their army withered from loss of courage, and they too were gently imprisoned and then released. One of them was Francis Stewart, Earl of Bothwell, son of a marriage between one of James V's bastards and a sister of that Bothwell long since dead in a Danish dungeon. He was a well-educated man but he walked along the dark edge of insanity, and was generally believed to be the warlock lord of half a dozen covens of witches. He lived for violent action, riding from Protestant or Catholic plot to Border brawl, and from that to a wild attack on the Edinburgh Tolbooth, liberating one of his men. When a number of crazed women in North Berwick were brought to trial for witchcraft they confessed that they knew the King's intimate bed-chamber talk with his wife, and that their satanic leader was Bothwell. James had a credulous belief in sorcery, which he shared with most of his subjects, and he ordered the Earl's arrest. Bothwell gaily escaped from prison, crossed the Border, and then rode back at Christmas, 1591. With maniacal daring he attacked Holyrood, hammering on the King's door and threatening to burn it down, until the townsfolk drove him out of the city. In his terror the King was given no comfort by the ministers, one of whom told him that the noise of Bothwell's hammering

---

[1] *Johnson.* "Sir, never talk of your independency, who could let your Queen remain twenty years in captivity, and then be put to death, without even a pretence of justice, without your ever attempting to rescue her; and such a Queen too! as every man of any gallantry of spirit would have sacrificed his life for.' – Worthy *Mr. James Kerr, Keeper of the Records.* "Half our nation was bribed by English money." – *Johnson.* "Sir, that is no defence: that makes you worse." ' James Boswell, *The Journal of a Tour to the Hebrides with Samuel Johnson, LL.D.*

had been a divine warning. With three hundred men Bothwell then attempted to abduct the King, and when that failed he came boldly to Holyrood again, demanding a trial for witchcraft, which neither Crown nor Kirk granted. This terrifying man was not entirely a lunatic, for behind his mad acts were the shadows of less deranged plotters, Protestant, Catholic and Spanish. When his passion burnt away his energy, he disappeared from Scotland, dying in poverty at Naples.

He was the indirect cause of a bloody murder that is still remembered in one of the most melancholy of Scottish ballads. In February, 1592, James ordered the arrest of the Earl of Moray, son-in-law of the old regent, on a charge of abetting Bothwell's violent December raid. Huntly was given the commission, which he accepted with delight, and probably with no intention of taking the Earl alive. James was aware of the old feud between the Gordons and the Moray family, and his foolish order to Huntly is inexplicable, unless one agrees with the ballad that Moray was the Queen's bonny lover. Forty Gordon horsemen, led by their earl, found their quarry at Donibristle on the northern shore of the Queensferry. He was alone in his house except for a few servants, and when the raiders set fire to it he ran out to their waiting knives, with his hair aflame it was said. Huntly first slashed his face with a dagger, and the plunging swords did the rest. Legend gave Moray a last arrogant taunt, 'Ye hae spoilt a better face than your ain, my lord!' There is a macabre painting of his naked and butchered body that shocks the eye and heart, and the ballad records the King's grieving anger.

> Nou wae be tae ye, Huntly,
> And wharfore did ye sae?
> I bad ye bring him wi ye,
> But forbad ye him to slay.[1]

And indeed he may have done, but the woe he brought upon Huntly's head was a week's imprisonment in Edinburgh Castle.

The bandit behaviour of great lords reflected or provoked less chivalrous disorders of riot and civil defiance, which the King's courts were too weak to suppress. The fear of Catholic plots was omnipresent, and although on his return from Denmark James had promised to maintain the Kirk as long as he lived, and had declared that the Church of England was 'an evil Mass said in English', his hatred of presbyterianism was well known. The murder of Moray, and the derisive punishment received by his assassin, produced an outcry which the ministers shrewdly encouraged from their pulpits. John Maitland, now Lord Thirlestane, had his brother Lethington's cold and machiavellian mind, and his uncouth face masked one of the most artful intellects in the history of the Scottish civil service. He was without religious attachments, and perhaps without religion at all, but he was dedicated to the preservation of Crown and State. The King respected and admired him, and it was upon his advice that James once more surrendered to the Kirk. In June, 1592, he agreed to the 'Golden Act', remembered as the Charter of the Presbytery, by which he and his parliament confirmed all the liberties, privileges, and immunities of the Kirk. Episcopal jurisdictions were abolished, and the government of the Kirk was given to its presbyteries, synods and General Assembly, which now had the right to meet as often as it wished and in the presence of the King or his commissioner.

[1] Version published in *The Oxford Book of Scottish Verse*.

James had surrendered, but he had not abandoned his intention to impose a form of episcopacy upon the Kirk. By guile and flattery, by bribery where necessary and with the advice of Thirlestane, he began to undermine the achievements of the Golden Act. A clause in the statute gave him the right to name the date and place of the General Assemblies, and to keep them from Edinburgh he called them in towns and cities lukewarm or unsympathetic to the Kirk. When a riot broke out in Edinburgh, for some unknown cause, he fined its citizens and declared that it was no longer his capital. Their purses thereby diminished, the burgesses naturally lost some of their sympathy for the ministers. He also separated some of the nobles from the Kirk, securing their support with grants from the temporalities that had been annexed by the Crown. It was at this time that Andrew Melville imperiously plucked at his sleeve and called him 'God's silly vassal', reminding him of the greater kingdom of Christ Jesus. But James knew that many of the ministers were more malleable, less extreme than Melville, and with kingly craft he played upon their ambition and vanity. He made some of them his advisers on Church affairs, and approved their suggestion that the Kirk should have representation in parliament. The ministers sat in the Estates as representatives of the vacant bishoprics, and although the General Assembly drew up the list from which the King selected them, and although it was insisted they should be known as commissioners without episcopal duties, a precedent had been made which the King boldly exploited. By 1600 he was appointing ministers of his own choice to empty sees, and they sat in parliament as the nucleus of a future episcopacy.

The Gowrie Conspiracy, which occurred in the middle of this ecclesiastical sparring, was a violent backward jolt to the behaviour patterns of the Middle Ages. That it was a conspiracy at all is not proven, but with sub-plots of a dark stranger, royal greed, and a suspicion of homosexuality, it is one of the best mystery stories in Scottish history. The Earl of Gowrie and his brother, the Master of Ruthven, were grandsons of that grim murderer of Riccio, and sons of the conspirator whom James had beheaded. They were also men who opposed his absolutist ambitions, and whose death would free him of one more fear. According to the King's account, virtually the only one, when he was hunting by Falkland in August, 1600, he was met by the Master of Ruthven, who told him a wondrous tale of an old man who had been discovered with a pot of gold. Intrigued by this, James rode with the Master to Gowrie House in Perth. He dined in amity with the brothers, and was then taken to a turret room by the Master. There he was shown no old man and no pot of gold, but a stranger in armour. When the Master told the King that he must die, James struggled to a window and called 'Treason!' to his servants below. In the brawl that followed the Ruthven brothers were killed by a valiant page. There were many who would not believe this story then, and many who have not since, and some who thought and think that by accompanying young Ruthven to the turret room James had a purpose unconnected with gold, one which the Master violently repulsed. But there was and is no substantiated alternative to the King's account. A few ministers refused his order to read it from their pulpits, but the rest dutifully obeyed.

The brilliant and tormenting Queen in London was nearing her death, and still she had not named James as her successor. He was ready to seize her throne by force if he had to, but there was no need for him to appear in the unnatural role of a warrior. Robert Cecil, the English secretary of state, was his partisan, the English Council was willing to proclaim him when the last Tudor was gone, and Protestants and Catholics

SVPER·EST

RELIGIO

PAX

THE
WORKES
OF THE MOST HIGH
AND MIGHTY PRINCE,
IAMES,
By the grace of God, Kinge
of Great Brittaine
France & Ireland
Defendor of the
Faith &c:
Published by Iames, Bishop of
WINTON & Deane of his
Mtie. Chappell Royall.
1 Reg: 3. 12. v. Loe I haue giuen thee
a wise and an vnderstanding heart.

LONDON
Printed by Robert
Barker & Iohn Bill
Printers to the Kings mos t
excellent Maiestie.
1616.

Cum priuilegio.

Renold Elstrack sculpsit

of both countries, for contrary reasons, were anxious for his succession. To James it was not a matter of rightful inheritance only. By the strength of the twin crowns he would be able to establish that absolute kingship he had justified in *The Trew Law of Free Monarchies*, which he wrote in 1598 and which his son Charles would later use as a step to the scaffold. In the Bible, it said, kings were called gods, 'because they sit upon God his Throne in the earth, and have the count of their administration to give unto him'. This was not Melville's silly vassal, but God's deputy. The King was *Dominus omnium bonorum*, 'without advice or authority of either Parliament or any other subaltern judicial seat'. Parliament was but the head court of a king, and there had been kings in Scotland before there had been other men of rank and estate. Between king and people there should be mutual duty and allegiance, but it was the monarchy and not the nation to whom James gave the adjective *free*. The concept was feudal, perhaps even benevolent, but it would be calamitous, and the *Trew Law* is more harrowing to read with hindsight than the King's entertaining treatise on sorcery and demonology.

More intimately, the divine right and personal responsibilities of a king were explained in *Basilikon Doron*, which James wrote for the instruction of his first son Henry.

> Therefore, my Son, first of all things, learn to know and love God, whom-to ye have a double obligation; first, for that he made you a man; and next, for that he made you a little God to sit on his Throne, and rule over other men. Remember that his glistering worldly glory of Kings is given them by God. . . .

A democratic form of government was a fantasy, designed to lead the people by the nose. Parliaments were ordained for making laws. 'Therefore hold no parliaments but for necessities of new Laws, which would be but seldom.' And the best laws, it would seem, were those that curbed the power of the nobles, and confined those fiery-spirited ministers who 'fed themselves with the hope to become *Tribuni Plebis*'. Young Henry was advised to be temperate in food and drink, modest in dress, jealous of his privacy and discreet in his choice of servants. He should be a good horseman and hunt with hounds, avoid violent games like football, and ban the wearing of arms at court. He could play cards, but dicing was a drumhead habit of common soldiers. History he should read, but not 'such infamous invectives as Buchanan's or Knox's Chronicles'. He should not be afraid of anger, for it was said in Proverbs that the wrath of a king was the roaring of a lion.

Toward dark on Saturday, March 27, 1603, Sir Robert Carey rode into Edinburgh with the news that the Queen of England was dead. Four days later another messenger reported that James had been proclaimed in London. Early in April he said goodbye to the Scots at St Giles's and then left on a slow journey southward, with a large following and a wife who was now a Catholic convert. His new subjects were neither sympathetic to him nor the country he was so abruptly leaving. Scotland, said a member of the Commons, was the 'most barren and sterile of all countries'. There was no promise of a serene and happy union in this thought, and less in the thistle-response that came from the Scots lawyer, Sir Thomas Craig.

> Though we have less money (and in that respect there is no comparison between us and our neighbours) yet we may console ourselves with the reflection that if our means are small, our needs are small also. . . . We do not mind our neighbours sneering at our lack of wealth. For wealth and material resources are not everything; otherwise we should long ago have lost our liberty and fallen under the dominion of the English.

*The elaborate title-page of the* Works of James VI, *the folio collection of 1616:*
*'Therefore, my Sonne,' he wrote, 'learne to know and love God . . . for that he made you*
*a little God to sit on his Throne, and rule over other men.'*

# PART VI

# One King and Parliament

'. . . to become one in hearts and affections,
as we are inseparably joined in interests'

James Graham, Marquis of Montrose, Covenanter and Royalist, the 'revolutionary moderate who can go no further
along the road his conscience has taken him, and in turning aside becomes the servant of reaction'.

The King's instructions to his son contained a short account of the boy's future subjects in the mountainous north. In the Highlands their savagery was softened by some civility, but in the Isles they were all utterly barbarous. Prince Henry was advised to 'reform and civilise the best inclined among them, rooting out or transporting the barbarous and stubborn sort and planting civility in their rooms'. It was not a new policy and it would be followed until the middle of the nineteenth century, when the harshness of its language would be modified but its purpose would be unchanged and its success finally achieved.

With the beginning of the seventeenth century the Highlanders may be seen in a recognizable form, the real material from which later men would tailor a romantic mockery. George Buchanan had already described them as a simple, pastoral people who lived by hunting, fishing and war, who boiled their meat before eating it, and sometimes devoured it raw, squeezing out the blood.

> They delight in variegated garments, especially striped, and their favourite colours are purple and blue. Their ancestors wore plaids of many different colours, and numbers still retain this custom, but the majority, now, in their dress, prefer a dark brown, imitating nearly the leaves of the heather, that, when lying upon the heath in the day, they may not be discovered by the appearance of their clothes; in these, wrapped rather than covered, they brave the severest storms in the open air, and sometimes lay themselves down to sleep even in the midst of snow.

They lived in crude huts, the floors covered with fern and heather, on which they rested in healthy ease. They were contemptuous of all civilized comforts, even when travelling outside their mountains, 'lest these barbarian luxuries, as they term them, should contaminate their native, simple hardiness'. They were a warrior people, delighting in danger and combat.

> Their weapons are, for the most part, a bow, and arrows barbed with iron, which cannot be extracted without widely enlarging the orifice of the wound; but a few carry swords or Lochaber axes. Instead of a trumpet, they use a bagpipe. They are exceedingly fond of music, and employ harps of a peculiar kind, some of which are strung with brass, and some with catgut. In playing they strike the wires either with a quill, or with their nails, suffered to grow long for the purpose; but their grand ambition is to adorn their harps with great quantities of silver and gems, those who are too poor to afford jewels substituting crystals in their stead. Their songs are not inelegant, and, in general, celebrate the praises of brave men; their bards seldom choosing any other subject.

In his Latin history of Scotland, published at Rome in 1578, Bishop John Leslie said the manners, clothing and tongue of the 'old Scots' had scarcely changed in two thousand years. Their peculiar and pestilential vice was seditious strife, and rather than be labourers and craftsmen all wished to be nobles, 'or at least bold men of war'. They were healthy and free from sickness, and those who survived their interminable conflicts usually died of old age. They could outrun the swiftest horse, and closed quickly with the enemy in battle, fighting skilfully with bow, lance and two-edged sword. Though quarrelsome and provocative, they were not lecherous, and abhorred voluptuous pleasures. The belted plaid, sole garment of most of them, was worn from necessity not vanity.

> The clothing of the women with them was most decent, for their coats hung down as far as the ankles, with mantles above, or plaids all embroidered cunningly; bracelets about their arms, jewels about their necks, brooches hanging at their throat, both comely and decent, and much to their decoration and

ornament. But that we pass not far from the men, when all their care was to excel in glory of warfare and victory, their labour and whole study in both peace and war was always set thereto, giving themselves, in a manner, wholly to that exercise.[1]

The economic and social basis of the Highland way of life was the clan system, tribal and patriarchal in origin. The *clann* was the family, the children of the chief, and he was *Ceann-cinnidh*, the head and leader of the family. The chiefs of some clans, such as the Frasers, Chisholms and Colquhouns, were in fact Norman-Scots or Anglo-Norman in origin, but although the belief in a common progenitor was fanciful in their case, intermarriage with their neighbours had long since made them as Gaelic as the rest. Since the coming of the Normans the great chiefs were also liege-lords, in law at least, and the feudal rights and jurisdictions of six earldoms overran the tribal divisions of the clans. But the people were an older civilization by practice and preference, and the exercise of feudal power upon the Highlands lasted as long and reached as far as the King's writ could be enforced by the sword. Though Bruce had made good use of Highlanders at Bannockburn, his authority over them had been tenuous, and they had used their swords in alliance rather than allegiance. At Flodden and at Pinkie they were the warrior rent-roll of the *Ceann-cinnidh*, not feudal levies of the Crown. He was their father and he protected them, and they defended his quarrels with their lives.

Though they were hostile to and contemptuous of the *Gall* – the Lowland man, the Saxon of the south – their struggle with him until now had been less bitter than their quarrels among themselves. He was the buyer of their horses and cattle, and only hard winters and cruel summers brought them raiding to the Mearns or the Stirling plain. Between all clans, immediate neighbours or distant, there was a history of feud, battle and treachery, but a major line of hostility may be drawn between the west and the east, as it was once drawn between Pict and Scot, and the strong heart of the *Gaidhealtachd* was still the west, sustained by the memory of Dalriada. Here the MacDonalds, as Lords of the Isles, had ruled the last Gaelic polity until 1493, and still claimed the leadership of the clans. At the zenith of their power they had held the great buckler of islands from the Butt of Lewis to Islay, dominated the western littoral from Loch Alsh to Kintyre, and marched their claims inland through Lochaber to the Great Glen and Easter Ross. The bardic genealogies of their chiefs, like the exultant clanging of shields, claimed descent through fifteen hundred years from Conn of the Hundred Battles, High King of Ireland. They were children of Colla Uais, a prince of the Isles before the sons of Erc beached their ships on the coast of Argyll, and they were the race of Fergus MacErc the founder of Dalriada. On firmer historical ground, they were descended from Somerled of the Isles, called Regulus of Argyll. When he was murdered, leading a great fleet of galleys against Malcolm IV in 1164, his lands were divided among his sons, and it was from a son of one of these, Donald, Lord of Islay, that the people acquired their patronymic. There was no joy without the men of Clan Donald, said one of its bards when the lordship of the Isles was lost. The hawks of Islay were renowned for their valour, their wisdom, and their nobility. No one was gentler with women, or bolder in war, no one more comely, patient and generous, more steadfast or more manly. Without Clan Donald there was no joy.

The successful challenge to the MacDonalds' leadership of the Gael, and by that to

---

[1] An anglicized version of the Scots translation made by Father James Dalrymple toward the end of the sixteenth century.

the lands they held, was made by the Campbells, who became the Highland arm of king or government for three centuries until Colonel Belford's cannon ended the story at Culloden. In the years that followed Red Harlaw they acquired what was lost by Clan Donald's stubborn intransigence. The MacDonalds' great power had begun with rewards given for service at Bannockburn, but thereafter they arrogantly resisted the Crown's authority. When they at last gave the House of Stuart their support, less for its sake than their own, it was already a lost cause and they were destroyed with it. The gratitude of Robert Bruce was also the foundation of Clan Campbell's mountain empire, and by involving themselves in the dynastic and religious struggles of the south its leaders preserved it with valour and with cunning. Campbell earls twice went to the scaffold, but it was during the temporary eclipse of the power they supported, and its ultimate triumph restored what had been lost with their heads. Though Clan Campbell called itself the race of Diarmid, from a shadowy lord of Lochow into whose family a Gillespic Cambel had married, the originator of its good fortune was Sir Neil Campbell, who transferred his allegiance from Balliol to Bruce at the right moment, and profited there-from with the grant of lands and castles in the west. From his descendants came the great families of Argyll and Breadalbane, a hundred and more cadet branches, with lands taken by battle or charter from MacDonalds, MacDougalls, MacGregors, Murrays, Macleans and MacNaughtens.

The first Earl of Argyll was created in 1457 and like the nine who followed him, until the family stepped higher to a dukedom, he was active and eminent in public affairs. Whenever MacDonald lands were lost by forfeiture, a Campbell earl or a member of his family was given a large share in their redistribution. The succeeding heirs of this Gaelic house married daughters of the great families of Hamilton, Gordon, Graham, Menteith, Methven, Lennox Stewarts and royal bastards. They were born into the government of Scotland. They were judicious and shrewd, and while they served their own ends they also brought order and law into the chaotic anarchy of the north. This was southern law and Campbell order, of course, and was neither invited nor desired by the *Gaidhealtachd*, but the King's peace was usually maintained in those areas where the Earl of Argyll's jurisdiction was backed by the bows and swords of his clan. In Argyll, it was said, both Lowlander and Highlander might come without fear to the courts and ask for justice. Elsewhere justice was dispensed by pit and gallows, by the supreme authority of the chiefs and often in contempt of the Crown.

Well served by his Chancellor, the second Earl of Argyll, James IV was able to bring a measure of peace to the Highlands, as much by the force of his own personality as by Campbell swords. The Earl died with him at Flodden, and the clans once more returned to wasteful quarrels. Never fully agreed upon the rightful heir to the lordship of the Isles while that title was a reality, the MacDonalds fought bitterly among themselves once it was abolished. In 1545 the last active claimant, Donald Dubh, gathered four thousand swordsmen and a hundred and sixty galleys to play his part in the Rough Wooing of his English allies. But sickness killed him, and the old claim was now scarcely heard in the noisy struggles between MacDonald chiefs of Dunyveg, Sleat and Clan-ranald. More than MacDonald pride was lost with the lordship of the Isles. It had been a centre of Gaelic independence and culture, a recall of the old Dalriadic kingdom of the Scots, and arguably a power that might have been able to impose government and order upon the Highlands. Without Clan Donald, said the bard, there was no strength.

Power and authority shifted southward to the Campbells and eastward to the Gordons, and they were feudal earls answerable to a Lowland crown, its weapons against the disorder and blood-letting that continued throughout the sixteenth century. In the far north Mackays fought among themselves, and then against the Keiths, the Gunns and the earls of Sutherland. When Lauchlan Mackintosh, chief of Clan Chattan, seemed inclined to accept the authority of the Crown, he was murdered by one of his own kinsmen, and the clan wars which followed were only suppressed by the hanging of two or three hundred Mackintoshes. The MacDonalds of Clanranald and the Frasers of Lovat disputed the lands that lay between them, and although Argyll was able to restrain the one for a time, and Huntly the other, they met at last by Loch Lochy. On a hot July day eight hundred men fought in their shifts, and when dusk came all but fourteen were dead, including the chief and eighty gentlemen of Clan Fraser. The Reformation scarcely affected the Gaelic north-west, and few of the new Kirk's ministers were ready to exile themselves in the wild mountains and isles. Clan Campbell, however, was accepting the new faith, grafting it upon that peculiar Gaelic hybrid of pagan myth and Christian ethic. Since the Gordons of Huntly adhered in fact, if not always by profession, to the Catholic Church, the house of Argyll grew stronger upon their indecision and treason. When Huntly murdered the bonnie Earl of Moray, and was further suspected of popish plots, the seventh Earl of Argyll was sent to bring him before the King. The Campbell was only nineteen, but he raised an army of twelve thousand men from his own clan and from the Macleans, Grants, MacNeils, MacGregors and Mackintoshes. They met the Gordons and their clan allies at Glenlivet, but the Campbells ran, Argyll wept in shame, and Huntly was forgiven by the King. Although James VI was grateful

*The weapons of the Highlanders were picturesque, but deadly, manifestations of their warrior culture. 'All their care,' Bishop Leslie wrote of the chiefs, 'was to excel in glory of warfare and victory.'* Right *Thomas Pennant's view of Castle Gordon, Moray, also known as the Bog of Gight, built by the Gordon Earls of Huntly.*

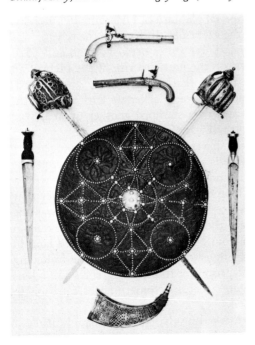 

to the Campbells for their police work, they were a potential army of the Kirk, and to keep a balance he raised Huntly to a marquisate and restored him to the lieutenancy of the north.

The King's opinion of the Highlanders, as expressed in *Basilikon Doron*, was almost a cry of despair. In 1597 – when Clan Donald and the Macleans were in feud, and the men of Sutherland and Caithness were hewing at each other in Strathnaver – he endeavoured to impose some order and control. He insisted that all chiefs and lairds should produce titles to the lands they held, and should stand surety for their own behaviour and that of their dependants. Admirable in concept though this was, it produced more bloodshed. Men without titles fought for what they held. Others, like the Appin Stewarts, the MacGregors, and the MacDonalds of Glencoe, refused to appear in Edinburgh to answer for the natural high spirits of their clansmen. To punish malcontents, and to suppress thieving and raiding, Writs of Fire and Sword were granted to other chiefs, and where possible they were executed with ferocious joy and savagery. By such commissions against their petty neighbours, the earls of Argyll, Huntly, Sutherland and Seaforth were able to cloak their own aggrandizement in the substance of royal authority. These were the years of the MacGregors' fall. Their narrow glens ran between the Campbell lands of Argyll and Breadalbane. They were proud, brave and intractable, cattle-raiders and mercenaries, but the government's reaction to their wild ways outdid them in savagery. They were struck from existence, their name proscribed and their lives forfeit when three or more assembled in arms. They were hunted as animals, not as noble beasts but as vermin, and the head of a MacGregor was valued no higher than the mask of a wolf. By royal orders to 'root out and extirpate all that race' they were hanged, shot and dirked. Their lands passed to the Campbells of Glenorchy, and their name was taken from them for nearly two hundred years.

The King's attempt to colonize the Highlands and the Isles was no more successful than fire and sword, but it was a template for imperial plantation. He originally intended to settle Lowlanders in Kintyre, Lochaber and the Hebrides. In Kintyre the scheme was briefly fulfilled, and in Lochaber it quickly died. Three times between 1598 and 1610 optimistic adventurers sailed from Fife to Lewis on the northern rim of the Hebridean shield, and three times they were driven out by the 'barbarous, bloody and wicked' Macleods. What they could not do was later done by the Mackenzie Earl of Seaforth, who had one foot upon Cromarty in the east and now stamped another upon Lewis, thus making himself the master of the north as Argyll was of the south.

The MacDonalds of the Isles and the mainland were linked by distant progenitors and recurrent marriage to the Catholic MacDonells in the glens of Antrim across the north channel of the Irish Sea. Their intriguing and their comradeship in arms were a constant threat to the Crown's authority, and the menace of the Celtic confederacy that might grow from it was the substance of unhappy royal dreams. Colonization was the King's answer again, and this time it succeeded, though the value of it would remain undecided by posterity. To divide MacDonald from MacDonell, he confiscated land in Ulster and settled it with Protestant Scots and Englishmen. Throughout the following century the colony would also be used as a work-prison for transported rebels and felons from England and Scotland, and would ultimately become something of a nation in itself, an albatross about the neck of the Irish Gael.

The early Highland policy of James VI was marked by the calamitous application of good intentions. By entrusting the suppression of disorder to great feudal magnates like Argyll, Seaforth and Gordon, and by encouraging one clan to hold another in check, he prepared the ground for enmities that would last for another century and a half. Andrew Knox, Bishop of the Isles, warned him that there was no sense in rooting out a pestiferous clan like the MacDonalds only to elevate another like the Campbells. Knox was a shrewd and intelligent man, and wisely led a commission to find an alternative to the original policy. He travelled with it to Iona in 1609, securing the promise of many chiefs, MacDonalds among them, that they would obey the King and his laws. They also agreed to admit reformed ministers, to build inns, suppress vagabonds, prohibit the carrying of firearms, send their heirs to the Lowlands for education, and to keep the peace within their bounds. They even agreed to stop the mouths of their bards, whose songs perpetuated the memory of old feuds and hatred. There is no great evidence that these promises were kept. A way of life sustained for a thousand years, rooted in racial pride and besotted with military valour, is not changed by parliamentary enactment. Nor was time given for change. The country was moving toward the violence of religious and political upheaval, and the Highlander's 'broad sword with a shearing sharp edge' would be needed in a war-game that was to be played from London to Strathnaver.

The chiefs who met Andrew Knox in conciliation on Iona had been bred in a tradition recorded by Bishop Leslie.

> Among them this was their manner, the greater of degree and the nobler of blood that any of them was, in the wars he was foremost, and gave the first onset in the field, and set first on the enemy: and this he did to move and inflame his company to stand stoutly, and without fear to gang forward.

## 2

When James said goodbye to his people at St Giles's on April 3, 1603, he asked them to think of him as going from one part of the island to another to secure their greater comfort. The congregation is said to have wept, but if these words were remembered later it may have been with sour humour. Scotland was sent little comfort by an absentee king, and his journey to that other part of the island brought him closer to his dangerous ideal of an absolute monarchy. The nation he left retained its parliament, kirk and savage pride, and of these only the last was not weakened by the transference of the royal presence to London. The English were in general unimpressed by this sad-eyed, harsh-tongued man who came southward on a tide of new knighthoods, and who hanged a thief without trial on the way. At his first address to their parliament, some of the Commons sat with their hats upon their heads, sullenly listening to his felicitous description of himself as the husband of Great Britain. 'I am the head and it is my body. I am the shepherd and it is my flock.' He was a Christian king under the Gospel, and it was unreasonable to think he should have two wives, that being the head he should have a divided body.

The English did not share his opinion that they could now be one with the Scots. That supercilious traveller Sir Anthony Weldon, admittedly extreme in his prejudices, said that Scotland was 'good for those that possess it, and too bad for others to be at charge to conquer it'. The air of the country would certainly be wholesome but for the odour of the people who inhabited it, and the earth might indeed be fruitful had they the wit to manure it. It was a wonder so brave a prince and king as James could be born in so 'stinking a town as Edinburgh in lousy Scotland'. The English parliament roughly rejected the King's suggestion that it should unite with the Estates, although a court decision did determine that all his subjects born after his accession to the throne of England had a common nationality. The Scots, no more enthusiastic for a parliamentary union, established common citizenship by statute. Delighted by England, impressed by the wealth of its nobles and the luxury of their great houses, James quickly forgot his promise to return to his native land every three years. He governed Scotland as if it were a province, through a Privy Council that grew smaller over the years until it was composed entirely of royalist officers. They were able men, but they were creatures of the King, and in time they controlled Parliament through its administrative committee known as the Lords of the Articles. Though this should have been elected by the Estates, James eventually submitted his own nominees, many of them members of the Privy Council. 'Here I sit,' he bragged, 'and govern by my pen. I write and it is done, and by a clerk of the Council I govern Scotland now, which others could not do by the sword.' The boast was no exaggeration. He was James I of Great Britain, realizing some of the hopes that had died with the great Plantagenet at Burgh-on-Sands three centuries before.[1]

Warmed by the flattering support of the Church of England, he struck at the Scots Kirk. He ignored the articles and the spirit of the Golden Act, and for two years successfully postponed a meeting of the General Assembly. In 1605 a further postponement was defied by nineteen bold ministers, who were tried for treason and exiled. Andrew Melville was called to London in the following year, with other leaders of the Kirk, and there subjected to lectures on the virtues of episcopacy. But a man who had called his king God's silly vassal was not one to be instructed by the Archbishop of Canterbury, and he became the master and the prelate his pupil. When he wrote a Latin lampoon, mocking the Anglican ritual in the Chapel Royal, he was first imprisoned in the Tower and then exiled. He never returned, dying in a Huguenot seminary at Sedan.

When Melville's voice was silent in Scotland, his inspiring courage gone, the Kirk lacked the muscle and sinew to resist the King. An Act of 1607 restored the prelates to their jurisdictions, the bishoprics were filled by royal nomination, and in 1610 James summoned Archbishop John Spottiswoode of St Andrews[2] to London, where, with two others, he received the Spiritual Touch from Anglican prelates. When they returned to Scotland they similarly consecrated their colleagues. A weak General Assembly accepted these reversals, and a subservient parliament confirmed them. Moderate Presbyterians, though they did not like the changes, accepted them without serious protest, and the ambitions of many ministers lifted their hopes toward sacerdotal vanities they had once condemned. James had achieved a remarkable victory, but it was not yet enough. In 1617 he paid his only visit to Scotland, with a great retinue of servants and courtiers, and although he left his English ministers in London he was accompanied by several Anglican advisers, including William Laud, the Dean of Gloucester. What further changes he proposed for the Kirk were made clear at the Chapel Royal of Holyrood. Its officiating ministers were ordered to wear white surplices, and a sweet-tongued choir of boys sang to

---

[1] In October, 1604, James adopted the title of King of Great Britain, France and Ireland. The Treaty of Union in 1707 confirmed the title, and the existence of one united kingdom only. The numbering of its monarchs should properly date from 1603, a fact which English custom has ignored.

[2] He was the son of John Spottiswoode, Kirk superintendent of Lothian, one of the commission which drew up the First Book of Discipline. The Archbishop's brother was an Anglican vicar.

the music of an expensive organ. Wooden images of the apostles flanked an altar upon which were placed two closed bibles and two unlighted candles. The King and his attendants knelt at Communion. A year later, against the cautionary advice of Spottiswoode and the uneasiness of the bishops, James asked a General Assembly at Perth to approve five articles of reform. The Sacrament was to be received kneeling, and to be available to the sick in private. Baptism should also be permitted in private houses, where circumstances demanded, and all children were to be confirmed by a bishop. Finally, the Birth, Passion, Resurrection and Ascension of Christ, with the descent of the Holy Ghost, were to be commemorated by all on the appointed days. Lords, prelates and burgesses sat at a long table while these articles were read, the ministers standing behind, and it was made plain that the King's authority was supreme and final, and that the behaviour and opinions of all present would be reported to him. The Articles were approved, but almost all who voted against them were ministers, unable to accept so blunt a contradiction of Reformed doctrine. Nor could the people in general be persuaded to stomach them. At the first festival following, Christmas Day, many stayed away from church and tradesmen opened their stalls. Men and women stubbornly refused to kneel for the Sacrament at Communion, and some of their ministers went bravely to prosecution for encouraging their defiance. In his last effort to impose the Church he desired, James had revived the stubborn spirit of opposition to it.

As the 'little God' of the *Basilikon Doron*, the King was determined to be the master of the Kirk, and his behaviour sometimes seems to have been the product of an intimate duologue between himself and the Almighty. Yet without his passionate concern for scholarship and religion, literature would be the poorer. The version of the Bible he authorized is unmatched in its beautiful, subtle and powerful use of the English language. A later age, enjoying the benefits that followed the exhaustion of sectarian conflict, may perhaps think it worth a Sacrament taken upon the knees.

Though the Highlands were never restful, the Borders were quietened, and the relative stability of the first years of the new century brought a slow prosperity in which all shared to a greater or lesser degree, although at the bottom of the social pyramid men still lived in hunger and despair. The husbandman had his sod-roofed hut, a chair and a

*Highland life, illustrated here in Pennant's* Tour, *was a warrior society based on cattle economy. Shielings were rough dwellings occupied by the people during the summer pasturing.*

table, pot and kettle, and a bible by the fire, but below him were the 'idle and sturdy beggars', wandering paupers whom the Privy Council could never satisfactorily control or effectively coerce. They were frequently dispossessed sub-tenants, or landless labourers and farm-servants whose livelihood depended upon the tenant as his did upon the laird, the first victims of weather and famine, death and debt. Castle and keep still dominated a bleak landscape, and there were as yet few graceful country houses like those that were rising in England and Europe, but the Reformation and its political consequences had produced a middle class of merchants and small gentry with a taste for comfort and for the vanities to equal their power and importance. In the burgh houses there were now dining-rooms and withdrawing-rooms, doors and cupboards of carved wood, panelled walls, upholstery of silk and scarlet leather, carpets and rugs, Dutch chairs that could be turned into gaming-tables, more glass, more silver, more damask cloth, and a stand of books rather than a bell of arms. An hour-glass stood on the chimney-breast, a tinder-box on a table, and a caged lark sang hopefully by an open casement. There were idle hours for golf and archery, for needlework and the tailoring of flower gardens. In the homes of bonnet lairds and country lords life and pleasure were less sophisticated, but they were robust in their self-reliance. In 1618 the English waterman John Taylor, self-styled Water-Poet to the King, set out on his 'moneyless perambulation from London to Edenborough', determined neither to beg nor borrow but presumably to keep himself alive on the liberal hospitality of the Scots lairds. He was well received, and probably paid for his free lodgings with the unconscious exercise of his comic conceit.

> I have been at houses like castles for building; the master of the house his beaver being his blue bonnet, one that will wear no other shirts but of the flax that grows on his own ground, and of his wives, daughters, or servants spinning; that hath his stockings, hose, and jerkin of wool of his own sheep's back; that never (by his pride of apparel) caused mercer, draper, silkman, embroiderer, or haberdasher to break and turn bankrupt: and yet this plain home-spun fellow keeps and maintains thirty, forty, fifty servants, or perhaps more, every day relieving three or four score people at his gate: and besides all this, can give noble entertainment for four or five days together, to five or six earls and lords, besides knights, gentlemen, and their followers, if they be three or four hundred men and horse of them; where they shall not only feed but feast, and not feast but banquet.

Anthony Weldon, the English gentleman, was less impressed than the Thames boatman. He came to Scotland with James in 1617, and obviously had his gentility stung by Scots pride. 'Their followers are their fellows, their wives their slaves, their horses their masters, and their swords their judges. . . .'

> They christen without the cross, marry without the ring, receive the sacrament without reverence, die without repentance, and bury without divine service. They keep no holy days, nor acknowledge any saint but St. Andrew, who they said got that honour by presenting Christ with an oaten cake after his forty days fast. They say likewise, that he that translated the Bible was the son of a maltster, because it speaks of a miracle done by barley-loaves; whereas they swear they were oaten cakes, and that no other bread of that quantity could have sufficed so many thousands.

Scotswomen rarely pleased the Englishman, whose usual complaint was that he could not see their faces, so wrapped about were they in plaids of the same woollen stuff 'whereof saddle-cloths in England are made'. Weldon thought they were all monsters, and none too clean at that. 'To be chained in marriage with one of them were to be tied to a dead carcass and cast into a stinking ditch.' The sinful use of cosmetics, he noticed, had newly arrived in Scotland, but he did not think it would last. English criticism was harsh and uncharitable, and did not hide a dislike of the union and a distrust of Scotland, but it was a Scot who wrote a more penetrating indictment of his countrymen, and that upon an occasion when a panegyric might have been expected. William Lithgow was a prototype of the peregrinating Scot, and had he been to a fraction only of the countries he claimed to have visited his opinion would still have been worthy of attention. In 1633 he wrote a jolting poem of welcome to Charles I, and its picture of his native land is perhaps closer to truth than is sometimes allowed. He complained of the shortage of coinage, of the Scotswoman's custom of walking abroad like a masked harlot or a spirit in a shroud, of the base and stinking habit of tobacco, and of debtors who threatened their creditors with sword and pistol. More pertinently, and speaking as if he were Scotland itself, he asked and explained why it was so bare,

> Thus void of planting, woods and forests fair:
> Hedges and ditches, parks and closed grounds,
> Trees, strips, and shaws in many fertile bounds:
> But only that the landlords set their land
> From year to year, and so from hand to hand:
> They change and flit their tenants as they please,
> And will not give them lease, tacks, times nor ease
> To prosper and to thrive; for if they should,
> As soon they thrust them out of house and hold:
> And he who bids most farm, still gets the room,
> Whilst one above another's head doth come:
> Or else to raise his rent, or kiss the door,
> This is the cause my Commons live so poor,
> And so the peasants cannot set nor plant
> Woods, trees and orchards which my valleys want,
> But leave me half deformed, so they're distressed,
> And by their greedy masters still oppressed.

The same complaint had been made in the previous century by John Major, and would be made again. Nobleman, bonnet laird and tenant lived upon rents paid in money or kind, and gave little back to the land. The great peasant mass of the Lowland population, husbandmen, sub-tenants and labourers, had no rights or security on the ground they worked, and none of the real or mythical kinship with their lord which gave the Highland peasant a feeling of family unity. In this context it is easy to understand why the levelling doctrines of the Reformers could excite a passionate loyalty and devotion among the common people.

The city of Edinburgh, swollen with sixty thousand crowded inhabitants, still excited admiration and disgust. Taylor thought the Royal Mile was the 'fairest and goodliest street' he had ever seen, though he hadn't a penny in his pocket when he first walked down it. A loch to the south was now gone, and that on the north was no more than a marsh. Held inside the Flodden Wall, the houses climbed high through a cloud of coal-smoke, eight, nine and ten storeys from the street before, and a dozen or more from the falling rock-face behind. The gabled roof-line from castle to palace was broken by the crown steeple of St Giles's, the rising masonry of Parliament House and Heriot's Hospital, the spires of churches, the walls of a prison, gildhalls and university. Merchants and tradesmen lived on the High Street above the Netherbow Port, but below on the Canongate approach to Holyroodhouse were the town-homes of the nobility with walls eight or ten feet thick, built not for a month or a year, said Taylor, but from antiquity to posterity. The gardens behind these houses, said another Englishman, had been created with 'such elegance, and cultivated with such diligence, that they easily challenge comparison with the gardens of warmer climates, and almost of England itself'.

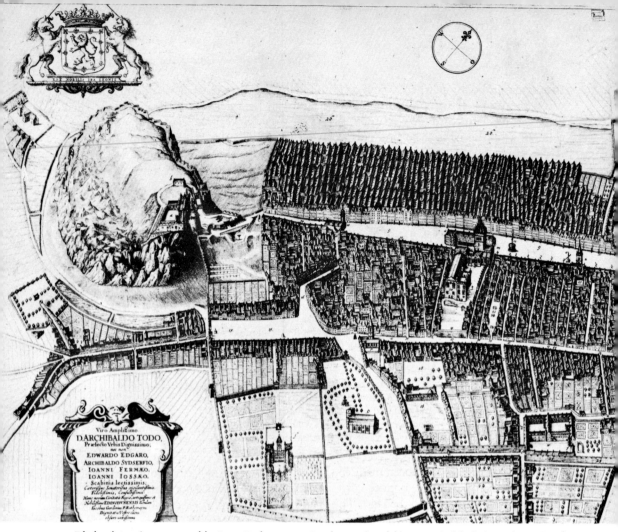

*Edinburgh in 1647, as mapped by James Gordon, pastor of Rothiemay. 'Doubtless a most healthful place to live in,' said an Englishman, 'were not the inhabitants most sluttish, nasty and slothful.'*

Comparison with England was inevitable, and rarely to Scotland's credit. Sir William Brereton, a Cheshire man, kept a journal of his visit in 1636, and it was he who said that Scotswomen wrapped themselves in cloth which Englishmen would place beneath their saddles. He too thought that Edinburgh's one great street was the most graceful he had ever seen, though it lacked fair glass in its windows and was disfigured by the wooden facings on its stone houses.

> This city is placed in a dainty, healthful pure air, and doubtless were a most healthful place to live in were not the inhabitants most sluttish, nasty and slothful people. I could never pass through the hall, but I was constrained to hold my nose; their chambers, vessels, linen and meat, nothing neat, but very slovenly; only the nobler and better sort of them, brave, well-bred men, and much reformed. This street, which may indeed deserve to denominate the whole city, is always thronged with people, it being the market-place, and is the only place where the gentlemen and merchants meet and walk, wherein they may walk dry under foot, though there hath been an abundance of rain. Some few coaches are here to be found for some of the great lords and ladies, and bishops.

He was disgusted by the unscoured pewter from which he was invited to drink, by the bare-legged wash-women who trampled in tubs on the High Street, by foul pots of

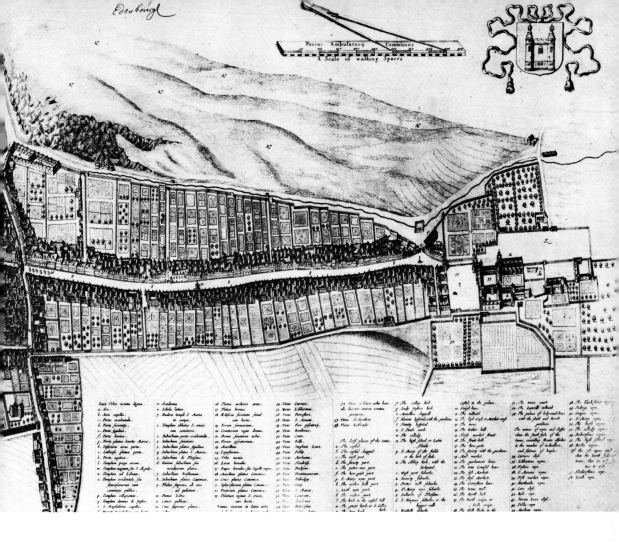

ordure at the openings to the wynds, and by the noisy disorder of the courts of justice. On the Lord's day he saw three women on stools of repentance below the pulpit, an adulterer in a hair shirt which he was condemned to wear for a year, a fornicator who confessed to the satisfaction of the congregation. And he was shocked by the poor, more than he had seen elsewhere in his travels, and the 'most miserable creatures in the world'.

Brereton saw the Reformed Kirk at its nadir. The extremist ministers had dwindled to a hard core of intransigents, defying the returned episcopacy and loyal to the teachings of Melville. Forbidden to preach in public, they did so in private, and circulated books and pamphlets among those whom they could trust. As their numbers decreased, so the fire of their faith burnt stronger, and they were loved and admired by the men and women who came discreetly to their meetings. The great social reforms, the educational programme proposed by the first Book of Discipline, had come to little in stagnant indifference. William Lithgow was no friend to the Reformers, condemning them for the destruction of beautiful churches and abbeys, but he lamented the decay in scholarship and knowledge.

237

So grammar schools are ruined, learning rare,
Boards are so dear, and stipends wax so bare;
That good householders, countrymen I spy,
Can hardly board their bairns abroad, and why?
Burghs are so fingering, school-masters so needy,
Love at such rate, and victuallers so greedy,
That now most bairns with sheep and ploughs are found,
Which makes so many ignorants abound,
With rustic courage, manners harsh and rude,
And decent comeliness is quite seclude.

In March, 1625, James had been attacked by a tertian ague at the great house of Theobalds, two hours' ride from London. It grew worse and he could not survive. He was almost fifty-nine and had been a king for all but a year of his life. In many respects he was an admirable man, although this judgment must be made outside the context of his kingship. Within it, the effect and the results of his work would be disastrous. For all his assumption of earthly godhead, as he grew older he was happier with his servants, withdrawing from court and state life, greedily indulging himself with melons, strawberries and grapes. He wrote more bad verse, and no longer burst into passionate rages. He had been the king he wished to be, and believed he should be, and if his horizon had been narrow, his course devious, his objective had remained constant. He died on the twenty-seventh day of the month, and was buried in Westminster Abbey on May 5. The last words of a funeral oration, spoken by the Bishop of Lincoln, were that Solomon now slept.

## 3

The Presbyterian Revolution began with a violent and probably contrived incident in the High Church of St Giles on Sunday July 23, 1637. The congregation, greater than usual, included a number of waiting-women who were hired to arrive early at the kirk and who kept places for their employers by sitting on their folding 'creepie-stools'. When the Dean of Edinburgh began to read from the new Service Book authorized by the King they shouted at him, and a gentleman who murmured a dutiful response to the liturgy was struck on the head with a bible and asked 'Dost thou say Mass in my lug!' David Lindsay, Bishop of Edinburgh, went to the pulpit to quieten the women, and was greeted with cries of 'Wolf!' and 'Crafty fox!' and 'Beastly belly-god!' According to some reports stools and bibles were thrown at the learned old man, and he was told that he had been begotten by the Devil and a witch, that he was a pest to God's Kirk, and that he would be better hanged. The Provost summoned officers to drive the women from the church, and there they remained for the rest of the service, hammering on the locked doors and throwing stones at the windows.

In London, King Charles was told that the riot was the work of the 'rascal multitude' and that good and decent men were disgusted by it. But it was too timely, and was exploited too well for it to have been no more than a spontaneous incident. Charles was not a man to recognize portents and warnings, or to be deflected by them if he did, and the nature of his beliefs argued that opposition to them could come from a minority only. He ascended the throne at twenty-five, a small and sallow man, shy and sensitive, aesthetic in tastes and totally without humour. When his elder brother died in 1612 he had accepted his future kingship with dedication, and with a determination to honour his duty to God and the Crown in the manner prescribed by his father. As king, he devoted his life to the establishment of an absolute monarchy and an episcopal Church, and since his stubborn defence of both was matched by the growing intransigence of his enemies – in both kingdoms – his death and that of thousands of his subjects became inevitable.

Within a few months of his accession Scotland discovered that he was a man without the wish for compromise. An Act of Revocation passed by his Privy Council in October, 1625, recalled to the Crown all Church lands that had been acquired by lay proprietors.

*Charles I, painted by Daniel Mytens. 'When his brother died in 1612, he accepted his future kingship with dedication and with a determination to honour his duty to God and the Crown in the manner prescribed by his father.'*

The King's honest conscience was involved, and he sincerely wished the rentals to be used for the benefit of the Church, to dignify its rituals and pay its stipends, but he immediately lost the sympathy of many great landowners, and it was not restored when they were allowed to keep what they had upon payment of a settled sum. Not un-naturally, they began to think of the common interests they might have with the uncompromising zealots of the Kirk. For the first eight years of his reign Charles had little interest in Scotland, controlling it as his father had done through a loyal Council, and he had trouble enough with the constitutional problems of England, most of which he thought he could resolve by dispensing with parliamentary government. His belief in an absolute monarchy was encouraged by its apparent success in France, and by the blessing of his spiritual adviser, William Laud. He wished to glorify the episcopal Church of his northern kingdom with material richness and elevating worship, to create a resounding ante-room to a heavenly temple, wherein he stood closest to the door of the Almighty, and he threatened condign punishment upon those bold Scots ministers who sent him a remonstrance against the obnoxious custom of kneeling before him. To make the city a fitting capital, he would create a new bishopric in Edinburgh, order the renovation of St Giles's that it might be a proper cathedral, and begin the building of a Parliament House beside it. Such things would be paid for by the heavy taxation of the city's inhabitants.

He came at last to Edinburgh for his coronation in 1633, and he brought Laud with him. The town did its best to receive him with respect. The filthy streets were cleaned, bone-white skulls were taken from the gates, and the gallows was removed from the links at Bruntsfield. The disquietening splendour of his crowning was arranged by Laud, who was said to have rebuked Archbishop Spottiswoode for appearing without a surplice. There was a table which all men could see was meant to be an altar, clasped books and candles, a tapestry of the Crucifixion before which the prelates moved in idolatrous reverence. On the following Sunday Charles went to St Giles's, where the Anglican service was read by Laud's chaplains. The tactless foolishness of such indifference to Scots feelings was repeated when Charles called a parliament, and a committee of the Lords of the Articles was elected by the votes of his bishops. In a single day the committee submitted a hundred and sixty-eight measures confirming the King's financial and ecclesiastical policies, and Charles was seen to be writing down the names of those who opposed them.

Nor was this all. After his departure to England arrangements were made to introduce

*The centre of the Old Town of Edinburgh, showing the High Kirk of St Giles, the resounding pulpit of Reform. Right The title-page of a 1662 edition of the Book of Common Prayer, engraved by David Loggan. Scots Episcopalians accepted this revised English liturgy, but it was rejected by non-jurant Jacobites.*

Laud's Anglican forms. All kirks were to be rearranged on the English model with the communion table as an altar. Ministers were to hear confessions. Those who opposed the rules of the Book of Canons, who challenged the Crown's right to order Church affairs, or who criticized the episcopal hierarchy were to be excommunicated. Archbishop Spottiswoode was made President of the Exchequer, appointed to the Privy Council with four other prelates, and given precedence over all the King's Scottish subjects. In 1635 the Kirk was ordered to use a new Prayer Book which was still in preparation and upon which no minister had been consulted.

It was two years before Dean John Hanna attempted to read this liturgy in St Giles's, and by then the growing opposition to it and all it represented had been given time to prepare for its reception, not only in Edinburgh but elsewhere. Throughout the country there were violent manifestations of outraged feelings. Those prelates who had approved the Prayer Book were pursued like animals whenever seen. One fled to England to escape summary hanging, and another was brutally mobbed for wearing a crucifix. The Provost of Edinburgh was stoned, and would have been killed had not his servants fired above the heads of the crowd. 'The whole people think Popery at the doors,' wrote the moderate minister Robert Baillie, 'I think our people possessed with a bloody devil. . . . I think I may be killed and my house burnt over my head.'

Much of the rioting was spontaneous, but that which was productive was undoubtedly inspired. The stool-throwing in St Giles's was followed by more serious disorder in the streets, during which Provost and magistrates were besieged in the city chambers, and it became necessary to treat with the mob as with an organized and controllable army. Upon a suggestion from the Lord Advocate it appointed a committee to negotiate with the Privy Council. Four lords, four lairds, four ministers and four burgesses were quickly found, and the revolution had begun. In December this committee, known as the Tables, insisted that it should be heard as the voice of the Estates, and it presented the alarmed Council with a petition from twenty-four nobles and between two and three hundred lairds, many of whom signed as representatives of the burghs as well as individuals. Well supported by ministers, the petition demanded the withdrawal of the offensive Liturgy and Canons, and the removal of the bishops from the Council. The Tables publicly disowned the mob which had brought them into being, but said that no action should be taken against its leaders.

The King was bewildered, and in the conceit of his own rectitude he decided that he was faced with no more than an outcry against Popery. He sent a declaration of his own disapproval of Catholicism, but he refused to yield to the demands of the petition and he ordered the signatories to disperse upon pain of treason. When this proclamation was read in Edinburgh there was a riot, and young James Graham, Earl of Montrose, climbed upon a barrel by the Mercat Cross and cheered on the mob. In a moment of merry prescience his friend, Lord Rothes, told him that he would not be content until he was raised still higher by three fathoms of rope. Hanging seemed to fascinate Rothes, and he was not always jovial when he talked of it. If bishops could not behave, he said, then 'noblemen, barons and burgesses would sit upon them and hang them'. The mobbing and the rioting, the easy talk of violence and the open purchase of arms, deeply alarmed men like Baillie. 'I am affrighted,' he wrote, 'with a bloody civil war.'

Confidently borne upon the wave of hysterical emotion, the Tables invited the nation to subscribe to a greater protest, a declaration of faith and purpose. The roots of this National Covenant were deep in Scotland's history. It had long been the custom for men to sign collective agreements, to enter into bands for their mutual protection. The Covenant was such a band by which a whole people, landed and landless, rich and poor, could declare its adherence to the Negative Confession of 1580 and its readiness to oppose all changes that had not been approved by a free Assembly and Parliament. More than a declaration of faith, it was a political manifesto that challenged the King's prerogative and by implication affirmed that the right to make and change the law rested in parliament only. It was first drafted in the early weeks of 1638 by two remarkable men. Alexander Henderson was the middle-aged minister of Leuchars, a product of Melville's reformed university of St Andrews, and a steadfast presbyterian with a statesman's cool and cunning mind. His colleague was a young advocate, Archibald Johnston of Warriston, whose feverish intelligence was close to insanity and who said that the product of their pens was a glorious marriage between God and the people. Revised by Lord Balmerino and the earls of Rothes and Loudoun, the band was first signed on February 28 by leading members of the nobility in Greyfriars Church. Ministers and burgesses signed on the following day and it was agreed that copies should be sent to every burgh, parish and university, and that the names of those who abstained should be recorded. It thus had the virtues of a national referendum and the vices of a tyrannical plebiscite.

There is more drama than truth in the legend of rich and poor crowding into Greyfriars Kirkyard, where the band was placed on a flat stone, but the response was immense, inspired by sermons to apposite texts: 'And they entered into a covenant to seek the Lord God of their fathers. . . .' In the south-west men were said to have signed in their own blood. When an Edinburgh minister urged his congregation to stand, to hold up their hands in a solemn oath of support, 'there rose such a yelloch,' said Warriston, 'such abundance of tears, such a heavenly harmony of sighs and sobs through all corners of the church, as the like was never seen nor heard of.' Johnston was himself transported by the moment. His nephew[1] said that he 'looked on the Covenant as the setting Christ on his throne', that he placed the Presbyterian cause before all others, even his family, and that he prayed without exhaustion for hours at a time. Elsewhere, particularly to the north, there was less enthusiasm. The Provost and two baillies of Inverness refused to sign, or to persuade others, and a third baillie called out the town drummer to march the people to the pen. In Aberdeen the magistrates resisted, claiming that the Covenant had no authority from the King, and at the universities some teachers were compelled to sign by the expulsion of more obstinate colleagues. Bold men asked for an assurance that they might still kneel for the Sacrament, and others for proof that there was no wish to overthrow the King. But the pressure was strong everywhere. Havering ministers were replaced, travellers were refused lodgings, and the known lukewarm were harried through the streets by young gallants with drawn swords, and by cries of 'Papist villains!' In this dangerous turmoil most of the bishops discreetly left for England. Archbishop Spottiswoode went with them. All that had been done in the past thirty years, he said, was now overthrown.

During that passionate summer Charles ordered the northern counties of England to muster their trained bands. The Covenanters raised funds for the purchase of arms, drilled volunteers on the hills, and sent appeals for help to Scots mercenaries abroad. In September the King was persuaded by his Council to withdraw the Liturgy and

---

[1] Gilbert Burnet, Bishop of Salisbury, *History of His Own Times.*

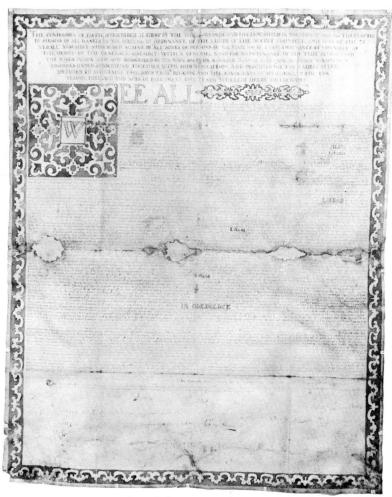

*The National Covenant of 1638 was more than a declaration of faith, it was a political manifesto by which 'a whole people could declare its readiness to oppose all changes that had not been approved by a free Assembly and Parliament'.*

Canons, and to promise a free Assembly and Parliament, but this promise was hedged with confusing conditions. He invited subscriptions to a Covenant of his own, repeating the Negative Confession, but though some men said it condemned episcopacy, others like Warriston described it as atheism and perjury. The time had grown too late for so suspect a compromise. The free General Assembly demanded was at last called, meeting at the High Kirk of Glasgow in November, but since the presbyteries had been persuaded to elect no delegate who approved of the Liturgy and Canons the one hundred and forty-two ministers were almost all Covenanters. They were also accompanied by seventeen lords, nine knights, twenty-five lairds and forty-seven burgesses, posing for the occasion as elders of the Kirk. Alexander Henderson was Moderator, and Warriston was Clerk, surrounded by an armoury of registers and proofs against episcopacy. The King's commissioner was James, third Marquis of Hamilton, a melancholy and inept young man, passionately ambitious but ill-equipped to control this bear-garden for his master.

'Truly, Sir,' he wrote to Charles at the end of the first day, 'my soul was never sadder than to see such a sight, not one gown amongst the whole company, many swords, but many more daggers, most of them having left their guns and pistols in their lodgings.' Robert Baillie called the delegates 'rascals without shame', and said that if they behaved in his house as they were now behaving in church he would have them thrown down the stairs.

The wrangling and argument, preaching and polemics, lasted for a week until Hamilton, unable to endure more of it, ordered the Moderator to dissolve the Assembly. When the order was ignored, he left, and Henderson told the delegates that they were now at war with the 'kingdom of Satan and Antichrist'. The Assembly finally dissolved itself on December 20, having annulled the Prayer Book, Canons and Articles of Perth, abolished the High Commission Court and deposed the bishops. King Covenant ruled, and Henderson was right. The country was at war.

*A standard carried by the Covenanters. 'There was the sound of pipes and fiddles, the singing of psalms, and before the Lord-General's tent was a great banner . . .'*

Home from Europe that winter came mercenaries who had been fighting for good pay and Gustavus Adolphus, and sometimes for a Protestant God. They were hard and disciplined veterans, and none harder than old Alexander Leslie, who had fought in the Swedish army for thirty years. Though he was a rough-bred, crooked little man, said Baillie, the leaders of the Covenant 'gave over themselves to be guided by him as if he had been Great Solyman'. As Lord-General, and making good use of the funds raised by the Tables, he gathered an army with astonishing speed, officered it with his returned comrades and marched it south to bar the Border against the King. 'Our soldiers were all lusty and full of courage,' said Baillie, who despite his earlier doubts now served the Covenant as a regimental chaplain. Throughout the Lowlands there was a fierce spirit of defiance, and in Edinburgh and Leith women carried baskets of stones to repair the walls. In the north the royalist Gordons were in arms under their splendid, braggart Marquis of Huntly, but they were outmarched and outridden by Montrose. To rival the scarlet show of the Gordons, the Graham ordered his men to tie knots of blue ribbons to their hats, and thereby gave the Covenant its badge.

This, the first Bishops' War, was also the first of Charles Stuart's many humiliations in the field. He had planned a trident attack for the spring of 1639 – his own march over the Border, a sea assault upon Aberdeen by Hamilton, and another upon Kintyre by his lieutenant in Ireland, Thomas Wentworth. To find the money for so grand a campaign he summoned an English parliament, quarrelled with it, and dissolved it without being a penny the richer. The twenty thousand men summoned to accompany him across the Tweed were thus unpaid and quarrelsome, more eager to loot, mutiny and desert than to fight. Officers were confused and contentious, equipment was defective, and the only spirited contingent of English Borderers was largely armed with bows and arrows. At Newcastle Charles was welcomed by joyous bells and thundering guns, but there was also Hamilton, sour of face and low in enthusiasm. Montrose's victorious men were in the north-east, and Hamilton wondered how they could be driven out by a fleet of colliers and five thousand men who scarcely knew how to close the pan of their matchlocks. He was sent instead to the Forth, but its shores were heavily defended and his Covenanting mother threatened to shoot him if he landed.

The King reached Berwick at the end of May, and there sent his scouts across the Border. They found the Scots army twelve miles to the east, camped about the gentle hill of Duns Law. There was the sound of pipes and fiddles, the singing of psalms, and before the Lord-General's tent was a great banner declaring his army's determination to fight 'For God, Covenant and Country'. There was no fight. Though they were strong and vehement, in Baillie's words, the Scots hesitated before battle with a King their Covenant had confusingly sworn to defend, and the English would not die for an empty belly and an unfilled purse. At Whitsuntide Charles agreed to meet a hectoring commission from Leslie's camp. By the Pacification of Berwick on June 18 he would not acknowledge the 'pretended' Assembly of Glasgow, but he promised another and a free parliament, both of which he would attend. He would also withdraw his army, but for their part the Scots should surrender the royal castles they had taken, disband their army, and dissolve the Tables.

There is little sincerity in a treaty concluded along the blade of a sword, and there was no honest observance of this. Charles attempted to bribe or persuade some Covenanters, and then went south without attending a new Assembly and Parliament. The first ratified all that had been decided at Glasgow, and compelled the Privy Council to make the signing of the Covenant obligatory. When Parliament was called in the autumn it would have gone further than the Assembly in duplicity had it not been prorogued by the Earl of Traquair, the Royal Commissioner. In June, 1640, it met again in defiance of King and Commissioner, abolished episcopacy, and declared itself capable of electing its own Committee of Articles. Kirk and Parliament were now the Crown's resolute opponents. Traquair was called traitor in the streets, Rothes declared that the Church of Scotland had power to excommunicate a king, and the people sang ballads in honour of Leslie and Montrose.

The second Bishops' War began in August, and the King's mutinous army was still at York when the blue ribbons of the Covenant came over the Tweed. Ten days later Leslie's guns blew away a small body of horse and foot that bravely barred a ford across the Tyne, and the Scots marched into Newcastle and Durham, cutting the supply of coal to London. Once more the King submitted, but since the Scots refused to treat with him unless their agreement were approved by an English parliament, Charles was forced to summon it, the Long Parliament which would eventually destroy him. The commissioners of both countries first met at Ripon – where it was agreed that Leslie's men would occupy northern England and be paid eight hundred and fifty pounds a day in subsistence by the counties they held – and then in London. The bargaining lasted a year, both sides united in a common hostility to the little man whose pride they were humbling, the Scots making allies among the political and religious extremists of the southern kingdom. When a treaty was finally concluded in June, 1641, Charles gave his bitter assent to all that had been done by his pretended Assembly and Parliament. The Scots were to receive an indemnity of three hundred thousand pounds and their soldiers would remain in England until the first instalment was paid. The ministers of Scotland entered their pulpits with swords and daggers at their waists, and gave thanks to God for His mercy and protection.

Charles came to Edinburgh in August, and in a desperate attempt to steady the world that was spinning about him. His English parliament, which had the Scots to thank for its recall, had already forced him to abandon much of his cherished absolutism, not the least being the power to summon and dismiss it as he wished. He was without money, and he had been compelled to surrender Archbishop Laud to the Tower, his loyal friend Thomas Wentworth to the block. To enlist allies in the inevitable war he must now fight with this parliament, he came to the land that had been the immediate cause of his misfortune. He had reason to hope that he would find them. The episcopalians were strong in the north-east, and there was doubt and dissension among the Congregation of Christ. Many men who had signed the Covenant remembered that it bound them to 'stand to the defence of the King's Majesty', and many lords resented the fact that power taken from the Crown was now being assumed by ministers and bonnet lairds. Graham of Montrose thought that changes made by Assembly and Parliament exceeded the rights given them, and a year earlier he and seventeen others had signed a bond at Cumbernauld, pledging themselves to uphold the true letter of the Covenant. But the Cumbernauld Bond was formed against a man rather than for an ideal, and that man was Archibald Campbell, eighth Earl of Argyll and the strong heart of the extremists. He was forty-three, eight years older than Montrose whom he hated, and he wore a divine's skull-cap above his red hair, but behind his long nose and pain-twisted face was a powerful and compelling mind. His clansmen called him King Campbell, and the nickname he had inherited from his father, Gruamach the Sullen, better described the disfiguring cast in his eye. When an ingenuous letter from the King to Montrose was intercepted in June, 1641, it was Argyll who urged the Graham's imprisonment and examination by Parliament.

Charles had no success in Scotland, and Montrose was not freed to advise him. He scattered fair words and titles, giving a marquisate to Argyll and the earldom of Leven to Leslie, upon that old mercenary's promise not to bear arms against him. But few men trusted him. Speaking with great emotion, he told the Estates that he had come to 'settle their religion and liberties'. But few men believed him. He talked wildly of ingratitude and of schemes against him, and he was suspected of complicity in a plot to kidnap Argyll and Hamilton. This rumour, encouraged by the ministers, finally discredited him. His enemies had accepted his bribes – Warriston had been knighted, and Henderson made dean of the Chapel Royal – but had promised nothing in return. On October 28 he was playing golf at Leith when a letter from London told him of rebellion and massacre in Ulster. He left for England, and once he was gone the Earl of Argyll recommended the release of Montrose.

When the English Civil War began nine months later both King and Parliament appealed to the Scots for help. None was immediately given to either, for while it had taken a constitutional shape Scotland's quarrel with Charles was religious not political. The intransigent Covenanters were already bigots, the Presbyterian Church was the only true faith and should be established throughout Great Britain, although Henderson conceded that a new form might be necessary. The abolition of English episcopacy was the price of Scots help. This the King was told at Oxford and Parliament informed in London, and since the latter was as anxious to reform the Church of England as it was to secure a supply of Scots coal, it struck the bargain. In the summer of 1643 it summoned an assembly of divines to Westminster to debate the 'reformation in Church ceremonies and discipline so much longed for'. Alexander Henderson headed a wordy and enthusiastic Scots delegation, and in August a General Assembly in Scotland drafted a Solemn League and Covenant binding the contracting parties to preserve the Kirk, to reform religion in England and Ireland, to extirpate popery and prelacy, and to assimilate all reformed churches into one. The Parliamentary commissioners who came to Edinburgh in September insisted that all this should be done 'according to the Word of God', thus opening a door through which cautious and prevaricating men might later step. Like its predecessor, this document was also presented to the people for signature. The English, said Baillie, were for a civil league and the Scots for a religious covenant, but each got what each desired, and twenty thousand horse and foot were mustered in Scotland to fight against the King.

Keeping his earldom but abandoning the promise that had secured it, Alexander Leslie led his army across the ice of the Tweed at the beginning of 1644. On the second day of July, Scottish pikemen stood on the right of the Parliament line at Marston Moor, and although many ran before a cavalier charge the rest held their ground in the stubborn schiltron of their ancestors. When Cromwell was wounded and his Ironsides in confusion, old Leven's namesake David Leslie took eight hundred Scottish horse against Rupert's triumphant squadrons, halted them in a slashing *mêlée*, and then drove them northward from the field.

Embittered by the small credit given them, their disappointment further soured by squabbles with the English, the Scots withdrew to Newcastle, where they sulked in angry inaction. The war would now spread to their own country.

## 4

Until the end of his life James Graham of Montrose believed in the spirit and letter of the National Covenant, in the religious and civil liberties it proclaimed, and it seemed to him that the King had agreed to all its demands. The Solemn League, however, went beyond the law in purpose and practice, and in his last days he accused its supporters of oppressing the poor and violently perverting justice and judgment. He was the revolutionary moderate who can go no further along the road his conscience has taken him, and in turning aside becomes the servant of reaction and one of its noble victims. The king to whom he offered his life was not the 'great, good and just' man he described, nor was the royal cause perhaps worthy of his devotion. But he was loyal to both, and to the promise he made his mistress, Scotland.

> I'll serve thee in such noble ways
> Was never heard before;

I'll crown and deck thee all with bays,
And love thee more and more.

He did not make his decision to oppose the Covenant without great doubt and pain. In the summer of 1643 he and Alexander Henderson met in a riverside meadow by Stirling to debate their differences, but although they parted in friendship there was no agreement between them. He went to Oxford, and was coldly received by a king who preferred the flattering advice of Hamilton, now a duke. Montrose offered to win back Scotland, telling Charles that 'your affairs will at any rate be in no worse case than they are at present, even if I should not succeed'. When Leven's army entered England, and Hamilton was betrayed by his own impossible intrigues, the King at last offered to make Montrose his Viceroy and Captain-General in Scotland. The Graham wisely refused titles that could only make jealous enemies, and accepted instead a marquisate and a commission as Lieutenant-General. He was offered no army, although he gathered some English Borderers, and two days after Marston Moor he found Prince Rupert in a Richmond inn. 'Give me a thousand horse,' he said, 'and I'll cut my way into the heart of Scotland.' But the humiliated Cavalier was mourning the rout of his own men, the death of his dog in battle, and it was he who took the Border horsemen whom Montrose had recruited. With two companions only, all disguised in the dress of Leven's troopers, the King's Lieutenant-General crossed the Border northward from Carlisle and rode toward the safety of his own country in Strathearn.

He raised his army in the Highlands, from clansmen who were ready to fight for King Charles if by doing so they could strike a hard blow at King Campbell. The strongest support came from Clan Donald, of course, though not immediately from its mainland glens where Argyll's grip was firm. Since the beginning of July, however, a thousand MacDonell kerns from Ireland, helped by six hundred Macleans and MacDonalds of the Isles, had been harrying Campbell settlements in Ardnamurchan. The Earl of Antrim had unleashed them for the King, and they were led by his distant kinsman Alasdair MacDonald. This splendid and heroic man, of giant build and cropped black hair, was the son of a Colonsay chief known as Colla Ciotach, Coll the Left-handed. Alasdair MacColla Ciotach, which Lowland pens simplified to Colkitto, was the darling of Clan Donald, and its bards would give all the credit for the miraculous year ahead to him and his followers, to 'the men with fair locks, with sharp cleaving blades, and red shield-bosses'. But at the start, their savage appearance and unwelcome Catholicism almost destroyed the royal cause. As they approached the rendezvous Montrose had called at Blair, accompanied by a mob of starving women and children, they so alarmed the central clans that the fiery cross was lit against them and not against the Covenant. Only the arrival of Montrose, tired and on foot, prevented a bloody struggle. He stood between them in tartan trews and plaid, a buckler on his arm and a badge of oats in his bonnet, and he charmed them into friendship and loyalty. Only three men were ever able to unite the clans, to persuade them to suppress their hatreds in a common cause, and naturally none was a Highlander. The second would be another Graham, and the third a Stuart prince.

The little army marched upon Perth, and westward of that town at Tippermuir, on the first day of September, it met seven thousand Covenanters from Fife and the midlands. It was the Sabbath, the ministers had promised the godly an easy victory, and their battle-cry was 'Jesus and no quarter!' Montrose was outnumbered by more than

Above *The prize of Bannockburn and the key to the kingdom: Stirling Castle overlooking the cockpit of Scotland.* Below *The Palace of Holyroodhouse, Edinburgh. Begun by James IV and continued by his successors, it stands by the ruins of an abbey founded in 1128. Overleaf The valley of Glencoe.*

two to one, bowmen were his artillery, and for cavalry he had the three poor nags that had brought him and his companions from England. His only muskets were carried by the Irish, and they with one round each, but he told the rest to gather stones from the moor, to stand in three ranks and to be of good heart. The battle, if that is the word, began with a walking advance of both armies, the one precious volley and a shower of stones that scattered the Covenanters' cavalry, and then a screaming charge by the clans. It was irresistible, and the pursuit was terrible. The killing continued until late that hot evening, and it was said that a man could have walked on the dead from the bloody moor to the town of Perth.

As was their custom, the mainland clans would then have gone home with their loot, but Montrose kept them together by the force of his personality and led them toward Aberdeen. He sent a messenger and a drummer-boy to demand the town's surrender, but the child was shot by accident or design, and in a bitter rage Montrose promised Colkitto the sack of the burgh once it was taken, though its sympathy for the Covenant was weak. There was a long, hard fight to break the army defending it, but once more it was done by an Irish charge, and for three days Highlander and Islander took what they wanted and did what they wanted in Aberdeen. Old and young were killed, sometimes stripped naked so that their blood might not soil their clothes. Women were raped and butchered, or taken away as captives. Contemporary accounts are partisan and suspect, but the harshest was written by the royalist John Spalding. 'The wife durst not cry nor weep at her husband's slaughter before her eyes, nor the daughter of the father, which if they did and were heard, then they were presently slain also.' To save their lives, some put the Graham's badge of oats in their hats. The killing was not as great as would be later claimed, fewer than two hundred, but this was not the bay-leaf honour Montrose had promised his mistress, and the Covenanters would in time take a ferocious revenge upon the Irish.

Though one or two Gordon gentlemen joined the royal army, Huntly kept the bulk of his clan at home, sulkily remembering his humiliation in the first Bishops' War. As Argyll advanced upon him with four thousand horse and foot, Montrose fell back into the Highlands. In the game of touch that was played among the October beauty of the eastern glens, the King's man was the superior general, and with less than a thousand Irish he turned to fight on the Braes of Gight, holding hillside ditches against Argyll's advance. Colkitto was away recruiting in the west, but his lieutenant Magnus O'Cahan was cast from the same Fingalian mould. He looked at the muskets taken by the first charge of the Irish and said 'We must have at them again, these stingy hucksters have left us no bullets.' Argyll withdrew, the first snows closed the valleys, and the campaign might have been over had not Alasdair returned with Camerons and Macleans, Stewarts and Farquharsons, MacDonalds of Keppoch, Glengarry, Clanranald and Glencoe. All had one desire, to strike at Clan Diarmid. Montrose responded with a wild and impossible proposal, that they should cross the central massif and fall upon Inveraray in the heart of Campbell land.

They went by drove-road and raiding-road in December, over saddles deep in snow, encouraged by a priest who promised God's help with the weather. A Glencoe man guided them on the last few miles, telling Montrose that his men would live well at the end 'if tight houses, fat cattle, and clear water will suffice'. Joined by MacNabs and MacGregors from Loch Tayside, and with the east wind at their backs, they reached Loch Awe before the news of their coming was heard in Inveraray. Argyll boarded a

*Parliament Hall, Edinburgh, with its hammer-beam roof of Fife oak. Here the Estates met for nearly seventy years, until they dissolved themselves in March, 1707.*

herring-boat, and the wind that carried the sound of pipes in Glen Aray also took him safely down Loch Fyne. He left his people and his town to the wild revenge of his ancient enemies. They killed a few men who resisted, burnt cottage and steading between Glen Orchy and Glen Fyne, lifted the fat cattle they had been promised, and celebrated Christmas in the warmth and comfort of the terrified burgh. The heather badge of Clan Donald at last triumphed over the wild myrtle of the Campbells.

From the southern safety of his estates at Roseneath, Argyll wrote angry protests to Edinburgh. The Estates mustered sixteen battalions of militia, but he would have none of them on his lands, for the rape of Inveraray had been a clan humiliation and should be revenged by the clan. Lamed by a fall from his horse, he went back to his town as soon as Montrose retired from it in January. Campbell galleys returned to the sea-lochs and Campbell fighters were summoned for the pursuit. The Mackenzies of Seaforth were raised in the north, and the eastern and southern passes were closed by General William Baillie and the Lowland militia. Within this steel chamber, Argyll and his clan came up the Great Glen like a piston-head, intent on forcing Montrose against Seaforth's men at Inverness, but the Graham did not retreat. In the worst weather that men could remember, avalanche, blizzard and waist-high drifts, he turned southward from Loch Ness on a spectacular flanking march, climbing twenty-five hundred feet over Carn Leac to Glen Roy and the valley of the Spean. In the early hours of Candlemas Day, February 2, his tired and hungry men came down the shoulder of Ben Nevis to the flat ground at the head of Loch Linnhe.

Though there had been some skirmish shots in the night, the Campbells did not believe that the whole of Montrose's army had come. Argyll was aboard a galley, too valuable to the Covenant to be risked in battle, but five thousand of his clan, with some Lowland foot, were grouped in battle order by the black tower of Inverlochy. In the darkness before dawn the fifteen hundred Royalists ate a bitter breakfast of oats mixed with snow, and at first light the Graham's trumpet sounded. On the right and left flanks the Irish crossed themselves and rose from prayer, walked toward the assembling Campbells, fired one volley and charged. They were quickly followed by the centre, MacDonalds, Camerons and Stewarts, and by some ragged horse under the Ogilvy Earl of Airlie. The Lowlanders immediately broke, but the Campbells were stout and gallant men, said Montrose's chaplain Wishart, 'worthy of a better chief and a juster cause'. Attacked on three sides, they fell back to the loch and were killed in the water until they too turned and ran. Fifteen hundred died in the fight, or in the running rout over the high braes toward Loch Leven, a fierce slaughter that destroyed the clan power of Argyll for a generation. The slender swords had been unsheathed, said the bard of Keppoch, and the claws of the Campbell lay on the ground with sinews severed.

The conceit of victory was infectious, and Montrose believed that he had also struck a mortal blow at the Solemn League. He told the King that he would soon bring a brave army south to 'make the rebels in England, as well as in Scotland, feel the just rewards of rebellion'. It was a foolish boast. Satiated with Campbell blood, the Lochaber clans soon left him, and for the rest of the winter he rarely had more than eight hundred straggling Irish. They were cold and hungry, and although he sacked Dundee to feed and clothe them, he was driven back into the hills by Baillie. In the spring he was joined by some welcome Gordon horse under Huntly's son, Lord Aboyne, and by some Keppoch and Glengarry MacDonalds whom Alasdair had persuaded to go to war instead of their summer shielings. In early May, at Auldearn on the Moray Firth, the little army defeated a superior force of Covenanters under a general with the inapt name of Hurry. Colkitto's Irish once more began the fight, but their charge was stoutly held in the pigsties of the village, and Alasdair's shield was studded with pike-heads, hewn from their shafts by his broadsword. Aboyne and his Gordons turned the doubtful battle into a rout. Two months later, southward at Alford on the River Don, Argyll was also defeated again, narrowly escaping death from the singing sweep of a MacDonald sword.

The King's cause had been terribly mauled at Naseby, and Montrose now came out of the mountains in a heroic and suicidal attempt to honour his promise. For a while it seemed as if he could never be beaten. In the Kilsyth hills north-east of Glasgow, on a hot and windless August day, he destroyed all but a few hundred of the six thousand men whom Baillie brought against him. But now his army deserted him, and the year of miracles was over. Nagged for disloyalty by a jealous father, and angered by imagined insults, Aboyne took most of the Gordons back to their own country. Nor would the Highlanders go any further. They had expected the rich sack of Glasgow after Kilsyth, and were disgusted when Montrose accepted a tribute of five hundred pounds instead. They had no sympathy for a king's cause in England, and no wish to leave their glens undefended. It would soon be time to bring the cattle down from the Lochaber shielings, and since no journey should be made without profit they went home by way of Kintyre, where Colkitto proposed a raid on the Campbells. Alasdair took half the Ulstermen with him, promising to return, and although he may have meant to keep his word, he never saw the Graham again.

With a hundred horsemen and five hundred Irish under the loyal O'Cahan, Montrose marched boldly across the Pentlands and down toward the Border by the valley of the Tweed. He appealed for loyal gentlemen to join him, but few came. He could not be forgiven for unleashing the clans on Scotland, or for allying himself with wild kerns who had massacred Ulster Protestants. On the flat meadowland of Philiphaugh, three miles from Selkirk he was suddenly attacked by six thousand Covenanters under David Leslie. The stubborn Irish fought in their mean trenches until four hundred of them were dead. Fifty of the little troop of cavalry were cut from the saddle by Leslie's riders, and Montrose would willingly have died with them had not his friends dragged him away from the field. The Irish who surrendered were sabred where they stood, or shot the following morning. O'Cahan was allowed to keep his life, until it was taken from him by a rope in Edinburgh. Urged on by their hysterical ministers, and in the name of God and the Kirk, the Covenanters butchered the three hundred women and children whom the Irish had brought from Ulster. Two hundred menial camp-followers, cooks and horse-boys, were also slaughtered. For days the hills were searched for wretched fugitives, and all were killed where they were found. Their throats were cut and their bodies mutilated. They were hanged. They were thrown into rivers and held down by pikes until they drowned. They were Irish and they were papists, and it was a royalist historian who said that they were 'without all shame, most brutally given to uncleanliness and filthy lust'. At last the murderers sickened of the killing and turned on their ministers, crying 'Have you not once gotten your fill of blood?'

This was the squalid end to Montrose's year of glory. His victories were perhaps never more than a bright glow at the extinction of the King's cause. His generalship is customarily believed to have been equal to that of great European captains, but it was never tested against them. He embraced the Covenant but confounded its logic with his belief in an absolute monarchy, by his claim that it was 'not meet the head should stoop unto the feet'. He was a superb leader of irregulars, but the reckless courage that was their strength was a dangerous weakness in him. He could inspire Highland hearts but he could not persuade Lowland minds, and the clans easily left him for their own feuds against the Campbells. They remembered him with love, but with no shame for their desertion, and the bard of the Keppoch MacDonalds reserved his highest praise for Alasdair MacColla Ciotach.

Montrose was hiding in the mountains in May, 1646, when the King surrendered himself to Leven's army at its siege-works about Newark-on-Trent, determined to exploit the growing differences between Scots and English. The Army now controlled the Parliament cause, and its factious Independents had no sympathy for the imposition of Presbyterianism, believing that each congregation should be allowed to worship as it desired. This tolerant disregard for the religious articles of the Solemn League outraged the Scots, and when Charles persuaded the royalist garrison of Newark to surrender, Leven withdrew his army to Newcastle. There the King allowed himself to be lectured by the dying Alexander Henderson, but although he had gone this far in duplicity he could not bring himself to sign the Covenant, and thus lost the one chance he had of persuading the Scots to fight for him. The English Parliament was tired of the obdurate conscience and wavering loyalty of its ally, and believing that Leven's army could become a Trojan horse, the Commons voted to buy it off with its arrears of pay. The Scots wanted two million pounds but they accepted an offer of four hundred thousand pounds, only half of which was ever received. Since Leven's army could no longer stay in England, nor return home with a man who stubbornly refused to take the Covenant, it left him behind in the hands of his enemies. Some effort was made to secure an assurance of his safety, but the scent of betrayal is strong.

Leven's troopers came home in bitter disappointment, and Scotland was disillusioned by the failure of the Solemn League with England. The Covenanters were still fervent in their desire for one Presbyterian Church throughout the kingdoms, and believed in the Crown as a necessary instrument to secure it. The country was divided, however, between those who would accept the King's promise to establish it in England for a trial period, and those who would have him impose it for ever. In December, 1647, three commissioners from the former party made a secret Engagement with Charles, now a prisoner on the Isle of Wight, promising him the help of a Scots army in return for his agreement to establish Presbyterianism for three years, and they did not ask him to make the Covenant obligatory. These commissioners were all earls, one of them the brother of Hamilton. With the exception of a few like Argyll, the nobles were Engagers, now alarmed by the threat to their power from a dictatorial and seemingly egalitarian Kirk, and for the same reason they were supported by a majority of lairds and burgesses in the Estates. There was also growing alarm for the safety of the King, and perhaps a sense of responsibility for his present predicament. The moderate compromise of the Engagement, with its contingent offer of equal commercial privileges with the English, offered some relief to a people weary of confusing loyalties, but it was strongly opposed by the General Assembly. Although this did not control the Estates, its ministers influenced the morale of twenty thousand soldiers who marched south under Hamilton in July, 1648. Both David Leslie and Leven refused to command this undrilled army, and had either accepted he might have saved it from disaster, or at least equipped it with artillery and enough ammunition.

Cromwell came upon the Scots when they were strung out along the road between Preston and Wigan, and after three days of skirmish and cavalry charge he brought them to the bloody push of pike. 'By the blessing of God,' he wrote, 'we killed about a thousand of them, and took, as we believe, about two thousand prisoners.' When the rest retreated, and then surrendered, Hamilton was sent to London. Seven months later, and with more spite than legal justification, the English removed his head.

Their army so miserably destroyed, the Engagers were also lost. From the south-western shires an armed band of six thousand intransigent Covenanters advanced upon Edinburgh, urging their horses with cries of 'Whiggamore!' and thus giving a name to themselves and to the political party that would inherit a dilution of their radical zeal. The ease with which they occupied the capital, and threw out the Engagers, was largely due to the fact that Cromwell had advanced into Scotland. In the manner of such invaders, he protested that he had no quarrel with its 'poor innocent people', providing they got rid of the faction that had led them into sin.

Argyll was now master of Scotland, leading a government of anti-Engagers and supported by agile turncoats like his clansman the Earl of Loudoun, who had been one of the commissioners sent to the Isle of Wight. In October Cromwell was invited to Edinburgh and was treated as a liberator. He supped with Argyll and Warriston in the Canongate, and there the squint-eyed Highland chief, the manic lawyer, and the God-tormented English yeoman settled the troublesome affairs of Scotland. 'Give assurance,' Cromwell had demanded, 'that you will not admit or suffer any that have been active in or consenting to the engagement against England to be employed in any public place or trust whatsoever.' The assurance was willingly given, and a common and expedient cause was made against a 'malignant' monarchy. Supported by three English regiments which had been left for their temporary protection, the Estates passed an Act of Classes on January 4, 1649, defining the enemies of the Covenant and barring them from office until they repented. Before that month was over, a masked headsman in Whitehall demonstrated what Cromwell had meant by relentless opposition to Malignancy.

The Scots were shocked by the execution of Charles I. Their parliamentary commissioners in London had made private and public appeals against it, telling Cromwell that the Covenant obliged both countries to preserve the King's life, and that to take it would be a breach of their alliance. 'Are small offenders to be punished,' he asked, with terrible logic, 'and the greatest of all to go free?' So the alliance was broken outside the Banqueting Hall, and on February 5 the Scots proclaimed Charles, Prince of Wales, King of Scotland. But the young man was in the Low Countries, and in his grief he was disinclined to come to a kingdom that had betrayed his father to the English, and which now demanded his acceptance of a Covenant that blessed martyr had rejected. For a year he resisted the nagging commissions sent to him, arguing with adroit and humorous skill. And he encouraged the exiled Montrose in a brave plan to invade Scotland, to take it for him without the hateful condition of the Covenant.

In the early spring of 1650, with no more than his new King's goodwill, a few hundred Danish mercenaries and a thousand Orkney levies, the Graham landed by Duncansby Head on the far tip of northern Scotland. Two weeks later, at Carbisdale on the Kyle of Sutherland, his unwarlike Orcadians were slaughtered by Lowland troopers, and he fled westward into the mountains of Assynt. A laird of the Macleods, from whom he asked shelter, sold him to the government for twenty-five thousand pounds Scots, part of which was paid in oatmeal. When he was brought into Edinburgh he was watched from a shuttered window by Argyll and Warriston, and in the afternoon of Tuesday, May 21, he walked to that ultimate elevation Lord Rothes had foreseen. Exquisitely dressed, with white gloves and brave ribbons, he was hanged thirty feet above the Mercat Cross, and his dying silenced the mob. A man who watched said that he looked more like a bridegroom than a felon.

In his bedroom at Breda, fourteen days before, Charles II had told the Scots commissioners that he would agree to the Covenants, and he accepted their formal invitation to come to Scotland for his coronation. His ship arrived in the mouth of the Spey on June 23, and there he surrendered his signature.

The Scots' stubborn adherence to a monarchy England had expelled left Cromwell with no choice but coercion. He entered Scotland with sixteen thousand men, reminding the members of the General Assembly that a popish army was at present fighting for their malignant king in Ireland, and beseeching them 'in the bowels of Christ, think it possible you may be mistaken'. Since they had never thought this before, they did not now. The foolish Act of Classes was not lifted, experienced men who might have defended the nation were forbidden to bear arms against the approaching enemy, and ministerial witch-doctors further purged the army which David Leslie gathered, but even so it trapped the over-confident Cromwell at Dunbar, between Doon Hill and the sea. The Englishman believed that he could not win this fight 'without almost a miracle', and if he prayed for one it quickly came. Leslie listened to the urging of his ministers and took the Scots down from their strong position on the hill, just as John Comyn had done three and a half centuries before against de Warenne. Cromwell broke the charge of their regiments, and counter-attacked with pike and sword. When they ran, his troopers sang two verses of the One Hundred and Seventeenth Psalm and rode in pursuit. Three thousand Scots were killed, and ten thousand were taken prisoner. The battle was fought in the half-light mists before dawn, on the third day of September.

Although Cromwell occupied the eastern Lowlands, and the town of Edinburgh if not its castle, the Scots refused to surrender. Charles was crowned at Scone on New Year's Day, a macabre ceremony in which the golden circlet of Bruce, now topped with jewelled arches, was placed upon his head by Argyll. After a sermon of three hours, during which he was advised to undergo public humiliation for his family's sins, he choked upon his pride and declared that he agreed to all the terms of the Covenant. That night Argyll prayed with him, and rejoiced to see the young man weep.

After Dunbar, and the defeat of a force of western zealots, moderate Presbyterians and Royalists allied themselves to secure the abolition of the Act of Classes, and early in the summer of 1651 the Estates formally rescinded the crippling statute. Malignant men who had been rejected before Dunbar were now welcomed into the great army which Leslie and Charles were assembling on the Stirling plain. Too weak to oppose it in Scotland, Cromwell cunningly left his flank open and allowed it to march deep into the hostile shires of England. He then followed it, gathering recruits until he had thirty thousand men. He marched them without respite, twenty miles a day in their shirts, their arms and armour carried by the bat-horses of the train, and at the end of August he surrounded the Royalists at Worcester. On the anniversary of Dunbar, he won another victory in five hot hours of bitter assault that filled the ditches and streets with Highland and Lowland dead, and floated a fleet of corpses on the River Severn. The tall, black King escaped to France, but not a regiment or troop of his army returned in order to Scotland. The prisoners who survived their wounds or gaol-fever, and who had not rank or influence to save them, were sold to the plantations of America, joining the men who had been taken at Dunbar. It was as stiff a contest as Cromwell had ever seen, and so he admitted. With a drawn sword he had led his men across the river bridge, and he thanked God for a crowning mercy.

Before Worcester was fought, Stirling and Dundee had fallen to the English, and the last royalist stronghold below the mountains, the tiny Bass Rock in the Firth of Forth, surrendered in the spring. That autumn England and Scotland were declared one commonwealth, and all public assemblies were banned, except those authorized by the parliament in London. George Monck, who now became Governor of the northern province, was a swarthy Devon soldier with a mature experience of war and women, and a growing taste for politics. Under his rule – interrupted for two years when he assumed the bizarre rank of admiral against the Dutch – English troops occupied Scotland as they had done under the Plantagenets. This time, however, their control was absolute, and they behaved with rough tolerance and good humour, treating the Scots as disobedient children. Though they thought that Scots ale was so thick it ought to be eaten with a spoon, and that Scotswomen were generally unwashed, the land was beautiful, the towns endurable, and garrison life a pleasure once one got used to the lice.

*When Charles II, in exile at Breda, agreed to sign the Covenant, the Scots formally invited him to Scone for his coronation. Their 'adherance to a monarchy expelled by the English left Cromwell no choice but coercion'.*

Scotland was not allowed to debate the union imposed upon it. In time, thirty voiceless representatives were sent to the parliament at Westminster, but their presence there was a token of equality rather than its instrument. Eight Englishmen replaced the old Privy Council, and seven English judges the Court of Sessions, and if the latter were known as 'kinless loons' it was also admitted that they could not be bribed, which was more than could have been said of their predecessors. Heavily taxed to pay for the army of occupation, the Scots were also governed more fairly and firmly than at any time in their anarchic history, and no Wallace arose upon the murdered body of an English tyrant. In the Highlands there was an appeal to those who remembered Colkitto

Perfidia.    TYRANNVS.    Crudelitas.

*A Restoration cartoon attacking Cromwell. Though it could not be claimed that Scotland suffered greatly under the Commonwealth, its people largely welcomed the return of the Stuarts.*

and Montrose, but the rising was easily suppressed, and English forts were built at Inverlochy and Inverness. There was no interference with the language, dress, and peaceful customs of the clans, and some chiefs like Cameron of Lochiel and MacDonald of Glencoe became the friends of the young Governor of Inverlochy, John Hill.

Scotland now had equal trading rights and privileges with England. Though the wars had robbed the nation of ships that might have taken advantage of these rights, and although legislation usually favoured English merchants and weakened Scottish commerce, there was a general rise in the standard of living among ordinary people. Burnet said it was a 'time of great peace and prosperity', a partisan exaggeration, but things were probably not as bad as Baillie maintained when he wrote: 'A great army in a multitude of garrisons bides above our heads, and deep poverty keeps all estates exceedingly under.' One of Monck's troopers, Richard Franck, was impressed by the 'splendour and gaiety' of Glasgow, by warehouses stuffed with merchandise and shops swollen with foreign goods. Thomas Tucker, an English exciseman, said that the country was admirably equipped for commerce, and would prosper but for the 'lazy vagrancy' of its people. English soldiers were appalled by the wretchedness of Scots poverty, but Cromwell was perhaps right when he told his parliament

The meaner sort live as well and are likely to come into as thriving a condition under your government, as when they were under their own great lords, who made them work for their living no better than the peasants of France. . . . The middle sort of people do grow up into such a substance as makes their lives comfortable, if not better than before.

What men enjoyed most under the Commonwealth was peace, a release from fratricidal hatred. The English were tolerant of religious congregations, providing they did not favour popery or prelacy, and they brought the moderates and the extremists to an uneasy truce. Scotland had eight years to reflect upon the value of compromise in religious matters, as it had time to think of the good that might truly come from a union that would protect its economy and laws. Cromwell died in 1658, on the anniversary of Dunbar and Worcester, and ten months later Parliament twice heard the reading of a Bill of Union introduced with Scots encouragement. It came to nothing, but next year when George Monck left Scotland, for the hard bargaining that was to restore the monarchy, the commissioners of burghs and shires presented him with a petition asking him to maintain the political union of the two nations.

## 5

The hysterical joy which greeted Charles II when he rode into London on his thirtieth birthday was echoed by the Restoration celebrations in Edinburgh three weeks later. The nineteenth day of June, 1660, was declared a Day of Public Thanksgiving. Wine ran from a waterspout by the Mercat Cross. The iron throat of Mons Meg belched thunder on the castle wall. There were trumpet salutes and singing bells, a drum-march from the Landmarket to Holyroodhouse, and a splendid illumination in which Cromwell was pursued by the Devil and went to perdition in an explosion of fireworks. It was not, perhaps, the return of a Stuart that caused this delirium of delight. The thought of freedom was a greater intoxicant than the claret that dribbled down the cobbles of the Royal Mile.

By the Declaration of Breda in April, before he went aboard the *Royal Charles*, the King had promised a 'liberty to tender consciences', declaring that no man would be called to answer for his religion or his politics, providing they did not disturb the peace of the kingdoms. Liberty was the word in all men's mouths. It had been in Monck's before Christmas, along with a quid of tobacco, when he assured the commissioners of burghs and shires that he was going south to restore the liberty of England, Scotland and Ireland. Liberty was the dominant thought of those Scots nobles who went to London to swear loyalty to the King, and to secure from him in return as many promises as could possibly be made in the elation of the moment. Liberty has many doors, and that which opens for one man may be closing upon another, but to the Scots in general freedom meant that they would be rid of an English army and the taxes that had supported it, that they would once more be an independent nation with their own parliament, the loyal subjects of a Covenanted King.

When the Commonwealth ended, England was a powerful country with a prospering economy, and with resources which even the wasteful ineptitude of the last Stuart kings would not entirely exhaust. Scotland was poor and would grow poorer still, paying a high price for the return of its parliament and independence. The paper privileges of the brief union would be destroyed under the Navigation Acts by which England successfully neutralized the commercial competition of its neighbour. The religious disputes of

England moved from pulpit and preaching-house into Parliament. In Scotland they once more soured and impoverished the nation's spirit. Compromise in all things clerical and secular, which was to become the greatest characteristic of the English, was impossible in Scotland while the arrogant dogma of religious faith was still the issue in dispute. The political power of the Scots middle class was limp compared with that of England, where a young mercantile capitalism had won its early parliamentary victories and would soon secure a greater triumph. Since the Reformation the parliaments of Scotland had been primarily involved in the conflict between Kirk and Crown, and at their most effective had frequently been the servants of the General Assembly. The first Restoration parliament was at least free from the control of the Kirk, and it became something of a debating-chamber with an emergent opposition, though it was still led by the nobility. Since that class was now potentially episcopalian, by expedience if not conviction, it cannot be said that God had left the floor of Parliament House.

The zealots of the Kirk were still faithful, and under the inspiration of James Guthrie, the embittered minister of Stirling, they met to frame a Protest against the dangerous slide toward episcopacy. Their leaders were arrested, and Guthrie, who had taunted Montrose and urged Leslie's army to leave the heights of Doon Hill, went to martyrdom on a rope. While the spirit of retribution was strong, and driven by the rough bullying of the King's Commissioner, John, Earl of Middleton, the Estates also ordered the arrest of Warriston and Argyll. The Campbell was in sympathy with the Protesters, but he was tried for aiding the Cromwellian occupation and for opposing the Highland

*The opening of a new assembly of the Estates began with the ceremonial 'Riding of Parliament'. Having viewed the rooms of the House the Constable, seen here in 1681, sat at the Lady Steps and saluted Members as they dismounted.*

rising against it. The King would have saved this man he hated, and who had prayed at him with such savage exultation, but Middleton insisted that clemency would be resented by the Estates. Argyll died with dignity and courage beneath the falling blade of a guillotine known as the Maiden. His head, soon to be straight-seeing from eyeless holes, was placed upon a spike that had recently carried the skull of Montrose. Warriston fled, but was extradited from France, and when brought before the Privy Council he threw himself on the floor and wept, swearing that he had lost his memory and could not even remember a word from the Bible. He was more composed when he was hanged at the Mercat Cross, but his address from the scaffold was unintelligible gibberish.

In a long session of six months Parliament passed nearly four hundred acts, bringing the Crown closer to absolutism than it had ever been, and by the Act Rescissory it annulled all legislation since 1633, thus restoring the episcopal system created by the previous Stuart kings. Bishops once more sat in the Estates, and all ministers appointed since 1649 were ordered to resign their offices and offer themselves for reinstatement by lay patrons of their parishes. As the powers of the prelacy were increased by successive legislation, most ministers accepted the changes without protest, comforting their consciences with the thought that if bishops had replaced the Assembly, synods and presbyteries had been retained. But a dismembered Kirk, the head removed and re-placed by the obscene mask of its enemy, was intolerable to the zealots. Three hundred ministers, most of them in the Whiggamore west, refused to accept the prelacy and left their churches in disgust. Their congregations supported them, climbing the hills on the Sabbath, attending conventicles in remote glens, and calling to God upon the wind. The King's Commissioners reacted with the stunted imagination of Ottoman satraps, believing that the swing of a dragoon's sabre was the most effective persuader of a troubled conscience. Fines were imposed upon the dissenters, and were collected where possible from a cavalry saddle. Hard veterans of continental wars like Sir Thomas Dalyell of the Binns and Sir James Turner led these dragonnades.

Turner's troopers provoked the first armed resistance. They had begun to relieve the boredom of fine-collecting by riding down upon known conventicles, and dispersing them with drawn swords. In November, 1666, the Galloway peasants rose in armed insurrection with banners and slogans of old wars. They captured the astonished Turner in Dumfries, and in a hysteria that was as terrifying as the brutality that had provoked it they marched upon Edinburgh. There were never more than three thousand of them, ill-disciplined if not undisciplined, and recklessly confident. At Lanark they issued a proclamation declaring their loyalty to the King but demanding the re-establishment of the Presbyterian Kirk and the observance of the Covenant. Now led by an old soldier with the felicitous name of Wallace, their numbers decreased as they approached the capital, and Dalyell's scarlet riders followed them at a watching distance. Four miles from Edinburgh, desertions had reduced them to less than a thousand men, but the captive Turner, frequently threatened by pistols, said that he had never seen 'lustier fellows or better marchers'. The capital was closed against them, and they turned into the Pentland Hills. An hour before sunset on November 28, Dalyell fell upon them at Rullion Green, and although they fought bravely, singing the Seventy-fourth and Seventy-eighth Psalms, they were scattered in the dusk. More than a hundred prisoners were taken, of whom two-thirds were sent to Barbados. The rest were hanged, ten of them on one gibbet in Edinburgh and the others before their own doors in their own country. At least two were first tortured, their feet crushed by contracting iron boots.

The High Commissioner Lord Rothes, the son of Montrose's friend, thought them all 'damned fools and incorrigible fanatics' for not saving their lives by renouncing the Covenant. The brutality of his repression, in which he was supported by Archbishop James Sharp of St Andrews, was partly the reaction of one compassionate faith to the rivalry of another, but it was also an expression of the government's naive fear that the rebels were in alliance with the Dutch, upon whom the King was waging a miserably unsuccessful war. Rullion Green added to the roll of Covenant martyrs, but the public's horror led to an indemnity for the fugitives and the recall of Rothes.

*After the Restoration, adherents of the Covenant were bitterly persecuted. This monument in Hamilton Kirkyard, Lanark-shire, commemorates four victims whose dismembered bodies were distributed about the country.*

He was replaced by John Maitland, Earl of Lauderdale, a big man with untidy red hair, a raw Scots voice, and a tongue so large that when he spoke he sprayed his listeners with spittle. His passionate temper was close to madness, and Burnet said that he was the 'coldest friend and violentest enemy I ever knew'. Until 1647 he had been a zealous Covenanter, and had been a prisoner from Worcester to the Restoration, but despite his rough manners and blundering body he was learned in Greek, Latin, divinity and history, and if he thought the mewing of a cat preferable to good music he was more shrewd than men of finer grain. The Letters of Indulgence which were issued upon his advice were an attempt to strike a difference between permissible non-conformity and political discontent. Banished ministers were allowed to return to their parishes without complete submission to the bishops, but those who accepted this indulgence were bold in their continued opposition, and those who refused were elevated still higher in the esteem of their congregations. Field-preaching was punishable by death, but the conventicles increased, and now the congregations came to their hillside meetings with sword and musket, drilling while they prayed. Landowners were made responsible for the behaviour of their tenants and dependants, for dispersing the conventicles and discouraging the assemblies of armed men. Those who refused to sign the bonds of responsibility, or failed to honour them, were heavily fined. Many were ruined by these impositions, or were driven into bitter and secret sympathy for the preachers.

Lauderdale now returned to the previous policy of persecution. He threatened to extirpate the conventicles, said Burnet, and 'ruin the whole country if a stop was not put to those meetings'. There was no longer a large standing army, but the chiefs and lairds of Argyll, Atholl, Breadalbane and Moray were ordered to muster their clansmen in arms, to bring them to the Stirling plain and then 'march to the west, to the places infested with these disorders'.[1] This Highland Host of four thousand five hundred men, reinforced by more than three thousand Lowland militia and regular foot, was quartered upon Ayrshire and the west from February 1678 until the spring, with orders to disarm the country and live free upon it. It was a bloodless occupation, but if the clansmen killed nobody they terrified and pillaged all, and when they departed with their booty they left the westland shires with an enduring hatred and contempt for the Highlander, an echo of which would be heard a century later in the verse of Robert Burns.

The western lairds had told Lauderdale that although the field-meetings were armed, there was no danger to the public peace, and after the Host had plundered their lands and spoilt the early ploughing they became stubbornly hostile to his policy of holding them responsible for the behaviour of their people. He called some of them to Edinburgh, shook a bared arm at them, and swore by Jehovah that they would obey. In this unhealthy mood the country moved inevitably to violence. It began in May the following year, and its first victim was the hated Archbishop of St Andrews. Sharp and his daughter were travelling home across Magus Muir, three miles from the city, when their coach was stopped by a group of horsemen. The meeting appears to have been accidental, but the riders, small Covenanting gentry, accepted it as a gift from God. They pistolled Sharp, slashed him across the face, cut off his hand, and rode over his body. He still lived. While his daughter knelt beside him, they crushed his skull.

They rode to the west, where they were welcomed as the Lord's good and faithful servants. On June 1, two of them commanded a body of armed horsemen in a large conventicle at Drumclog, to the north of Loudoun Hill, where Bruce had destroyed the armoured charge of Aymer de Valence. Three troops of Life Guards and dragoons left Hamilton to disperse them, commanded by John Graham of Claverhouse, the dark and gay young man who would soon take his place in the gallery of Jacobite heroes. He was outnumbered, and his troopers could not ride through the lochans and marsh that protected the conventicle. When the Covenanters attacked, with pitchfork and halbert, thirty-six cavalrymen were unsaddled and the rest galloped to Glasgow. The few prisoners taken were shot by the preaching baronet Robert Hamilton, who blessed the Lord for

---

[1] Clan Donald was not invited to this great foray, but with nice irony Sir Donald MacDonald of Sleat, Laird of MacDonald, chief of the name and a descendant of the Lords of the Isles, was told that while the other chiefs were away he would be held responsible for the security of the Highlands.

*Greyfriars' Kirkyard, Edinburgh, where the Covenant was first signed in February, 1638. After Bothwell Brig in 1679 more than a thousand Covenanter prisoners were confined here, and are remembered by the Martyrs' Memorial.*

this opportunity to glorify His name. Thrown out of Glasgow when they entered it in pursuit, the Covenanters gathered an army of five thousand and more, but wasted time in schismatic debate and jealous quarrels. On June 22, at Bothwell Brig on the Clyde, they were attacked by dragoons and foot under the King's bastard, James, Duke of Monmouth. The insurgent cavalry soon left the fight with their commander John Balfour of Kinloch, one of Sharp's murderers, but the infantry bravely defended the barricaded bridge, inspired by the valour and leadership of David Hackston of Rathillet. When they were at last overcome, twelve hundred prisoners were marched to Edinburgh and close-herded in Greyfriars Kirkyard, where their Covenant had first been signed. Two ministers were hanged in the city, and other men were executed on the sacred ground of Magus Muir. Monmouth was distressed by the barbarity of the repression, and generously secured an indemnity for those who would promise to live in peace, but more than two hundred would not accept it. They were shipped for the plantations, and it may be that the Orkney storm in which they were drowned was a providential mercy.

Ill and discredited by a policy that had been worse in effect than his predecessor's, Lauderdale resigned, and few but his favoured kinsmen and friends regretted his going. The King's brother, James, Duke of York, was now sent north, though by religion, temperament and ability he was no better equipped than other commissioners. But his conversion to Catholicism, a fact for nearly twenty years and public knowledge for ten, had become an embarrassment in London, where there was already a Bill to exclude him from the throne. The Scots Parliament was more elastic in its logic. In 1681 it recognized his right to the throne of Scotland, and then passed a Test Act obliging all holders of public office to swear to maintain the Protestant religion as set forth in the Confession, to disown popery and the Covenant, and to recognize the supremacy of the Crown. James was exempted from taking this oath which outlawed his faith but confirmed the absolute power of his future crown.

The indemnity and indulgences secured by Monmouth had not stopped the persecu-

tion, the heavy impositions of fines. Though reduced in numbers, by death, imprisonment and indulgence, the Covenanters grew stronger in defiance. In 1680 a young field
preacher, Richard Cameron, declared war upon King and government below the Mercat
Cross of Sanquhar in Dumfries. A dedicated and passionate man, who seemed driven by a
crazed death-wish, he gathered a little band of zealots who called themselves the Society
Folk, although the name Cameronians given to them by others soon replaced that title,
and lasted until it died with the beat of disbanding drums three centuries later.
Cameron was killed in a skirmish at Aird's Moss, but his successor, Donald Cargill,
gathered the survivors in the hills and impudently excommunicated the King, the dukes
of York and Monmouth, Sir George Mackenzie the Lord Advocate, and Thomas Dalyell
of the Binns. He was quickly caught and executed with four others. One of them was
Hackston, the brave defender of Bothwell Brig and the only rider present at Sharp's
murder who had refused to strike a blow. He was too weak from wounds to be tortured,
but his hands were cut off before he was hanged. The zealots darkly concluded that his
suffering was a divine punishment for his failure to join in God's work on Magus Muir.

As might have been expected, the contradictory articles of the Test Act confused and
split the country. Eight episcopalian clergymen resigned, ministers were deprived for
refusing to take the oath, and men like Sir James Dalrymple, President of the Court of
Session, surrendered their offices and went into exile. The Earl of Argyll, less resolute
than his father, first said that he would take the oath 'as far as it was consistent with
itself' and then refused it, a prevarication that sent him to prison under sentence of
death. He escaped in the unlikely disguise of his stepdaughter's page and fled to Holland.
Many men now found asylum in the Low Countries, ministers and lairds, lawyers and
soldiers. In pleasant, red-bricked towns where Royalists had once endured an impoverished exile, they talked the years away in argument and plot, encouraged by the
sympathy of the young Stadholder, William of Orange, and making uncertain alliances
with English refugees. The Cameronian peasants and artisans could not escape, and when
caught they chose to die rather than save their lives by crying 'God bless the King!'
There was no king but Christ. They were now led by James Renwick, a militant student
from Edinburgh and Groningen who believed the Society Folk were the only true
Church, and who before his execution in 1688 would excommunicate all other ministers.
In November, 1684, the *Apologetical Declarations* of his followers were posted on church
doors and market crosses in the south-west, promising that any man who attempted to
take their lives would do so at the expense of his own. The challenge was accepted with
equal ferocity. A prisoner taken by the dragoons was asked to denounce the *Declarations*,
and if he would not he was often shot as he stood by the stirrup of his captor. There are
stories of men sabred while they knelt in prayer, of conventicles destroyed by musketry,
of women drowned. These were the bitter 'killing times' when the Lord Advocate
became Bluidy Mackenzie, and James Graham was Bluidy Clavers. There is no record
that more than ten Cameronians were shot on the Graham's orders, but one man
summarily killed is perhaps enough to justify the adjective, and the western dragonnade
stains the reputation of Claverhouse, as the sack of Aberdeen darkens the memory of
Montrose.

Few men could swallow the extreme doctrines of the Cameronians, but their courage
was admired and their resistance was an inspiration to wider discontent, although this
was as yet unwilling to overthrow government or Crown. When Charles died of an
apoplectic stroke in Feburary, 1685, his Catholic brother was proclaimed in Scotland

with conventional expressions of joy, and a revolt that was meant to support the Duke of Monmouth's rising in England shared its dismal failure. Argyll had returned from Holland to raise his clan, but got little response from it or other men, and his own son offered to lead his tribal children against him if the act of forfeiture were lifted from the earldom. The miserable army was wasted by dispute, and Argyll was captured by two militamen while crossing a burn in peasant disguise. After a bungled attempt to shoot himself, he died with resignation under the Maiden that had killed his father. He had never been quite sane, it was said, since the trepanning of his skull. With the government's approval, Clan Donald and its allies once more descended upon Campbell lands, hanging, burning, and looting from Roseneath to the Firth of Lorne. The men and women who had supported Argyll were crowded into subterranean prisons, tortured or brutally neglected, and then transported to the Americas.

The new king was long-jawed and thin-nosed, his youthful good looks lost in an arrogant and disagreeable face. He had no sense of humour, and pursued his passion for women and foxhunting with the dedication of a priest. He believed that the monarchy was answerable to none but God, and that he had been called to the throne to protect the Catholic faith. His haughty obstinacy had increased with age, and in what must have been a mental decline he now proceeded to destroy the house of Stuart. All his virtues of moral and physical courage, diligence, loyalty to his friends, were spoilt by a blind arrogance. His desire to give equal liberties to his co-religionists is just and reasonable in twentieth-century terms. In his age it was disastrous. Protestant faiths which could not yet endure each other were not ready to tolerate a common enemy, nor it them. If he understood this, he ignored it. Though the Scottish parliament somehow found the strength to resist his proposal to repeal the penal laws against popery, he used the Privy Council to annul them. The monarchy, he had once written, 'has no dependency on parliaments'. In contempt of the Test Act, he removed Protestants from office and replaced them with Romanists, alienating men he would have need of later. He punished ministers who preached against Rome, and deprived two prelates who opposed him. The Chapel Royal at Holyrood was refurnished for Catholic worship, and Jesuit teachers were established in the palace with a printing-press. The first of his proclamations of Indulgence in 1687 suspended all laws against Catholics, and to make this acceptable, Presbyterians were given freedom to worship in private houses. The second Indulgence removed all penal laws against non-conformity, giving the dissenters the right to meet in house or chapel, provided no sedition was preached. Conventicles, however, were still punishable by death.

There was little sympathy for the king who had granted the indulgences. His supporters were reduced to the Catholic minority, a few dedicated Royalists, and a handful of trimmers who would desert him at the first cold wind. The Episcopalians of the Established Church were sullenly resentful of the liberties given to their rivals on both flanks, and were angered by their own loss of office and influence. Though the Cameronians were still outlawed, exalted by suffering, many men who had unwillingly accepted the ecclesiastical changes since 1660 could now hope for the return of the old Kirk. Using the freedom given them, non-conforming preachers opened meeting-houses in competition with established ministers, attracting large congregations. Scenting change and opportunity, exiles came home from Holland and slowly began the restoration of the old presbyterian system. The spirit of Henderson and Melville was awoken by the call for a True Kirk, No Popery and No Prelacy.

*James II, the last Stuart king, all of whose virtues 'of moral and physical courage, diligence, loyalty to his friends, were spoilt by a blind arrogance'.*

269

The Glorious Revolution was made by the English, and the Scots caught at its coat-tails. The birth of a son to James's second wife, with its depressing promise of a Catholic dynasty, and his foolish coercion of the Church of England, made an inevitable fall immediate. His aloof and asthmatic son-in-law, William of Orange, had been ready twelve months for a call from the English Whigs, but his offer to rid the Scots of the tyrant James had been coldly received. He was in London, and James was on his way to France, before the Edinburgh mob came out of the wynds. Joined by the trained bands of the city, and by a group of enthusiastic gentlemen, it overcame the soldiers defending Holyroodhouse, harried the Jesuits, destroyed the printing-press, sacked the Chapel Royal, and drove the Lord Chancellor from his house. In the south-west on Christmas Day, two hundred episcopalian curates were ejected from their homes and parishes, and the Cameronians marched upon Edinburgh, where the Earl of Angus would later muster a thousand of the youngest and boldest into a redcoat regiment. The last exiled saints of the Covenant had returned with William, their offices and preferment already decided, and one of the three divisions of his invading army was the mercenary Scots Brigade under old Hugh Mackay of Scourie. In February, William accepted the throne of England for himself and his wife Mary, having made it plain that they would reign jointly and that he would not be his wife's 'gentleman usher'. Even then the Scots made

*An anti-Catholic cartoon of 1688 on the natal arrival of the Old Pretender. The birth, with 'its depressing promise of a Catholic dynasty, made the inevitable fall of James II immediate'. Right Successors to the thrones abandoned by James II were his daughter Mary and her husband William of Orange.*

no offer of their crown, only a request that he undertake the administration of the country until it could decide its future.

He summoned a Convention of the Estates, and it met in March as if the crown were in auction, hearing letters from both William and James. To help it toward a proper choice, three regiments of Mackay's veterans were disembarked at Leith, and the new Earl of Argyll brought in a band of Highlanders from his glens. The only armed opposition to this show of democratic force was a troop of fifty horsemen gathered by Graham of Claverhouse, recently created Viscount Dundee. When the supporters of Orange elected their own candidate as President of the Convention, King James's men withdrew from Parliament House and Dundee wisely rode northward to his ultimate place in Jacobite hagiolatry. Further protected by the young Cameronians, the Convention resolved that by vacating the throne James had forfeited his right to it, and it could therefore be offered to his son-in-law and daughter. As if preparing an inventory and a new lease, the Estates drew up a *Claim of Rights* and *Articles of Grievances*, listing the offences of the retiring tenant and imposing fresh terms on the new occupiers, asking them to protect the laws, religion and liberties of the nation, to root out the enemies of the True Kirk. In May, the necessary pieces of the Regalia of Scotland were carried to London in the baggage of three commissioners from the Estates, and the coronation oath was modestly taken in the Banqueting Hall at Westminster.

The northern kingdom so casually re-assigned was already at war. A month earlier, Dundee had raised James's standard outside the city of his new title, but finding little support for it had ridden on to the Highlands. There the MacDonalds of Keppoch, indifferent to Orange or Stuart but conducting a successful feud against the Mackintoshes, were holding the town of Inverness to ransom. Dundee bought them off with a promise of two thousand seven hundred pounds Scots and led them down the Great Glen to Lochaber. On the green field of Dalcomera by the River Lochy, he was at last able to assemble an army, mostly drawn from the western clans, from Clan Donald and Camerons, Stewarts and Macleans. As with Montrose before him, his valour and charm persuaded them to set aside their touchy differences for a common purpose, but loyalty to the Stuart cause meant less to them than older dreams and hatreds. The Earl of Argyll had returned from the make-shift coronation in Whitehall with his titles and estates restored, and with a commission to raise a regiment of his clansmen in the service of William. It was a time to bloody the head of King Campbell again, to recover all that Clan Diarmid had taken.

The Jacobites marched to the south and east, and in the Pass of Killiecrankie on July 27 they met four thousand men under Hugh Mackay, Lowland Scots and veterans of the Dutch wars. The Williamites outnumbered Dundee by nearly two to one, but they broke under the storm-charge of the clans, running in panic through the pass. It was a hard tussle, said Iain Luim the bard of Keppoch, many a cocked hat and periwig was smashed by the terrible swords of Clan Donald. Red blood flowed in waves over the grass, and a thousand spades would be needed to level the graves of the enemy. It was an empty victory, however. Six hundred Highlanders were also killed, and Dundee was dead from an unlucky musket-ball. Without the one leader who could have effectively used them, the grieving clans moved southward to the cathedral town of Dunkeld.

It was held by a single regiment, the newly-mustered Cameronians, twelve hundred men behind the walls of the cathedral precincts. Their lieutenant-colonel was William Cleland, a brave young man who had once mocked the Highland Host in derisive

*Pennant's view of Dunkeld, which Kenneth MacAlpin made his joint capital with Scone, and where the Cameronian regiment bloodily repulsed the Jacobite clans in August, 1689.*

doggerel, and who had fought with the godly at Drumclog and Bothwell Brig. He was killed by a bullet in the liver and another in the head within an hour of the first assault, but his men set fire to the town and drove the clans from it at push of pike. A few months before these Covenanting zealots had been outlawed men, but now they were the saviours of the Revolution, standing in the smoke and their bloody red coats, singing psalms of praise to a triumphant Sabbath.

Dispirited by defeat, the clans made pacts of mutual assistance, robbed Campbell lands in Breadalbane, and went home to their glens. They would not rise again in strength for twenty-five years.

6

Within a year of the fierce battle in the streets of Dunkeld, a new parliament abolished prelacy and established Presbyterianism. William's support for the True Kirk was not the result of pious sympathy. The refusal of Scots bishops to accept the Revolution had left him no choice. When the first General Assembly met in 1690 he told its members that moderation would become them as much as it would please him, but bitter memories of the killing-times were not to be set aside by the sensible advice of an invited king. One intolerance was replaced by another, and the victims were now the episcopalians, 'all insufficient, negligent, scandalous and erroneous ministers' whom the Assembly was determined to remove. The holy work begun by the western mob in December, 1688, was continued in the purging of parish and university by Kirk commissions, until the King's indignation and Parliament's intervention regularized the witch-hunting, protecting those episcopalian office-holders and ministers who took an oath of allegiance to the Crown, and outlawing those who would not. After one hundred and thirty years the Kirk was finally victorious, but preoccupation with the long struggle had stunted the artistic and intellectual growth of the country south of the Highland line, hampered its industry and economy, wasted the blood of its young men, and given it a tradition of hard, self-sacrificial intolerance that would dominate its spirit for another century and more. The triumph of Presbyterianism came toward the end of Scotland's political independence, and in the few years left the nation's pride would reach its zenith in a splendid and suicidal gesture, falling to a shameful nadir of spiteful revenge.

The changes that had taken place in the people's way of life were more evident in the top strata of society, small creature-comforts of carpets in the homes of the middle-class and gentry, marble chimney-pieces and bold stairways in great houses, glazed windows, painted ceilings, tailored gardens, but all were little compared with England. Highways were so bad that men and women preferred the saddle to the discomfort of a coach. Agriculture was poor and primitive, and the growth of the population had outmarched the ability of land or husbandry to support it, increasing the suffering and hardship of the peasantry. Harbours, naturally among the finest in Europe, were neglected or ill-developed. Except for a few coastal vessels of light burden there was no shipping, and the English Navigation Acts discouraged the building of a merchant navy. Towns were still pestiferous and stinking from overcrowding and wretched sanitation, and were remarkable abominations even at a time when all urban communities were incubators of disease and epidemic. The city of Edinburgh, said the English chaplain of a Scots regiment, 'is likened by some to an ivory comb, whose teeth on both sides are very foul, though the space between 'em is clean and sightly'.

A million people now inhabited Scotland, and if most of them were truly as slothful

*The Study, in the little Royal Burgh of Culross, Fife, a well-preserved example of the gentler 17th-century domestic architecture. Right After the Revolution Scotland suffered bitterly from famine and disease. This contemporary remedy for the plague, an omnipresent menace, was found in the Medical Book of the Duke of Argyll.*

About the 14th of September, the following Receipt was publish'd about the Country against the Plague.

Take common Salt Petre 4 Scruples; Flower of Brimstone one Scruple ; Saffron and Cochineal of each Six Grains ; all in fine Powder mix for a Dose.

This (faith the Author) was repeated Night and Morning, fo long as need required ; and of fome Thoufands that took it not one died.

He advifes the keeping of moderete Fires, in the Houfes and the burning of Rofemary, Sweet Herbs, Gums, &c. in a Pan of Coals, in Rooms where fick Perfons are ; who muft be kept clean, for he fays that Naftinefs and Dirt encreafes this Diftember.

Dr. Butler of Cambridge his Prefervative against the Plague.

TAke of Wood Sorrel and pick it from the Stalk, and pound it very well in a Stone Morter ; then take to every pound of beaten Sorrel, a Pound of Sugar finely beaten, and two Ounces of Mithridate ; beat them very well together, and put it into Pots for your Ufe : Take every Morning before and after the Infection, for fome Time together, of this Conferve as much as a Wallnut.

London, Printed by J. Smith.

and self-indulgent as the English claimed, they should still be admired for their will to survive. The dragoons of war and persecution had been accompanied by those other apocalyptic horsemen, pestilence and hunger, and there had been two terrifying visitations of plague, one of them when men were killing each other for King or Covenant. After the Restoration there were years of good harvests and benign summers, and by some providential mercy Edinburgh escaped the bubonic horror that turned London into a death-house. But as the century ended there were seven terrible years of near-famine, each worse than the last, sickly summers and lingering winters, failing crops and little seed for the spring sowing. The Kirk said the disaster was God's punishment upon a wicked people, the Episcopalians recognized it as divine justice upon the Presbyterians, and no one saw it as the collapse of primitive husbandry before the natural forces of the weather. Ministers reported that a fifth, a third, and sometimes half of their parishes had died of hunger and disease. Other men wrote of bodies found by the roadside with grass in their mouths, of hordes of emaciated beggars, children sucking at empty breasts, diseased carcasses eaten by the desperate, the dying dragging themselves to the kirkyard in hope of burial. Andrew Fletcher of Saltoun, one of the nation's best patriots and poorly remembered, wrote of these years with anger.

> We voted His Majesty a standing army, though we had more need to have saved the money to have bought bread, for thousands of our people that were starving afford us the melancholy prospect of dying by shoals in our streets, and have left behind them reigning contagion which hath swept away multitudes more, and God knows where it may end.

It ended where he would not have wished it to end. He believed that Scotland would flourish if only the bonds that tied her to England were loosened. Other men recalled the promise if not the achievement of the Commonwealth union, and were convinced that the future prosperity of the country could come when those knots were tightened, when the Scots would enjoy equal rights and equal privileges with the English. A proposal to treat with England for a political union had been one of the earliest resolutions put before the Convention of the Estates in 1689, and although it had been rejected the small support for the idea slowly grew. One of its subtle supporters was Sir John Dalrymple, Master of Stair and the King's principal Secretary of State for Scotland in 1691. Though his political and religious convictions were malleable, he and his family had suffered in the name of Kirk and Covenant. He was the intellectual superior of most of his countrymen, a cunning administrator and a cynically accurate judge of men. The Jacobites accused him of being the main instrument of all the misfortunes that fell upon Scotland, and if the Treaty of Union, for which he killed himself by self-denying work, is one of them, he is usually seen through the red mist of the Highland massacre he planned and ordered.

Once its principal leaders had been adequately bribed, the King had little interest in his northern kingdom except as a source of supplies and recruits for his wars in Flanders. The greatest obstacle to his sympathy for Scotland, and to the English parliament's readiness to take the thought of a political union seriously, was the lawless state of the Highlands. In the pleasant suburban sprawl of London, westward from Holborn and Charing Cross, it was also easy to see little difference between a Lowland laird and a mountain savage, and to have no wish for union with either. Since the defeat of the clans at Dunkeld, and a comic rout at Cromdale later, the peace of the mountains had been uneasily kept by Colonel John Hill, the old Cromwellian recalled to a new fort at Inverlochy. The Whig clans of the north-east and the south-west outnumbered those who still supported the exiled Stuart for selfish or selfless reasons, but the risk of another rising, of a second front inspired by the French, prevented William from withdrawing those Scottish regiments he had raised for use in the Low Countries.

The original scheme for the pacification of the clans, involving men of sincere good-will, was to buy their loyalty, and the Master of Stair supported it and worked for it as long as it seemed practicable, though he did not disguise his contempt for the High-landers. Most of the chiefs were ready to accept the money, and some disputed the amount promised them, arguing that their rank and importance deserved more. The plan failed, partly from the King's reluctance to buy what he thought he should be given, and partly from the contrived bungling and dark double-dealing of its principal negotiator, the slippery and ambitious Campbell Earl of Breadalbane. From the royal camp in Flanders on August 17, 1691, William then offered a pardon to all rebels provided they took an oath of allegiance to the Crown before January 1, threatening those who did not with the 'utmost extremity of the law'. Caught between honour and survival, the Jacobite chiefs sent an urgent message to James in France, asking to be released from their oath to him so that they might take another to his son-in-law. As the weeks passed into winter without a response, and without the oath being sworn by any chief, Stair briskly and secretly prepared for bloody coercion. With the cautious advice of Argyll and Breadalbane, he proposed the punitive use of 'fire and sword and all manner of hostility' upon several clans, but particularly the MacDonalds, for few men, he thought, would regret what happened to them. 'Let me hear from you,' he wrote to the deputy commander of Fort William at Inverlochy, 'whether you think this is the proper season to maul them in the cold long nights.'

In the last week of December a messenger arrived in the Highlands from the irresolute exile at St Germain. The loyal chiefs, said James, could 'do what may be most for their own safety'. At so short a notice, and in the bitterest of weather, less than a hand's-count were able to travel to the sheriffs of their shires, and there submit to the oath in time.

The victims finally chosen for a terrible lesson were not the great MacDonald clans of Keppoch or Glengarry, but a small branch living in a narrow valley between Loch Leven and Rannoch Moor. These Glencoe MacDonalds were renowned as great poets, archers, lovers of dogs, and incorrigible rogues. They had few, if any, friends, but a long history of robbing, burning, murder and rebellion. Cattle-lifting was a way of life in the mountains, an economic necessity, and the poverty of their own valley forced the Glencoe men to raid deep into the east and south-west. Their only loyalty was to that which served Clan Donald, to the ancient and lost power of the Lords of the Isles, and they were thus hostile opponents of the Campbells – though they had not been above taking Clan Diarmid's pay for the killing of its other enemies. Stair believed that it would be a lesson to the laggards and a mercy to the nation if this 'thieving tribe were rooted out and cut off', and since they were said to be papists as well as thieves the great charity of their extinction would be doubly blessed.

The chief of Glencoe was a valiant old giant with a curled moustache and a mane of white hair, Alasdair MacDonald, known as MacIain. Delayed by a fierce blizzard, and by the absence of the sheriff-depute of Inveraray, he did not take the oath until January 6, and he wept as he asked for his word to be accepted. Orders for the extirpation of his clan, subscribed and superscribed by the King, had been sent to Scotland before his tardy submission was known, but the news of it did not change Stair's mind. 'I am glad Glencoe did not come in within the time prescribed,' he wrote, 'I hope what's done there may be in earnest.' The work of charity he desired was carried out by two companies of the Earl of Argyll's regiment under the command of Captain Robert Campbell of Glenlyon. The use of Campbell soldiers had little to do with their ancient feuds, they were the only disciplined and reliable force in John Hill's district, but the selection of the bankrupt and drunkard Glenlyon was perhaps deliberate. Despite the fact that he was related by marriage to MacIain's second son, he had particular reasons for hating the Glencoe men. On their way home from Dunkeld, they had burnt and looted his glen for the second time, completing a financial ruin begun by drink and gambling, and forcing him to take service in his kinsman's regiment at the age of sixty.

He took his companies into Glencoe at the beginning of February, asking for quarters. He was welcomed agreeably and generously, for Highland hospitality was traditionally inviolable, whatever the bitterness between guest and host. At dawn on Saturday, February 13, the soldiers turned upon the MacDonalds. The massacre was bungled, a snowstorm and Glenlyon's ineptitude prevented him from destroying all males under seventy as he had been ordered. MacIain was killed in his own bed-chamber, while he was calling for wine to be brought to his guests, and thirty-six of his men were slaughtered in their huts or against the walls outside, with three or four women and children. The rest of the clan, no more than four hundred, escaped to the high braes, where the bitter weather continued the work of the Argyll pikes and bayonets.

There had been more brutal massacres in the Highlands, in some of which the Glencoe men had taken part, but this, as a Commission of Enquiry later declared, was 'murder under trust', planned and ordered by the King's servants, a deliberate attempt at genocide. Though William's guilt was ignored, Stair was condemned by the Scots parliament and resigned his secretaryship, but his work had been effective, and the laggard chiefs came quickly to take the oath of submission. Jacobite hacks and agents made good use of the incident in plot and propaganda, but the Glencoe men, with a tolerance unknown to their sympathizers over the next two centuries, soon put it in perspective. In 1715 they fought beside the sons and tenants of Glenlyon.

Parliament's courage in addressing the King in the matter of Glencoe, declaring the responsibility of his minister and asking for the trial of his officers, was another stage in their uneasy and frequently hostile relationship. Against his wish the Committee of Articles had been abolished in the first year of his reign, and as parliamentary representation was widened so it became more independent in temper. The greatest cause of bitterness was the heavy burden which Scotland was carrying in the long and unpopular war with Louis XIV. The contribution in men was out of proportion to the population. Of twenty British battalions which fought in the bloody battle of Steinkirk, for example, eight were Scots, and both Mackay's and the Cameronians were all but destroyed. The persistent demands for more men and more supplies exhausted a famine-stricken country. All its meagre industries suffered from privileged English competition or restrictive English legislation. English shipmasters had exclusive rights to foreign trade, and the great English trading companies had rich monopolies in Africa, Asia and America. Scotsmen were held upright by their pride, but there was little else they had that had not been sold to them by the English at English prices. The belief that all this might be changed by a political union was steadily growing, but before then Scotland made an heroic and disastrous attempt to become as great a colonial and mercantile power as England.

In June, 1695, when it was waiting to debate the report of the Commission of

*Eilean Donan Castle, Ross and Cromarty, the ancient home of Clan Macrae. Bombarded by the British in 1719, it was largely restored in this century. Overleaf Sibbald's Circulating Library, by W. B. Johnstone, 1786. Among other literary figures are Robert Burns and the boy Walter Scott.*

Enquiry into Glencoe, the Scots Parliament passed an act authorizing the establishment of a Company of Scotland Trading to Africa and the Indies. The Marquis of Tweeddale was the King's Commissioner, and knew his master's disapproving mind, but he bent his ageing and rheumatic back to the pressure of the Estates, touched the Act with the sceptre, and thus gave it the royal assent without first giving William the opportunity to read it. The dream of a Scots merchant colony was not new, and although previous attempts to fulfil it in Nova Scotia, New England and Carolina had been miserable calamities, the spirit and challenge of this 'noble undertaking' inflamed the imagination of the country. Fletcher said that men and women seemed moved by a Higher Power toward the 'only means to recover us from our present miserable and despicable condition'.

In its original form, the scheme for the Company had been drawn by a group of Scots merchants in London and principally by William Paterson, a Dumfries wanderer whose creative intellect was in advance of his time, and whose simplicity of faith had scarcely emerged from childhood. He and his companions proposed a joint Scots and English venture, but this was effectively squashed by the English trading companies and the impeachment of its founders before the Commons. A following attempt to enlist the support of the Hanseatic towns was also stopped by the English, and Scotland went bravely ahead alone. In an atmosphere of feverish enthusiasm, Scots men and women, burghs, corporations and associations subscribed four hundred thousand pounds toward the Company, believed to be half the available capital of the nation. Patriotism was married to profit, and the issue was assured. 'Trade will increase trade,' Paterson had said, 'and money will beget money.' The Council-General of the Company abandoned its earlier thoughts of Africa and decided to establish a colony and an *entrepôt* on the coast of Darien, the most inhospitable and unhealthy part of the Isthmus of Panama. No one, not even Paterson who had suggested this site from the beginning, had ever been there. What information there was about it came from the journals and papers of a young buccaneer-surgeon, Lionel Wafer, and his warning that it was the wettest place in the torrid zone was blithely ignored.

Ships were bought, built or chartered in Holland and Hamburg, and the Company's warehouses at Leith and Glasgow were slowly filled with a bizarre collection of goods which, it was confidently believed, could be exchanged for the spices, silks and gold of the Orient. All men south of the Highlands wished to share in the glory and the rewards, offering their purses or their sons as an investment. Darien, said Paterson, would be the 'door of the seas, the key of the universe', reducing by half the time and expense of navigation to China and Japan, and bringing peace to both oceans without the guilt of war. This wondrous scheme was premature, not impossible, and two centuries later men would realize part of it by cutting the cord of the Isthmus with a canal.[1]

In July, 1698, five ships left Leith upon a great wave of emotion. They sailed north about and down the Atlantic, made a landfall off the coast of Darien in November, and claimed it as the Colony of Caledonia. Many of the colonists were already dead from flux and fever, and their leaders were inefficient and quarrelsome. The splendid harbour chosen was a trap for vessels that could not sail to windward. Ambition, pride and envy, aggravated by ignorant stupidity, destroyed the spirit of those who survived the killing

---

[1] Seventy years later still, the Darien coast where the Scots established their colony may be chosen as the eastern end of a new Panama canal, to be cut by nuclear force.

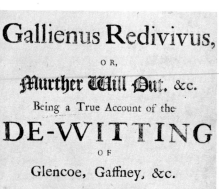

*Gallienus Redivivus was a contemporary account of the Massacre of Glencoe written by the Jacobite minister and hack, Charles Leslie. Centre Robert Campbell of Glenlyon, seen here as a young man, was a bankrupt drunkard whose ruin was made complete by raiding Glencoe men. Right This contemporary map of the Darien settlement gives no indication of the rain-soaked, fever-ridden reality of the peninsula.*

fevers. Paterson's wife died within a few days of the landing, and he went slowly out of his mind with despair. The town of New Edinburgh was never more than a few palmetto huts, and the ramparts of Fort St Andrew were washed away by the pitiless rain. The Spaniards' claim to Darien had been acknowledged by William and the English government, but their attempt to retake it was repulsed by the Scots in a little jungle skirmish. When the English colonies of America and the Caribbean were ordered to give no help to Caledonia, the survivors lost their courage and abandoned the huts, the fort and the bay. Relief ships from the Forth were welcomed by four hundred lonely graves. Despite the bitterness of famine, and the shortage of money and supplies, Scotland had assembled another expedition of four ships, and it was already at sea before the failure of the first was known. It reached Caledonia in November, 1699, and found only a 'vast, howling wilderness', but the huts were rebuilt and the fort reoccupied. From the beginning there was jealousy and disunity, fever, desertion and mutiny, and the ministers sent by the General Assembly violently abused the sick and dying for their 'atheistical cursing and swearing, brutish drunkenness and detestable mockery'. Once again the Spaniards attacked, and were once again thrown back in the green wet mist of the jungle. When they blockaded the colony by sea and land, advanced their guns and trenches to the rotting ramparts of the fort, the Scots resisted bravely for a month and then surrendered. On April 12, 1700, Caledonia was finally abandoned.

The Darien Venture was perhaps the worst disaster in Scotland's history, greater than the bloody defeats of Flodden and Dunbar and Worcester. There had been no glory, no valour, and few nations can withstand the terrible loss of pride and money. Its exchequer and storehouses were empty, and its challenge to the mercantile power of England was now a mockery. Nine ships which the Company had bought or chartered were sunk, burnt or abandoned. A call had been made upon three-quarters of the subscribed capital, and it was all lost. Only three hundred of the colonists, soldiers and seamen returned to Scotland. Two thousand men, women and children had been sacrificed to a national *hubris*, drowned at sea, buried in the foetid earth of Darien, abandoned in Spanish prisons, or lost for ever as indentured servants in English colonies. The anger of the people was intense, and was not reduced when the King said that their colony had been a threat to peace. Nor was his promise to promote their trade, to repair their losses if possible, more than bitter comfort. Few men blamed the failure of the colony upon the stupidity of its location, the contentious inefficiency of its leaders, or the blind ignorance of its promoters. English treachery was responsible. Great men who knew this to be false, or at least an exaggeration, publicly agreed rather than challenge the outraged emotions of the nation. Five years after the capitulation of Fort St Andrew, the Privy Council submitted to a violent mob outside the locked doors of Parliament House and agreed to the hanging of the captain, the mate and the gunner of the English merchantman *Worcester*. The charge of piracy laid against these young men, of looting and burning a Scots ship, was the imaginative creation of the Company's embittered secretary, but most men believed it, and some of the few who did not were glad to see the humbling of English pride. This squalid judicial murder was Scotland's last gesture of defiance before it surrendered its political independence.

The death of the childless, asthmatic and widowed King in 1702 had left the crown of both kingdoms to his sister-in-law Anne. With a gynaecological history of unhappy accouchements she was unlikely to leave an heir, and the problem of further succession had been resolved by the English parliament a year before William's death. The crown was to go to the Electress Sophia of Hanover, granddaughter of James VI. Scots opinion was not consulted, and the Estates made their resentment plain in 1703, declaring that unless the security and privileges of Scotland were assured it would choose its own sovereign. The implication was that he might well be the young son of the recently deceased exile of St Germain. William had foreseen this squabble, and upon his death-bed had urged the English parliament to accept a political union. Negotiations did begin in the first year of Anne's reign, but were abandoned when the English would not give the Scots the equal trading privileges they now demanded as their price for accepting the Electress. Anne at first refused to accept the Scots Act of Security, whereupon the Estates voted her no supplies until she submitted a year later. In this blustering game of intimidation by statute, the English held the powerful hand, and by an act of February, 1705, they banned the importation of cattle, coal and linen from Scotland, and declared that all Scots would be treated as aliens unless their parliament accepted the Electress within a year, or treated for a union. It was during this passionate mood of mutual hostility that the young officers of the *Worcester* were ritually murdered by the mob and Privy Council of Scotland.

Brave defiance and cowardly reprisal were useless. 'We are utterly ruined should those laws take effect,' said the Earl of Roxburgh, joint Secretary of State, and after four weeks of envenomed debate the Estates at last voted to treat for a union. Having served its bullying purpose, the most offensive clause of the Alien Act was withdrawn by the Commons, despite protests from the English public. In April, 1706, commissioners from both countries met with unconscious irony in the Cockpit at Westminster, and two months later they were agreed upon the terms of the treaty. Scotland's earlier hope for some form of federal union had collapsed before English obduracy and the pressing needs of the nation's poverty, and the advantages to be got from equal trading privileges with the English outweighed all other considerations. There was further solace to a country still suffering from the shock and the debts of the Darien Venture. By Article Fifteen of the Treaty, England agreed to give Scotland nearly four hundred thousand pounds sterling for the liquidation of its public debts, the improvement of its monetary standard, and the repayment of the capital stock of the Company with interest at five per cent. William Paterson was glad that the colony had not been entirely in vain. 'No good patriot,' he wrote, 'would have been angry when even the miscarriage of that design hath contributed to the Union.' Most men were just thankful to have their money back.

The draft of the Treaty was presented to the Scots parliament on October 12. During the three months it was under debate Scotland was in ferment, and English regiments were marched to the Border, to be called across it should the Queen's Commissioner believe there was a need for them. Daniel Defoe, who came as a spy for the English government, reported a 'most confused state of affairs'. Since an election earlier in the year the Whigs again dominated the Estates, but not one party or group – Tory and Whig, Presbyterian or Episcopalian – could stomach all the articles, and the mob outside Parliament House shouted with one voice this day, and another tomorrow. In a November riot, windows were broken and coaches overturned on the Royal Mile until soldiers were brought down from the Castle. Passion in the House was sometimes at the same heat, with John Hamilton, Lord Belhaven, launching himself upon a wave of execrable rhetoric and describing a vision in which he saw Scotland's ancient mother Caledonia dying from the murderous blow of the Union, murmuring *Et tu quoque me fili!* Posing as a fish-merchant, and sometimes as a linen-manufacturer, Defoe went among mob and gentry. The Episcopalians, he said, were all rebellious. The Presbyterians were mad at the worst, and at the best dissatisfied. Some of the northern lairds had brought their men from the mountains in the manner of their ancestors. Never had so many Highlanders been seen in Edinburgh, 'each man armed with a broadsword, target, pistol or perhaps two'.

Outside the capital, the Queen's soldiers were troubled and disaffected, and their officers had no faith in them. Copies of the Treaty were burnt before the market cross at Dumfries, surrounded by armed men, and there were unlikely stories that the clans of the north and the Cameronians of the south-west were ready to unite in the common cause of an independent Scotland. Two hundred dragoons were sent to Glasgow, where ministers were inspiring riot with cries of 'Up and be valiant for the city of our God!' When the soldiers were withdrawn, the mob held the city for a month, and the Provost hid in his bed-cupboard. Night-riders called for rebellion, and a minister told Defoe, now pretending to be a glassmaker, that but for the rain fifteen thousand men would march upon Edinburgh. No one at that moment saw the humour of the report.

While the country was in uproar, the Scots Parliament went painfully ahead with its suicide, a weak but determined opposition insisting that all of the twenty-five articles of the Treaty should be debated. On January 16, 1707, it was finally ratified by one hundred and ten votes to sixty-seven, and the work was done. When the Treaty passed through Westminster without opposition the parliaments of Scotland and England ceased to exist. There would now be a Parliament of Great Britain consisting of five hundred and thirteen representatives from England in the Commons, and forty-five from

Scotland. Sixteen elected Scots peers would sit in the House of Lords. Something of Scotland's independence remained. It was to keep its own Kirk, courts and legal code, the royal burghs their particular privileges, and the great lords their heritable jurisdictions. But the seat of government was moved four hundred miles to the south, and like a magnet it would alter the polarization of Scotland's economy, politics and culture. 'We are bought and sold for English gold!' sang a Jacobite ballad, but the complaint was an over-simplification. The Queen sent twenty thousand pounds to pay the arrears and expenses of her government officers, and men who had opposed the Union took their share. Bribes and inducements were undoubtedly given and taken during the long debates, but this was the custom. The independence of the country was not sold, it reluctantly surrendered to a belief that it could no longer survive, and what the heart of Scotland had resisted for four hundred years was at last accepted by its stomach.

The Estates met for the last time on March 25, 1707. All passions were exhausted and all protests stilled. Before the members were dismissed, their valediction was spoken by the High Commissioner James Douglas, Duke of Queensberry. He was confident that posterity would reap the benefit of the Union they had concluded, and that they would

> . . . promote a universal desire in this kingdom to become one in hearts and affections, as we are inseparably joined in interest with our neighbour nation.

One of the last acts passed by the Scots Parliament, and one which was to be regarded as part of the Treaty, secured the Protestant religion and the presbyterian system of Church government. Five years later the Westminster parliament passed a Toleration Act which gave some freedom and justice to those episcopalian clergymen who took an oath of allegiance and abjuration. Although most of the Scots clergy refused the oath, the Presbyterians were alarmed by the old chimera of prelacy. That alarm became an outraged protest when the parliament next restored lay patronage to the Kirk, contrary to the Act of Security that had been passed with the Treaty. It was the worst of a series of worrying grievances since the Union, which had included the continuing drain of Scots blood in the French wars, the apparent disparity of tax burdens, the abolition of the Privy Council, and the discovery that the House of Lords had jurisdiction in Scotland as the ultimate court of appeal.

In June, 1713, the Scots peers introduced a bill to repeal the Union. It was narrowly defeated, but it is doubtful if anyone would have known what to do had it been passed. The horse was gone, and there was no stable door.

PART VII

# North Britons

'*The* Rights of Man *is now well kenned*'

The Rebellion of 1715 was already over when James Stuart, the Old Pretender, landed at Peterhead.
He established an unhappy court at Scone, but retreated before Argyll and left for France in February, 1716.

Looking from his window one evening during the great debate, Daniel Defoe saw a 'terrible multitude' on the Royal Mile, marching behind a drummer and shouting 'No Union! No Union! . . . English dogs!' and the like. He decided later that the riot had been inspired by the Lord Chancellor, the Earl of Seafield, to justify a call for English troops, but he did not say that the same influence was at work when the Treaty was passed and an 'universal joy of the friends of both nations' ran through the city. Another English spy, less considerate of his masters' feelings, reported that most Scots cursed the nobles who had betrayed them into the Union, and that for every man who supported the Treaty there were fifty against it. 'I never saw a nation so universally wild.'

For more than a quarter of a century it did seem as if Union were a greater disaster than the Darien Venture, and that the surrender of Scotland's political independence would bring it no relief from hardship and suffering. Between a fifth and a third of the nation, it was estimated, had died from starvation or disease during the famine years, and the effect of this upon the economy could not be immediately improved by closing the doors of Parliament House. Scots merchants and manufacturers now had equal privileges in law with the English, but the latter had the powerful advantage of established and resilient industries, as well as the sympathy of a predominantly English parliament. A rise in taxation, which the English could accept, was a wounding hardship to Scotland, and an impost upon salt all but destroyed its moribund fisheries. The manufacture of linen was of no great consequence in the south, but it was a staple industry in Scotland, and when Parliament proposed a heavy export duty the Scots members asked for it to be given the same preference as English wool. The Lord Treasurer's answer reflected the arrogant mood of his countrymen. 'Have we not bought the Scots, and a right to tax them?' When English merchants persuaded the Crown to subsidize Irish linen manufacture, in which they had an interest and which would import yarn from Scotland, the Scots again protested. The export of the yarn would impoverish Scottish weavers, and would be contrary to Scots law. They were given another illustration of the English interpretation of the Treaty. 'Whatever are or may be the laws of Scotland, yet now she is subject to the sovereignty of England, she must be governed by English laws and maxims.'

England's lack of sympathy for Scotland's particular needs seemed sometimes perverse and malicious, the triumph of a small boy who is winning a game he has himself devised. A Scots proposal to drive roads into the Highlands, to exploit their great stands of timber for the benefit of both nations, was bluntly rejected, and English ships continued to bring wood from the American colonies. The export of English coal to Ireland was freed from duty, and although Scots fields were included in the first two readings of the Bill, they were cunningly excluded from the third. This was not a union of equal peoples. Hot tempers on both sides provoked unreasonable and ill-judged words, but the depth of English arrogance was evident in the linen debate when the Speaker told the Commons that they had 'catcht Scotland and would keep her fast'.

The English had inherited four centuries of contempt for Scotland, and saw no reason to change their minds because their most exclusive club had just admitted forty-five new members. It was well known that the Scots were improvident and backward, that their established Church was impudent and bigoted, and their claim to equality with civilized nations was laughable since a great number of them were half-naked savages who lived by murder and robbery. Their miserable soil, where it was capable of bearing fruit, was either overworked or choked with weeds, wasted for want of proper drainage, and too often farmed in uneconomic strips. Ownership of the land was ridiculously disputed by hereditary feuds or dragging lawsuits. Debts that were the running sores of the land-owning class were paid in wadsets, in mortgages of rents, and quarrelsome chiefs in the Highlands still demanded military service as well as payment in kind from their tenants. Poverty was endemic, and long after the famines some men were still living on weeds plucked from kirkyards. In 1727 an English visitor could still write that the Scots were not only poor but *looked* poor, 'dejected and discouraged, as if they had given up all hope of ever being otherwise'.

Even in this state the Scots' will to survive began to assert itself over a belief that the English intended to use the Union to destroy them. In fact, England was largely indifferent to the problems of its partner, and North Britain[1] was left to recover if it could, to prove itself in hard competition. The challenge was accepted by a number of dedicated patriots, such as the three hundred who formed the Honourable Society of Improvers in the Knowledge of Agriculture, in 1723. Many of the improvements in management and husbandry were introduced by a gentry inspired and shamed by the comparison between their meagre lands and the richness of English estates. Turnips first grown for the table in 1716 were soon used as cattle food, reducing the great Martinmas slaughters, and the cultivation of the potato on the Stirling plain in 1739 promised a reliable diet upon which the common people of the Highlands and Lowlands would exist for a hundred years. Highland glens which had once supplied Border spearmen with their little horses, now began to send more beef to the south, black cattle on the hoof moving over a network of drove-roads from Caithness and the Outer Isles to a great tryst at Falkirk, giving Scotland one of its greatest industries until the coming of the Cheviot Sheep.

The Honourable Society and its imitators experimented in crop rotation and enclosures, new farm tools, English ploughs, milling machinery. Improvement brought profit, town houses and travelling coaches, commissions in English regiments and marriages across the Border. These things for the great lord, but for the bonnet laird there was also greater comfort and a deeper purse. But change also brought the fencing of common pastures, the amalgamation of small farms, the eviction of unwanted tenants and the unemployment of a superfluous peasantry. There was wide public sympathy for the men who resisted these changes, who plucked a name out of the past and called themselves Levellers. They were mostly small tenants, angered by eviction and embittered by poor harvests and heavy rent arrears. They rose inevitably in the south-west, armed with a few guns, with forks and flails, and united by a covenant that echoed the defiant spirit of their Cameronian grandfathers. For a few months in 1724 they resolutely

---

[1] This term was first used with the best of motives and some innocent justification, since the country was now part of the United Kingdom of Great Britain, governed by the Parliament of Great Britain. The 21st Regiment of Foot, Royal Scots Fusiliers, was referred to as the North British Fusiliers as late as the 'Forty-five, and the Scots Greys were the North British Dragoons. Resentment of the title was already strong in 1762 when John Wilkes produced his *North Briton*, attacking Lord Bute and the Scots, but it was used in the nineteenth century by the North British Railway, and has lingered into this with the North British Hotels. It is not used in this book as a gratuitous insult, but because it does indicate the slow surrender of the Scots governing classes to the influence of British – and by definition English – customs, manners, aspirations and culture. At no time was England seriously called South Britain.

broke down enclosures and ignored the shocked denunciations of ministers who were now serving both God and Property. When magistrates read the Riot Act against them, they gloriously responded with the words of the Solemn League and Covenant, and gathered again in Sanquhar, where Richard Cameron had declared war on Charles II. Dragoons eventually broke them up, but this time without the ferocity of Dalyell or Turner. Some prisoners were transported, the rest were released, and within fifteen years the south-west was enclosed and their spirited resistance was forgotten except at a winter fireside. Theirs was the only serious opposition to the harsh compulsions of Improvement.

The peace which followed the death of Anne and the accession of George I, son of the Electress Sophia, turned the Lowlands away from the dynastic squabbles of the past and toward the future that might come from industry and trade. The benefits of union were slow in arriving, the great flowering of energy, spirit and invention was still forty years away, and men who had been born in an independent Scotland died in the belief that the Treaty had robbed them of pride and liberty. The past was also still alive north of the Highland line, and perhaps it had to be destroyed before the future could be released.

2

After the punitive shock of Glencoe the clans turned their backs to the south, believing that they could continue to live as they had always done, despite tax collectors and redcoat garrisons. Until his retirement from Fort William, John Hill also kept them in a good humour, using a little strength and a 'little forbearance'. With the exception of the Earl of Argyll and MacFarlane of that Ilk, none of the chiefs subscribed to the Company of Scotland, although a third of the Darien settlers were Highlanders, disbanded men from the Whig regiments of Argyll, Strathnaver and Mackay. They were wild men, according to their ministers, 'that cannot speak or understand Scotch, barbarians to us and we to them', and if one of the colony's most virulent critics is to be believed, the clans also made a more bizarre contribution to the venture. The trade goods sent to the isthmus had included hundreds of bob-wigs, periwigs and campaign wigs, made from Highland hair. Catholic and episcopalian chiefs took little part in the great Union debate and riot, and although they were opposed to the Treaty no real attempt was made to exploit their resentment while the nation's temperature was at fever level. In March, 1708, when the heat was beginning to cool, a French fleet arrived at the mouth of the Forth with six thousand men and the pretender James Edward Stuart. There was panic in England and Scotland, a run on the banks, but when twenty-eight English men-of-war entered the firth under Sir George Byng, the French cut their cables and fled northward before a crippling storm. It was the first attempt at a French landing since 1560, and it was also the last. The Jacobites and Louis XIV might have been wiser had they chosen the Isles or the western sea-lochs, but past history had shown that little was gained from relying upon the Highlander alone, and to have unleashed him from his hills might have lost the support of Lowland sympathy.

The last clan battle had been fought between the MacDonalds and the Mackintoshes at Mulroy in 1688, and bloody quarrels survived in braeside murders only, but the old way of life was largely unchanged in the Highlands. It was still a warrior society, tribal at the bottom and quasi-feudal at the top, dressed in tartan swagger and ennobled by a splendid oral culture. Land was now held by the chief in law, and he distributed it among his kinsmen upon tacks, leases of nominal rent with the obligation to serve him in arms. Below these tacksmen, each a *duine-uasal*, a gentleman of touchy pride, tenants and sub-tenants had no security of possession, paid their rents in kind and supplied the blood and bone of the clan regiment. Supported by a black cattle economy, and inspired by a thousand years of legend and mythology, the patriarchal society was both tyrranous and benevolent. The chief was still the father of the clan, with the terrible powers of his ancestors, and if there were no alternative better than his protection there was no appeal against his authority. In this century a Clanranald chief would punish a thief by tying her hair to the sea-weed on his coast, leaving her to drown in an Atlantic tide, and a MacDonald of Sleat and a Macleod of Dunvegan would drive a hundred of their disobedient people aboard a transport for America. But there was also love and sacrifice, and a common clansman who shared his mother's breast with the child of a *duine-uasal* became his foster-brother's henchman, placing his own body before the fall of an enemy's sword. 'May your chief have the ascendancy!' said a Highlander, wishing another good fortune, for the chief gave all, defended all, was all.

But already he was closer to a Lowland laird than he was to his hereditary bard or shield-bearer. He travelled abroad more often than his father had done, sometimes spoke French and Latin as well as Gaelic and English, wore velvet and lace above his tartan trews, drank claret from glass and whisky from silver, tied back his hair with a ribbon, and matched his gentility against a Lowland peer. The hand that caressed or chastised his clan was controlled by a mind awakening to new opportunities, and he had taken the first unconscious steps toward the great betrayal of his children.

The Highlanders were a monoglot people, cherishing the richness of a language that was older than Scots or English. It was also the greatest obstacle to their subjugation by or acceptance of a southern authority, and at the beginning of the seventeenth century Scots parliaments had passed three unsuccessful acts designed to destroy it. Highland bishoprics were abolished with the rest after the Revolution, and it was proposed that their rents should now be used for the establishment of schools and the 'rooting out of the Irish language'.[1] Little came of this either, and when the Society for Propagating Christian Knowledge was founded in 1708 one of its principal aims was the replacement of Gaelic with English. In a report of the same year the Society clearly expressed the desperate need for Christian knowledge in the mountains.

> Many of those Highlanders etc., are in an interest absolutely inconsistent with the safety of the Government, for they are bred in principles of tyranny, depend upon the Pope as Head of the Church, upon a Popish Pretender bred up in the arbitrary maxims of France as their rightful sovereign.

This was an exaggeration. Few of the clans were now Catholic, although Roman missionaries to the mountains had increased since the disestablishment of the Episcopal Church. The influence of the Presbyterian Kirk was weak among the Campbells of the south-west, Mackays and others in the north, and although their chiefs were Whigs the clansmen's bloody experience as regular soldiers in Flanders, their terrible losses in

---

[1] Lowlanders and Englishmen at this time, and until the end of the century, invariably referred to Gaelic as Irish. Although it is an acceptable, if loose, term, in its historical context it was an emotive and pejorative word, betraying a common feeling that the Highlanders were an alien and savage people whose way of life placed them beyond the virtues and mercies of civilization.

Darien, had soured their enthusiasm for faraway loyalties. All the clans were stubbornly attached to their ancient way of life, and all were an uneasy military threat. In a report to William III, the Earl of Breadalbane had said that at least thirty thousand men could be quickly called to arms in the Highlands, and that by their deep attachment to their chiefs they would be far more reliable than any standing army. Anticipating the future by sixty years, he said that they should be mustered as regiments of the Crown, for if their leaders could be persuaded to join in seditious union they would overthrow King and government with ease. Divided by old jealousies, however, the Highlanders were incapable of such unity, and under Montrose and Dundee's successors they had twice shown that they would abandon a national cause when it no longer gratified their personal ambitions.

Time had eroded some of the influence of the chiefs, and many customs of past significance had fallen into disuse, yet the core of the clan system was still strong and defiant. Left to themselves the Highlanders might have dragged themselves in the tail of change, and in time adapted themselves to it, but to argue this is perhaps to believe that the quick will patiently wait for the slow, that a numerically strong and industrially potent society does not always destroy a more primitive people who hamper or obstruct its progress, be they Gael, Zulu, or Comanche Indian. To such people themselves there eventually comes an unconscious realization that a final challenge is being made to their existence, and the more resolute among them go to meet it in arms, innocently confident of victory. The Stuart cause was already lost before the Jacobite rising of 1715, and thirty years later it was an anachronism, but the independence of the clan system and the Highland way of life was still in dispute. Grape-shot would first destroy its defiant valour, statutes would outlaw its proud customs, and the Cheviot sheep would inherit its emptied glens.

With the accession of George I in 1714 the Jacobites had good reason to believe that the exiled house might now be restored by rebellion. There was bitter disappointment with the Union, and many Scots believed that the breach of some of its articles gave them the right to choose their own king. Whig repression which had followed the invasion threat of 1708 had been foolish and spiteful. The Habeas Corpus Act had been suspended. Known Catholics and those who voted against the Union had been arrested, or compelled to surrender bonds of three or five thousand pounds against their good behaviour. Edinburgh Castle was filled with Lowland peers and Highland chiefs, including the two MacDonalds of Keppoch and Glengarry, Stewart of Appin, and Ewen Cameron of Lochiel, 'old and weak past four score years'. All were ultimately released, and the trial of five Stirling lairds ended in a verdict of not proven, but the bloodless reign of terror left a lingering resentment against the government and the Union. The disaffected of the Highlands and the Lowlands could make common cause in a demand for the repeal of the Treaty, and although their banners would declare their allegiance to James Stuart, the broadswords of some would be engraved with the words *Prosperity to Scotland and No Union*.

On September 6, 1715, the Stuart standard was raised on the Braes of Mar in Aberdeenshire, watched by a small group of armed men. The ineptitude of the rising was comically manifest in its chubby-faced leader, John Erskine, sixth Earl of Mar. Known ribaldly as 'Bobbing John', he had been one of the commissioners sent to London to treat for a union, had actively supported repressive measures after the failure of the French invasion, and was Secretary of State for Scotland when Anne died. In a letter thick with flattery he offered her successor his continuing loyalty in the same post, but was asked for his seals of office instead. He embarked upon a collier for Newcastle, and by the time he arrived on his native Deeside he was a zealous Jacobite. His autumn proclamation called upon good men to fight for their rightful king, for the 'relief of our native country from oppression and a foreign yoke too heavy for us and our posterity to bear', and this more than his unattractive personality brought in most of the chiefs from the western and central Highlands. A common detestation of the Union imposed some extraordinary alliances. The Mackintoshes, who had supported the Revolution, were now ready to fight beside the Keppoch MacDonalds who had defeated them at Mulroy, and the Glencoe men were brigaded with the followers of Glenlyon. The chiefs raised their clans in the old way, by appeal and by threat, and Mar himself told his tenants that he would burn out those who would 'come not forth with their best arms'.

The Jacobites occupied Perth and Inverness, but no French ships brought them assistance. Nor was there a sympathetic rising in southern England, despite the riots

*Whig hacks and cartoonists usually had more broad wit and invention than their Jacobite opponents, and this carto-graphical fancy was perhaps more effective than sterile emphasis on Stuart legitimacy.*

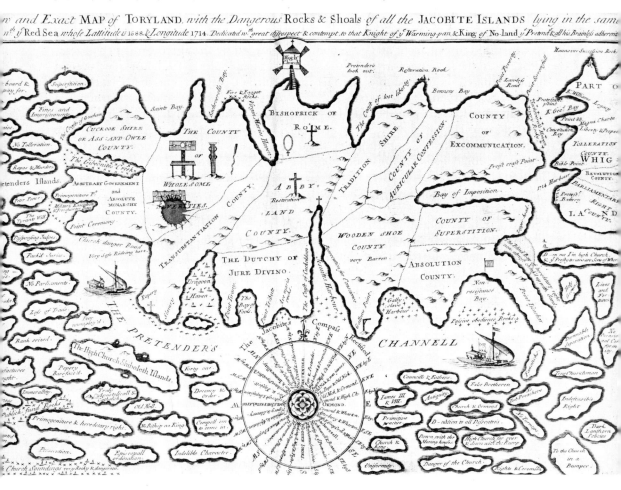

293

that had welcomed George I. Less than five thousand men under the Duke of Argyll held the Stirling plain for the government, but although Mar now commanded twice that number his havering indecision kept him in the Highlands until October. Upon word of support from Jacobite lords along the Border, and from the Earl of Derwentwater and other English Catholics across it, he at last sent two thousand men southward under William Mackintosh of Borlum, a middle-aged but redoubtable soldier who should more properly have commanded the whole enterprise. Borlum crossed the Forth to North Berwick, frightened Edinburgh, and marched to Kelso and Jedburgh without losing a horse or a man. There he was joined by the Borderers under Viscount Kenmure and the Earl of Nithsdale, and by a few hundred Englishmen who had come north with Thomas Forster, Member of Parliament for Northumberland. Bobbing John was well matched by this honourable and gallant gentleman. He had been given command because he was the only Protestant among the English Jacobite leaders, and it was hoped that the influential value of this would compensate for his defects in other respects, such as his custom of retiring to bed when the problems of command became too great.

The Earl of Derwentwater wanted to attack Newcastle, ill defended by a crumbling wall and broken gates, but Forster insisted upon a march against Liverpool, saying that the whole of Lancashire was waiting to greet them. They accordingly marched south, and were welcomed by cautious but hostile bands of Westmorland militia, armed with pitchforks. By the time Preston was reached, five hundred of the Highlanders and Borderers had turned about and gone home. Threatened by the approach of two government forces, the Jacobites barricaded the streets, cut loop-holes in the houses, and pressed fifteen hundred of the county's citizens into reluctant service. The first Hanoverians attacked on November 12 and were stubbornly held at the barricades, where two hundred of them were killed, Derwentwater fought stripped to the waist, and the Highlanders were bloodily entangled with the 26th Foot. This was Dunkeld again, for the 26th were the Cameronians, but although their predecessors had held a town against the clans they could not take this one from Borlum's broadswords. The next day, when Preston was surrounded by more Hanoverian battalions and three regiments of dragoons, Derwentwater and Mackintosh were ready to cut their way out, but Forster consulted his conscience and surrendered everybody to the enemy.

On that same Sunday at Sheriffmuir, where the Ochil hills hang above Dunblane, the Earl of Mar was fighting his only battle, too late and upon ground chosen by an enemy he outnumbered two to one. After a morning discharge of musketry, ten battalions of Highlanders threw off their plaids and charged half-naked across the frosted grass and heather. On the right, the MacDonalds broke the regular foot who faced them, and routed three squadrons of horse, but the left wing was stopped and thrown back by a flanking attack from the rest of Argyll's cavalry. The Duke himself joined in the pursuit, believing he was driving the whole of Mar's army upon its camp by Allan Water. This revolving wheel of a battle, noisy with the scream of pipes and bright with red coat and tartan, requires no tactician's description. A wry-mouthed ballad is enough.

> A battle there was that I saw, man.
> And we ran, and they ran,
> And they ran, and we ran,
> And we ran, and they ran awa', man!

If none could claim the battle a victory, Mar retreated to Perth, and Argyll held the

Stirling plain and the roads to the south. The tragically comic rebellion was over, the blood uselessly spilt, and the clans went back to their glens. Three days before Christmas, James Edward Stuart arrived at Peterhead on the Buchan coast. His reserve and coldness of manner disappointed the few hundred men remaining with Mar, and had he not been weakened by a feverish cold he might not have issued a mad order to burn the country ahead of Argyll's advancing army. He regretted it later, and said that any money remaining after his soldiers had been paid should be given to those whom the burning had left without food or shelter. He believed that the rebellion could be continued, but he lacked the offensive daring his son would have, the ability to make an ingenuous and defenceless appeal for loyalty. At the beginning of February he submitted to the pessimism of his advisers, wrote a plea for clemency to Argyll, and left for France. He never returned.

The suppression of the rebellion was mild compared with what would follow thirty years later. Nineteen Scots and two English peers lost their estates. Eight were condemned to death, but only Derwentwater and Kenmure went to the block on Tower Hill. The melancholy Englishman died with nobility, asking God to accept his life as a small sacrifice for his country's happiness, but there was no dignity in the hanging of twenty-two common men taken at Preston, the transportation of hundreds more. In defiance of the Disarming Act, the Highlanders hid their broadswords, axes and guns, and surrendered broken and useless weapons. The Clan Act attempted to destroy the bonds between the chief and his children, relieving the rents of those who refused to support him in rebellion, but now that the rising was over it had little effect. Juries refused to convict Jacobites *in absentia*, and a wide sympathy for the political motives of the rebellion, if not for the dynasty it had wished to restore, persuaded the government from extreme

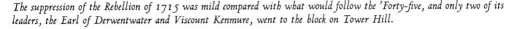

*The suppression of the Rebellion of 1715 was mild compared with what would follow the 'Forty-five, and only two of its leaders, the Earl of Derwentwater and Viscount Kenmure, went to the block on Tower Hill.*

measures. The sale of forfeited estates also revealed the sad personal troubles that had forced their owners into the desperate gamble. The prices realized scarcely exceeded the debts and mortgages by which many of them were encumbered. In 1717 an Act of Grace pardoned all rebels except the outlawed, persecuted and reviled children of Clan Gregor.

Four years after the 'Fifteen, James Stuart found an ally south of the Pyrenees, and two Spanish frigates brought three hundred white-coat soldiers to the far shore of Loch Duich below Eilean Donan Castle. Five thousand had originally sailed from Corunna, with arms for thirty thousand more, but the fleet had been dispersed by the usual providential storm. Except for some Atholl men and Mackenzies, Lochiel's Camerons and the MacGregors under Rob Roy, the cautious clans stayed at home. Opposed in the narrow gorge of Glen Shiel by a resolute force of regulars and Whig levies, the Jacobite Highlanders drifted away, leaving their Spanish allies to the falling mortar-shells and to inevitable surrender.

When the call for a rising came again, a quarter of a century later, only an old man had any clear recollection of life under the last Stuart King, and only a man in middle age could remember the bitterness and anger of the great Union dispute. The busy travels of Jacobite agent and Roman priest, money and pride, memory and ambition, all kept the old hopes warm in the Highlands, but it was now a game more than a serious political cause. Claret was solemnly passed over water before the royal toast, visits were secretly or boldly made to the exiled court, younger sons served in the Scots regiments of France, and hard winters were agreeably passed in plot and intrigue. But the answer to any proposal that James should come again, that the clans should once more rise, was always 'Not now, not yet.' There were strong government garrisons in the Great Glen, linked by military roads which Major-General George Wade was driving across the central massif to Lochaber and Inverness, unconsciously fulfilling the dream of Julius Agricola. Some of the labourers on these roads were Highlanders, working for unaccustomed wages and in defiance of their chiefs, but most of the clansmen hated the choking threat of the roads and resented the omnipresence of red coats. There was no physical resistance to the garrisons or the road-builders, and Edward Burt, an Englishman who worked for Wade, thought the Highlanders had little taste for king-making. 'Were it not for their fond attachment to their chiefs, and the advantage those gentlemen take of their slave-like notions of patriarchal power, I verily believe there are but few of them that would engage in an enterprise so dangerous to them as rebellion.'

This was not to say that the glens were orderly and peaceful. The rise in the beef trade to the Lowlands and England had increased cattle-thieving and blackmail,[1] and such lawlessness was usually unchecked by the chiefs and unpunished by the government. In four years one man only was hanged at Inverness, and Burt said that the worst offenders came from the Keppoch MacDonalds, the Camerons, and of course the outlawed MacGregors. There was no standing army large enough to police the mountains, and in the pattern of imperial conquest the government used the militant spirit of the Highlander against himself. Independent companies from the Whig clans had first been raised during the Revolution, and although John Hill had been disgusted by the Grants

---

[1] The levying of blackmail was an old Border and Highland custom. *Mails* were the rents paid in money and kind on Scottish estates, and blackmail was the tribute paid by law-abiding men to freebooters or raiding clansmen, in return for a promise that their stock would not be lifted or their steadings burnt.

*There were frequent mutinies in Highland regiments, dignified refusals to accept broken promises. The first was in the Black Watch in 1743. Farquhar Shaw was one of three mutineers shot in the Tower.*

*The squalid tragedy of Charles Edward Stuart, hero of Scottish romanticism, is perhaps no better illustrated than in these two portraits – the hopeful boy and the drunken wife-beater of middle-age. He lived forty-two years after his wild attempt to restore his father. His brother, Cardinal Henry of York, then accepted an English pension, and when this last of the Stuart exiles was dead the Prince Regent paid for a monument to their memory in St Peter's, Rome.*

and Munros sent to him at Fort William, the practice had been continued, and the companies fought against their Jacobite cousins at Sheriffmuir and Glenshiel. They were then disbanded, but in 1725 the chiefs of the central and south-western Highlands were given commissions to raise six companies of a Watch, a police force for the supression of cattle-lifting. The young gentlemen of both Jacobite and Whig clans eagerly took service in *Am Freiceadan Dubh*, the Black Watch, so-called from its dark government tartan, each coming to the muster with a tail of servants to carry his arms and support his dignity. In 1739, the Watch was increased by four companies and reorganized as a regular 43rd (later 42nd) Regiment of Foot. After a noble mutiny, which was perhaps encouraged by Jacobite agents and was certainly justified by the government's ignorant indifference to their special qualities, these Royal Highlanders fought as valiantly in Flanders for the house of Hanover as their grandfathers had done at Killiecrankie for the Stuarts.

Though it might be argued that it would have been better had he not come at all, Charles Edward Stuart at least came to Scotland to begin a rebellion and not when it was already over. Accompanied by a handful of ageing companions, this handsome, self-centred and tragically reckless young man landed on the white sand of Arisaig in July, 1745. He was strong and healthy, ill-educated and charming, and he had come against the wishes of his father, the disapproval of Louis XV, and the advice of his sympathizers in Scotland. He brought little but the innocent appeal of his personality, and the wiser chiefs were those who refused to meet him lest his charm seduce them into their own destruction. In later years of drunkenness and self-pity he would remember the Highlanders with maudlin affection, but at the time he seemed to share the usual civilized opinion of them. When he first dressed himself in Highland clothes he said that he needed only the itch to be taken for the real thing.

The clansmen raised for him were in many cases reluctant recruits, particularly those from the glens of Atholl, and they were brought in by threats of eviction and roof-burning. But almost all were inspired by the ease of their early victories, by the gay confidence of their young leader, and by a defiant contempt for the alien and hostile society to the south of their mountains. When the Campbells were raised for the government, as independent companies and a regular regiment of the line, an old bitterness was reawoken, and the strong core of the Jacobite army came from those clans whose hatred of Argyll was fiercer than their loyalty to the Stuarts: the Macleans of Mull and the Isles, MacGregors from Balquhidder, MacDonalds of Keppoch, Glengarry, Clanranald and Glencoe, the Stewarts of Appin and the Camerons of Lochiel. They were the last to defend the Highland way of life with the sword, but they were a minority. From the raising of his standard at Glenfinnan to his defeat at Culloden nine months later, Charles never commanded more than ten thousand men, and sometimes only half that number. Before the rebellion was finally crushed, there were more clans hostile to him, and more Scotsmen in arms against him than had ever sworn to die with him. He had come too late, even to the Highlands, and his stubborn adherence to the Church of Rome would lose him all but derisive support in the Lowlands and England.

He came down to the Stirling plain in September, and eastward on the Firth of Forth at Prestonpans his terrible swordsmen scattered the only government army in Scotland. Though the castle of Edinburgh was closed against him, he occupied the city, danced at Holyroodhouse, and prepared his tartan army for the invasion of England. The emotional enthusiasm he aroused in the capital was like a tidal wave that is larger and higher than the rock from which it must eventually recede. Wherever he went he inspired admiration, and whenever he was gone he was remembered with caution and

*He came down to the Stirling plain in September, and at Prestonpans his terrible swordsmen scattered the only Government army in Scotland. Nineteenth-century Jacobitism here re-fights the battle.*

doubt. His army was inactive during the five weeks he spent at Edinburgh, although there was some fighting against the Hanoverian garrisons and levies in the mountains, and many of his clansmen went home to lard their slaughtered cattle for the winter. The government in London spent this time profitably, recalling seasoned regiments from Flanders, and though the Black Watch was among them it was not used against the clans.

Charles crossed the Esk into England on November 8, wading through its water with fewer than six thousand men. His lieutenant-general was Lord George Murray, son of the first Duke of Atholl, a staunch Jacobite and a brave mercenary. He was the only able tactician in the Prince's service, and had fretted over the delay in invading a country where, according to reports, all was confusion and alarm. Now, as the Jacobites marched south by way of Carlisle, Preston and Manchester, two British armies had assembled against them, each outnumbering the clans. One was by Newcastle with George Wade, and the other lay across the London road under King George's young son, the Duke of Cumberland.

An ill-fated regiment was raised at Manchester from the non-jurant episcopalians of Lancashire. They were issued with buckler and broadsword, sashed with tartan, and bonneted with white cockades, but no other Englishmen joined the Prince. He reached Derby on December 5, where it was learnt that Wade was at Wetherby across the Pennines, Cumberland was twenty-four miles to the south-west at Lichfield, and a third army was assembling on Finchley Common for the defence of London. That evening Charles faced an unhappy council in the pannelled drawing-room of Exeter House. He wanted to march on, and had gaily discussed what he should wear for his entry into London, but the chiefs would not support him, and Murray said that a further advance would be dangerous now that there was no hope of an English rising or a French invasion.

Black-humoured and bewildered, the little army turned about for the Border. It fought a spirited rearguard action at Clifton to the south of Penrith, where Murray drew his sword, cried 'Claymore!' and led the Macphersons and Glengarry MacDonalds against an assault by Cumberland's dragoons. The Manchester Regiment was left behind to defend Carlisle, a futile gesture that ended with its inevitable surrender, the hangman's rope and the American transports. The Esk was recrossed on the Prince's birthday, and the clans marched by way of Nithsdale to Glasgow and Stirling. On January 15 they were drawn up on the field of Bannockburn, to receive an attack by a British army under the foul-mouthed, flogging cavalryman Henry Hawley. He did not leave his camp at Falkirk, so they fell upon him instead, when his battalions were blinded by a gale of rain. The screaming victory, in which Flanders veterans ran without fighting, or were hewn apart with little resistance, could not be exploited, and in early February the dwindling Jacobite army turned northward into the mountains.

At dawn on Wednesday April 16, 1746, fewer than five thousand hungry and exhausted men limped into their battle-line on a bleak moor above Culloden House – clansmen, foothill tenantry, and a few newly-arrived Irish and Franco-Scots.[1] A Falkirk

---

[1] An exact estimate of the Jacobite strength cannot be made. Its muster-master, Patullo, put the figure at less than five thousand. Since his arrival in the north, Charles had been reinforced by a contingent from Clan Chattan, by Grants, Frasers, Chisholms and Macleods among others, and also by the arrival of the Scots and Irish mercenaries from France. He had made an abortive night attack toward Nairn, however, and many of his men lay exhausted in the grounds of Culloden House throughout the battle.

gale was now driving sleet into their faces, and they stood upon ground which no senior officer but Charles believed could be defended. Below on the Moray Firth to their left were English transports and men-of-war, and advancing toward them from Nairn were nine thousand men under the Duke of Cumberland, sixteen battalions of foot and another of militia, three regiments of horse and a company of artillery. Three of the regular battalions were Lowland Scots, a fourth and the militia had been largely raised from Clan Campbell. Within an hour of noon the battle was over. Winnowed by Cumberland's guns, the clans at last charged through musketry and grape, and where they could reach the enemy they slashed their way into three ranks of levelled bayonets. Held back by volley-firing, Clan Donald did not engage the right of the red-coat line, and the men of Keppoch, Clanranald and Glengarry tore stones from the heathered earth and hurled them in impotent fury. The stubborn withdrawal from the charge became an hysterical rout, and the British marched forward to take ceremonial possession of a victorious field, bayonetting the wounded before them, and cheering their fat young general. 'Lord,' he said, 'what am I that I should be spared, when so many brave men lie dead upon this spot?' The long brawl of Scottish history had ended in the terrible blood of its best-remembered battle.

This time the policy of repression was inexorable. It began immediately with an order for the extermination of the wounded who still lay upon the field. It was continued by the harsh imposition of martial law, the shooting and hanging of fugitives, the driving of stock, the burning of house and cottage. Lowland and English graziers came to Fort Augustus to buy the cattle driven in from the glens, and the Navy and the Army co-operated in a ruthless search for the fugitive prince, brutalizing those who were thought to have information about him, and hanging a few who would not give it. In this sustained terrorization, Lowland regiments were as active as men from English shires, and three officers long remembered for their bitter cruelty were all Scots. The only government forces to show compassion for the homeless and the hunted were the Campbell militia from Argyll. The prisoners taken were tried in England, lest Scots juries be too faint-hearted. The axe was nobly busy on Tower Hill, and the gallows rope sang at Carlisle, York, and Kennington Common. One hundred and twenty common men were executed, a third of them deserters from the British Army, but nearly seven hundred men, women and children died in gaol or in the abominable holds of Tilbury hulks, from wounds, fever, starvation or neglect. Two hundred were banished, and almost a thousand were sold to the American plantations.

This time, too, the structure of the clan system was torn down and left to its inevitable decay. The ancient authority of the chiefs was taken from them, by the abolition of heritable jurisdictions which had given them power of 'pit and gallows' over their people, and since the friends of the government as well as its enemies had possessed these rights, a scale of compensation was agreed. The Duke of Argyll received twenty-one thousand pounds, but the attainted Jacobite chiefs were naturally given nothing. The forfeited estates of the dead or exiled were placed under the management of approved factors, and although these men were usually more efficient and productive than the chiefs had ever been, they replaced the emotional bond between father and children with the cold obligations of an economic unit. The clansman himself was stripped of the tangible manifestations of his pride. The carrying of arms was forbidden under penalty of death. The wearing of tartan, kilt or plaid was banned, with transportation for a repeated offence, and suspected men were forced to swear upon the holy iron of a dirk that they had neither weapons nor tartan in their miserable huts. They dipped the traditional cloth in vats of mud or dye, and sewed the kilt into ludicrous breeches. Five years after Charles Stuart boarded a ship for France, from the same white shore where he had landed, kilted fugitives were still being hunted by patrols, and Lieutenant-Colonel James Wolfe was considering a plan for the massacre of the Macphersons. 'Would you believe I am so bloody?' he asked a friend, '  'twas my real intention.' When the proscription on Highland dress was lifted in 1782, few of the common people accepted it. It became the affectation of their anglicized lairds, the fancy dress of the Lowlanders, and the uniform of the King's Gaelic soldiers.

The wearing of a red coat, a belted plaid of black government tartan, enabled the young men of the hills to keep some of their pride, and to follow the military example of their ancestors. Their eagerness and their valour were prodigally expended by successive governments. In 1757, William Pitt adopted a policy suggested seventy years before by the Earl of Breadalbane, and repeated in 1738 by Duncan Forbes, Lord President of the Court of Session. The raising of Highland regiments, upon commissions granted to their chiefs, took sullen and resentful men away from their despoiled glens, and used them in the creation of an imperial Britain. One of the first, mustered by Simon Fraser of Lovat, chief of the name, contained many men who had fought at Culloden, and some of them died with James Wolfe on the Heights of Abraham. During the next fifty years, the Crown drained the Highlands for twenty-seven line regiments and nineteen battalions of fencibles: Frasers, Macleods and Campbells, Macleans, MacDonalds, Camerons and Mackenzies, Gordons, Grants, Rosses and Munros, Atholl men, Sutherlanders and Mackays. In the French wars at the turn of the century the Highlanders supplied the British Army with the equivalent of seven or eight infantry divisions. They were raised in the old way of clan levies, each chief and his tacksmen bringing in so many of their young tenants, by persuasion or by force. They were a unique and splendid corps. Crime and cowardice were rare, and when they mutinied, as they sometimes did, it was with dignity and because the promises made to them by their chiefs had been broken by the government.

The last tragedy of the clans may not be the slaughter of Culloden, but the purchase and wasteful expenditure of their courage by the southern peoples who had at last conquered them.

3

Scotland's golden age of intellect, invention and industry was all the more remarkable in a small and peripheral European nation. As if a water-gate had been opened, the pent force of ages burst through in flood and exhausted itself in the shallows of the next century. It fertilized and enriched the growth of an imperial Britain with talent and blood, and made a practicable return to independence forever impossible. Between the present and the heroic past stand these astonishing years when the material and spiritual promise of the Union was triumphantly realized, and the foundation of a future Scotland was laid. An expanding middle class dominated trade, industry, the arts and sciences with a vigorous confidence in itself, willing to debate the moral responsibility of power and profit. The agricultural revolution created a competitive farming class from the old gudeman tenant, and a land labour-force from a peasantry with no nostalgia for its brutal past, and with no serious resistance to change after the defeat of the western

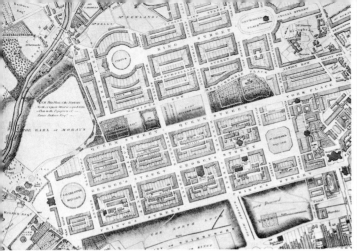

*'Edinburgh broke from its medieval chrysalis on the rock and sunned its grey-white wings to the north.' Part of the plans for the New Town, drawn by James Craig and published in 1767. Right Robert Adam's façade for the north side of Charlotte Square is one of the most magnificent features of Edinburgh New Town. The rest of the square was completed by Sir Robert Reid.*

Levellers. Industry and industrial revolution also produced a working-class which would in time accept a union beyond anything imagined by the articles of the Treaty, and would supply the British socialist movement with much of its muscle and sinew.

The boldness of the new age was nowhere more nobly manifest than in the metamorphosis of the capital. Edinburgh broke from its medieval chrysalis on the rock and sunned its grey-white wings to the north. Six years after Culloden there were proposals for the enlargement and improvement of the city, and its adornment with public buildings of national benefit, but the suggestion that private men should adventure 'schemes for public good' was finally answered by the lord provost, George Drummond, and the town council. From six submitted plans they accepted that drawn by the young architect James Craig. He published it in 1767, a broad grid of long, classical streets, serene squares and elegant crescents, grand houses and green gardens, a breathing lung to replace the bronchial congestion of the old town. The site chosen, from which the design would later spread, was the low ridge above the Nor' Loch, which would be finally drained and delicately bridged. Exposed to the sun and wind between the castle and the Forth, each house would be a residential temple to the Age of Reason, solidly built of good Scots stone. Craig was inspired by his own vision, and at the foot of his engraved plan he sang a little verse of wonder.

> August, around, what PUBLIC WORKS I see!
> Lo, stately streets! Lo, squares that court the breeze!
> See, long canals and deepened rivers join
> Each part with each, and with the encircling main
> The whole entwined isle.

Glorifying Church and Crown, the names of streets and squares were taken from the kingdom's saints and royalty, but when George III was told what the longest of all was to be called, he tutted with disapproval. 'What, what? . . . *St Giles* Street? Never do, never do!' It was renamed Princes Street in honour of his sons. Splendid though the vision was, few men were willing to leave their ancient ant-heap, complaining that the project was too cold, too English. The town council offered a premium of twenty pounds to the first who would build a house, and a haberdasher who was the original resident on Princes Street was exempted from burghal taxes. The transfer was slow in the beginning, but a curiosity became a compulsive fashion and then a social necessity. Craig died in 1795, as his wonderland was growing, and thirty years later, when there were five thousand houses in the New Town, some of his original ideas were still being executed. But there was no marriage between old and new as Drummond had hoped, and the bed of the Nor' Loch became a class gulf. Rank and privilege, profession and trade, paraded their manners on George Street and Princes Street, and the tall lands they had left became the homes of the diseased and the poor, of wheelright, furniture-seller, French teacher and chairman. The gentry who remained were old, said Robert Chambers, and 'did not think it worth while to make any change till the great one'.

One of the earliest residents of the New Town was the philosopher David Hume, who built himself an elegant house in a side street by St Andrew Square. A gentle, self-deprecatory man, he was not only one of the greatest minds his country had produced, but also one of the most influential in Europe, working upon the body of belief with the scalpel of scepticism. His *Treatise of Human Nature* and *Dialogues Concerning Natural Religion* were received with hostility, but they compelled other men to re-examine their cherished ideas upon rational belief and causation, and are still a chilling wind upon the heat of philosophical debate. Objects have no discoverable connexion, it is only by 'custom operating upon the imagination that we can draw any inference from the appearance of one to the experience of another'. But Hume was a warm-hearted man, and his desire to see the favourable rather than the unfavourable side of life was part of the abounding optimism of the age. His dear friend and stern critic was Adam Smith, who published his *Wealth of Nations* in 1776, the year of Hume's death, originating the science of political economy and arguing that the hand of some unnamed divinity directed men toward happiness, whatever their motives. A flourishing mercantile capitalism was assured that if its growth were unrestricted and unfettered, the natural order of things would inevitably work for the public good, and the thought that God, or a beneficent providence, was guiding free enterprise would continue to sustain its high moral justification in the face of the terrible proletariat it ultimately produced.

Hume and Smith were the peaks of a mountain range that included such lesser figures as Thomas Reid, Adam Ferguson and William Robertson. If the business of Scotsmen had sometimes seemed to be the breaking of men's heads, it was now the emancipation of their minds, and the twin cities of Glasgow and Edinburgh blossomed with literary, philosophical, scientific and political societies. Some were philanthropic as well as self-indulgent, and the Select Society for the Encouragement of Arts, Sciences, Manufacturers, Etc. gave awards for particular achievements in these fields. The country was soon too small to contain or employ the abundant energy released, and it flooded over the Border and beyond the oceans . . . philosophers and historians, surgeons and physicians, statesmen and jurists, booksellers and journalists, the entertaining gossip James Boswell and the compassionate soldier John Moore, explorers like James Bruce and Mungo Park in Africa, Alexander Mackenzie in north-west Canada. Scots architects were the most splendidly creative in the united kingdom, and the hitherto arid field of painting was now enriched by young men whose minds were opened and inspired by visits to Italy, paid for by aristocratic patrons. Some of them, like Alexander Runciman and Gavin Hamilton, became classicists, but Jacob More painted beguiling landscapes, and David Allan was famous as an illustrator of Burns. Allan Ramsay, however, was an original, a portraitist who evolved his own technique, recording the faces of his time with heart-stopping sympathy. He alone would justify the prodigious expenditure of

*Prince Charles Edward Stuart and the Irish Jacobite Antoine Walsh on the shore of Loch nan Uamh, July, 1745. Walsh's ship, the* Du Teillay, *had brought the Prince to Scotland. Overleaf* A detail from Culloden, *in which captured clansmen are believed to have posed for David Morier in 1746.*

paint and canvas by his forgotten contemporaries, but his genius was perhaps outmatched by Henry Raeburn, who stepped into money and society by way of marriage, and used a dramatic brush to immortalize men and women whose principal claim to remembrance must be that they were his rewarding subjects.

Like the nation itself, families had an excess of talent. The father of Ramsay was another Allan, a wig-maker turned bookseller and poet who opened the century with the sweet felicity of his verse. The sons of a poor Glasgow family, Robert Foulis and his brother Andrew produced fine printings of the classics, and founded an Academy of Arts. The agriculturalist George Rennie was the elder brother of the great John Rennie, constructor of docks, harbours, bridges, and canals, progenitor of a dynasty of civil engineers. The brothers John and William Hunter were born on a Lanarkshire farm within a few years of the Union, and scarcely able to read or write in their boyhood, but they became pre-eminent surgeons and anatomists, scientists and teachers, and if they alone were all that Scotland had produced for the benefit of mankind, humanity would be in its debt. William Adam, a Kirkcaldy architect, rebuilt the country houses of the nobility and gentry in a manner that fitted their new wealth and arrogance, but he was eclipsed by his brilliant sons. Robert, the greatest of the four, returned from a Mediterranean tour to create a revolution in style, from architecture to pottery, that is not yet exhausted. Greek, Roman and Renaissance ideas, synthesized by his own inventive genius, changed the exterior face of Britain, redirected its ornamental arts, made elegance and taste the partners of design, and beauty the servant of utility.

The creative voice of Scotland, in poetry and prose, had been silent or subdued since the Reformation. The Scots tongue, which Mary Stuart is said to have spoken better than English, was now the language of the poor and uncouth, and what was thought to be a civilized and increasingly anglicized society endeavoured to avoid the worst of its idiom and accent. The age of reason and debate expressed itself in classical English. The poet James Thomson and the novelist Tobias Smollett not only used the language of the south but found it preferable to live there also. But a robust Scots communicated the honest thought and virile emotion of street and field, and the best of Scots poets were inspired by it: Allan Ramsay, the tragic Robert Fergusson who wrote in the vernacular of Edinburgh outside the walls of the asylum in which he died, and of course Robert Burns. Yet even Burns thought that English was the proper medium for serious thought, and the worst of his poems are written in it. Scottish poetry, as opposed to poetry written in English by Scots, reached its brilliant zenith with Burns, but the peasant society which inspired him, and the urban class which read him were becoming increasingly influenced by England. English was the medium of genteel and intellectual communication, of trade and good manners, and at the moment when the example set by Burns might have been followed by others, the language he had used was crushed by the monumental work of his admirer, Walter Scott. Though this unique and tormented man had an accurate ear for the common speech of the Scottish people, he could not or would not use it in verse or narrative prose. His novels are rich and diverse, teeming with imagination and subtle invention, but they are English literature. The best of them express Scott's romantic and nostalgic pride in his country's past, and may have helped to anaesthetize the pain of its surrender to the present. Consciously or unconsciously, they appeal for England's respect and admiration, where the poetry of Burns could provoke bewilderment or laughter only, and the door they closed upon the literary use of native speech was as stout as a studded postern at Abbotsford.

*Raeburn's portrait of Alasdair Ranaldson MacDonell of Glengarry, the apogee of Highland romanticism.*

*Two water-colours by David Allan,* A Fireman *and* The Prize of the Silver Golf. *Sometimes called the 'Scottish Hogarth', Allan was the son of an Alloa shoremaster, and the illustrator of works by Burns and Allan Ramsay.*

In the Highlands, the last of the great Gaelic bards were also singing to a dwindling audience. John MacCodrum, who was born on the west shore of North Uist in 1693, was still composing shrewd and witty verse when Burns reached manhood. He was the bard of MacDonald of Sleat, and one of his jealous admirers was Mac Mhaighstir Alasdair, Alexander MacDonald, the passionate and humourless poet of the 'Forty-five. He was the lyricist of war and love – bloody, bawdy, and beautiful – the husband of a Glencoe girl, and the last defiant voice of Clan Donald. Duncan Ban Macintyre, the forester of Dalness, was known as the 'maker of songs to sing', composing poems to fit the lingering music of the hills. He served with the Argyll militia in the Rebellion, and wrote in praise and lament for the Campbells, but he was non-partisan in his concern for all the pleasures and pains of his race. Such men, with Dugald Buchanan from Balquhidder, and Rob Donn the moralizing satirist of Durness, were strong voices in a closing darkness, but they were unheard in the literary salons of Edinburgh and London. There, and throughout Europe, society was entranced by the bogus Celtic mythology of *Fingal*, said to be the translation of verses written by Ossian, but in fact the bold forgery of James Macpherson of Kingussie.[1]

The richness of Scotland's golden age of arts and sciences would have been impossible without its prospering middle class, and this, in its turn, was the product of an impres-

---

[1] Macpherson's industrious hoax was paralleled in the next century by the Sobieski Stuart brothers, who claimed to be the grandsons of Charles Edward. They published a fanciful account of the origin and nature of Highland dress, based upon manuscript sources which they never produced. Like *Fingal*, their *Vestiarium Scoticum* was widely accepted by a romantic and gullible public.

sive economic growth, the remarkable expansion of industry and commerce, the development of overseas trade and the bold use of capital by thriving banking-houses, encouraged by the memory of past deprivation and stimulated by the teaching and discipline of the Kirk. The combination of Scots money and English skills which had begun to change the nature of agriculture and the rural classes before the Rebellion, was soon applied to industry and the natural resources of the country, although in this case it was primarily English money and Scots skills. When they finally received the payments which the Treaty had said they should have from the Equivalents – sterling sums to balance the increased revenues from Scottish customs and excise – fisheries and the wool trade were unable to show much improvement, but linen spinners and weavers at last flourished in the towns about Glasgow, forming their own company to market their product in Africa and America, and a bank for the extension of credit. In the last quarter of the century, the cotton industry of Lanarkshire and Renfrewshire was revolutionized by the inventions of the Englishmen James Hargreaves, Richard Arkwright and Samuel Crompton, by the building of mills and by the employment of dispossessed Highlanders. The long wars with France forced Britain to find most of its food from its own earth and waters, and the traditional Scottish fishing industry began to prosper. For the same pressing reason, sheep replaced cattle in the Highlands, and the wool trade grew with the increasing flocks.

More complex means of production had demanded greater power. Burning with ideas and the fever of chronic illness, James Watt improved the steam-engine by the invention of the separate condenser and air-pump in 1765, and gave the industrial age its muscle and lungs for the next century and a half. It was first used in the coalfields of the Lowlands, and these fed the great ironworks at Carron, where cherry-white cauldrons poured metal for a frigate's guns and factory machines. Change also demanded improvement in transport, roads that were not a medieval penance. An Ayrshire man, John Macadam, spent his own fortune in the development of a system that would give them a smooth surface, and although Thomas Telford was contemptuous of their shallow foundation, it is Macadam's name that survives in the vocabulary of the nation. Telford was the son of an Eskdale shepherd, an apprentice mason who became one of his country's greatest civil engineers. He built a thousand miles of roads and a hundred new bridges, most of them in the Highlands. He created harbours and canals, of which the finest is still his monument, the Caledonian which scissors the Great Glen and links the North Sea to the Atlantic. Robert Stevenson properly belongs to the nineteenth century, but he was born in 1772 and was the product of the enlightened and curious minds that worked in the Andersonian Institute of Glasgow. An eccentric and devout man, he was the third generation of a family that encircled Scotland with marine lights and breakwaters. He designed and constructed twenty lighthouses, including the Bell Rock and Skerryvore, and he invented intermittent and flashing lanterns. His sons succeeded him in the work, and his grandson, Robert Louis, lit brilliant and lasting lamps with his pen.

Edinburgh was the cultural centre of the nation, of professional and polite society, law, literature and politics, the germinal ground of publishing and critical journalism, but Glasgow was the country's purse. For much of its existence a frontier town, menaced by raiders from north and south, its population was no greater than twelve thousand five hundred in 1707. By mid-century this had doubled, and was eight times as large in 1800. The first ships for Darien had sailed from Leith on the Forth, but the second expedition wisely left from the Clyde. Eighty years later, nearly four hundred merchantmen were trading in and out of the firth, a quarter of them owned by Glasgow and Greenock merchants. They carried away cloth, iron, leather, glass and timber, and brought back tobacco, sugar and rum, limes, lemons and mahogany. Much that was imported from the colonies was resold to Europe, the Tobacco Lords built great fortunes, and all but a few of them were resilient enough to survive the collapse of their trade at the outbreak of the American Revolution. Glasgow was the natural heart of the surging industrial growth of Renfrew and Lanark, and the Clyde its powerful artery. Its manufacturing hierarchy, more public-spirited than is sometimes believed, encouraged the study of the sciences, widened the nation's narrow banking system, and founded the first Chamber of Commerce for the study of markets and the promotion of trade. Powered by Clydeside capital and inspired by a national genius, Scots merchants and manufacturers, shipmasters, road-builders and canal-diggers, miners and factory-workers, carried their country into the nineteenth century.

In the past, Englishmen had rarely visited the northern kingdom without handkerchiefs to their faces, despising the stench and poverty, the sloth and indolence of the Scots, and barely acknowledging their generous hospitality. Now visitors began to write of their neighbours' industry and charm, their lively spirit and inventive minds. At the time of the Union, the Scot had been an improvident buffoon, ungraciously admitted as a junior partner for his own good and the protection of English interests. In the mid-century, at the time of the Rebellion, he was a traitorous ingrate, and Tobias Smollett kept his mouth closed during the triumphant victory celebrations for Culloden, lest his accent should cause him to be mobbed. Thirty years later the happy investment of English capital in the Scottish industrial renaissance brought a tolerant acceptance of an ancient enemy. More than Johnson or Boswell, Thomas Pennant excited English interest in this unknown land to the north, and a visit to its mountains and lowlands became as important as a Grand Tour. Pennant's splendid accounts of his note-taking tour of Scotland, his honest and impartial record of its topography, history, trade and industry, were the first and finest of many such books which the English would write during the next three-quarters of a century. This flow of tourist curiosity was eventually choked

*'The clear and wondrous aquatints of William Daniell . . .' A view of Liveras, near Broadford on the Isle of Skye, 1819, and Princes Street, Edinburgh, from Calton Hill, 1822.*

by the romanticism of Scott's imitators, the maternal sentimentality of Victoria. The clear and wondrous aquatints of William Daniell, which had revealed the beauty of the Highland coastline, were soon obscured by wild engravings and extravagant canvases of Gothic monstrosity, and the old lies of England's hostility were replaced by the patronizing fictions of its genuine friendship.

Before the end of the eighteenth century the Scots middle class was moving freely in English society, and was using its money to create a little England on its estates and in its houses. Coming from the lower strata of society, as many of its members did, from Border shepherd and Lowland artisan, it gave more to England than perhaps it took, vigour and spirit, respect for success by achievement rather than influence and preferment, but it would soon think and act as part of the English middle class. It had bought its ticket of entry early in the rise of its material prosperity, to the satisfaction of Samuel Johnson.

> The conversation of the Scots grows every day less unpleasing to the English; their peculiarities wear fast away; their dialect is likely to become in half a century provincial and rustick, even to themselves. The great, the learned, the ambitious, and the vain, all cultivate the English phrase, and the English pronunciation, and in splendid companies Scotch is not much heard, except now and then from an old lady.

## 4

'All the lower ranks,' wrote a government spy from Scotland, 'particularly the operative manufacturers with a considerable number of their employers, are poisoned with an enthusiastic rage for ideal liberty that will not be crushed without coercive measures.' In that same year, 1792, another informant said that troops in Edinburgh had been so inflamed by seditious propaganda that those on guard at Register House had shouted 'Damn the King!' The effigies of Henry Dundas and his nephew Robert – both Scots, the one Home Secretary and the other Lord Advocate – were burnt before 'several hundreds of the lower class', while boys shouted 'Liberty, Equality, and no King!' Throughout the country, upon news of French victories against the Allies, green firs were planted as symbolic Trees of Liberty.

Mob-violence and persuasion by threat had been part of Scotland's political life since the Reformation, but until now it had been contained within the structure of society, exploited and directed from above. Equality before God had at last led to a demand for equality among men, and like most of the ideas that have influenced Scotland it came from without. The liberal-minded section of the middle class, anxious for reforms that would give it political rights equal to the economic burden it carried, was sympathetic to the principles of the French Revolution and encouraged by their success. More passionate, more desperate and more in need, was the anger of the new worker class, cottage operatives, spinners and weavers, colliers and ironworkers upon whose labour the country's prosperity fundamentally rested. The golden age had created them, but they received little from its luminous rewards, the victims of child labour and brutal exploitation, falling wages and rising prices, powerless to affect the organization that controlled the simplest of their needs. Though the authorities feared and believed in the chimera of political unity among these lower classes, and crushed it wherever it was suspected with the same ferocity that had been directed against the Jacobites, the leaders of the radical reform movement came from the middle class and from artisans and small tradesmen. The worker class was spoken for rather than heard from, and in this early stage of its development it depended upon the sympathy and goodwill of its social superiors.

In the ten years before 1790 the press in Scotland had increased from eight newspapers and journals to nearly thirty, and by 1792 many of them were violent advocates of reform, opposing the war against France, ridiculing the extravagance of court life, attacking the greed of landlord, banker and industrialist, and questioning the system of government that had existed since 1688. Authority naturally decided that this inflamed passion was the fever of an alien disease, and looked no further than the Border for its source. 'An evil spirit seems to have reached us,' the Lord Provost of Edinburgh told Henry Dundas, 'which I was in hopes John Bull would have kept to himself.' The *Caledonian Mercury*, once a Jacobite sheet and now a warm supporter of the establishment, said that a madness from England 'pervades the whole of Caledonia, societies are every-where formed, and clubs instituted for the sole purpose of political debate'.

A mild reform movement had been in existence since the American Revolution, supported by small gentry who protested against the harsh exploitation of the new worker class and the evils of excise laws. What had been a subject for the drawing-room was now brought into the public arena by the triumph of reason in France, and by the appearance of the *sansculottes* on the sacred floor of political debate. Liberty was a word which a mob could shout more easily than a gentleman could define it, and a cry for equality was more compelling than a polite discussion of Tom Paine and Edmund Burke's *Reflections on the French Revolution*. When the Edinburgh mob brought the cause of reform on to the streets in 1792, celebrating the King's birthday by burning the Dundases in effigy, the riot lasted for three days, and in the following month a Society of the Friends of the People was formed in Edinburgh.

It was a popular movement with constitutional aims, in touch with the London Corresponding Society which had been formed by the Scots shoemaker, Thomas Hardy, and it quickly spread to Glasgow and other towns. Its rank and file came from the artisan

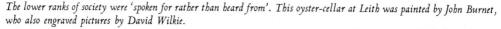

*The lower ranks of society were 'spoken for rather than heard from'. This oyster-cellar at Leith was painted by John Burnet, who also engraved pictures by David Wilkie.*

*At the beginning of the 18th century the population of Glasgow, seen here by Johannes Kip, was less than 15,000. By 1800 it was eight times as great, and nearly four hundred merchantmen traded from the Clyde.*

class and the more politically conscious weavers, but its title better described the character of its restraining middle-class leaders, enlightened and patronizing, high-minded and presumptuous. They also included two soldiers, Lieutenant-Colonel Dalrymple of Fordell, and Lieutenant-Colonel Norman Macleod, who was the Member of Parliament for Inverness. The single representative of the nobility was Lord Daer, heir to the Earl of Selkirk, and he was a nationalist more than a reformer. 'Scotland had long groaned under the chains of England,' he said, 'and knows its connections there have been the cause of its great misfortunes.' More violent in feeling than these moderates was the young advocate Thomas Muir, who had defended one of the birthday rioters, and who was present at the Star Inn for the inaugural meeting of the Glasgow Society. His short and meteoric life would leave a more brilliant trace than any of his companions.

When a 'General Convention of the Friends of the People in Scotland' met in December, one hundred and sixty men representing thirty-five societies in towns and villages, the divisions between them were as sad as the lofty desire of Muir and others to restore the constitution to the 'purity of King Alfred's days'. Although an oath was taken to 'live free or die in the French manner', the only unanimous agreement was that the franchise should be extended to all males over twenty-one, and there was a paradoxical resolution to assist the civil power in the suppression of riots. The passion which compelled common men to join the societies, and the violence which would be its only outlet, frightened the gentry who endeavoured to control the movement, as much as it alarmed the government. The artisans and peasants of Scotland, said Colonel Macleod, were 'marked by the finger of God to possess, sooner or later, the fullest share of liberty', but the Almighty naturally wished this to be compatible with the 'good order and institutions of a well-regulated community'. When some men began to speak of pikes rather than principles, he entreated them to 'be not rash, be not impetuous, search only for loyal and gentle correction.' Such caution came naturally from a man who had been brought into the movement by his conscience only, and Alexander Paisley, the weaver poet, was closer to the real emotions of the deprived.

> The *Rights of Man* is now well kenned,
> And read by mony a hunder;
> For Tammy Paine the buik has penned,
> And lent the court a lounder.
> It's like a keeking-glass to see
> The craft of kirk and statesmen,
> And wi' a bauld and easy glee,
> Guid faith, the birky beats them
> Aff hand this day.

But the birky Paine was a fugitive in France, and the government was determined to silence the English and Scots radicals his writing inspired. Robert Dundas and his uncle had the unqualified support of most of the landed gentry and middle class, and were well served by agents and informers. Thomas Muir, whom the Lord Advocate had sworn he would 'lay by the heels on a charge of High Treason', was arrested in January, 1793. Released on bail, he promptly left for London to attend a meeting of radicals there, and although he was outlawed, he came boldly back from another meeting in Dublin. He was once more arrested, and in the words of Lord Cockburn his trial was 'one of the cases the memory whereof never perisheth, history cannot let its injustice alone'. Memory and history have not been that loyal, perhaps, but the travesty of the trial was at least remembered for half a century. The Lord Justice Clerk referred to the brave young man as a 'demon of mischief' and a 'pest of Scotland', and the judge Robert Macqueen, Lord Braxfield, expressed the opposition to radical reform in one dazzling and illuminating paragraph.

> A government in every country should be just like a corporation, and in this country it is made up of the landed interest, which alone has a right to be represented. As for the rabble, who have nothing but personal property, what hold has the nation on them? What security for the payment of their taxes? They may pack up all the property on their backs and leave the country in the twinkling of an eye. But landed property cannot be removed.

To the astonishment of the jury, which had petitioned for leniency, Muir was sent to Botany Bay for fourteen years. He escaped from the penal colony in 1796, and from then on his life was a boy's adventure story. He went to America, to Mexico and to Cuba, and was returning to Europe on a Spanish ship when he lost an eye in a sea-fight with two British frigates. In France, where he was welcomed as 'The Brave Scottish Advocate', he supplied the Ministry of Foreign Affairs with an estimate of the help the French might expect should they invade Britain. There would be no assistance from the English lower classes, he said, but the Scots, particularly the betrayed Highlanders, longed for French aid in the establishment of liberty, justice, and religious freedom. Gallant and hot-blooded, he died before the century was out, but he was not forgotten. When the Reform Bill was passed in 1832, his portrait was publicly illuminated in Glasgow, and the Edinburgh Trades Council draped an empty chair with black for his memory.

In October, 1793, a third general convention of the Friends was attended by representatives from England, and described itself as 'The British Convention of Delegates Associated to Obtain Universal Suffrage and Annual Parliaments'. It was dispersed by force and three of its members were transported. The government's fierce determination to crush the reform movement was supported by the weight of the middle class, now alarmed by the nightmare of republican terror. Counter-reform clubs clashed in public with the mob and the radicals. Walter Scott was involved in an affray at an Edinburgh theatre, where rival factions sang '*Ça ira!*' and 'God Save the King', and Burns took part in a Dumfries riot. Burns's original sympathies had been with the French government, and as an excise officer he had sent it four carronades he had taken from a smuggler's schooner in the Solway. Now his sentimental, histrionic nationalism was stronger than free-thinking goodwill, and what had been a cloak for the Jacobin inspiration of *Scots Wha Hae* became the substance of *Does Haughty Gaul Invasion Threat?*

The reformers were confused and disunited, split between retreating moderates and stubborn zealots, and a small group of the latter were driven to desperate action when the government suspended *habeas corpus* in England, and an act against wrongous imprisonment in Scotland. The Pike Plot of 1794 had more reality in the authorities' imagination than it had in fact, and its principal was a misty and ambiguous man, Robert Watt, once a government spy and now, it would seem, a sincere revolutionary. A store of pikeheads discovered in Edinburgh were said to have been gathered by him upon orders from the British Convention, and he was hanged before the Tolbooth. His execution or martyrdom stiffened the resolve of the zealots, who now formed themselves into societies of United Scotsmen, inspired by the example of the United Irishmen. Once more the leaders were young advocates, small merchants and skilled artisans, but a strong body of support came from the weavers, extraordinary men with firm radical and Calvinistic convictions. Many of them, particularly about Paisley, were lyric poets, and they had a joyous enthusiasm for the arts and sciences. They were also more prosperous than any other worker group.

The United Scotsmen met in secret, using cabalistic signs and melodramatic passwords, and they did not come into the open as a revolutionary force until 1797. This was the year when the peasant and proletarian classes of Britain were closest to insurrection, the year of bad harvests and high prices, of a French landing in Wales and a threatened invasion of Ireland, of the great naval mutinies at Nore and Spithead, and the mobbing of the King's carriage by ragged men who cried out for bread and peace. In Scotland there was fierce bitterness against a Militia Act, which proposed the raising of a home defence force by ballot, ostensibly to resist invasion but plainly for use in civil disorder if necessary. The burden of service fell upon the lower classes, for the middle class could buy exemption with a substitute, or serve instead in the play-acting regiments of fencible volunteers. The United Scotsmen organized the militia riots where they could, and according to government agents they also planned an independent Scottish Republic with a provisional leadership that included the exiled Thomas Muir, Colonel Macleod and the Earl of Lauderdale, though whether these gentlemen's approval had been obtained was not known.

The sporadic outbursts of violence and protest lasted from May to August, and were widespread between Ayr and Aberdeen. In many cases the rioters did no more than frighten the session clerk and burn his parish register, from which the offensive ballot was drawn. Where mobbing was more dangerous in intent, it was effectively controlled or suppressed by the militia that had caused it, and if the United Scotsmen were as active as their sentimental sympathizers would later claim, they were also singularly inept. In Perthshire, however, it seemed as if they might actually launch their republican insurrection. Sixteen thousand men, it was said, were raised by Angus Cameron and John Menzies, the one a wright and the other a small merchant. They had sufficient military sense to capture Castle Menzies, to strip the armoury of another at Taymouth, and to begin the organization of a cavalry squadron, but when the government sent regular battalions against them, their little army drifted away without a fight.

*Thomas Muir, immortalized here in John Kay's portrait, is the best remembered of the reforming Friends of the People. He died before the 18th century was out, but his name was honourably recalled at the passing of the Reform Bill in 1832.*

In East Lothian there was bloodshed. The colliers of the area were rough-hewn men with none of the cultural subtlety of the weavers. They drank hard and were crippled by debts. Their standard of living was higher than it had ever been, or would be again for another fifty years, but men and women and children worked below ground like animals, with candles between their teeth, their shoulders broken by the black weight they carried, and when they came to the sunlit surface many of them wept with pain and despair. Such men, who worked in killing darkness for their country's prosperity, saw no reason to wear its red coat as well. They gathered at Tranent behind a drum, shouting 'No Militia!' and advancing upon the soldiers sent against them. Eleven were killed and twelve wounded by the sabre-charge of hysterical dragoons, and when the murdering was over the soldiers raped and pillaged the colliers' villages.

The United Scotsmen were disillusioned by their failure to turn the militia riots into rebellion, and were weakened by an act of July, 1797, which declared them all liable to transportation. In November one of their leaders, a Dundee weaver splendidly named George Mealmaker, was found guilty of sedition and the administering of unlawful oaths, and was sent to the penal colonies for fourteen years. More trials and more transportations followed during the next five years, and the last man to go in shackles to Botany Bay was a weaver from Fife. By then most of the societies had been disbanded, and many of their members were in exile. The government's harsh repression had been accepted with apathy or approval by a population that could now hate Napoleon Bonaparte, as the enemy of Britain or the betrayer of the Revolution. The United Scotsmen had produced no great leaders, only humble martyrs, but their country would be the worse for forgetting their noble spirit.

They were not, however, the last victims of militant protest. Five years after Waterloo their inheritors, the Scottish Radical Reform Movement, were planning a bold and suicidal attempt to establish an independent government. The end of the long wars had brought industrial depression and creeping unemployment throughout Britain, riot and disorder, repressive Acts, the Peterloo slaughter, and the Cato Street conspiracy to murder the cabinet. The red cap of Liberty made a startling reappearance at a Paisley meeting for reform, and five thousand regulars were marched into the south-west. Young Radicals had begun their military training in 1819, but the movement was weak and ill-armed, and its leaders did not think a rising would be possible before 1821. The establishment could not wait this long, and on March 21, 1820, upon information laid by its busy spies, it arrested all twenty-eight members of the hopeful Provisional Government in the Gallowgate house of a Glasgow vintner. Since they had been careful to keep most of their names and much of their activities secret, the body of the movement was unaware that its head had been removed.

Eleven days later, a proclamation was posted in the streets of Glasgow and the towns about it, calling for a national strike and equality of rights. 'Liberty or Death is our motto, and we have sworn to return home in triumph or return no more!' Its origin is unknown, but the Radicals' claim that it was a trap set by the government makes more sense than the counter-assertion that it was posted by the reformers. The response was ill-organized, diffuse, and tragic, and its only success was the opportunity it gave the government. On April 5, the day named for the strike, redcoats lined the streets of Glasgow, and although there was an evening skirmish with the cavalry there was no bloodshed. Earlier that Wednesday, a small party of weavers had left the city for Carron, where they hoped to seize guns from the iron works and to meet a mythical force of

*The central figure of this group, by John Kay, is Adam Smith, whose* Wealth of Nations *originated the science of political economy and gave mercantile capitalism a moral philosophy that sustained it for more than a century.*

rebels from Northumberland. They were met instead by hussars and yeomanry on Bonnymuir, and after a brief resistance they fled with four wounded.

Throughout the rest of the week there were little clashes between troops and radicals in the south-west, burning reprisals against the houses of hostile gentry. Greenock prison was stormed on Saturday, and five of the imprisoned leaders were released, but frightened musketry in the streets, the killing of men, women and children, broke the spirit of the revolt. The trials for treason which followed were held in defiance of bitter protest, and in violation of the Treaty of Union, for they were conducted by English law and prosecuted by an English barrister. Of twenty-four men and boys sentenced to death, all but three were eventually transported for life. These three were weavers: James Wilson, an old Jacobin from Strathaven in Lanarkshire, Andrew Hardie of Glasgow, and John Baird, who had once been a soldier. Twenty thousand people watched the death of Wilson at Glasgow, and his scaffold was guarded by two regiments of foot, and two of horse. On the walls of Scotland a placard cried *Murder! Murder! Murder!*

The Movement's middle-class sympathizers now abandoned it, and took the cause of reform to the Westminster parliament. Weavers, wrights, and colliers had learnt a harsh but memorable lesson in unity, in the power of labour when it is withheld, for sixty thousand of them had answered the strike call, if not the summons to arms. But the nationalism, the heady dreams of political independence that had inspired the reformers since 1792, quickly faded, and the emerging working class of Scotland would soon look southward for solidarity with its English brothers.

5

The year in which the Friends of the People formed their first society was remembered in the Highlands as *Bliadhna nan Caorach*, the Year of the Sheep. In July, the month of the first inaugural meeting, the men of Ross from Strath Oykel and Strath Carron, Glen Achany and Strath Rusdale, gathered the great Cheviot flocks that grazed on braes where they had once pastured their black cattle, and would have driven them south from the county had they not been stopped by mounted gentry and three companies of the Black Watch. This simple and hopeless protest, which Sheriff Donald Macleod and others believed to be inspired by Jacobins, was the only organized and spirited resistance the Highlanders would make to the changes that were taking place now, and which would continue for the next sixty years. The bitter story had already begun, eviction and clearance, the substitution of men by sheep, the betrayal of their children by anglicized chiefs. When it was finished the founding race would no longer occupy the glens, and the English-speakers would dominate the hills.

The end of the warrior society in 1746, and the loss of their hereditary powers, had placed many of the chiefs below the economic level of a Lowland laird or an English squire, and their pride alone could not pay the debts of their poverty. Nor could they be paid by a barren land and an abundant people. Over-population had been a problem before the Rebellion, when blackmail and cattle-lifting could fill empty bellies once in a season, but now it was an embarrassment, and if men could no longer be counted in broadswords they must be valued in shillings and pence, and dispensed with when the reckoning was unprofitable. Since his people were his tenants-at-will, cotter or tack-holding kinsman, the chief solved part of his financial difficulties by demanding money instead of rents in kind, by redistributing tacks at increasingly higher rates. The resentment this caused, the first serious break between father and children, began the wide Diaspora that was to fill the emigrant ships for the next hundred years. The first to go were tacksmen who could no longer stomach the rack-renting of their cousinly chief, and who took their own tenants away to the Americas. Those who remained grew poorer on a black cattle economy that barely supported them, and rarely paid for their chiefs' ambitions. The dispossessed became vagrants, wandering southward to Lowland factories. 'Look around you,' John MacCodrum said, 'and see the gentry with no pity for the poor creatures, with no kindness to their kin.'

The Great Cheviot Sheep, richer in fleece and mutton than any other, was brought to the glens of Perthshire at the beginning of the golden age, and by 1790 it was on the Caithness hills. It was a simple and infallible answer to the laird's problems. Nor need he trouble himself with the tedious business of herding and shearing, for Lowland and Northumbrian graziers were ready to lease his land. Before they would bring their sheep, however, their shepherds and dogs, men must go, their townships from the glen and their cattle from the brae. The increasing demand for meat during the French wars made mutton more economic than beef, and profit supplanted the paternalism of Keppoch, Glengarry and Clanranald, Breadalbane, Strathglass and Lochiel. 'Our fathers,' said a Lochinver man, 'were called out to fight our master's battles, and this is our reward.' The wise and enlightened agriculturalist Sir John Sinclair of Ulbster was the first man to graze the Cheviot in Caithness, and he urged caution and consideration, the absorption of the native people in the new economy, but he was ignored. The ease with which a glen could be emptied, a lease sold and debts paid, encouraged the chiefs to think of immediate rewards not future obligations, and in valleys where a hundred young swordsmen had once been raised there was soon no more than a Border shepherd and his dog.

The Highlanders called the Cheviot their chief's 'four-footed clansman', and they went sadly to their exile in the Lowlands and the colonies. Whatever the laird may have become, they were still for the most part the creatures of a tribal and patriarchal society, and having no rights in law to challenge his decision to remove them, they had even less by tradition. Yet they went with bitterness, and with sorrow that a father should so cruelly abandon his children. 'Our chief,' said a bard of Clan Chisholm, 'has lost his feeling of kinship, he prefers sheep in the glen and his young men in the Highland Regiments.' He had not, however, lost his arrogant pride, and money now enabled him to indulge its pretentious conceits. Led by that ludicrous romantic, Alasdair Ranaldson MacDonell of Glengarry, whom Raeburn magnificently immortalized, the chiefs formed the Society of True Highlanders, covered their bodies with fantastic elaborations of their ancient dress and arms, observed delicate points of honour and precedence, and barred all but an accepted *duine-uasal* from membership. The true Highlanders whose removal made this expensive play-acting possible, took their grief to the slums of Glasgow and the emigrant ships at Fort William and Greenock. 'I see the hills. the valleys, and the slopes,' cried a Mackenzie bard,

> But they do not lighten my sorrow.
> I see the bands departing
>     on the white-sailed ships.
> I see the Gael rising from his door.
> I see the people going,
>     and there is no love for them in the north.

At the beginning of the nineteenth century the indiscriminate and selfish practice of eviction and clearance was transformed into what many landowners believed to be a benevolent plan for the national good. The influence of Adam Smith, and the fashionable study of political economy, persuaded them that if they exacted the maximum profit from their land the majority of the population must ultimately prosper. Since so religious a devotion to economic wealth needed a devil, the bewildered Highlander who stood in the path of advancement was condemned as unproductive, slothful, superstitious and ignorant. The Policy of Improvement in the Highlands was largely created, industriously applied, and vigorously defended by James Loch of Drylaw. In 1813 he was appointed Commissioner of the English and Scottish estates of George Granville Leveson-Gower, the dazzlingly rich and ineffably dull Marquess of Stafford. By marriage to Elizabeth, Countess of Sutherland, Stafford had acquired a vast area of land between Cape Wrath and the Dornoch Firth, its annual rental of fifteen thousand pounds being less than he sometimes spent in one day at Christie's. Loch's intention, as he later described it, was 'to render this mountainous district contributory as far as it was possible to the general wealth and industry of the country, and in the manner most suitable to its situation and peculiar circumstances'. Improvement was to depend primarily upon the introduction of sheep.

Eviction and sheep-walks had been started on the Sutherland estates in 1800, and Loch now accelerated the process. His policy, in essence, was to remove the people from the inland valleys and to resettle them on the coast. There they would be employed in fisheries which, at the time the policy was begun, had not yet been built. Those who could not, or would not, change a pastoral way of life for the sea should leave the country altogether. 'The idle and lazy,' he said, 'alone think of emigration.' Loch's improvements, which he believed would also 'emancipate the lower orders from slavery', cannot be faulted in theory nor on the premise of their intent, but like most of the schemes of early enlightenment they were characterized by a cruel inhumanity in their execution. The first great clearances began in 1814, *Bliadhna an Losgaidh*, the Year of the Burning. The greater part of Strathnaver, where the original battalion of the 93rd Highlanders had been raised, was emptied of men, women and children, houses, stock and meal, and the roof-trees of many cottages were fired before their occupants had begun their confused march to the northern coast. The factors employed to carry out the evictions were excessively brutal in their indifference to the weeping people, and one of them placed his own sheep on the ground that was cleared. There were also two, perhaps three, deaths, aged people who surrendered to shock and exposure. The factor Patrick Sellar, who was later charged with murder, was acquitted by the Circuit Court at Inverness, and the Sheriff-Substitute who brought him to trial wrote a letter of humble apology.

The major clearances on Stafford's estates continued for the next five years, in Kildonan, Clyne and Rogart, Lairg and Strathnaver again, until most of the valleys were under sheep. The fisheries, where they were established, were rarely as successful as the policy had proposed, and the life of the people was little better than the slavery from which Loch believed he had liberated them. Their lives were regulated and directed, and to prevent over-population a factor's approval was necessary before a young man could marry the girl he wished. Many of the people left for the Earl of Selkirk's colony, on the Red River prairies of Canada.

Stafford was English, and although his wife was called Ban mhorair Chataibh, the

Great Lady of Sutherland, she was a Gordon by descent and an Englishwoman by choice. But the men who cleared Strathglass were the chiefs of Clan Chisholm, and the evictors of Knoydart were MacDonell lairds of Glengarry. Lochaber was emptied by the guardians of the young heir of Lochiel, and the MacDonalds were soon gone from Glencoe. The great dispersal lasted until the middle of the century, and the sheep empire endured until it was destroyed by the wool and mutton of Australia, where many of the exiles had gone. What little opposition there was to eviction and burning came from the women of the townships. The memory of *Bliadhna nan Caorach* was kept alive in Ross, but when the women of Strath Carron and Glencalvie barred the advance of sheriff's officers and soldiers, they were beaten down with truncheons. For some years the kelp industry of the Isles sustained a large population, and even encouraged immigration, but in the end it decayed and was replaced by sheep. Once again the women resisted, at Sollas on North Uist, and their defiance persuaded their men to join them, but the truncheon was triumphant. Emigration was now regarded as a noble purpose, and it was supported by the government and by private subscription. Proprietors contracted with shipmasters before they issued writs of eviction against their people, and the men of South Uist and Barra were dragged to the transports by constables. 'The clearances came upon us,' said an old Isleswoman, many years later to a Government Commission. 'There was neither sin nor sorrow in the world for us, but the clearances came upon us, destroying all, turning our gladness into bitterness. . . . Oh, dear man, the tears come upon my eyes when I think of all we suffered, and of the sorrows, the hardships and the oppressions we came through.'

There were frequent famines, and the worst was that which followed the potato blight of 1846. There were epidemics of cholera, and whole families were found dead on the rotting straw of their huts. And in the food riots which followed both blight and pestilence, Highland regiments marched against Highland men and women. The last clearances of all, in Knoydart, were perhaps the most terrible of all, for their purpose was not to empty the glens but to remove a vestigial pauper population before it could become the Poor Law liability of the incoming graziers. There were chiefs who resisted the compulsions of a sheep economy and clearance, like Alexander, the twenty-third of Clan Chisholm, but Strathglass was emptied by his successors. Godfrey MacDonald of Sleat, fourth Baron of the Isles, was a humane man and deeply regretted the evictions his debts demanded. He did what he could to help his starving people during the famines, and it was thus an irony that the most bitterly-remembered clearance in the Isles took place on his lands. Once begun, the policy of Improvement could not be halted, and few of the chiefs and lairds believed that it could be imposed without the removal of what Loch admitted was the 'ancient population of the country'. Sinclair's advice had been ignored at the beginning, and that given by *The Times* in 1845 was perhaps too late.

What, then, is the remedy? Employment. Give employment to the people. Create employment. Pursue a course directly the opposite in its tendencies to that now pursued. Do not make employment more scarce by turning the hills and glens into sheep-wilds. Make many yeomen out of one sheep-farmer. . . . Promote factories; surely with waterpower costing nothing, and wool at your doors, you can make cloth as cheaply as it can be made in Yorkshire? This will employ your population instead of driving them to Canada. . . . Abandon the tenant-at-will system; give leases, or make such agreement as shall secure the tenant as well as the landlord; and independence of spirit, and improvement, and enterprise, will rapidly follow.

With a few noble exceptions, most Presbyterian ministers defended the lairds from

*Dr David Welsh, the retiring Moderator who refused to constitute the General Assembly of 1843. From an original collotype by D. O. Hill and Robert Adamson, used as a guide to one of six hundred faces in a painting of 'The Disruption'.*

whom they had received their Highland parishes, threatening the people with damnation if they did not obey the writs of eviction. The clearances, and the support given them in the name of God, were contributory factors in the great disruption of the Kirk. Since the re-establishment of the Presbyterian Church in 1690 there had been two major secessions in 1733 and 1761, and the first had been split still further. The common ground of protest between them had been the reintroduction of patronage five years after the Treaty of Union, and the full effect of this was perhaps not apparent until Highland ministers enlisted the wrath of God upon behalf of the proprietors. In 1784, when the General Assembly abandoned its annual protest against patronage, there was already a clear division between the moderates – who disgusted their critics by their taste for cards and the theatre – and the later-known Evangelicals, among others, who wished to reawaken the Church's concern for the doctrines of sin, grace, and redemption. The humanitarian and reform movements in the early part of the nineteenth century, the partisanship of Highland ministers, the growing strength of the Evangelicals, brought the Kirk to its third and greatest secession.

At the General Assembly of 1843 the differences between the two parties were wide and complex, but the real issue at their heart was the spiritual and humanitarian responsibility of the Kirk. No minister, said the rebels, could be appointed over a congregation except by the consent of the heads of its families, and conversely they had the right to reject such an appointment if they wished. Though this was in defiance of the law, the Evangelicals refused to be deflected. Before the proper business of the Assembly began in St Andrew's Church, Edinburgh, the retiring Moderator, Dr David Welsh, said that he and others could not acknowledge it as a free body, and were therefore determined to leave it. Nearly two hundred ministers and elders followed him into Hanover Street, and they walked in procession through a cheering crowd to Tanfield Hall, where they constituted themselves as the first General Assembly of the Church of Scotland Free. A third of the people and nearly forty per cent of the ministers of the old Kirk joined the new, and it prospered on the generosity of wealthy supporters and the enthusiasm of its congregations. The Disruption, said Lord Cockburn, was the 'most honourable feat for Scotland that its whole history supplies'. It was also its last revolution of conscience.[1]

And what was perhaps the last voice of an independent Scotland was heard in 1854. Fittingly, it came from the race that had given the nation a name and a beginning. With the declaration of war against Russia, recruiters were once more sent to the Highlands. The chiefs who remained, and the southern proprietors who now owned the glens of those who were gone, appealed for men to fill the depleted battalions of Alma and Balaclava. They could scarcely raise a platoon. 'Since you have preferred sheep to men,' they were told, 'let sheep defend you.' The Earl of Seafield, one of the principal supporters of the Treaty of Union, is believed to have said that it was the 'end of an auld song', but the great echo-chamber of Scottish history held the notes for another century and a half, until they were lost in the brassy anthem of an imperial Britain.

[1] The Patronage Act of 1874 restored to the congregations of the Church of Scotland the right to elect their ministers, but there was no immediate reconciliation. Most of the seceding groups were united in 1900, and were further united with the established Church in 1929. One hundred and fifty Highland congregations stubbornly refused to accept either union.

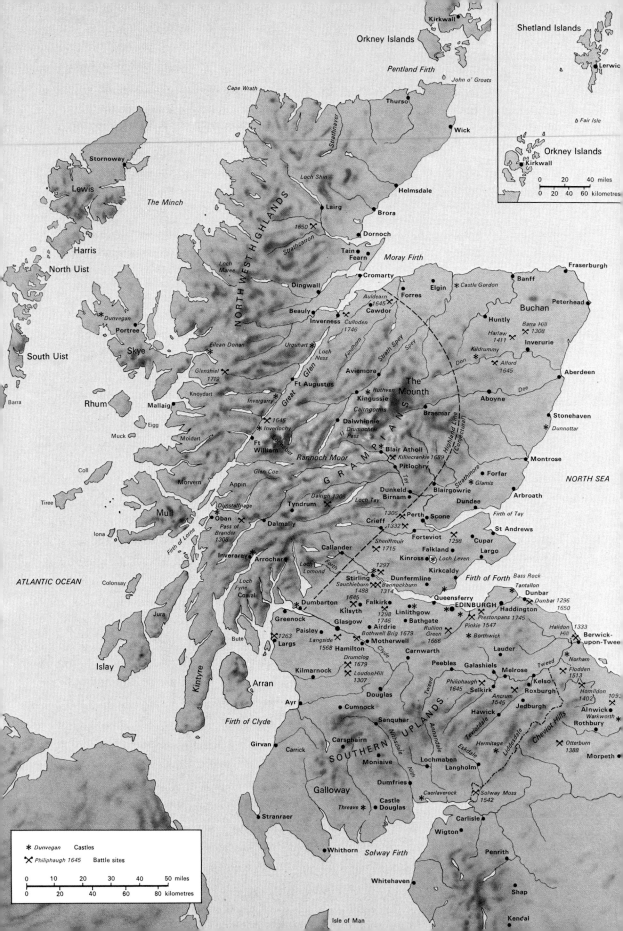

Shetland Islands

Lerwic

△ Fair Isle

Orkney Islands

Kirkwall

0    20    40 miles
0  20  40  60 kilometres

Kirkwall

Orkney Islands

Pentland Firth

John o' Groats

Cape Wrath

Thurso

Wick

Helmsdale

Stornoway

Lewis

The Minch

Harris

North Uist

Lairg

Brora

Dornoch

1650

Strathcarron

Tain
Fearn

Cromarty

Moray Firth

Elgin

Forres

Castle Gordon

Banff

Fraserburgh

Peterhead

Buchan

South Uist

Dunvegan

Portree

Skye

Eilean Donan

Glenshiel
1719

Knoydart

Invergarry

Dingwall

Beauly

Inverness

Auldearn
1645   Forres

Cawdor

Culloden
1746

Findhorn

Urquhart

Loch
Ness

Aviemore

Ruthven

Kingussie

Cairngorms

Strath Spey

Spey

Huntly

Harlaw
1411

Kildrummy

Alford
1645

Don

Barra Hill
1308

Inverurie

Aberdeen

Dee

Aboyne

Stonehaven

Dunnottar

Montrose

Rhum

Mallaig

Eigg

Muck

Moidart

Coll

Tiree

Iona

Mull

Morvern

Appin

Glen Coe

Dunstaffnage

Oban

Pass of
Brander
1308

Dalmally

Firth of Lorne

Colonsay

Jura

Islay

Kintyre

Arran

Bute

Ft Augustus

Dalwhinnie

Drumochter
Pass

Blair Atholl

Killiecrankie 1689

Pitlochry

Dunkeld
Birnam

Blairgowrie

Braemar

Highland Line

The Mounth

GRAMPIANS

Rannoch Moor

Dalrigh 1306

Tyndrum

Loch Tay

Tay

Crieff

1306
1332

Perth

Scone

Forteviot

1298

Strathmore

Glamis

Forfar

Dundee

Arbroath

NORTH SEA

Callander

Sheriffmuir
1715

Falkland

Cupar

St Andrews

Largo

Firth of Tay

Kinross

Loch Leven

1297

Stirling

Sauchieburn
1488

Dunfermline

Bannockburn
1314

Kirkcaldy

Firth of Forth

Bass Rock

Tantallon

Dunbar

Dunbar 1296
1650

Inveraray

Arrochar

Loch
Fyne

Loch
Lomond

Cowal

Dumbarton

1645

Kilsyth

Falkirk
1298
1746

Linlithgow

Queensferry

EDINBURGH

Haddington

Pinkie 1547

Prestonpans 1745

Halidon
Hill 1333

Berwick-
upon-Tweed

Greenock

Paisley

Glasgow

Airdrie

Motherwell

Bathgate

Rullion
Green
1666

Borthwick

Lauder

Norham

Langside
1568

Hamilton

Drumclog
1679

Bothwell Brig 1679

Clyde

Carnwath

Peebles

Galashiels

Melrose

Tweed

Flodden
1513

Kelso

Roxburgh

Homildon
1402

Alnwick

Warkworth

Rothbury

Largs
1263

Kilmarnock

Loudon Hill
1307

Douglas

Cumnock

Ayr

Firth of Clyde

Girvan

Carrick

Sanquhar

Carsphairn

Moniaive

Galloway

Castle
Douglas

Threave

Stranraer

Whithorn

Solway Firth

Douglas

Hawick

Ancrum
1545

Jedburgh

SOUTHERN UPLANDS

Nithsdale

Annandale

Teviotdale

Lochmaben

Langholm

Dumfries

Caerlaverock

Solway Moss
1542

Carlisle

Wigton

Penrith

Whitehaven

Shap

Kendal

Isle of Man

Philiphaugh
1645

Selkirk

Eskdale

Liddesdale

Hermitage

Cheviot Hills

Otterburn
1388

Morpeth

Ft
William

Ardwhinnie

Inverlochy

1645

Lochaber

Great Glen

NORTH WEST HIGHLANDS

Loch Shin

Strathnaver

Loch
Maree

ATLANTIC OCEAN

Drumlog

Knoydart

Confeqarar

* Dunvegan    Castles

✕ Philiphaugh 1645    Battle sites

0    10    20    30    40    50 miles
0   20    40    60    80 kilometres

# Scotland's Line of Kings

*Alpin to David I*

A.D. 843–1153

r.   reigned
=   married
——  father – son
----  descent of crown

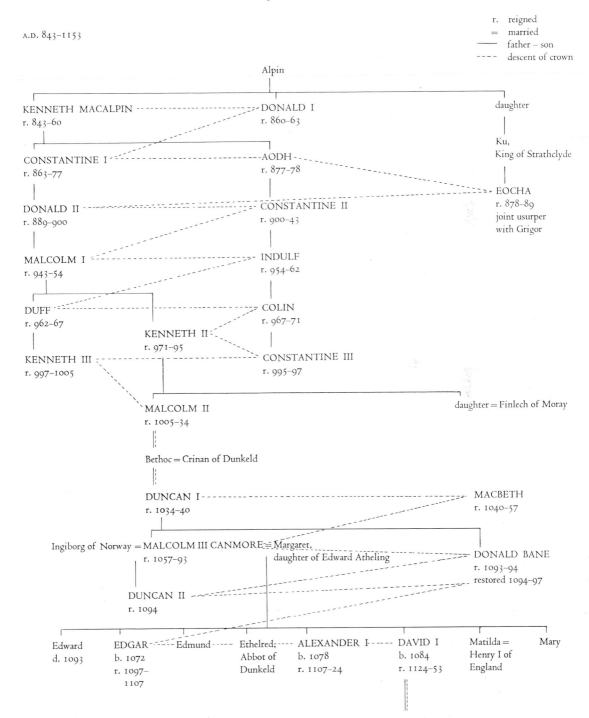

Alpin

KENNETH MACALPIN - - - - - - - - - - - - - - - DONALD I
r. 843–60                                        r. 860–63

daughter

Ku,
King of Strathclyde

CONSTANTINE I - - - - - - - - - - - - - - - - - AODH - - - -
r. 863–77                                        r. 877–78

DONALD II - - - - - - - - - - - - - - - - CONSTANTINE II
r. 889–900                                  r. 900–43

EOCHA
r. 878–89
joint usurper
with Grigor

MALCOLM I - - - - - - - - - - - - - - - - - - - INDULF
r. 943–54                                        r. 954–62

DUFF - - - - - - - - - - - - - - - - - - - - - COLIN
r. 962–67                                        r. 967–71

KENNETH II
r. 971–95

KENNETH III - - - - - - - - - - - - - - - CONSTANTINE III
r. 997–1005                                r. 995–97

MALCOLM II
r. 1005–34

daughter = Finlech of Moray

Bethoc = Crinan of Dunkeld

DUNCAN I - - - - - - - - - - - - - - - - - - - - - - - - MACBETH
r. 1034–40                                                r. 1040–57

Ingiborg of Norway = MALCOLM III CANMORE = Margaret,
                      r. 1057–93            daughter of Edward Atheling

DONALD BANE
r. 1093–94
restored 1094–97

DUNCAN II
r. 1094

Edward        EDGAR - - - - Edmund - - - -  Ethelred,  - - - - ALEXANDER I - - - - DAVID I        Matilda =        Mary
d. 1093       b. 1072                        Abbot of          b. 1078             b. 1084        Henry I of
              r. 1097–                       Dunkeld           r. 1107–24          r. 1124–53     England
              1107

# David I to Robert Bruce

A.D. 1124–1306

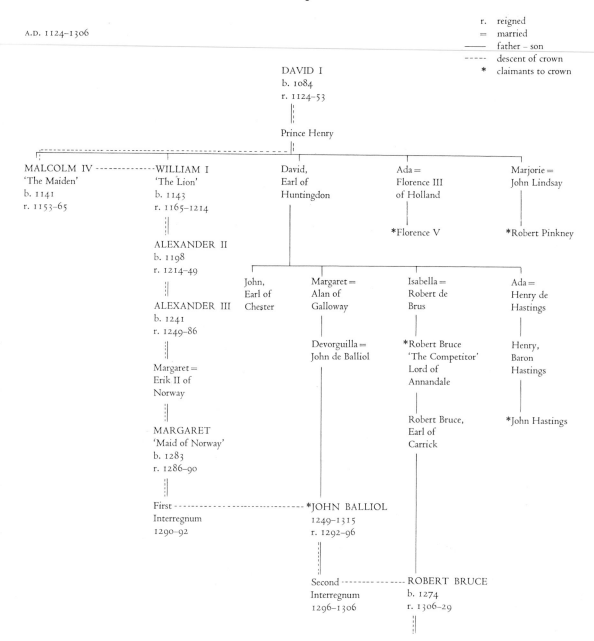

DAVID I
b. 1084
r. 1124–53

Prince Henry

MALCOLM IV ------------ WILLIAM I
'The Maiden'            'The Lion'
b. 1141                b. 1143
r. 1153–65             r. 1165–1214

David,                 Ada =
Earl of                Florence III
Huntingdon             of Holland

                       *Florence V

Marjorie =
John Lindsay

*Robert Pinkney

ALEXANDER II
b. 1198
r. 1214–49

John,          Margaret =       Isabella =        Ada =
Earl of        Alan of          Robert de         Henry de
Chester        Galloway         Brus              Hastings

ALEXANDER III
b. 1241
r. 1249–86

               Devorguilla =    *Robert Bruce     Henry,
               John de Balliol  'The Competitor'  Baron
                                Lord of           Hastings
                                Annandale

Margaret =
Erik II of
Norway

                                Robert Bruce,     *John Hastings
                                Earl of
                                Carrick

MARGARET
'Maid of Norway'
b. 1283
r. 1286–90

First ---------------------------- *JOHN BALLIOL
Interregnum                        1249–1315
1290–92                            r. 1292–96

                Second -------------- ROBERT BRUCE
                Interregnum           b. 1274
                1296–1306             r. 1306–29

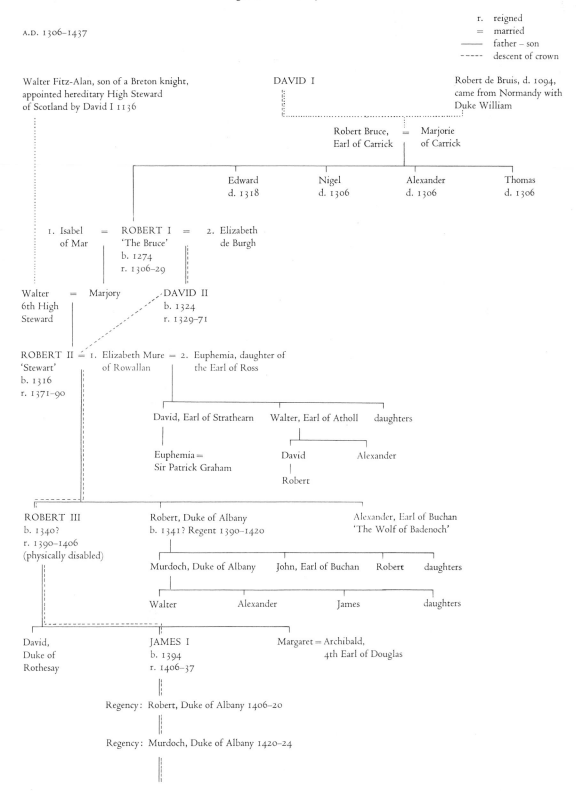

# Robert Bruce to James I

A.D. 1306–1437

r. reigned
= married
—— father – son
----- descent of crown

Walter Fitz-Alan, son of a Breton knight, appointed hereditary High Steward of Scotland by David I 1136

DAVID I

Robert de Bruis, d. 1094, came from Normandy with Duke William

Robert Bruce, = Marjorie
Earl of Carrick    of Carrick

Edward          Nigel          Alexander          Thomas
d. 1318          d. 1306          d. 1306          d. 1306

1. Isabel    =    ROBERT I    =    2. Elizabeth
of Mar            'The Bruce'         de Burgh
                  b. 1274
                  r. 1306–29

Walter    =    Marjory          DAVID II
6th High                        b. 1324
Steward                         r. 1329–71

ROBERT II = 1. Elizabeth Mure = 2. Euphemia, daughter of
'Stewart'      of Rowallan           the Earl of Ross
b. 1316
r. 1371–90

David, Earl of Strathearn    Walter, Earl of Atholl    daughters

Euphemia =                    David          Alexander
Sir Patrick Graham
                              Robert

ROBERT III              Robert, Duke of Albany          Alexander, Earl of Buchan
b. 1340?                b. 1341? Regent 1390–1420        'The Wolf of Badenoch'
r. 1390–1406
(physically disabled)

Murdoch, Duke of Albany    John, Earl of Buchan    Robert    daughters

Walter          Alexander          James          daughters

David,          JAMES I              Margaret = Archibald,
Duke of         b. 1394                         4th Earl of Douglas
Rothesay        r. 1406–37

Regency: Robert, Duke of Albany 1406–20

Regency: Murdoch, Duke of Albany 1420–24

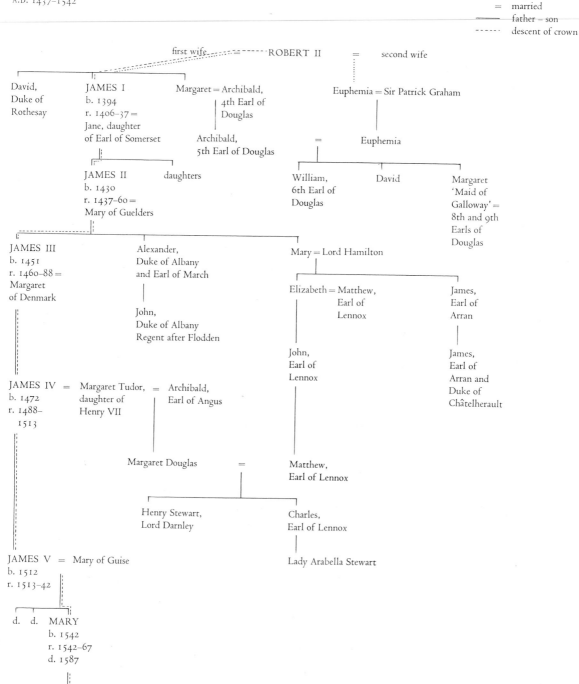

# The Stewarts

A.D. 1437–1542

r. reigned
= married
——— father – son
------ descent of crown

first wife ........= ------ ROBERT II = second wife

David,    JAMES I    Margaret = Archibald,      Euphemia = Sir Patrick Graham
Duke of    b. 1394         4th Earl of
Rothesay    r. 1406–37 =       Douglas
         Jane, daughter
         of Earl of Somerset    Archibald,       =      Euphemia
                        5th Earl of Douglas

         JAMES II        daughters       William,       David       Margaret
         b. 1430                    6th Earl of              'Maid of
         r. 1437–60 =               Douglas                 Galloway' =
         Mary of Guelders                                 8th and 9th
                                                           Earls of
                                                           Douglas

JAMES III        Alexander,          Mary = Lord Hamilton
b. 1451          Duke of Albany
r. 1460–88 =       and Earl of March
Margaret
of Denmark                        Elizabeth = Matthew,       James,
                                      Earl of          Earl of
         John,                              Lennox        Arran
         Duke of Albany
         Regent after Flodden              John,               James,
                                     Earl of          Earl of
                                     Lennox        Arran and
                                                          Duke of
JAMES IV =   Margaret Tudor, = Archibald,                                Châtelherault
b. 1472      daughter of     Earl of Angus
r. 1488–     Henry VII
1513

                 Margaret Douglas        =       Matthew,
                                           Earl of Lennox

                 Henry Stewart,           Charles,
                 Lord Darnley            Earl of Lennox

JAMES V =   Mary of Guise                         Lady Arabella Stewart
b. 1512
r. 1513–42

d.   d.   MARY
        b. 1542
        r. 1542–67
        d. 1587

# The Stewarts: to the Commonwealth

A.D. 1542–1649

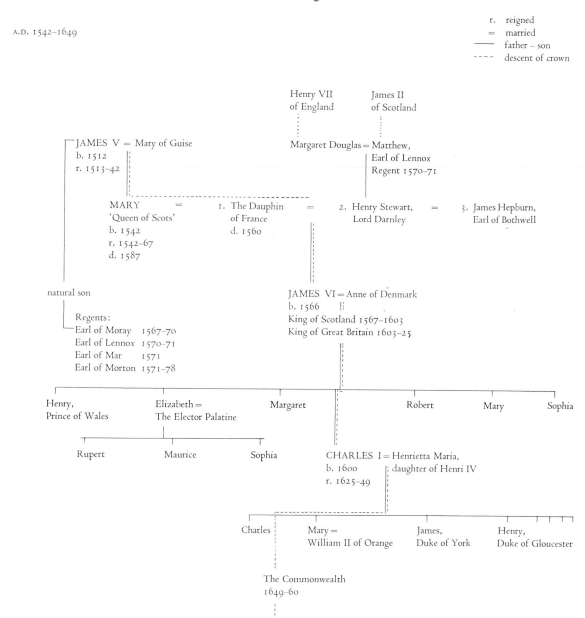

Henry VII
of England

James II
of Scotland

Margaret Douglas = Matthew,
Earl of Lennox
Regent 1570–71

JAMES V = Mary of Guise
b. 1512
r. 1513–42

MARY          =          1. The Dauphin     =     2. Henry Stewart,     =     3. James Hepburn,
'Queen of Scots'         of France                 Lord Darnley                 Earl of Bothwell
b. 1542                  d. 1560
r. 1542–67
d. 1587

natural son

JAMES VI = Anne of Denmark
b. 1566
King of Scotland 1567–1603
King of Great Britain 1603–25

Regents:
Earl of Moray   1567–70
Earl of Lennox  1570–71
Earl of Mar     1571
Earl of Morton  1571–78

Henry,            Elizabeth =          Margaret                  Robert      Mary      Sophia
Prince of Wales   The Elector Palatine

Rupert            Maurice            Sophia            CHARLES I = Henrietta Maria,
                                                       b. 1600     daughter of Henri IV
                                                       r. 1625–49

Charles           Mary =                        James,              Henry,
                  William II of Orange          Duke of York        Duke of Gloucester

The Commonwealth
1649–60

CHARLES II
b. 1630
crowned at Scone 1651
restored 1660
d. 1685

# The Union of the Crowns

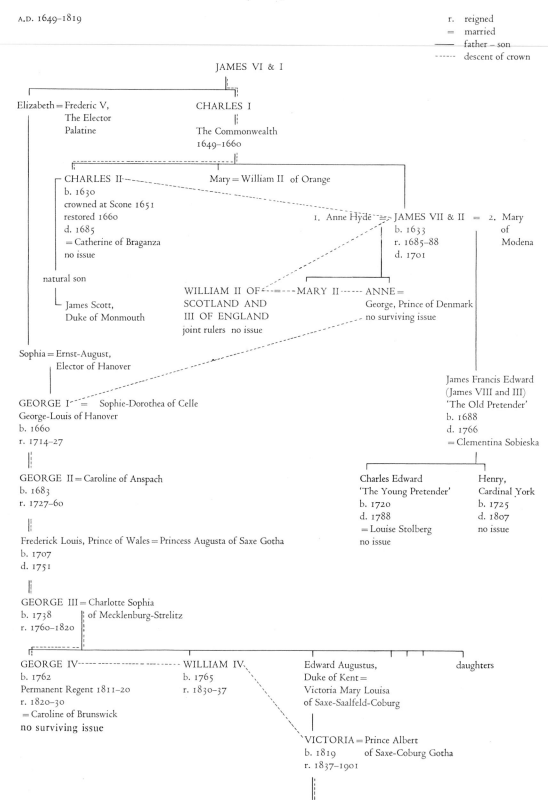

JAMES VI & I

Elizabeth = Frederic V,
The Elector
Palatine

CHARLES I
The Commonwealth
1649–1660

CHARLES II
b. 1630
crowned at Scone 1651
restored 1660
d. 1685
= Catherine of Braganza
no issue

Mary = William II of Orange

1. Anne Hyde = JAMES VII & II = 2. Mary
b. 1633                          of
r. 1685–88                       Modena
d. 1701

natural son

James Scott,
Duke of Monmouth

WILLIAM II OF = MARY II ANNE =
SCOTLAND AND          George, Prince of Denmark
III OF ENGLAND        no surviving issue
joint rulers no issue

Sophia = Ernst-August,
Elector of Hanover

James Francis Edward
(James VIII and III)
'The Old Pretender'
b. 1688
d. 1766
= Clementina Sobieska

GEORGE I = Sophie-Dorothea of Celle
George-Louis of Hanover
b. 1660
r. 1714–27

GEORGE II = Caroline of Anspach
b. 1683
r. 1727–60

Charles Edward
'The Young Pretender'
b. 1720
d. 1788
= Louise Stolberg
no issue

Henry,
Cardinal York
b. 1725
d. 1807
no issue

Frederick Louis, Prince of Wales = Princess Augusta of Saxe Gotha
b. 1707
d. 1751

GEORGE III = Charlotte Sophia
b. 1738        of Mecklenburg-Strelitz
r. 1760–1820

GEORGE IV
b. 1762
Permanent Regent 1811–20
r. 1820–30
= Caroline of Brunswick
no surviving issue

WILLIAM IV
b. 1765
r. 1830–37

Edward Augustus,                daughters
Duke of Kent =
Victoria Mary Louisa
of Saxe-Saalfeld-Coburg

VICTORIA = Prince Albert
b. 1819        of Saxe-Coburg Gotha
r. 1837–1901

r.    reigned
=     married
      father – son
----- descent of crown

# Selected Bibliography

As its sub-title clearly states, this book is a personal view of Scotland's history, but although it is frequently subjective in comment, and sometimes partisan perhaps, I hope that it is honest enough for its conclusions to be disputed upon the evidence it gives, if the reader so wishes. The library of Scottish history is vast, its manuscript archives extensive, and no man could study them all in one lifetime. A general work such as this depends upon secondary sources and is in debt to the pioneer work of others, although where it touches upon the Highlands, and upon the Darien Venture, it is naturally influenced by the original research I have done for earlier books upon these subjects. To acknowledge all the source material that has been consulted would be impossible within the space available, but my particular gratitude must be expressed for the recent work of such eminent scholars as T. C. Smout, Gordon Donaldson, William Ferguson, and William Croft Dickinson. The following selected bibliography is given with apologies for what may seem to be lamentable and unforgivable omissions. Unlisted, but no less important, are the many volumes of papers, diaries, memoirs, and records published by the Scottish History Society and others.

## GENERAL

Brown, P. Hume. *History of Scotland.* 1911.

Browne, James. *History of the Highlands and the Highland Clans.* 1838.

Burton, John Hill. *History of Scotland.* 1853.

Cunningham, Audrey. *The Loyal Clans.* 1932.

Dickinson, W. Croft. *Scotland from the Earliest Times to 1603.* 1961.

Donaldson, Gordon. *Scotland, James V – James VII.* 1965.

Ferguson, William. *Scotland, 1689 to the Present.* 1968.

Lang, Andrew. *A History of Scotland.* 1900–7.

Linklater, Eric. *The Survival of Scotland.* 1968.

Mackenzie, Agnes Mure. *A History of Scotland, Vols. I–VI.*

Mackenzie, W. C. *The Highlands and Isles of Scotland: A Historical Survey.* 1949.

Mackie, J. D. *A History of Scotland.* 1964.

Mackie, R. L. *A Short History of Scotland.* Edited by Gordon Donaldson. 1962.

Smout, T. C. *A History of the Scottish People 1560–1830.* 1969.

## POLITICAL, RELIGIOUS

Burleigh, J. H. S. *A. Church History of Scotland.* 1960.

Cunningham, John. *The Church History of Scotland.* 1882.

Grub, George. *An Ecclesiastical History of Scotland.* 1861.

Mackenzie, W. M. *The Scottish Burghs.* 1949.

Rait, R. S. *The Parliaments of Scotland.* 1924.

## SOCIAL, ECONOMIC

Brown, P. Hume, editor. *Early Travellers in Scotland.* 1891.

Brown, P. Hume, editor. *Scotland before 1700 from Contemporary Documents.* 1893.

Chambers, Robert. *Traditions of Edinburgh.* 1868.

Chambers, Robert. *Domestic Annals of Scotland.* 1874.

Cruden, Stewart. *The Scottish Castle.* 1963.

Fyfe, J. G. *Scottish Diaries and Memoirs 1550–1746.*

Graham, H. G. *Social Life of Scotland in the Eighteenth Century.* 1899.

Grant, I. F. *The Social and Economic Development of Scotland before 1603.* 1903.

Innes, Cosmo. *Scotland in the Middle Ages.* 1860.

Mackenzie, W. M. *The Mediaeval Castle in Scotland.* 1927.

Rogers, Charles. *Social Life in Scotland from Early to Present Times.* 1886.

Warrack, John. *Domestic Life in Scotland, 1488–1688.* 1920.

# SECTIONAL

## THE UNION OF PEOPLES

Adamnan. *Life of Columba.* Edited by A. O. and M. O. Anderson. 1961.

Anderson, A. O. *Scottish Annals from English Chroniclers.* 1908.

Anderson, A. O. *Early Sources of Scottish History.* 1922.

Chadwick, H. M. *Early Scotland.* 1949.

Chadwick, Nora K. *Celtic Britain.* 1963.

Collingwood, R. G. *Roman Britain.* 1937.

Henderson, Isabel. *The Picts.* 1967.

Piggott, Stuart. *Scotland before History.* 1958.

Skene, W. F. *Celtic Scotland.* 1886–90.

Wainwright, F. T., editor. *The Problem of the Picts.* 1955.

Dalrymple, David, Lord Hailes. *Annals of Scotland.* 1819.

Fergusson, Sir James. *William Wallace.* 1948.

Fordun, John. *Chronica Gentis Scotorum.* Edited and translated by W. F. Skene. 1871–2.

Gray, Thomas. *Scalacronica.* Translated by Sir Herbert Maxwell. 1907.

Linklater, Eric. *Robert the Bruce.*

Maxwell, Sir Herbert, translator. *The Chronicle of Lanercost.* 1913.

Palgrave, Sir Francis, editor. *Documents and Records Illustrating the History of Scotland.* 1837.

## THE NORMAN INVASION

Coutts, J. *The Norman Invasion of Scotland.*

Ritchie, R. L. Graeme. *The Normans in Scotland.* 1954.

## THE WAR OF INDEPENDENCE

Barbour, John. *The Bruce.* Translated by A. A. H. Douglas. 1964.

Barron, Evan Macleod. *The Scottish War of Independence.* 1934.

Bryant, Arthur. *The Age of Chivalry.* 1963.

## THE STEWARD'S HOUSE

Bain, Joseph, editor. *Calendar of Documents relating to Scotland, 1108–1509.* 1881–8.

Donaldson, Gordon. *Scottish Kings.* 1967.

Dunbar, William. *Poems.* Edited by John Small and A. J. G. Mackay. 1893.

Henryson, Robert. *Poems.* Edited by C. Gregory Smith. 1906.

Lindsay, Robert, of Pitscottie. *Historie and Cronicles of Scotland.* Edited by A. J. G. Mackay. 1899–1911.

Lyndsay, Sir David, of the Mount. *Poetical Works.* Edited by David Laing. 1879.

Major, John. *History of Greater Britain.* Edited and translated by Archibald Constable. 1892.

Mackie, R. L. *King James IV of Scotland.* 1958.

## REFORMATION

Buchanan, George. *The Tyrannous Reign of Mary Stewart.* A translation of Books XVII–XIX of Rerum Scoticarum Historia by W. A. Gatherer. 1958.

Donaldson, Gordon. *The Reformation in Scotland.* 1960.

Fraser, Antonia. *Mary Queen of Scots.* 1969.

Knox, John. *History of the Reformation in Scotland.* Edited by W. Croft Dickinson. 1949.

Ridley, Jasper. *John Knox.* 1968.

Willson, D. Harris. *James VI and I.* 1956.


## ONE KING AND PARLIAMENT

Buchan, John. *Montrose.* 1928.

Defoe, Daniel. *The History of the Union between England and Scotland.* 1786.

Firth, C. H. *Scotland and the Commonwealth.* 1894.

Firth, C. H. *Scotland and the Protectorate.* 1899.

Lane, Jane. *The Reign of King Covenant.* 1956.

Mackenzie, W. C. *Andrew Fletcher of Saltoun.* 1935.

Mackinnon, James. *The Union of England and Scotland.* 1896.

Mathew, David. *Scotland under Charles I.* 1955.

Mathew, David. *James I.* 1967.

Smout, T. C. *Scottish Trade on the Eve of Union, 1660–1707.* 1963.

Wedgwood, C. V. *The King's Peace, 1637–1641.* 1955.

Wedgwood, C. V. *The King's War, 1641–1647.* 1958.


## NORTH BRITONS

Campbell, R. H. *Scotland since 1707.* 1965.

Ellis, P. Beresford, and Mac a' Ghobhainn, Seumas. *The Scottish Insurrection of 1820.* 1970.

Gray, Malcolm. *The Highland Economy, 1750–1850.* 1957.

Hamilton, Henry. *The Industrial Revolution in Scotland.* 1932.

Hamilton, Henry. *An Economic History of Scotland in the Eighteenth Century.* 1963.

Mathieson, W. L. *The Awakening of Scotland, 1747–1797.* 1912.

Meikle, Henry W. *Scotland and the French Revolution.* 1912.

Petrie, Sir Charles. *The Jacobite Movement, The First Phase, 1688–1716.* 1948.

Petrie, Sir Charles. *The Jacobite Movement, The Last Phase, 1716–1807.* 1950.

Prebble, John. *The Highland Clearances.* 1963.

Youngson, A. J. *The Making of Classical Edinburgh.* 1966.

# Notes on Illustrations
## and Acknowledgments

Where the following abbreviations appear in the notes, they are intended to indicate the locations of pictures, and to acknowledge permission to reproduce photographs that the museums, art galleries and other institutions (or specifically their governing bodies) have granted in cases where they hold the copyright.

*BM:* The Trustees, British Museum, London. *NGS:* National Gallery of Scotland, Edinburgh. *NLS:* The Trustees, National Library of Scotland, Edinburgh. *NMAS:* National Museum of Antiquities of Scotland, Edinburgh. *NPG:* National Portrait Gallery, London. *Pennant's Tour: A Tour of Scotland and a Voyage to the Hebrides,* 1772, by Thomas Pennant (Author's collection). *SNPG:* Scottish National Portrait Gallery, Edinburgh. *SRO:* Scottish Record Office, Edinburgh.

*page*

90 Tomb, mid-14th cent. *Westminster Abbey*. Reproduced by permission of the Dean and Chapter. Photo: John Freeman.

92 *NMAS*.

94 Photo: A. F. Kersting.

99 (Left) *Royal Scottish Museum, Edinburgh*. (Bottom) *Canterbury Cathedral*. British Crown Copyright: reproduced by permission of the Department of the Environment. (Right) *Tower of London*. British Crown Copyright: reproduced by permission of the Department of the Environment.

101 *SRO*. Archives Nationales, Paris.

103 Wood and bronze, 7th cent. *NMAS*.

104 T. Stalker-Miller, MSIA.

105 (Left) T. Stalker-Miller, MISA. (Right) British Crown Copyright: reproduced by permission of the Department of the Environment.

107 Oil painting, 1476, ascribed to Hugo Van der Goes. Copyright reserved: reproduced by gracious permission of Her Majesty the Queen.

108 Fresco, 1505, by Pinturicchio. *Opera Metropolitana, Siena, Italy*. Photo: Scala.

111 Miniature, early 15th cent., from *The Travels of Sir John Mandeville. B.M.*

113 Photo: J. Pugh.

115 British Crown Copyright: reproduced by permission of the Department of the Environment.

121 Electrotype from the gilt-copper tomb effigy (*c.* 1377–80) in Westminster Abbey. *NPG*.

122 Photo: Institut Géographique National, Paris.

124 Engraving, 17th cent., by Wenceslaus Hollar. *BM*.

126 Engraving, 17th cent., *SNPG*, Department of Prints and Drawings.

129 *Pennant's Tour*. Photo: John Freeman.

132 (Left) Oil painting, late 16th cent. *NPG*. (Right) Oil painting, late 16th cent. *NPG*.

134 *St Andrews University Library*.

135 (Left) Oil painting, 16th cent., based on an earlier work, now lost. *SNPG*. (Right) Manuscript, *c.* 1490. *The Curators, Bodleian Library, Oxford*. Arch. Selden, B.24.

141 Photo: A. F. Kersting.

143 *SNPG*, Department of Prints and Drawings.

145 (Left) *NMAS*. (Right) Oil painting, mid-16th cent. *NPG*.

147 Photo: J. Pugh.

150 *Central Public Library, Edinburgh*. Photo: F. R. Inglis & Son.

157 Oil painting, 17th cent., by Daniel Mytens, based on an earlier work. Reproduced by permission of Colonel Stirling of Kier. Photo: *SNPG*.

158 (Left) Illumination from *The Hours of James IV*, *c.* 1503–13. *Österreichische Nationalbibliothek, Vienna*. (Right) Embroidery, *c.* 1520. *NMAS*.

159 *NLS*.

161 Oil painting, early 17th cent. *NPG*.

164 T. Stalker-Miller, MSIA.

166 Wood engraving, 1580. From Beza's *Icones*. *SNPG*.

169 Oil painting, 1578. *Hatfield House*. Reproduced by permission of the Marquess of Salisbury. Photo: Derrick Witty.

170 Oil painting, *c.* 1605, ascribed to John de Critz. Reproduced by permission of J. R. More-Molyneux, Esq. Photo: Derrick Witty.

171 Oil painting, *c.* 1605–10, ascribed to Marcus Gheeraerts the Younger. *Woburn Abbey*. Reproduced by permission of the Duke of Bedford and the Trustees of the Bedford Settled Estates. Photo: Derrick Witty.

172 (Above) Miniature, 1566. *SNPG*. (Below) Oil painting, 1591. *Darnaway Castle, Morayshire*. Reproduced by permission of the Earl of Moray. Photo: Tom Scott.

175 (Left) Oil painting, 16th cent. *SNPG*. (Right) Oil painting, 16th cent., in the style of Corneille de Lyon. *SNPG*.

181 (Left) Oil painting, 16th cent., School of Holbein. *SNPG*. (Right) *Pennant's Tour*. Photo: John Freeman.

182 (Left) Miniature, mid-16th cent. *The Trustees, Victoria and Albert Museum, London*. (Right) *BM*. Photo: John Freeman.

186 Manuscript, *BM*.

189 *Bibliothèque Nationale, Paris*.

192 Engraving, 1559, by J. Tortorel and J. Perrissin. *BM*. Photo: Radio Times Hulton Picture Library.

195 Oil painting, 1563, by Hans Eworth. British Crown Copyright: reproduced by gracious permission of Her Majesty the Queen.

197 Oil painting, *c.* 1575, ascribed to Arnold van Brounckhorst. *SNPG*.

198 Painted ceiling, 1625–48. British Crown
–9 Copyright: reproduced by permission of the Department of the Environment.

200 *SNPG*.

202 Oil painting, *c.* 1575, ascribed to Arnold van Brounckhorst. *SNPG.*

204 Drawing, 10 February 1567. British Crown Copyright: reproduced by permission of the *Public Record Office, London.*

207 Photo: J. Pugh.

214 (Left) British Crown Copyright: reproduced by permission of the Department of the Environment. (Right) Photo: J. Pugh.

222 *NLS.*

224 Oil painting, *c.* 1634, after Honthorst. *SNPG.*

229 (Left) Weapons, 18th cent. *NMAS.* (Right) *Pennant's Tour.* Photo: John Freeman.

233 *Pennant's Tour.* Photo: John Freeman.

236 *Central Public Library, Edinburgh.* Photo: F. R.
–7 Inglis and Son.

239 Oil painting, 1623. British Crown Copyright: reproduced by gracious permission of Her Majesty the Queen.

240 (Left) *BM.* Photo: John Freeman. (Right) *BM.*

243 *NMAS.*

244 Embroidery, early 17th cent. *NMAS.*

249 (Above) British Crown Copyright: reproduced by permission of the Department of the Environment. (Below) Photo: Albert Barber.

250 Oil painting, 1847, by Horatio MacCulloch,
–1 R.S.A. Private owner. (Jacket subject.)

252 Reproduced by permission of Perfecta Publications Ltd. Photo: Sidney W. Newbery.

259 Oil painting. *NPG.*

260 Satire, 1661. *SNPG*, Department of Prints and Drawings.

262 Drawing, 1681. *NLS.*

264 Photo: Gilbert Bell.

266 Photo: British Travel Association.

268 Oil painting. *NPG.*

270 (Left) *NGS*, Department of Prints and Drawings. (Right) *BM.* Photo: John Freeman.

272 *Pennant's Tour.* Photo: John Freeman.

273 (Left) Photo: J. Pugh. (Right) *NLS.*

277 Photo: J. Pugh.

278 *Lady Stair's House Museum.* Reproduced by
–9 permission of the Edinburgh Booksellers Society. Photo: *Treasures of Britain*, Drive Publications Ltd. L to R: Dr Hugh Blair, Henry Mackenzie, Robert Burns, Alexander Naysmith, David Allan, James Bruce, Lord Monboddo, Miss Burnett, James Sibbald, Dr Adam Fergusson, Walter Scott.

281 From 'The Scottish Regalia': reproduced by permission of the Controller of Her Majesty's Stationery Office.

282 (Left) *Author's collection.* Photo: John Freeman. (Centre) Oil painting, mid-17th cent. *SNPG.* (Right) *Author's collection.* Photo: John Freeman.

286 Engraving, early 18th cent. *SNPG*, Department of Prints and Drawings.

293 Engraving, early 18th cent. *SNPG*, Department of Prints and Drawings.

295 Engraving, early 18th cent. *SNPG*, Department of Prints and Drawings.

297 Engraving, 1743, published by John Bowles at the Black Horse Inn, Cornhill. *Scottish United Services Museum, Edinburgh.* Photo: Tom Scott.

298 (Left) Oil painting, 1732, by Antonio David. *SNPG.* (Right) Oil painting, 1775, ascribed to H. D. Hamilton. *SNPG.*

299 Engraving by R. C. Bell after Sir William Allan. *Scottish United Services Museum.* Photo: Tom Scott.

303 (Left) *Central Public Library, Edinburgh.* Photo: F. R. Inglis and Son. (Right) Photo: A. F. Kersting.

305 Oil painting (detail), 18th cent., British School. Private owner.

306 Oil painting, 1746, by David Morier. Copy-
–7 right reserved: reproduced by gracious permission of Her Majesty the Queen.

308 *NGS.*

310 *NGS.*

312 *Author's collection.* Photo: John Freeman.

314 *NGS.*

315 Engraving, *c.* 1714. Photo: Radio Times Hulton Picture Library.

318 Drawing, 1793. Photo: Radio Times Hulton Picture Library.

319 Drawing, *c.* 1787. Photo: Radio Times Hulton Picture Library.

324 Photograph, 1843. *SNRG*, Department of Prints and Drawings.

326 T. Stalker-Miller, MSIA.

Special thanks are due to the author for allowing us to photograph many items in his personal collection. We should also like to acknowledge the help of Ian Larner, photographer to the National Museum of Antiquities of Scotland, and Tom Scott, who photographed paintings and prints for the Scottish National Portrait Gallery and the National Gallery of Scotland. We are indebted for guidance in planning the maps to the National Trust for Scotland's publication *Bannockburn*, and to Moray McLaren's *If Freedom Fail*.

# Index

Page numbers in **bold** type refer to colour plates; page numbers in *italics*, to black-and-white illustrations.